DANCING WITH EMPTY POCKETS

Dr Tony Moore is a writer, historian and academic based in Melbourne. He has a PhD in Australian history from the University of Sydney and is a senior lecturer at and Director of the National Centre for Australian Studies, Monash University. Tony's career has spanned political activism, documentary making at the ABC, journalism and book publishing. He is the author of two other books: *The Barry McKenzie Movies* and *Death or Liberty*.

DANCING *with* *Empty* POCKETS

Australia's Bohemians Since 1860

TONY MOORE

For my children, Joseph, Eliza and Samuel

Published in Australia in 2012 by Pier 9, an imprint of Murdoch Books Pty Limited

Murdoch Books Australia
Pier 8/9
23 Hickson Road
Millers Point NSW 2000
Phone: +61 (0) 2 8220 2000
Fax: +61 (0) 2 8220 2558
www.murdochbooks.com.au
info@murdochbooks.com.au

Murdoch Books UK Limited
Erico House, 6th Floor
93–99 Upper Richmond Road
Putney, London SW15 2TG
Phone: +44 (0) 20 8785 5995
Fax: +44 (0) 20 8785 5985
www.murdochbooks.com.au
info@murdochbooks.co.uk

A cataloguing-in-publication entry is available from the National Library of Australia at www.nla.gov.au.

ISBN: 978-1-74196-144-7

Cover image: Dulcie Deamer in leopard skin costume, 1923. Photograph by Swiss Studios. Courtesy Mitchell Library, State Library of New South Wales (Call no. P1/Goldie, Dulcie)

Cover design by Design by Committee
Typeset by Emma Gough and Russell Whittle
Index by Richard McGregor

Printed in Australia by Griffin Press, an accredited ISO AS/NZS 14001:2004 Environmental Management System printer.

CONTENTS

ACKNOWLEDGMENTS

This history of Australian bohemia was a team effort. I thank Monash University and its School of Journalism, Australian and Indigenous Studies for grants that helped with research and permissions. It was a privilege to engage with the knowledge and skills of research assistants Stephen Mead, Nicole Davis, Chris Mikul, Jen Jewell Brown and Emma Price and the wonderful staff at Pier 9. I am also grateful to colleagues John Arnold, Daniel Angel Bradford, Nick Dyrenfurth, Liz Conor and Bruce Scates. The book would not have been possible without the collections of the State Libraries of Victoria and New South Wales and the Libraries of Monash University and the University of Sydney. This book had its origins in doctoral research, and I thank the University of Sydney and its School of Philosophical and Historical Inquiry for unflagging support, and pay tribute to my supervisor Richard White, who taught me that critical thinking and accessible storytelling go hand in hand. Authoring books is not conducive to family life, and it is to my understanding wife Lizbeth and children that I owe the greatest debt. My interest in bohemia began in the 1990s while directing a documentary on the topic at the ABC, and I thank the creative people who worked with me back then, especially Peter Kirkpatrick whose scholarship on the 1920s sparked the thoughts 'but didn't my mates and I experience a similar bohemian life of inner city pubs and parties in the 1980s? Maybe bohemia is alive still?'

INTRODUCTION:
THE BORDERS OF BOHEMIA

Bohemia was first named by Henri Murger, a struggling Parisian journalist who hit a popular nerve with *Scènes de la Vie de Bohème*, his serialised stories about the unconventional and impoverished artists of the Latin Quarter. Writing in the latter 1840s, he was romanticising the community of young and aspiring writers, painters, poets and philosophers that had formed in Paris between the revolutions of 1830 and 1848. Murger, like most chroniclers of bohemia since, was writing about his own lost youth.

For the nineteenth-century French, the word *bohemiens* conjured the primitive, exotic and mysterious power of gypsies, its original meaning.[1] By the 1830s the adjective 'bohemian' described, in Britain as well as France, any nomadic or vagabond character, with strong hints of poverty and even criminality. At the same time artists full of the ennui of romanticism's revolt against industrial capitalism were attracted to the gypsies' determined nomadism, non-conformity and spontaneity in the face of modernity. Young French artists were first called bohemians in the 1830s. In 1834 journalist Félix Pyat explained how the 'mania of young artists to wish to live outside of their time, with other ideas and other customs, isolates them from the world, renders them strange and bizarre, puts them outside the law, banished from society. These are today's bohemians.'[2]

It was, however, Murger's stories about young artists in the journal *Le Corsaire* that brought the association of artists and bohemians to public attention. His achievement was to describe bohemia as an artistic sensibility where the making of art was less important than both the gypsy lifestyle of being an artist and belonging to a sharing creative community critical of the wider work-a-day world around them. Murger's garret-dwelling characters embraced the major arts of poetry, painting, music and philosophy, but spent more time scraping a living together, partying and experimenting with sexual and other freedoms beyond the censure of bourgeois morality. Crucially, in Murger's portrayal, bohemians had moved from being wastrels and scally-wags to an embodiment of the romantic idea of the artist hero.[3]

Scènes de la Vie de Bohème, published in 1851, was all the more appealing for being nostalgically set in the recent past of the 1830s and it became a guidebook of bohemia. Its international popularity, which lasted well into the twentieth century, was no doubt assisted by Giacomo Puccini's 1896 opera *La Bohème*, and the popularisation of the romantic conception of the artist by a succession of other bohemian storytellers.[4] The bohemian label has since been applied to disparate groups in Europe and North America. Paris was a stage for a succession of bohemian groups, including the writers Balzac, Baudelaire, Gautier and de Nerval in the 1840s, 50s and 60s, the impressionist painters of the 1870s and 80s, symbolists, who burst into literary florescence with the vagabond poet prodigy Arthur Rimbaud and his lover Paul Verlaine, and climaxing in the *fin de siècle* demimonde of the Moulin Rouge. Well-known British bohemians include the Pre-Raphaelite Brotherhood, Oscar Wilde, Aubrey Beardsley and the Aesthetic and Decadent movements. In America there was Edgar Allen Poe in the 1840s, Walt Whitman and the 'Pfaffians' in the 1850s and the early twentieth century Greenwich Village scene.[5]

European bohemia continued to surprise and entertain in the first decades of the twentieth century, reinventing and revitalising itself through a series of hard-edged 'modernist' avant-garde art movements such as the fauves, futurists and cubists. The First World War and its aftermath produced the shocks of dada and the carnival of Cabaret Voltaire in Weimar Germany, the genteel intellectual non-conformity of Britain's Bloomsbury set, and the challenge of the surrealists radiating out from France. Then, following the war from the 1950s through to the end of the century, bohemia colonised new media and especially youth counter-cultures, explicitly in America's beats, Britain's Angry Young Men, France's existentialists and situationists, and more nebulously through a succession of dissident movements such as beatniks, hippies and punks on both sides of the Atlantic.

What is Australia's experience of bohemia? An early proselytiser was journalist and author Marcus Clarke, who claimed to have imbibed London and Parisian bohemia as a youth before emigrating from Britain to the colony of Victoria in 1863. 'I am a bohemian,' he declared. 'I live, I walk, I eat, drink and philosophise.'6 And so from that time, in Australia a bohemian identity was associated with networks, subcultures and movements across most creative arts and media that persisted through the nineteenth and twentieth century, leaving traces and echoes to this day. For more than a century and a half our cities have spawned networks of creative iconoclasts – poets, painters, novelists, journalists, philosophers, actors, filmmakers, rock'n'roll stars, comedians, tricksters, hackers – as famous for their eccentric lifestyles as for the work they produced, and many of them will be discussed in these pages.

Most artists' memoirs and histories focus on a particular bohemian group, a frozen moment of their youth perhaps, while I conceive of a bohemian tradition re-inventing itself through time. Across generations creative, often subversive, young people have congregated in similar urban spaces to make cultural products and to experiment with lifestyle, reaching for or being assigned the label 'bohemian' to describe their aesthetic and intellectual non-conformity. But because an essential characteristic of bohemias is the claim to be different and groundbreaking, it is very much a tradition in denial. The bohemian twin peaks of avant-gardism and nostalgia have meant that young cultural rebels disregard those who have gone before them and then when older fail to see those who come after them.

Bohemian artists like to characterise themselves as outsiders, dissidents operating beyond society's conventions, bravely speaking the truth and free of the mundane marketplace and work-a-day world where the rest of us must earn our living. But even if most of our cultural rebels begin on the margins, railing against establishment gatekeepers, a significant number in Australia make good, converting notoriety into celebrity, respect, wealth and even power. In Australia bohemians are important because many of the people who lay claim to this label or one its ever morphing avatars – various avant-gardes, libertarians, beats, 'the underground', counter-cultures, punks, indie – have been at the forefront of aesthetic or intellectual change.

Historically, the bohemian identity has helped young creative people feel free to take risks, enjoy pleasure and push (or in some cases demolish) the boundaries of middle-class respectability. Bohemia has also been a public performance to promote one's cause and career, a media strategy where emerging writers, painters, critics, filmmakers or activists might attract attention, distinction and even notoriety. In this sense the youthful adoption of a bohemian identity has helped the artist in their journey from fringe to famous, outsider to insider. Then there is the other bohemian fate of the *enfant terrible*, whose youthful promise is squandered in hedonism or excess, ending in obscurity, despair or even death. This is the hazy, hazardous point at which bohemia becomes too much of a good thing, a liability rather than a muse. Yet the thrill of walking on the wild side, the flirtation with danger, the fear of falling off the edge, is part of bohemia's enduring allure.

Defining such diversity of social and cultural practice as bohemian and connecting it within a tradition is a challenge, requiring not only a sceptical attitude to artists' romantic claims about themselves and their work but also a critical engagement with the favoured form of bohemian evidence, the memoir, and those commentators who too readily accept bohemians' own mythmaking.[7] The early French writers' attempts at defining the bohemia in which they participated were vague, poetic and romantic. Murger depicted it as 'a stage of the artist's career' that leads to 'the Academy, the Hospital or the Morgue'.[8] For Alphonse de Calonne bohemia was 'bordered on the north by need, on the south by misery, on the east by illusion and on the west by the infirmary'. For another, its frontiers were 'cold, hunger, love and hope'.[9] The idea of bohemia as a mythical country allowed the indulgence of metaphor, but did not explain how bohemia assisted artists to make a life in a hard-nosed world where, according to Murger, 'the five-franc piece is Empress'.[10]

From its origins in Paris in the 1830s, bohemia was caught up in romanticism's revolt against the impact of the growing market economy and mass urban living. For me the bohemian identity is a response to capitalist modernity and the accelerating industrial revolution in the West – a romantic strategy for dealing with the intrusion of market relations into the making of culture. Artists were loosened from the bonds of aristocratic patronage that characterised the *ancien regime* and subjected to market forces – art itself became a commodity to be bought and sold. This new status could be liberating, re-orienting artists towards the people and hitching artistic development to capitalism's progress. But most artists bemoaned their subjection to 'philistine' bourgeois tastes, work-a-day hours and intermittent poverty. Murger conceded that bohemia allowed the artist to live a 'double life' where they 'keep one life for the poet in them – the dreamer ... and another for the labourer that contrives to provide the daily bread'.[11] Almost as compensation for having to prostitute their talents, bohemianism was adopted by writers and artists as a performance of the self, a new identity in which they declared their freedom from the market by seeking to outrage or subvert the dominant *bourgeois* culture.

French sociologist Pierre Bourdieu has written at length on how the illusion of artistic independence from economic values can actually make the work more valuable to consumers.[12] Whether it is avant-garde painting, jazz, new wave theatre and cinema, 'alternative' or 'indie' music, the middle class enjoys consuming cultural products labelled with anti-commercial values. But rather than being 'co-opted', bohemians can be active manipulators of labels and consumer distinction. They create an aura of authenticity around their products that obfuscates the reality of their creation being produced for commercial gain.

Bohemianism has always allowed emerging artists and writers to parade their street cred, genius, unconventionality or innovation while tarnishing competitors as sell-outs, fake or obsolete. Bohemian groups also helped in daily life, providing a sense of belonging, and encouraging risk-taking to increase creative skills and ideas. They shared a sense of fun and carnival as well, offering young cultural workers, often new to the city, an opportunity to laugh in the face of economic hardship – to both symbolically and literally dance with empty pockets.

Murger's canny evocation of *joie de vivre* and noble suffering for one's art gave bohemia the popular appeal and the inspirational power to move off shore and into the future. By the 1860s the global movement of ideas, media and people even carried the identity to the far-off British colonies of Australia, where it found a receptive audience in the cocky young metropolis of Melbourne.

1

ROMANCING THE CITY:
MARCUS CLARKE'S AUSTRALIAN BOHEMIA
1860–1880

When Australians today hear the name Marcus Clarke they might – at a pinch – recall that he wrote *For the Term of His Natural Life*, the convict saga that became an international best-seller in the nineteenth century. Many who have admired the book's psychological insights and gothic darkness imagine it to be the work of a worthy older Victorian gentleman. In fact Clarke was in his twenties when he wrote the classic, and the book's provenance was far from worthy; first serialised in a magazine, at one stage Clarke's editor had to lock him in an office with a supply of tobacco and other creature comforts to force chapters out of the wayward author.

Having migrated to Australia as an adolescent, Clarke spent his twenties writing satire, reviews, literary essays, journalistic exposés into Melbourne's underclass, plays, short stories, novels, melodramas and even musicals. He edited newspapers and magazines and published his own literary journals to provide a platform for new Australian writing. With an ironic Wildean wit, Clarke ate, drank and scandalised his way about Melbourne in the 1860s and 70s, setting up a string of underground literary clubs, mocking respectable society and keeping one step ahead of his creditors. Along the way he invented a new Australian character to challenge the bushman – the urban bohemian writer.

'I myself am only a shoeless vagabond … and associate only with Bohemians,' Clarke declared in his opening column for the *Argus* newspaper.[1] He made no secret of the centrality of bohemianism to his identity. In 'Austin Friars', a short story based on his years living in a convivial Melbourne boarding house, Clarke's narrator boasts: 'you have never tried Bohemianism, you have never lived like a Prince of the blood one day, and subsisted on a pipe and a pint of beer the next'.[2] In another story, 'La Béguine', he confesses that, while still at school, 'I strayed into Bohemia, and acquired in that strange land an assurance and experience ill suited to my age and temperament.'[3]

In response to both a nostalgic longing for the metropolitan culture of London and Paris and his surprise at the energy and modernity of a still-forming Melbourne and its rambunctious media, Clarke spent the 1870s fashioning a bohemian way of life – textually through his fiction, humorous sketches and urban journalism; collectively through café life and mock gentlemen's clubs; individually as a dandy in high society; and, more transgressively, by mixing with an underclass of outcasts he exoticised as 'lower bohemia'. The supercilious satirist was transformed by his experiences of crossing the class divide: he became a passionate critic of the convict system and its 'power for evil' in his greatest novel. Clarke also took aim at urban poverty, the war on Tasmanian Aborigines and even religion, by declaring the death of God. Eventually he paid the price for picking too many fights.

Clarke's life raises questions about how the bohemian identity changed through separation from the metropolitan culture of Paris and London and its encounter with the very different conditions of colonial modernity – especially the rapidly growing immigrant cityscape of Melbourne, and the anxiety to establish the civilising cultural institutions Europe took for granted. Colonial modernity was the story of disparate peoples uprooted from their homelands; undertaking epic travels across oceans to settle a strange new land. Marcus Clarke, like many Australian writers and journalists of his generation, experienced separation, transplantation and resettlement, harnessed to a project of imperial capitalist settlement. Brian Elliot's sophisticated and thoroughly researched 1958 biography of Marcus Clarke is distinguished by its depiction of a colonial literary environment in which empire rather than nation is the chief source of belonging, but perceives his subject's bohemianism as a recreational diversion from writing rather than considering how it helped him be a writer.[4]

Bohemia emerged in Melbourne in tandem with the expansion and professionalisation of the press, driven by the desire for culture by the growth in a literate, cashed-up market. Newspapers such as the *Argus* and the *Age* made the still-young colonial city a magnet for educated young people – both native born and 'new chums' like Clarke – ambitious to make their living as writers. It was just such a migration of young men seeking work in journalism to Paris that led to bohemia first being named.[5] Modernity in Australia shared the old world trends of market capitalism, urbanisation, mechanisation and bureaucratic regulation. Nevertheless there were colonial peculiarities, notably the sense of separation from the imperial centre, the generation of wealth on the frontier, the urgency of institution building and the vulnerability to imported culture. Colonial modernity produced its own versions of optimism, but also an accentuated longing for home.

A CHILD OF BOHEMIA

Marcus Clarke was born into the privileged ranks of Britain's upper middle class, a scion of a Protestant Irish family that had secured military honours, land, wealth and high office in the service of Empire. His father, William Clarke, was a successful lawyer in London, one of his uncles a judge in South Australia and another a governor of Western Australia, while his cousin Andrew had been Surveyor-General in Victoria and an MP. Marcus's mother died while he was only an infant and William raised the boy on his own, never remarrying. An eccentric child enamoured of gothic literature, Clarke and his London school friends Cyril and Gerard Manley Hopkins (the future poet) collaborated on horror stories about reanimating the dead (illustrating their fascination with Mary Shelley's *Frankenstein*). As he matured, Clarke excelled academically in the classics and languages. Fluent in French, he was especially fond of Honoré de Balzac and modelled his flamboyant personal style on the French writer. He was a larger-than-life schoolyard personality, described by boyhood friend Gerard Manley Hopkins as a

'Kaleidoscopic, Parti-colored, Harlequinesque, Thaumatropic being'.[6] Clarke later claimed in his semi-autobiographical short stories to have been initiated into the demimonde while still an adolescent, recalling how his father had lived 'indifferently in Paris and London, patronised by the dandies, artists and scribblers who form in both cities the male world of fashionable idleness', so that 'I was suffered at sixteen to ape the vices of sixty'. Looking back to childhood, he claimed to have been 'thrown when still a boy into the society of men thrice my age, and was tolerated in all those witty and wicked circles in which virtuous women are conspicuous by their absence'.[7]

The wickedness that Clarke attributed to his father's society was certainly an exaggeration, but it would seem that as an adolescent he was exposed to a full social life courtesy of adult cousins, the dandyesque 'middle-aged Mephistopheles' of his fictionalised account of London bohemia. His father and other relatives also took him out to the theatre, opera, pantomimes and burlesques. His friend Hamilton Mackinnon later observed that young Marcus 'began his Bohemian career in Australia with a zest not altogether surprising in one who had been negligently allowed to drift into London Bohemianism'.[8]

William Clarke regularly ventured to Paris on business, occasionally taking his French-speaking son, and at the end of his schooling Clarke had every expectation of a position in the Foreign Service with a posting to Paris. But a family tragedy put paid to these dreams. In the early 1860s William Clarke succumbed to a mental disorder, and was committed to a mental asylum, at which point the near bankruptcy of the family estate – perhaps through financial speculation – was exposed. His sixteen-year-old son was compelled by relatives to migrate to the far-flung colony of Victoria in 1863.

This sequence of events meant a loss of 'home' for Clarke in every sense, and on his arrival in Australia he mourned for London and the career he had imagined for himself, considering himself in exile. But Victoria wasn't entirely the backwater he had anticipated. 'Melbourne has become a city already of some wealth and importance,' he observed in 1865. The 'drunken, blaspheming diggers' and soldiers of the gold rushes had 'given place to merchants, bankers and civilians, many rich beyond the average of their class, nearly all respectable and prosperous'.[9]

Clarke had the good fortune to arrive in Melbourne distinguished by his elite public school education and an air of sophistication beyond his years. This, along with his family connections, gave him an entrée to Melbourne society, encounters he later fictionalised in the story 'Human Repetends':

> During the first six months of my arrival I was an honorary member of the Melbourne Club, the guest of those officials to whom I brought letters of introduction, the temporary lion of South Yarra tea parties.

But he was not impressed with what passed for the gentry, concluding that 'the pursuit of wealth is the chief characteristic of the present age [and] its results are everywhere the debasement of national character, the undermining of principles and the corruption not only of taste but of virtue'.[10]

His disdain for Melbourne's moneyed class was exacerbated by a job the hard-up Clarke was compelled to take as a clerk in the Bank of Australasia, through family connections. Here he saw up close the booming colony's get-rich-quick speculators, developers, traders, hucksters and middlemen – the self-made colonial businessmen whom he would deride as a 'sham aristocracy', inferior to the natural aristocracy of writers and others who had 'culture'.[11] He complained bitterly of his exile among philistines: 'I was fond of Art and Literature, I came to where both are unknown; I was conversant with the manners of a class, I came where "Money makes the gentleman"; I hated vulgarity, I came where it reigns supreme … My mind is becoming cynical.'[12]

In his first published semi-autobiographical story 'Austin Friars' (1866), the Clarke-like narrator, lonely and unappreciated among the 'money-men' and 'philistines' of the new city, finds solace in the company of a rambunctious collection of itinerant eccentrics who come together in the dining and drawing rooms of his boarding house, fictionalised as 'Austin Friars'. It combined 'a hostel, a tavern, and eating-house, a spot sacred to the memory of the jolliest six months that I ever spent' characterised by 'pints of ale, "tobacco parliaments", Haymarket plays, Bohemianism, and "jolly-good fellows everyone!"'.[13]

Clarke's early writing promoting bohemia suggests that for him this identity was a cultural life raft in the new land; a creative attempt at reclaiming the metropolitan cultural capital he felt he had lost, closing the personal distance he felt from Europe. In his early articles and stories he portrayed himself as nurtured at the breast of the authentic Parisian bohemia. In the story 'La Béguine', set in Paris, Clarke draws on the language of Murger and Gautier to describe artistic 'bohemia' as a land of the mind, 'a curious country', peopled by 'wicked, good-hearted inhabitants'.

• • •

Clarke's time in the bank proved unsuccessful, boring and brief. In a later article recalling his many mishaps with ledgers and easy distraction attending to his fashions, he concluded 'I was no business man'. Securing more adventurous employment as jackeroo, he bolted for the bush. There he imbibed the Australia of coach inns, drovers and stockmen, Irish louts and corrupt police, tent towns and Chinese diggers, which he later reckoned knocked the 'humbug' out of him. A photograph of Clarke at twenty years of age from this time says a lot about him: a cocky young gentleman dressed in frock coat, riding breeches, high boots and hat, holding a silver-tipped cane and smoking a cigar. Decoding this image, researcher of Melbourne bohemia Stephen Mead notes the stylish accoutrements of the aspiring dandy and 'young man who has arrived', including the cabbage tree hat wound in a muslin veil (as worn by the artist Whistler), the nonchalant sitting legs-sideways on a fashionable balloon-back chair, the sardonic gaze directly to camera and the overt public display of smoking, a bohemian signifier at this time.[14]

He worked on a sheep station in the Wimmera, mastering horsemanship, squaring up to the characters on the frontier and learning about the country which he would famously describe as having a 'weird melancholy'. Steeped in the gothic tradition that had seen him graduate from *Frankenstein* to Edgar Allan Poe, Clarke found the bush to be a 'funereal', primeval and humbling place. In a preface to a collection of poems by Adam Lindsay Gordon, he wrote: 'In Australia alone is to be found the

Portrait of the writer as a young dandy – Marcus Clarke at twenty on a visit to Melbourne from 'up country' c. 1866. His outfit and pose were carefully arranged to convey his bohemianism.

Grotesque, the Weird, the strange scribblings of Nature learning how to write.'[15] He used the time spent in relative isolation to write and began having work published in the *Australian Monthly Magazine*. It was during this rural induction that he did the research that would later result in the colourful characters of a series of bush stories, 'Tales of Bullock-Town'. Clarke delighted in the curious, creative slang of the nomadic bush workers – many of them ex-convicts; it was a vernacular he would lace through his journalism and fiction.

At first, inspired by the opportunities that might be squeezed out of the vast land, the new chum imagined he would make his career and fortune as a grazier, cattleman or even miner. However the novelty of station life ultimately wore off and the grim reality of the harsh environment dealt a body blow to Clarke's rural ambitions when he mounted an ill-fated expedition into outback Bourke that ended in debacle and the death of a companion. An ill and dehydrated Clarke made his way back to Ledcourt Station, resolved to quit the unforgiving bush for the gaslight and drawing rooms of Melbourne. Luck was on his side, for a guest at the station took a shine to Clarke and his writing, and successfully lobbied the *Argus* to take the young man on. The station manager was not sorry to see Clarke go, for the overeducated jackeroo was deemed a bad influence on the other workers, to whom he had taken to reading saucy French novels during too-frequent siestas.

In 1867, aged twenty-one, Clarke returned to Melbourne to start a career in big-city journalism. At the time Melbourne was only thirty-two years old, but had already outgrown Sydney to become Australia's largest city, and would see its population double to 260,000 by 1881, when it would be dubbed the 'metropolis of the Southern hemisphere' and 'Marvellous Melbourne'. Considering Clarke's writing in an essay on Melbourne in 1886, another immigrant Francis Adams was surprised by the city's 'metropolitan tone', observing 'something of London in her, something of Paris, something of New York and something of her own ... The look on the faces of her inhabitants is the metropolitan look. These people live quickly.'[16]

Development, driven by the pastoral industry, then gold, followed by import replacement industries and an urban land boom, had been rapid and uneven, with wide streets based on the colonial grid pattern, gardens and large public buildings adjacent to hastily erected slum dwellings and dismal back lanes. Poet Hugh McCrae recalled his father's memories of Melbourne in the sixties as 'a hefty city': 'Bourke Street, packed with foreign cafés represented a cosmopolis by night … There were brawls: doors flying open, drunks crashing on to footpaths, figures silhouetted against squares of light, sailors with their doxies, constables in belltopper-hats, diggers, soldiers, ticket-of-leave men, and aboriginals [sic].'[17]

Melbourne was a far cry from the dowager weighed down with tradition that she would become in the twentieth century. Most of its inhabitants were immigrants and a good many of the labourers and poor had been convicts. Some of the free working-class immigrants had been radical Chartists in Britain. They joined with liberals, early trade unionists, manufacturers and reform-minded European émigrés from the failed European revolutions of 1848 in the political agitation that led to Victoria becoming one of the first polities in the British world to extend the right to vote to all men regardless of wealth. Yet alongside this early assertion of egalitarianism in politics was a spirit of greed unbound by a sense of the past or deep community roots. This produced a city in flux, where fortunes and reputations rose and fell with rapidity, and the cityscape itself was in a state of perpetual reconstruction driven by developers and debt.

Clarke's letters reveal a young town booming through gold, sheep and land speculation, brimming with energy and ambition, new money, new identities and the clash of immense wealth cheek by jowl with poverty worthy of Dickens' London. But a thin crust of bourgeois respectability was beginning to form, and Clarke was to make it his business to stir, shame and mock the pretensions of this bunyip plutocracy.

Clarke's complaints on arrival about Melbourne's paucity of culture were an exaggeration. The self-made men of the city had lavished it with the gilt of civilisation – art galleries, libraries, theatres. 'Victorians' in the truest sense, the civic fathers believed that art was good for the moral improvement of the colonial rabble. But a new generation coming of age in the 1860s had less lofty ideas. In the northern hemisphere young writers were finding employment with new popular 'magazines' featuring serialised stories about the sights, sounds, sleaze and the spectacle of the modern city. Where the good burghers of Melbourne wanted virtuous works, the mood blowing in from Europe was sensationalist, melodramatic, gothic and escapist.

The times suited the quick and the young and, on the strength of his references and portfolio, Clarke became the *Argus*'s new theatre critic – only to be sacked when he submitted a made-up review that lambasted an actor who had actually missed the performance. No nine-to-fiver, he became a freelance journalist and immediately landed the regular weekly column on the *Argus*'s weekly literary companion, the *Australasian*, that made him famous.

Scalpel in one hand and rapier in the other, young Marcus carved out a journalistic niche for himself as the 'Peripatetic Philosopher', a slightly bemused, cynical observer of the goings-on of Melbourne society. Clarke's topical, blasé style resonated with the city's humour. His targets included sharebrokers, 'new chums', 'our boys', the working man, politicians, squatters, art connoisseurs, journalists, sporting men, Victorian ladies and larrikins, complete with their own peculiar slang or jargon. The ear for voice and mannerism and ironic exposure of hypocrisy in Clarke's parodies make them a colonial precursor to Barry Humphries' rogues' gallery of a century later.

Like his hero Balzac, Marcus Clarke liked to watch, and while scribbling from his Collins Street café he succeeded in Australianising the Parisian flâneur, a wandering recorder of urban life and spectacle, whose spirit he invoked in his opening column in 1867: 'There is much to be learnt from the street life, and one's "daily walks abroad" are instructive as well as amusing … I am a bohemian … I live, I walk, I eat, drink and philosophise.'[18]

He used the French word flâneur in his mission statement but in this piece and elsewhere conflated the concept with his preferred term 'bohemian'. He offered Balzac to Melbourne readers as the 'the incarnation of Parisian Bohemianism' because of his boulevard blazing 'as a realist writer of modern city life', who 'grasp[ed] the anomalous life of the Parisian of the day'.[19] What connects the two terms is the idea of the gypsy, or *bohé-mien* in French – a metaphor for nomadic freedom – leading the Peripatetic Philosopher to claim kinship with 'tinkers of other men's kettles, patchers of other men's garments, ragpickers and snappers up of unconsidered trifles'.[20]

The flâneur's itinerancy and the romantic fantasy of

becoming one with the diversity of the city's people became central to Clarke's personal identity. He also owed much to French flâneur, poet and prose writer Charles Baudelaire, who turned his gaze on the leisure sphere of the café and shopping arcades, and did much to expose the ironies in modern life, using humour to skewer different types he observed in the Paris of the 1840s, 50s and 60s in journals such *Le Corsaire*, *La Tribune Nationale* and *Salut Public*. The flâneurs had a radical edge and, while critical of the urban condition, its alienation and poverty, they were alive to the possibilities of modern city life, from the visceral to the intellectual. By arriving at the vision of the flâneur, the second generation of French bohemians overcame nostalgia for the failed revolutionary hopes of their youth and joined the revolution of capitalist modernity itself, pursuing extreme personal liberty and self-realisation. The sensibility of the flâneur suited a generation more comfortable with rapid social, technological and economic change that wanted to push at the extremes of bourgeois society, to stroll the city's arcades rather than escape to a lost arcadia. Clarke's own bohemianism in Australia followed this tendency, avoiding the extremes of despair or naïve worship of progress in favour of a prickly, curious, amused engagement with the ironies of the colonial city.

Clarke's prose, with its staccato style, is a Victorian precursor of the hardboiled urban crime fiction that was to follow in the next century. An early letter back to England recounts a night out in Melbourne:

> On each side are covered bars, where some twenty or thirty girls dispense with lightning rapidity, the 'brandies hot', 'glass of ale', 'cold without', 'colonial wine', 'nobblers for five', 'whisky's hot', 'sherry's bitters', 'two glasses claret', 'nobblers for two', 'dark brandy' etc, which expectorating crowds of men and boys call for on all sides. White-coated waiters shoot like meteors through the mass … Walking up the street we meet a knot of station-men from the Murray with cattle runs … they have just put up their horses preparatory to 'goin' on the bust', and walk down the pavement four abreast, all booted, breeched, and

smoking violently ... Presently we come upon a group of Celestials, pig-tailed, blue-coated, and mandarin-capped, chattering in their teeth-breaking lingo ... These turn down Little Bourke Street into an opium house and will probably spend the remainder of the night in gambling away their hard-earned gains.[21]

'The Peripatetic Philosopher' was a hit with the public, and its young creator quickly became an established journalistic identity in Melbourne, becoming the centre of a circle of younger reporters and writers attracted to his promotion of bohemianism. Clarke brought a new ingredient to colonial writing and journalism – his own bohemian personality, which was explicitly marketed in his columns and performed in the social setting of Melbourne's cafés, theatres and drawing rooms.

In the second half of the 1860s his small band gathered daily in the Theatre Royal's Café de Paris, dubbed 'Café Lutetia' by Clarke in a story of the same name and identified as the 'resort of higher Bohemia'. Blurring the Victorian bourgeois distinction between work and play, 'the morning was spent in scribbling, the afternoon in tobacco, the evening in dinner, theatre and gaslight. I fear we did not lead virtuous lives. I am sure that we were often out of bed after the small hours.'[22]

The Theatre Royal offered theatrical performances, a bar and restaurant as well as the café, where prostitutes were rumoured to conduct business in the stalls. With its combination of entertainment, food, alcohol and possibly sex, it was something of a Victorian-era pleasure dome for the gentlemen on the town.

It was from the cafés that the flâneurs of Paris liked to watch the passing parade, so it is hardly surprising that Clarke boosted Melbourne's emerging café culture, writing an early article on 'My Café and People Who Go There'. While Melburnians are wont to think café society was brought to Australia's shores by post-war 'continental' immigrants, Clarke's reviews and fiction reveal a much earlier provenance. In the late 1860s new cafés included the Nissen, Café des Variétés, Café Gunsler, Clement's Café in Swanston Street, the Academy of Music Café and numerous eating houses, many of which were reviewed by

Clarke in the press. Melbourne was presented as a smorgasbord of sensations, distractions and amusements for those like him with modern, cosmopolitan sensibilities. As literary historian Andrew McCann has argued, the Peripatetic Philosopher aka Clarke was finding a sense of belonging in the city of Melbourne, evolving a bohemianism that made it familiar; seeking out, and exaggerating, what the colonial city shared with the cities he had left behind.[23]

CAFÉ DE PARIS.—(SEE PAGE 98).

Café de Paris in Melbourne's Theatre Royal on Bourke Street – a Victorian era 'pleasure dome' of the 1860s and 70s where Clarke's bohemian circle toasted 'Love! Youth! Happiness!' Wood engraving by Edgar Ray, reproduced in the *Illustrated Australian Mail*, 24 May 1862.

Clarke introduced to Australia the paradoxes of *la vie de bohème* – luxury one minute, poverty the next, and intense bouts of work combined with a healthy respect for indolence. At its core his bohemianism, like his journalism, involved transgression across the barriers of social class and middle-class morality. He revelled in 'an atmosphere of wit, poverty, luxury, champagne, tripe, tobacco, billiards, pawn-tickets, the drama, the gutter, beef and cabbage, oysters and chablis, lavender gloves and coats at elbows'. In 'Cafe Lutetia', Clarke celebrates the *joie de vivre* of 'witty conversation', 'hectic mirth', debates about art and naval victories, and exotic reminiscences by journalists just returned from 'New Guinea, the Algerian Services and India', rounded off with a toast to 'Love! Youth! Happiness!' before decamping to the 'latest burlesque'. Out of bohemian fun came inspiration: 'We absorbed wine and women, and hate and love into us, that we might be able to write those magnificent articles.'[24]

And write he did. What surprises about Clarke's varied body of work is the modernism and playfulness in his writing, whether the satirical columns of social observation; sensational documentary investigations of the city's underbelly; literary stunts, such as hoaxes (orgiastic religious cults, an optical device to broadcast the Melbourne Cup); and his sophisticated literary essays, short stories and novels. Long before Melbourne had the *Monthly*, Clarke inaugurated *The Colonial Monthly*, a national magazine of ideas to push new writing and emerging writers before there was even an Australian nation. When this failed he started a humorous magazine called *Humbug* and a pantomime starring his actress wife Marian Dunn. And across Clarke's diverse oeuvre, linking and centring the different plots and genres flits his greatest creation – himself.

BOHEMIA, AUSTRALIAN STYLE

One of the preconditions for bohemia in Melbourne was the growth of a newspaper and magazine market able to provide a living for a critical mass of professional writers, who previously had to rely on private patronage for support. The number of professional writers was increasing with the expansion in circulation and numbers of newspapers in Sydney and Melbourne, driven by the growth in the middle-class market, the increases in general literacy and improved distribution via the expanding railway network. Between 1855 and 1860 the circulation for the *Age* more than trebled, from 4000 to 14,500.[25] By 1874 it had increased to 23,000 and 120,000 by 1899, outstripping the *Sydney Morning Herald*. By the 1860s capital city-based newspapers aimed at a bourgeois and educated readership were carrying weekly supplements that published social sketches, longer articles, essays, reviews, short stories, serialised novels and columns, such as Clarke's 'Peripatetic Philosopher'. By providing publishing opportunities and a source of income for writers who were willing to accept commercial realities and limitations, the colonial press, as with the Parisian equivalent in the 1830s and 40s, created the subclass of jobbing journalists nursing literary ambitions who were attracted to bohemia as a way to negotiate a compromise between literary writing and its commodification in the press; to balance interesting collegiate cultural workplaces and resentment at business imperatives. The press gathered together young recruits in hectic offices in the inner city precincts and in nearby cafés and hotels after deadlines had been met. Though entry to most was at the 'grub street hack' level, the flavour of the magazine supplements offered some journalists the opportunity to spread their creative wings, and negotiate limited editorial determination. This is what Clarke quickly achieved with his weekly column.

Still, newspapers were privately owned organisations characterised by proprietorial fiat, editorial control, long hours and the profit motive. It usually meant writing copy to order, surrendering control to an editor or the news agenda. Creativity was subordinate to routine and measured out in column inches and arbitrary word lengths. In correspondence and *Humbug* Clarke complained that he felt like a machine that churned out copy – and that was on a magazine he controlled![26] Employment was precarious and not usually well paid in the early years of a career, when aspiring writers lived hand to mouth between articles while attempting to establish their worth and name.

In the 1860s and 70s two broad approaches emerged in the bid for autonomy: seeking freedom outside the press or asserting it while working within journalism in a way that made it both tolerable for the writer and attractive to readers. For Melbourne journalist Maurice Brodzky, the worst aspect of the popular press was the debasement of art to public taste, which meant the modern writer 'must descend from the elevated spheres of thought and imagination and mingle amongst gross natures, the inhabitants of the toiling, money-making world, and condescend to cater for the amusement of unthinking, unimaginative utilitarians.'[27]

Poets, too, yearned to be able to live off their art without compromise. The somewhat tragic poet Henry Kendall, who called himself a 'Wandering Bohemian', lamented that being 'in the midst of a novel society … true genius on the arts remained unacknowledged'. 'Genius,' he noted bitterly in 1877, 'would have to depend upon newspapers for publicity.'[28] Kendall failed to garner either income or publicity from Melbourne journalism, complained of being a 'literary hack' and drew an image of a victimised bohemia in his poem 'On a Street':

> I tell you this is not a tale
> Conceived by me, but bitter truth!
> Bohemia knows it pinched and pale
> Besides the pyre of burnt-out Youth![29]

This was a bohemia of consolation, where failure to achieve fame or fortune signified autonomy. In contrast, the bohemianism promoted by Clarke in writing and through individual and group activities was more complex and followed the injunction of the Parisian flâneurs to produce a modern art of the people in the mass media. He noted that there was little choice, because the colony lacked the 'lettered and leisured class who can afford to pay for a purely imaginative literature'.[30] Clarke, like Baudelaire would be simultaneously an artist *and* a journalist. But how could bohemia's romantic quest for freedom from the market be expressed within journalism?

One way was to be self-reflexive about the commercialisation of the arts in which he was involved, laughing at himself to demystify the creative process. In the introduction to *The Peripatetic Philosopher* (1869), a collection of his columns, Clarke apologises for 'thrusting himself into print every week': 'I do not publish this volume because I have a "high moral purpose in view"; … I do not even publish it because I "feel that it will supply a long felt social want"; I publish it simply because I think it will SELL.'

This confession is not atypical of Clarke's work. As revealed by Andrew McCann, Clarke was fascinated by the processes of production, distribution and marketing, referring in editorials, articles and short stories to the business of writing.[31] He explained to readers the importance of self-promotion: 'If you want to succeed in this world, you advertise yourself. It is no use hiding your light under a bushel; not a bit. If you do, your light goes out, sharp. You must stick yourself into a candlestick, and set your candlestick on a music stool … and then stand the lot on the piano, if you want to be seen.'[32]

Bohemianism was an important part of the salesmanship, with its hint of decadence and danger, suggested by admissions in his writing of such transgressions as taking cannabis or wandering through the city's red-light district. The creation of one's self as a work of art was a bohemian strategy implicit in the French texts of Murger, Balzac and Baudelaire. Michael Wilding points out that in Australia this was new because '[a]s a columnist [Clarke] was establishing a character, a recognisable personality, a cross between a brand name and a commodity'.[33]

Like a nineteenth-century Andy Warhol or Malcolm McLaren, Clarke liked to wear his pecuniary motives on his sleeve and introduced into his journalism literary devices that exposed the artifice of commercial writing itself, textual mutinies from the frontline of commodification critiquing his own role as a cultural hack. In one amusing tale Clarke comes close to a postmodern death of the author. As his character writes a potboiler he is assailed by the various stock characters of colonial fiction, rebelling at playing popular stereotypes like the 'digger', begging for liberation from the prison of their predictable plot.[34] Compared to writers and painters such as Brodzky and Kendall, who used bohemianism to (publicly) allude to their genius and muse, Clarke exhibited a fascination with the political economy of writing to make a living, and gave a knowing wink to his readers.

Thanks to his profile, in five years Marcus Clarke came close to achieving a balance between an editorial freehand and writing to a deadline and formula at a time when it was rare for a freelance writer to be able to earn a living. After taking a full-time job as a civil servant he continued to freelance for nearly a decade, contributing to every major newspaper and periodical in the country. Other columns featuring a similar bohemian persona were the 'Bunkle Correspondence' series in the *Argus*, the 'Atticus' morals column in the *Leader* and a series called 'The Wicked World' in the *Daily Telegraph*. In the competitive environment of the colonial press this was a privileged position not available to most, though Clarke's use of bohemia to market himself set a precedent for future writers and illustrators.

Clarke combined the flâneur's habit of anonymously strolling, observing and reporting with more social performances of bohemianism then current in Europe, notably playing the 'dandy' about town, and joining with others in mock clubs of mainly pressmen. One observer of the day noted how the diminutive Clarke 'looked in his carefully-fitting costume, as a full-sized British dandy of the period might look if viewed through the wrong end of an opera glass'.[35] Clarke, Kendall observed, affected 'the cynicism of a Coldstream' and sought 'to look, talk, and write like a "blasé libertine"'.[36] The image of the dandy first emerged in Regency England among young men of the gentry with liberal, Whiggish political leanings and elite tastes. They sought to use style and sensibility, literally wearing consumption on their sleeves, to distinguish themselves from bourgeois life. Two items of consumption with which Clarke was obsessed in his writing were fashion and food. His columns, reviews and short stories were littered with references to feasting with fellow bohemians on exotic gastronomic delights such as 'filet Chateaubriand aux champignons' or 'shark fin soup' in restaurants, and his eccentric and 'modish' clothing. Coloured waistcoats, pantaloons, 'lavender gloves' and ties are fussed over.

But the nineteenth-century dandy should not be mistaken for a superficial dilettante. In France of the 1830s and 40s Balzac refined the Parisian dandy style in terms of an aesthetic discernment, expressed in connoisseurship of the arts and eccentric fashion sense. The ostentatious, over-the-top style of the dandy was, paradoxically, a way to opt out of the world of commerce by refusing to take anything too seriously. While for Baudelaire, dandyism was 'an expression of opposition and revolt', it is best understood as a revolt into style.[37]

Clarke acted the dandy to cock a snook at respectability and the middle-class work ethic. He made a show of spending sprees, poverty, sloth and his addiction to credit, noting with approval that his hero Balzac 'was alternately between poverty and wealth, between a debtor's prison and a palace'.[38] By alternating the hedonistic living expected of the aristocrat with the hand-to-mouth existence of a vagrant, Clarke performed the fiction of being déclassé and accentuated his difference from the well-to-do he was otherwise socialising with at the Melbourne Club.

Bohemianism was in part calculated to annoy the older generation of entrepreneurs and improvers who reified values and skills associated with business investment and institution-building, such as the Victorian ensemble of thrift, hard work, piety and moral seriousness. During the 1840s and 50s men of learning and independent income like Nicol Stenhouse in Sydney and James Smith in Melbourne dispensed cultural and sometimes economic capital to protégés trying to make a mark in some branch of the arts in small, still-divided colonial markets regarded as generally hostile to home-grown literature. As well as contributing resources and administrative support to erect 'civilising' cultural institutions such as universities, public libraries and art galleries, both Stenhouse and Smith provided salon-like environments within their own homes to offer stimulation, criticism, contacts and advice to young poets, novelists, musicians, painters and intellectuals. Writers who later rallied around Clarke in Melbourne, notably Henry Kendall, found in the 'Stenhouse circle' literary nourishment and stimulation, encouragement to produce their own work and criticism of the results. But Stenhouse had a great aversion to dancing and late hours and preferred seclusion to socialising; he discouraged bohemianism in favour of education, study and hard work.

The emerging generation of younger writers, journalists and other artists of the 1860s, on the other hand, were interested in pleasure, consumption and irony, which was why Clarke's latest ideas from French bohemia appealed. Whereas the men who built Melbourne over the previous three decades, like

Smith and chairman of the Melbourne Public Library and judge Sir Redmond Barry, advocated good works to improve the city's cultural amenity, the younger men would signify their cultural capital by making a show of wasting it. '[L]oafing, when properly understood,' Clarke observed, 'adds a charm to the innocent sports of boyhood, gives zest to the healthy enjoyments of middle age and is a profound solace to one's declining years.'[39] This pose was a controversial alternative to both the prissy middle class and the grin-and-bear-it bushman, but Clarke's prodigious publication output belies the slacker image.

CLUB BOHEMIA

The collective expression of bohemia was encouraged by the shared public spaces of the city and the colonial press, which brought young people with common economic and cultural interests together in work and play. Marcus Clarke's writing and example helped inspire other men engaged in journalism and the arts to 'try bohemianism', creating the group experience essential for bohemia to emerge in Melbourne.

Unlike the ad hoc, itinerant literary wannabes that moved through the dining rooms of boarding houses like 'Austin Friars', Melbourne's first bohemian circle was self-selected from the ranks of pressmen and other writers, including Clarke, who were friendly with the young editor of the *Argus*, Frederick Haddon. Throughout 1867 and 1868 a loose network of 'the press, literary freelancers, actors, artists and poets' gathered on Saturday nights in Haddon's Spring Street rooms for a 'Symposium' that would be the nucleus for Australia's first bohemian club. The Yorick Club was founded when this group officially proclaimed its distinction and became serious about nurturing a bohemian identity by controlling membership and inventing rituals. Clubs like this became the organising structure for bohemian groups from the 1870s to the 1930s. The first gathering of the group that would become the Yorick – at the Nissen Café in Bourke Street in April 1868 – was shortlived owing to conflict with other patrons, described by the official history of the Yorick Club as 'stolid men' who took pleasure 'in silently playing dominoes, chess and draughts' and made known their objection to boisterous recreation 'by grunts, frowns, growls of "hush"'.[40]

Hugh McCrae, whose father George was an early member, pointed out the anti 'trade' prejudice of the group, claiming that: 'To share a public drinking-room with lime-and-cement merchants, trade-mark attorneys, estate agents, crumpet-and-doughnut manufacturers distressed their ardour and imagination.'[41] Indeed, at the time he led the charge to form the Yorick, Clarke's *Colonial Monthly* was running a hard line against the 'mercantile' class, claiming that Australia exceeded Britain in the 'vulgar administration of wealth, the greed of gain, and the unscrupulousness in seeking it'. The official Yorick history records, with a hint of irony, that '[t]he bohemians resolved' to provide a space where 'the flow of genius ... if nothing else, might have full play without interruption and intrusion from those deemed outside the particular and shining pale.'[42] Those 'outside' included the 'philistine', the 'respectable' and also the 'stolid' (not to mention all women and the working class). Declaring that they should form a club 'where they could cavort in freedom', Clarke rented an apartment in the offices of *Melbourne Punch* – appropriately enough – for £1 per week, furnishing the rooms with chairs made of old newspaper bundles. Thus was Marcus Clarke the instigator of the first formal bohemian association, although he would be a member for less than two years.

Clarke introduced a pipe-smoking human skull as mascot and that gave the club its name – though he pushed for the more sacrilegious name 'Golgotha', the 'place of the skull' where Christ was crucified. The first meeting of the Yorick was held in May 1868, with the official history recording that Clarke, being elected secretary, insisted that the club 'should be absolutely bohemian'.[43] In the first year this involved customs nostalgically revived from the eighteenth-century alehouse – drinking beer from pewter mugs and smoking long-stemmed pipes known as churchwardens. He jested that such proletarian props distinguished him from the 'bluest skimmings of the milk of colonial society': 'I am of the earth, remarkably earthy, and prefer a pot of porter (foaming mind you, and in a pewter – none of your dilettante glasses) and a black clay pipe, to all the fashionable eccentrics of the fashionable world.'[44]

Most of the club's founders were journalists who had worked

within the imperial media sphere and civil service. All had strong literary interests. The original rules stated that a member should have written a book but, mindful of the shortage of actual published authors, the membership was extended to 'the fellowship of the press', a loose definition that would also cover freelancers and occasional contributors who thought of themselves as 'men of letters'. The majority were essentially dabblers who were looking for market opportunities to do more paid writing, with a smaller hardcore leadership working full time in the press and more determined to make a living and identity out of writing.

John J. Shillinglaw was a one-time water policeman who rose to shipping master of the Port of Melbourne before leaving the position in 1869 to try to earn an income as a freelance writer. Perpetually clad in 'nautical' blue and a spirited singer of sea shanties, he wrote six books – some about the sea – and collaborated with Clarke in publishing the *Colonial Monthly*. Londoner and Cambridge-educated Richard Birnie was the Advocate-General of Western Australia and then a Melbourne barrister, but gave up his failing legal career to write for the *Australasian*. A close friend of Clarke who shared his gentrified background, the witty conversationalist was a link with the literary life of early nineteenth-century London, having associated with Thackeray and Dickens. Medical doctor and former gold prospector James Neild was a one-time *Age* journalist, theatre critic for the *Australasian*, as well as a lecturer at the University of Melbourne. Neild fell out badly with Clarke in the mid-1870s, and the pair conducted a very public feud through their columns. Another doctor, Irishman Patrick Moloney, wrote for *Melbourne Punch* and the *Australasian* and was personal physician and friend to Clarke, sharing his macabre sense of humour, and provided him with the club's skull mascot. George Walstab, the son of a plantation owner in the West Indies, had served with the mounted police in India and edited the Calcutta *Englishman* before taking up journalism in Melbourne. A close friend of Clarke who was with him when he died, Walstab became secretary to the Minister of Lands in 1874 and editor of the Melbourne *Herald* in 1882.

Another friend and sometime flatmate of Clarke was

Alfred Telo, an Englishman of Slavic or Spanish descent 'with the face of an artist and beard of a sheik', who spoke Russian, French, German and Italian, cultivating a cosmopolitan European style and an air of mystery. Clarke wrote that 'the wildest legends were afloat about this man of mystery. He had been a Russian spy. He had been a diplomatic agent … He had worked in the mines … He had married a countess. He had been – heaven only knows what he had not been!'[45] Telo translated Russian tales for the *Colonial Monthly* and the *Age*, adapted novels for the stage and was dramatic critic for *Australian Town and Country Journal*.

Hamilton Mackinnon, another Clarke confidant, worked at the *Argus*. He was a founding member of the Yorick and became Clarke's literary executor and his first biographer. Julian Thomas was the assumed name of John Stanley James, a London journalist who had come to Australia via the United States. A rival rather than friend to Clarke, he wrote a well-received series on the poorer inhabitants of Melbourne for the *Argus* under the pseudonym 'The Vagabond'. Thomas played with his identity as much as his name, embellishing an adventurous global back story in the colonies, covering for periods of extreme poverty.

A number of poets also became Yorick bohemians. Adam Lindsay Gordon had family connections to the British officer class and local squatters, moved in elite circles (becoming a parliamentarian) and was at the centre of Yorick activities. A champion horseman, steeplechaser and one-time mounted policeman, Gordon cut a gallant figure that suited his galloping, masculine verse. He became close friends with Clarke, the context in which the latter penned the famous preface to Gordon's collection *Sea Spray and Smoke Drift*, describing the 'weird melancholy' of the Australian bush.

In contrast to Gordon and most of the Yorickers, Henry Kendall, who grew up on the south coast of New South Wales, had not enjoyed a privileged life, although his mother had a keen interest in literature which was transferred to her son. After leaving school at the age of twelve he had various careers – as a shopboy, a sailor, a confectioner's assistant and an attorney's clerk – in Sydney, regional New South Wales and further abroad. Nurtured by Stenhouse's circle in Sydney, he enjoyed critical success with *Poems and Songs* in 1862, which opened up the possibility of being a full-time author. But Kendall's relative poverty and the indiscreet behaviour of his family ultimately excluded both him and his poetry from Sydney society. Fleeing to Melbourne in 1869 he found in the bohemian fraternity of the Yorick Club a surrogate family and a sounding board for his work. '[F]inding friends in Bohemia,' he explained in an amusing article about the club, 'I was baptized and became one of the glorious brotherhood who live on their wits.'[46] But this did not help when his second collection of verse *Leaves from an Australian Forest* failed financially in September 1869. He returned to Sydney and struggled for a number of years with severe depression and alcoholism, before rebuilding his career and reputation to become one of Australia's best-known poets, prior to his premature death in 1882.

One of the Yorick's leading lights, George Gordon McCrae, was raised in a creative, privileged family in Scotland, his father a prominent solicitor and aristocrat, his mother a professional artist. The family immigrated, acquiring a Victorian cattle property in 1843, and their household became a magnet for those with literary and artistic interests. Though active as a poet, novelist, painter and illustrator, McCrae remained a civil servant, working in the offices of the Auditor-General and Registrar-General, eventually being appointed Deputy Registrar-General himself. Nevertheless, McCrae was still considered a bohemian owing to the eccentric spirit, boyish exuberance and sense of humour that he brought to the Yorick, as well as his acknowledged literary achievements.

• • •

If café bohemia was an opportunity to perform a cosmopolitan, French and consumer-driven idea of bohemianism, the Yorick and its successors were inspired by a long British tradition of literary clubs that enjoyed a nineteenth-century incarnation in London's Savage Club. Clarke's self-published *Colonial Monthly* proudly observed that 'the club is ... conspicuously an English institution'.[47] Expanding on Dr Johnson's 1755 definition of a club as 'an assembly of good fellows, meeting under certain conditions', the magazine understood a club as 'generally based on the cooperative system of throwing together wit and information for the common benefit', with a meeting place and a means of scrutinising new members.

The Yorick and its Australian progeny parodied the rules and procedures of conservative gentlemen's clubs and the Masonic lodges with mock rituals and arcane names such as 'The Noble Captain' and 'The Worthy Ancient'.[48] They provided a regular meeting place where the group could eat, drink, talk and perform for each other. They were ambiguous spaces, private and public, productive and recreational, where entertainment and creative work merged. In their mockery of the Melbourne Club's pretensions the Yorick brought a sense of the carnivalesque into the new colonial bohemia – a topsy-turvy destabilising of authority and convention.

The Yorick held a monthly 'beef steak supper', sponsored lively conversation and earned a reputation for trips through the city in which the drunk members would engage in practical jokes, such as changing brass plates from business fronts or collecting door knockers from respectable people's homes.[49] Club bohemia valued japes and hoaxes as a form of recreation and, through harmless tricks, ridiculed earnestness or pretension. On one occasion, following a late night's carousing through the city streets, a member who took himself a little too seriously awoke to find his house adorned with a fishing rod, a gilt fish, a pawnbroker's sign and an undertaker's board.

New members to Clarke's next club, the Cave of Adullam, had to skull a quart of beer from a gigantic pot. In fetishising alcohol as a marker of their unconventionality, the bohemian clubs of the 1870s helped make drunkenness acceptable among journalists and writers, as it had been in Georgian society. But in his column Clarke refuted the accusation that 'the members sit on tubs around the room, smoke green tea [marijuana], and drink neat kerosene out of pewter pots.'[50]

The Yorick was a public relations exercise, attracting fame and a hint of notoriety that rubbed off on those lucky enough to be members. But after mocking the businessman and the family, the Yorick bohemians returned to their employers and home life. Mock meeting procedures, silly names and makeshift furnishings could be read as subversive only because they were performed by gentlemen in the class context of a club. Nonsense rituals, hoaxes and japes mocked the bourgeois view that entertainment should seek to improve. The male-only revelry was also celebrated as an escape from the bosom of the family life. But sexual custom was not challenged. Neither the Yorick nor Cave of Adullam ventured into erotic pleasures such as pornography, prostitution or promiscuous sex. The absence of women of any class precluded heterosexual promiscuity or adultery in the space of the Yorick and fortified its 'boys' own' ambience. Nor is there evidence that the club bohemians were interested in challenging Victorian taboos on homosexuality.

The rhetoric of soulmates pitted against a philistine society suggests that one of the main purposes of the bohemian club was to bring together creative people who might otherwise have been isolated. While some of the journalists were based in the office of a newspaper, freelancers such as Clarke appreciated the opportunity to socialise with colleagues. Journalists, writers and poets could share discourse about their arts and establish networks of support to help with careers. A club could help introduce newly arrived writers and reporters to Melbourne media circles, as happened with Kendall when he moved from Sydney.

The club offered material resources as well. It provided a berth close to the press offices in which to work, eat, talk, entertain and occasionally sleep. Melbourne newspaper offices worked late into the night, sometimes till 1 am when parliament was sitting, and the pressmen 'in town at all hours, busy at one time and free at another … found the Yorick a handy place to drop into when off duty'.[51] Friends were on hand to amuse, swap advice, and even to lend money during hard times. Financial insecurity attended the vagaries of the literary life. Clarke, for example, was a profligate borrower, though also a generous lender. Kendall frequently had to ask his friends at the Yorick for loans but there were limits to how far bohemian bonhomie or credit could compensate for Kendall's poverty. Clarke observed that '[h]e was of course, welcomed by all literary men; but welcome, however sincere, is not bread and cheese.[52] Nor could the companionship of the Yorick overcome

Adam Lindsay Gordon's melancholic personality, which was accentuated by poor sales and increasing indebtedness, leading to his tragic suicide while out riding at age thirty-seven.

Such was the Yorick's reputation as Melbourne's cultural hub that on his royal tour to Melbourne in 1869, Queen Victoria's son Prince Alfred was rumoured to have made a bee-line for the club (perhaps oblivious to the ridicule the Peripatetic Philosopher column heaped on HRH). Not surprisingly, its popularity spread from the journalistic community to anyone with a vague connection to writing. Rules were widened to include non-literary correspondents in industry and professional journals, a concession Kendall found laughable.[53] Hugh McCrae complained that 'it became apparent that there existed more potential authors in Melbourne than anybody had dreamed about': 'Mute inglorious Miltons, doctors who had published treatises on whooping-cough; even lawyers, responsible for indigestible digest began to drift in; also there is the particular instance of a Gentleman who once edited the Police Gazette.'[54]

Alarmed at this dilution of bohemianism, Clarke abandoned the Yorick after two years to form his own popular club for the purist bohemian, the Cave of Adullam (the refuge of David from the Philistines), which convened in Oliver's Café underneath the Yorick. As represented in *Twixt Shadow and Shine*, Clarke's 1875 comic novel caricaturing the new club, the Cave had refined the absurdity of the rituals and joke titles, and enhanced the theatricality of these performances. Despite the mock-secret password 'Honour! No Frills', the new club kept a tight rein on membership and it became known as an 'exclusive brotherhood', maintaining its reputation for both literary distinction and fun. This brotherhood comprised Clarke's cabal of Birnie, Walstab, Shillinglaw and Patrick Moloney, together with poets Kendall, McCrae and Adam Lindsay Gordon. Lasting well into the 1870s, younger bohemian journalists such as Maurice Brodzky, by then editor of the popular arts magazine *Table Talk*, Arthur Patchett Martin, lawyer, journalist and art patron Theodore Fink and Victor Daley were admitted. Other clubs followed in the 1870s, including the Garrick and the Bohemian, in which Clarke and his friends also participated.

In distinguishing the budding colonial profession of

journalism and authorship so loudly from the despised bourgoisie did Clarke and his fellow bohemians protest too much? While criticising merchants and businessmen, the truth is that many of them emerged from the propertied class, and as journalists, editors, publishers, writers proved themselves to be enterpreneurial risk takers, growing their own 'cultural capital' – to use Bourdieu's term for the mix of education, talent, connections, entitlement and plain chutzpah of artists and intellectuals – to establishing their brand in the cultural market place. Some like Clarke who got their hands on real cash through borrowing, became publishers of bold enterprises like the *Colonial Monthly* or *Humbug*, and like other businessmen, had to sell when costs exceeded profits (and enthusiasm). Resented that they were insufficiently acknowledged or rewarded for their creative contribution, the writers of the Yorick and Cave of Adullam embraced the bohemian identity to stake their claim as a cultural aristocracy. By declaring their distinction as the elect in a bohemian club, they were asserting their growing but still precarious status as professionals at what they did. The Yorick's fate symbolised the split personality of the bohemian and the bourgeois. At heart Clarke knew this to be so, and it drove him to explore 'lower bohemia'.

DESCENDING AN OCTAVE TO 'LOWER BOHEMIA'

Clarke shared with Balzac, Baudelaire and Gerard de Nerval a voyeuristic attraction to the lower classes that was translated into journalistic exposés of what he called 'lower bohemia'. He liked to hit the streets, slums and saloons with society's outcasts, spending 'A Night at The Immigrants' Home', drinking incognito in a sailors' pub and, on another occasion, sampling the 'Oriental' temptations of an opium den. 'I have an affection for unvarnished humanity,' the Peripatetic Philosopher declared, 'I like to see human life with its coat off, and to descend an octave on the social scale.'[55] His series of reportage-style articles for the *Australasian* spanning 1868 and 1869 placed him amid the poor, the unemployed, the homeless, alcoholics, prostitutes, the criminal, the infirm and the insane. Forsaking his trademark satire, the Peripatetic Philosopher takes the reader down Melbourne's backstreets after midnight, each sketch describing a lane, rookery, pawnshop, bar or trick being turned in a hansom cab. The idea of 'crossing over' the barriers of class, if only to observe, became an obsession of Clarke's journalism, and the subject of his finest novel, *For the Term of His Natural Life*.

Clarke differentiated the upper bohemia of artists to which he belonged from 'lower bohemia':

> The kingdom of Bohemia is divided into two parts. There is Upper Bohemia ... This is the land of sweet wickedness and unlawful delights ... and of freedom and wit, and pleasure; sparkling with supper parties, and radiant with beauty. But there is another Bohemia – very different to this ... where there are few suppers and no supper parties, where no songs are sung and no wine cups circulate, where vice is vice without the tinsel, and vagabondage is stripped of its poetry. This is the real Bohemia.[56]

Nomadism was a shared experience that linked 'lower' and 'upper' bohemia – the vagabonds who had no choice and the artistic bohemians who chose to be free. Upper bohemia had to step out of the comfort zone and shame the bourgeoisie. Virgil-like, Clarke advises, 'if you would absolutely know what Bohemia means ... hire a loafer's suit of clothes, leave your watch on the mantle piece, and come with me ... through a real Inferno'. He subscribed to Balzac's belief that by dressing 'like a workman' and journeying in his footsteps, an educated writer could actually 'live the life of another': 'My power of observation seemed to be intuitive; it penetrated into the souls of others without overlooking their bodies; while listening to these people I was wedded ... to their life.'[57] This type of romantic identification with down-and-outs persists in the Australian bohemian tradition, and has an echo today, as young students, artists and hipsters seek out the frisson, colour and cred of poor, seedy or immigrant inner-city precincts, unknowing harbingers of gentrification.

For Clarke and other writers of his generation the fascination with social descent had less to do with social justice than a hunger for sensational experiences stimulated by new developments in the European gothic aesthetic as well as the anonymity of the modern city. In addition to freeing one from consequences, anonymity could also facilitate identity play, a creative performance by the bohemian where the city literally becomes a stage and, in the manner of a method actor, the writer might imagine he is walking in the shoes of another.

The labyrinthine spaces of the modern city were a physical manifestation of class divisions and also a reflection of the ethnic patchwork of an immigrant population. Clarke's excursions into 'China Town' conjure romantic, exotic images of a 'feast of lanterns', the 'Great Wall', 'Timour the Tartar', 'pirate junks', 'willow-pattern plates' and the perils of opium addiction and racial miscegenation.[58] Melbourne was depicted as a 'city-wilderness' that tests men and women just as nature tested Robinson Crusoe.[59] The mid-nineteenth century gothic found 'the Other' within the familiar urban context, rather than in strange foreign lands or in the past. The exoticisation should not be confused with embrace of the Chinese as equals but rather an orientalist romanticisation of difference, which could just as easily manifest itself in the racial prejudice of some of Clarke's anti-Semitic and anti-Irish satire. Clarke asked readers to 'imagine a hunter of men instead of a hunter of beasts, a desert of locked doors instead of a desert of sand, a pavement instead of a prairie, a policeman instead of a Comanche, and you have your Bohemian'. By journeying into the backstreets where gentlemen seldom tread, a bohemian as flâneur could convince himself that he was flouting the conventions of bourgeois society, even if the reality was vicarious research for an article.

Lower bohemia was a libidinous place full of temptation for the unwary gentleman. Clarke is particularly good at describing sexualised zones of the city that are both public and private, such as brothels, drinking houses and even cabs. He observed drivers, doubling as pimps, luring unsuspecting passengers into temptation by picking up a prostitute who 'frequently succeeds in inveigling the pigeon into her house'. Sex was traded as another commodity, as '[d]irty and draggle-tailed women begin to appear at the ends of right-of-ways, and the popular music-halls have just vomited forth a crew of drunken soldiers … while in some of the door ways flaunting, but shabbily dressed women peer forth, like spiders from their web, on the look-out for prey'.[60]

Drawn since childhood to 'whatever was strange, mournful or grotesque', Clarke was especially fond of Edgar Allan Poe.

He enjoyed the earlier English gothic wave of ghost stories, medieval castles and dungeons, but in adulthood was excited by the new wave of realist gothic, including works by Dickens, that found terror lurking in the slums and rookeries of the modern city, and in the twisted recesses of men's minds. The mid-Victorian gothic argued that evil had an environmental dimension, so that if men were treated like beasts they would behave like beasts. Clarke found evil in man's injustice to man, in slums and crime and modern despotisms like prisons, asylums and work houses. It was in the tangle of alleyways, brothels and opium dens of Melbourne and, ultimately, in the prison system on which the colonies were built that Clarke believed modern evil was to be found and which he began to critique.

In a series of articles on Port Arthur he would focus on alienating aspects of nineteenth-century modernity such as the bureaucratic regulation of human beings, the institutionalisation of the poor and an industrialised convict 'system'.[61] An unlikely crusader, Clarke found himself at the infamous prison on a retainer from the *Australian Journal*. By then transportation had long ceased but some old lags, still serving out their sentences, were trotted out as virtual exhibits for what had already become a tourist attraction. The articles reminded readers of the brutality of transportation at a time when the convict stain was shameful and nice people preferred this fag end of the convict system to be kept out of sight, out of mind. But Clarke reckoned 'the smell of it remained – remains'. He then turned his research into the gothic gulag masterpiece initially titled *His Natural Life*, in serialisation to make sure that no one would forget that 'for half a century the law allowed the vagabonds and criminals of England to be subjected to a lingering torment, to a hideous debasement, to a monstrous system of punishment, futile for good and horribly powerful for evil'.[62] For Clarke, the barbarity of convictism still festered behind the facade of the colony's material progress. His belief that 'the law makes the criminal' was radical for the day, and his humanist critique of 'the system' remains a powerful corrective to the Australian obsession with locking away our undesirables.

• • •

Another border Clarke was tempted to transgress was his own inner consciousness via psychotropic drugs – a gothic theme that would reappear in subsequent generations. Asked whether he liked absinthe he replied: 'Not particularly, but I'm experimenting with it. They say it'll drive a fellow mad in a month and I want to find out if that's fact … I've tried opium smoking and I rather liked that. There are lots of lies told about these things, you know.'[63] In 1868 he wrote an article while under the influence of cannabis, claiming that 'no man had ever willingly given to the world a poem or story composed while under the effects of a narcotic', though he must have been aware of the promotion of such experimentation by Samuel Taylor Coleridge, Thomas de Quincey, Théophile Gautier, Baudelaire, Balzac and Victor Hugo. While his account of eating hashish adhered to the conventions of a gothic narrative, conjuring monks, black forests and witches, Clarke modernised de Quincey's *Confessions of an English Opium-Eater* by presenting the exercise as a scientific experiment into 'psychology' conducted under medical supervision.[64] Claiming 'the drug seems to unlock the doors of thought', Clarke reached for the metaphor of travel across inner and outer landscapes that a later generation would call a 'trip', a journey into his subconscious, as he 'seemed to be two persons in one', his 'ordinary self … listening to some newfound self, of which [he] had been hitherto ignorant'.

DOWNFALL

'[D]escending an octave on the social scale' was not without risk, and therein lay part of the attraction. Some of the desperate and poor Clarke encountered were once respectable 'gentlemen', those trammelled in the gold rush, driven mad by grog or personal tragedy, crippled through illness or bankrupt professionals. Clarke's reportage and fiction tapped into the nineteenth century bourgeois nightmare of downward mobility, disgrace and ruin. One of the attractions of bohemianism was the risk that it posed to an orderly middle-class life, but hedonistic consumption, debt, alcohol and idleness could and did throw respectable gentlemen and artists alike into poverty, bankruptcy, disgrace and ill health – a fate that befell Clarke in the last year of his life.

By the mid-1870s Marcus Clarke's youthful commitment to

living as a bohemian was coming up hard against the limitations
of social status, career and family. In 1869, at the height of his
celebrity, he married Marian Dunn, an actress and daughter of
the popular Melbourne actor, comedian and impresario John
Dunn. Clarke enjoyed theatre and performance across its various
genres, and found writing for the stage, whether original scripts
and librettos or adapting European works into English and local
conditions, to be easy money for not too much labour. His relationship with Marian grew out of this immersion in Melbourne's
energetic, robust theatrical life. While more comfortable in burlesque, she had won glowing reviews and quite a few admirers
playing Ophelia in *Hamlet*, and met Clarke while performing in
the play *Extremes* with the 'Press Amateurs', a group that included
some of the Yorick bohemians. The Irish immigrant Dunn
family, whose real name was O'Donoghue, was something of a
troupe, with sister Rosa and one brother also treading the boards.
The alliance clearly accentuated Clarke's championing of the
carnivalesque and his own tendency to act out identities, and
represented a further shot across the bows of respectability. Even
in the antipodes marriage to an actress was not considered quite
the done thing for a man of Clarke's social class.

Children appeared in quick succession and Clarke tried
to settle down to family life. Indeed, he made an ostentatious
show of this new phase by acting the colonial gentleman:
obtaining 'a little farm of eight hundred-acres and orchard' in
Melbourne's hinterland, engaging a cook, groom and nurse,
and declaring himself 'fully determined to turn over a new
leaf and forsake Bohemian Melbourne'.[65] However, it appears
Clarke was funding this and other extravagances by borrowing
against a property he was managing for an absent cousin serving
as Governor of the Straits Settlement and then in India. Giving
the appearance of settling down, he wrote to Cyril Hopkins
in 1877, lamenting that '[w]hen one is thirty-one and has five
children, two of whom are girls, one begins to think seriously
of the duties of life.'[66] His new responsibilities entailed taking on
the highly respectable position of sub-librarian at the Melbourne
Public Library (now the State Library of Victoria) at £350 per
annum. Clarke enjoyed the support of the library's Chairman
of Trustees, Sir Redmond Barry, who wanted his well-read and

curious mind at the disposal of Melbourne's premier cultural institution. For his part, Clarke was thrilled to have the largest collection of books in the continent at his disposal, and conceived his role as something of a public intellectual, digging into Australia's history and transforming his research into accessible and educative publications, such as *Old Tales of a New Country* (1871), while also recycling material into his magnum opus. Yet, according to Hugh McCrae, he was unable to adapt to the discipline and attention to detail and administrative diligence required of a librarian. He reported to George McCrae that he 'coveted his freedom so much that he would rather scintillate outside than be earning his salary locked up among books'.[67] Clarke's presence at his desk could never be guaranteed, as he continued to work as a freelance journalist and to attend to his various publishing endeavours about town. It is said that he signalled his presence in the library to friends by leaving a cigar in the mouth of a lion statue that guarded the building.

Although he had moved his growing family into an expensive country estate that was beyond his means, he continued to live a bohemian half-life of freelance journalism, keeping a flat in the city and indulging in excessive drinking. His emotional resources were stretched too, by an infatuation with his wife's married sister Rosa, with whom he entered a romance in 1872, manifest in surviving love letters that paint a picture of shared passion for literature, ideas and each other.[68] They also suggest that guilt prevented sexual consummation of the relationship and strained Clarke's marriage until Rosa's departure for England the next year.

Clarke was not one to avoid a fight. He stirred up controversy with his condemnation of the war against the Tasmanian Aborigines.[69] He was shortly thereafter condemned by the Bishop of Melbourne as an atheist for writing a pamphlet exulting in the slaying of religion by science and, in 1880, his musical farce lampooning the Victorian government was performed despite being banned. He was moving beyond the cynical superciliousness of the Peripatetic Philosopher. The colonial gentleman was condemned as a hypocrite: 'Gentleman! How that grand old word has been prostituted. "Gentleman" once meant an honest, courteous, brave and liberal man – a man who had an arm to strike at oppression and vice, and a heart to pity the repentant and the weak ... Now it means – money.'[70]

Money, or want of it, was a constant problem for Clarke. His addiction to the high life meant that he and his large family were perennially broke. 'It is no use borrowing if you mean to pay', he had once advised readers of *Humbug*. In 1874 he was declared insolvent and endured the public shame of appearing on the bankruptcy list. This led to the sale of his treasured book collection and the evaporation of much goodwill from benefactors who had until now tolerated his eccentricities. He had picked one fight too many with the colonial elite and was frozen out. Denied an expected promotion, Clarke endured his second bankruptcy and the compulsory sequestration of his estate, making his position at the library untenable.

Clarke complained that he attracted both envy for an assumption of superiority, and ostracism for breaking accepted codes.[71] But destabilising the codes of class was a real threat in an insecure society where some of the rulers and businessmen had emerged only recently from petit bourgeois, working-class or even convict origins. As long as bohemia was confined to the spirited antics of the gentlemanly bohemian clubs it was easily comprehensible as entertaining, if at times disrespectful, but in venturing outside class and other boundaries – such as solvency and sobriety – that distinguished a gentleman, Clarke's bohemianism became offensive to the rules of social intercourse. Ultimately the attempt to be both a libertine and respectable could not be sustained, as the excesses of Clarke's lifestyle undermined his purse, his reputation and his health.

Rapidly descending into poverty and his spirit broken, Marcus Clarke died prematurely from the sudden onset of the bacterial disease erysipelas in a rented St Kilda tenement in 1881. Manning Clark was to reflect a century later:

'Clarke's own dissolution foreshadowed the shape of things to come, the power of the conservative, petty-bourgeois view of the world to render impotent all those who, like Clarke, dreamed a great dream, only to see it fade away before the stern facts of Australia's past.'[72]

Yet Marcus Clarke did not have a tragic approach to life and should not be judged by the ignominy of his demise. Apart from

penning the first great Australian novel, his achievement was
to show future aspirants a new way to be an artist, by making
one's own life a work of art. Marcus Clarke imagined a curious
bohemia not content with the insular elitism of its own kind,
but stimulated by risky experiences, at least as an observer, from
the exotic to the narcotic, the criminal to the erotic – while
remaining always the cultured dandy dedicated to conversation,
clothes and café society. His writing and example made an
impression, and ensured that bohemianism in Australia would
strive for more than the japes of the club and the cosmopolitan
conviviality of the café and experience social difference. While
bohemia helped the writers of 1860s and 70s Melbourne to stake
their own distinction, it had the potential to shake up society's
larger system of distinction.

Over the next two decades this bohemian legacy took off
like Paterson's Curse as a distinctly native-born style of bush
yarns developed around the new *Bulletin* magazine and there
was an efflorescence of Australian painting produced out of
painters' colonies in Melbourne and Sydney. For the young
journalists, writers and visual artists emerging in the 1880s and
90s, Clarke's style provided both a model and a standard against
which to rebel.

But Clarke preferred the city to the bush. Longing for what
was modern and new in the Paris of Balzac and Baudelaire, he
introduced the style of the flâneur to Australian journalism,
revealing the literary potential of the colonial city. Clarke's use
of bohemianism to cultivate carnival and celebrity, to inspire
self-publishing experiments and to expose media artifice itself
through social and textual play was especially influential for
successive generations of literary bohemians who wanted to
be simultaneously journalists and artists. Henry Gyles Turner
had despaired that a country without moss-grown abbeys or
castles was ruinous of the romantic.[73] However Clarke found
colonial romanticism in bohemia itself and his creation became
an inspiration for future writers, journalists, poets, painters
and philosophers who came to believe that an artist should be
bohemian.

BUSH BARDS AND ARTIST HEROES

1880-1914

When Henry Lawson first visited the *Bulletin* offices overlooking Sydney Harbour at Circular Quay in the early 1880s he was wearing his work overalls, which were splattered with paint from his day job painting coaches. The young man had grown up in the bush. He was the only son of a Norwegian sailor who struggled to scratch a living out of panning for specks of gold in unyielding creek beds and farming a dry, scrubby selection until hardship and drink broke up his marriage. Harry was a shy, awkward boy, perhaps on account of being deaf in one ear. But, despite these handicaps, he had the ability to see and hear what others did not. His mother Louisa brought him to Sydney, where she grasped with both hands the new ideas and opportunities of the age, transforming herself into a publisher of radical ideas. Harry was stimulated by the creative milieu that gathered around his mother to kindle their idealism into verse, but he would not forget what the Australian bush could do to men's dreams.

Bulletin editor J.F. Archibald, himself from a humble country background, had been inspired by his own democratic ideals to tap into the talents of the pubs and shearing sheds to give shape to a distinctive national culture. After first throwing an unsolicited poem of Lawson's in the wastebasket, Archibald reconsidered it and the *Bulletin* found perhaps its greatest bush bard – a balladeer of mateship who found comedy and dignity in the little things of life. And at the chaotic offices of the magazine Henry Lawson discovered the antidote to his shyness and loneliness, in 'the breezy, careless, humorous comradeship that made up the Bohemian life of writers and artists'.[1] The *Bulletin*'s 'new romanticism' of the common man spawned a larrikin bohemianism in which Lawson's humour and eccentricities thrived into the new century. Yet the boys'-own bonhomie that Lawson dubbed 'beerhemia' would prove a curse as well as a muse.

• • •

At the same time in Sydney a handsome young man, also paint-stained, was observed daubing away in his studio enjoying 'a careless existence – eating when he felt like it and working all hours as the mood took him. Dressed anyhow, with wisps of long hair hanging over his forehead and a cigarette for ever drooping from his mouth, Charles Conder looked the embodiment of one of the heroes of his reading at that time – Murger's *La Vie de Bohème*.'[2]

Would-be artist Conder was a child of Empire, having spent part of his youth in India amid the exotica and pampered privilege of the Raj. Like Marcus Clarke he had immigrated from England to Australia while still an adolescent and spent dreary days as apprentice to his uncle, a geological surveyor, dreaming of painting rather than measuring the landscape. He abandoned surveying, took up art classes under Julian Ashton and began working as an illustrator in the Sydney press. What the young Conder lacked in money he made up for in charm, wit and a way with women. A chance meeting with Melbourne illustrator and painter Tom Roberts in 1888 led to the two painting *en plein air* around Coogee beach and a resolution by Conder to join his new friend in artists' camps in the bush and coastal hinterland of Melbourne.

The slightly older and debonair Roberts, known for the sartorial refinement of his red satin-lined cape and 'crush topper', was the bright centre of a collective of visual artists that tempted the pleasure-seeking Conder with a colourful palette of salons, studio soirees, artists' societies, 'smoke nights', exhibition parties and bush camps. In Melbourne Conder, who was influenced by the Aesthetic Movement, a British vogue promoted by the impressionist painter Whistler and playwright Oscar Wilde, made an immediate impression: 'One evening after the life class was started, the door opened and Tom Roberts appeared with a young man from Sydney. This was Charles Conder, in corduroy pantaloons of brown velvet, brown velvet coat, open shirt with a Shelley collar, a flowing tie in a bow, and a wide scarlet cummerbund.'[3]

In the bohemian clubs and studios of inner Melbourne and the camps around Heidelberg, Conder and his new friends found companionship in art, as well as the originality and savvy to launch themselves on the public as an emerging school of Australian painting. But their landscape impressionism would not be enough for Conder, who would push on with playful experiments in 'symbolism' and celebrity in the bohemian milieus of Paris and London.

• • •

While the bush bard and the urbane aesthete might appear to have little in common, they both thought of themselves as bohemians. The late nineteenth century was a golden age for Australian bohemia, stimulating art, journalism and nascent national visions. New variants on romanticism were gathering young converts but pulling in contrary directions, towards an elite 'art for art's sake' of the sort championed by Conder, and a more egalitarian folk nationalism that Lawson made his own. The playful literary bohemia evolving from the 1870s was joined by a visual arts bohemia that overlapped with journalists and writers, but also charted a different course, concerned with the painter as a new type of modern hero. Marcus Clarke's schizophrenic identities as the harlequin trickster and refined dandy diverged into a new larrikin carnivalesque of the romanticised common man associated with the press and the other a cosmopolitan aestheticism that was cultivated by painters. The bohemians of pen and brush did come together – in their obsession with the Australian landscape, in new media on which they collaborated, and at great public parties – but painters made their mark in the salon while the writers were more at home in the saloon.

A TRADITION BEGINS

Bohemia was central to the writers and visual artists of what literary critic Vance Palmer called the 'Legendary 90s'. It was a way of life they celebrated in articles, fiction, poems and social gatherings at the time, and recalled later with nostalgia in memoirs and articles. Journalist and academic Arthur Jose recalled the 'romantic' 1890s as 'the epoch of the band of brothers, Bohemians'. Cartoonist and entrepreneurial inventor George Taylor described the 'joy of living' for that decade's 'Bohemian Boys'.[4] In *Bohemians at the Bulletin* cartoonist, painter, writer, and all-round multimedia libertine Norman Lindsay wrote humorous (and bitchy) reminiscences of the eccentric writers and visual artists with whom he worked.

French bohemian style was important to the youthful identities of both press and artist bohemians. Bohemian texts came to the Australian colonies from Europe via an internationalising cultural market, winning new readers and audiences. Henri Murger's novel *Scènes de la vie de Bohème* enjoyed a revival in the 1880s and 90s with aspiring artists, who found its stories resonated with their attempts to begin careers. In the 1890s an English translation was published in Melbourne by Fabian socialist Henry Champion, and Puccini's operatic version *La Bohème* was regularly performed in both Melbourne and Sydney. A brand-new bohemian novel, George du Maurier's *Trilby*, struck a chord with the young in the 1890s.[5] Aspiring illustrators Lionel and Norman Lindsay became obsessed with the theatrical version that played in Melbourne, writing about 'Trilbyana' in the *Free-Lance* magazine. Lionel claimed in his memoir that *Trilby* 'introduced me to a new way of life altogether'.[6]

Young people in this period also imbibed writing, models and legends from Australia's first bohemian generation. Marcus Clarke's writing about art and bohemia was part of the word-scape of 1870s metropolitan colonial culture that urbane young men like Archibald, Roberts and Conder would have devoured. His comic novel *Twixt Shadow and Shine* enjoyed several reprints in the 1890s and Archibald wrote about his thrill, on first arriving in Melbourne from Warrnambool, at catching glimpses of his hero Clarke strolling the streets 'in a white suit'.[7] Clarke's contemporary and friend the tragic poet Adam Lindsay Gordon became an important model for Conder, who admired both his poetry and persona.

The transmission of bohemianism from one generation to the next could be more direct. Clarke died in 1881 but his collaborators in the Cave of Adullam, journalists Victor Daley and Theodore Argles, aka Harold Grey, brought the carnivalesque spirit and style of Melbourne's literary bohemia to Sydney. They were at the heart of the print media bohemianism of the second generation, working at the *Bulletin* and establishing the seminal Dawn and Dusk Club, which counted both Henry Lawson and Tom Roberts among its members. Irish-born Daley provided a direct continuity with Melbourne's first bohemian groups and a living example into the twentieth century of the carnivalesque style of literary bohemianism of the 1860s and 70s. Daley, who Archibald saluted as 'the rising poet of this country' in 1882, is a lynchpin identity not just between bohemian generations, but also between Europe and Australia, and Melbourne and Sydney, as well as between different groups and artistic professions. In 1902 he was still reminiscing in the *Bulletin* about his initiation into Clarke's bohemia: 'I was in Paradise – a Paradise that smelt of whiskey and cigar smoke, and echoed with light-hearted laughter. I had previously read the *Vie de Boheme*, and I said to myself, "This is Bohemia indeed". And it was.'[8]

Harold Grey helped put the *Bulletin* on its feet, and exposed younger journalists to the bohemian tradition of stunts and japes. Grey and Daley were typical of many of Clarke's journalist friends who became the editors and publishers of the 1880s and 90s, and were responsible for introducing younger colleagues to bohemianism within media workplaces. In Melbourne, Maurice Brodzky kept the flame alight, publishing the influential art magazine *Table Talk*. Likewise, Cave of Adullam member Theodore Fink, grown wealthy through the Melbourne *Herald* and land speculation, became a prominent patron of the arts in Victoria, influencing the younger generation of painters with whom he participated in the cosmopolitan bohemianism at Fasoli's café.

Melbourne poet Hugh McCrae had a more intimate connection to the first generation of bohemians. As the son of George McCrae – Melbourne writer, Yorick founder and friend of Clarke – Hugh boasted a proud bohemian pedigree. In *My Father and My Father's Friends* he claimed to have sat on Clarke's knee as a child, where he absorbed stories of the larger-than-life characters of the Yorick and Cave of Adullam. With nostalgia and humour McCrae carried their inspiration into the next generation in the 1890s and beyond, reminiscing in 1935 that '[t]hrough a stroke of fate, I constitute a living link between our present literary life and that of the sixties and seventies'.[9]

Despite these continuities there were profound changes in bohemianism that distinguished the second generation of bohemians from the first. The very first sentence of Arthur Jose's *The Romantic Nineties* suggests a stand-off between his generation and 'the upholders of Kendall and Holdsworth and Marcus Clarke and George Gordon McCrae – in whose minds the new boisterousness roused even more alarm than disgust'. Tensions between bohemians of different generations arose because of competition for position, but also due to the different environments each had experienced in their youths and the different cultural markets in which they practised their arts in early adulthood. Most men in the first generation of bohemians had grown up in Britain in the 1840s and 50s in privileged, educated families. Journeying far from home they found a sense of belonging in the new bohemian groups, but also in the British Empire and the status of gentlemen in a stratified class system. The second generation, especially journalists and writers, were overwhelmingly native born, some with lower-class and more provincial origins. Most felt a strong attachment to the landscape of their birth, an affinity to a 'rising generation' and enthusiasm for a coming nation. For some the bush, its people and slang were the natural measure against which English toffs and local swells would be judged and even ridiculed. As they reached maturity in the 1870s and 80s they enjoyed the security of already-established cultural institutions and a growing literary and visual marketplace. Improved travel by steamship meant that many were able to visit Britain and France, returning with new ideas about bohemianism and the aesthetics of their arts and mediums.

CHANGES IN THE CULTURAL MARKET

The cultural market established by the institution builders, publishers and impresarios of the 1860s was transformed by rising circulation and a concomitant increase in career opportunities on newspapers and magazines.[10] Circulation increase was driven by the growth of the reading market through natural population increase, immigration, urbanisation, better distribution, improved literacy and more leisure time in which to read. Whereas the bohemians of Clarke's circles had written for periodicals and literary supplements with a bourgeois market, writers of the second generation increasingly found employment on magazines and newspapers targeted at working-class or cross-class readerships. Most important for changes in bohemia was the diversification in print media forms and styles, especially the growth in popularity of 'new journalism' in tabloid newspapers and magazines, and the emergence of both an illustrated and a radical press.

The catalyst for media innovation and the formation of a new bohemia in Sydney was the *Bulletin*, established in 1880 by a consortium in which Archibald played the creative lead. Norman Lindsay hyperbolically described it 'the only cultural centre this country possessed'.[11] Jose believed that the *Bulletin* 'bards and artists ... were assuredly the motive power in the new romanticism', which he termed 'the romance of common things'.[12] The *Bulletin* applied the stylistic techniques of new journalism from the United States, Britain and France to a national weekly magazine (before an Australian nation existed), which also took an intelligent and satirical approach to cultural, social and political debate. It broke new ground in its strong preference for Australian content written in local vernacular and styles, but it was the ensemble of material, design layout, and generous deployment of black-and-white illustrations that marked the *Bulletin* as distinctive. During its first two decades the *Bulletin* engaged with radical agendas of the day, but it was in the magazine's sense of fun, disruption of expectations and topsy-turvy mockery of authority that it was most subversive.

This new hybrid succeeded in winning a mass cross-class audience by promoting its version of a burgeoning Australian identity, and targeting the city and the bush, the fashionable

cosmopolitans and the literature-hungry readers of parish
pumps, shearing sheds and selections. Under co-founder and
editor-in-chief Archibald (from 1886 to 1903), and literary
editor A.G. Stephens (from 1896 to 1906), it quickly became a
magnet for young aspiring writers and illustrators from around
Australia and a centre for many of the bohemian networks that
formed in Sydney in the late nineteenth and early twentieth
centuries. Rather than a single '*Bulletin* bohemia', the periodical
was the centre for a number of cliques and networks, dominated
by particular personalities, that gathered together during work
hours and socially in what stalwart Roderic Quinn called 'a
genial company of artists, verse-makers and prose writers'.[13] Key
bohemian identities at the *Bulletin* in this period were Henry
Lawson, Victor Daley, Edwin J. Brady, John Le Gay Brereton,
Roderic Quinn, Fred J. Broomfield, Hugh McCrae, Christopher
Brennan and cartoonists Phil May, Ed Dyson and later Norman
and Lionel Lindsay.

The *Bulletin* brought talented people together and encouraged a degree of creative freedom and iconoclasm. As well as
promoting a democratic sense of ownership of the paper, the
innovative policy of inviting contributions from the readership
enabled the editors to tap a rich vein of anecdote and language
and to talent scout an outstanding group of characters. The
enigmatic Archibald was an imaginative and generous mentor to
his contributors, appreciating a diversity of personalities, styles,
stories and themes united by their illumination of an emerging
Australian people. His biographer Sylvia Lawson likened
Archibald's role to that of a 'circus ringmaster' – coordinating,
cajoling and, where necessary, controlling his performers.[14] A
policeman's son who started out on the *Warrnambool Examiner*,
Archibald's regional lower middle-class background helped
him gauge popular taste, but through bohemia he acquired the
cultural capital of the dandy, adopting a Gallic style and even
obscuring his common origins by replacing his baptismal names
John Fenton with the exotic Jules François.

Archibald's achievement was, for a time, to change the rules
of the game for writers and illustrators, so that his own class trajectory and hybrid experience as an Australian-born, bush-bred
cosmopolitan became the new criteria for success. Some people

from lower-class backgrounds with creative talent were given a go, and his team sought to turn the tables on English cultural condescension and local forelock tuggers alike. Whereas in the 1860s and 70s bohemia was an English gentlemen's club, it now tried to be a democratic elite in dialogue with a newly-imagined Australian people.

• • •

Magazines, newspapers and other media, then as today, were vitally important as projects around which the bohemian milieu was given purpose, providing a physical space in which creative people gathered to produce a collective text that reflected their individual ideas, aesthetics and skills. Deadlines focused activity, and their fulfilment provided occasions for recreation. The constant grind of criticism and control by editors like A.G. Stephens, which 'could be very cutting and really nasty' according to freelance illustrator George Taylor, suffocated dreams of artistic freedom at work that had to be resuscitated in the leisure sphere where the bohemian was in charge.[15] Journalism also provided an audience for writers and illustrators, from which they could carve celebrity. Just as important as long-lived institutions such as the *Bulletin*, were shorter-lived or more marginal publications such as Brodzky's *Table Talk* (established in 1885), *Bull-Ant* and *Free-Lance*, as well as a vast array of labour and radical papers, including colourful titles like the *Hummer*, *Boomerang*, the *Worker*, *Clarion*, the *New Order* and *Tocsin*.

The newspaper office of the time was being transformed by new technology such as linotype machines, telephones and, at the beginning of the twentieth century, image wiring and typewriters, which slotted journalists and illustrators into an assembly line for the mass production of newspapers and magazines. The biggest change for both writers and journalists in larger enterprises was the speeding up, specialisation and routinisation of tasks. The effect was a proletarianisation of the entry-level positions in journalism, with improved career paths and pay for those who succeeded in the new workplace. Wages in journalism improved from the 1880s, rising from around £2 per week (the average wage) for general reporting to between £4 and £6. But a career based on freelance writing remained precarious. Freelancers were as subject to editorial control and reader taste as full-time employees. A magazine hungry for copy like the *Bulletin* provided opportunities for the novice writer, but also reduced the art of poetry to payment by line. A sure way to increase your rate and secure promotion was to enhance your fame and market appeal. But even celebrity writers such as Lawson remained at the whim of editors who commissioned stories, poems or illustrations from freelancers according to their estimation of popular taste rather than the creator's desire for expression. E.J. Brady complained in verse that

> You may hold your own opinions and hold them dearly, too
> The journal that you live on has a 'policy', and you?
> Why, you barter these opinions for the things you wear and
> eat,
> And you sell your very virtue, like the woman of the street.[16]

Most literary writers of poetry, prose and criticism had their work published in mass-market magazines but the rise of publisher Angus & Robertson in the 1890s provided another avenue for Australian writers, although it remained common for a commissioned author to subsidise a book's production out of their own pocket. The poor compensation or recognition for writing was a constant complaint of litterateurs in late-Victorian Australia. A cynical Lawson famously advised the aspiring author to swim overseas to more lucrative markets, or execute a well-aimed shot to the head.[17] In reality life was difficult for writers everywhere, including the metropolitan centres, which is why most earned their principal income in journalism.

THE RISE OF THE VISUAL ARTISTS

Prior to the 1880s the laws of supply and demand meant that there were too few artists in Australia to constitute their own bohemia. Due to lack of systematic local training, immigrant painters already advanced in their careers, such as Eugene von Guérard, Nicholas Chevalier and Louis Buvelot dominated the small market for paintings but lacked a community of fellow artists akin to the writers of the time.

The increased circulation of periodicals such as the *Bulletin*, as well as innovation in mass reproduction of images such as lithography, etching and photographic printing, were crucial for the growing number of visual artists in Australia. These new technologies, introduced from the late 1870s, enabled the production of image-rich specialist periodicals like the *Illustrated Sydney News*, the *Australian Sketcher*, sports papers such as the *Arrow* and the *Referee*, and longer-term projects, especially the *Picturesque Atlas of Australasia*. Magazines such as the *Bulletin*, *Melbourne Punch* and many labour journals thrived on the black-and-white arts, especially satirical cartoons of news and social issues and caricatures of public figures.

The common pattern was for black-and-white artists to move between publications, or to work as freelancers. On the back of a black-and-white art boom, the number of visual artists able to make a living from commercial illustration grew from 461 in Victoria in 1881 to 1502 in 1891 (according to the Victorian census in that year), challenging the literary cast of Australian bohemia. In the 1880s aspiring painters Tom Roberts, Julian Ashton, Charles Conder and Arthur Streeton were typical of young artists working as freelance illustrators in the popular press and commercial art. When starting out Conder and Frederick McCubbin also held down regular jobs with lithographers and Roberts worked in a photographic studio. From the mid-1890s Lionel and Norman Lindsay worked as jobbing illustrators for the Melbourne *Hawklet*, the socialist *Tocsin*, and even a Sunday school text, before following the work to Sydney's *Bulletin*.[18]

While print media workplaces brought illustrators together in the journalistic environment, in the 1880s a collective way of life among artists was first cultivated then reinforced by art school lessons, sketching excursions and shared studios. Art colleges established by the governments of Victoria and New South Wales, and the schools associated with the National Gallery of Victoria and the Art Society of New South Wales, began the process of encouraging a visual arts collective distinct from literary bohemia. Public visual-art training produced skilled young draughtsmen, commercial artists and painters. Some of the first students recruited to the local colleges, such as Roberts, Streeton and McCubbin, would graduate to the National Gallery School and become leading painters in the 1880s.[19]

The life of the art student offered aspiring illustrators and painters an oasis of discourse, experimentation and social free-for-all. Students were fortunate to have among their teachers in the 1870s and 80s older immigrant painters from Europe such as Buvelot, who taught in Victorian technical schools, and, in New South Wales, Julian Ashton, who established the private Sydney Art School. They introduced new techniques such as painting *en plein air*, then fashionable in France, where artists left the studio to paint outdoors. Importantly, these instructors exposed students to European romantic ideas about the artist that went beyond the utilitarian artisan ambitions of the colleges' founders. In 1914 the *Lone Hand* detailed the rite of passage experienced by a grocer's son attending a painting class who, on receiving a crash course in the bohemian literary classics, 'yearned to paint lovely models in the Latin quarter … developed the habit of abusing his mother … for being a Philistine' and entered the National Gallery School 'full of undigested *la Vie de Bohème* and high hopes of artistic life'.[20] Another student at the school, Hugh McCrae, 'took a room in town and matriculated in smoking and drinking', 'hired dirty models' and 'had uncomfortable adventures and mixed with all sorts of decadents'.[21] This happened in the regional areas as well as the capitals. George Cockerill recalled how as a young journalist and art student at the Ballarat Academy of Art he imbibed *Trilby* and Murger.[22] These schools became sites in which bohemianism was passed on from established artists to younger students over many decades well into the twentieth century.

• • •

At the same time that the mass readership for print publications was providing visual artists with livelihoods as illustrators, the market for purchasing paintings was growing, especially in 1880s Melbourne, thanks to wealth generated by the land boom and the evangelism of galleries, art dealers, art teachers and art magazines such as *Table Talk*. Commissions for portraits increased and from the 1870s public exhibitions were supplemented by a growing number of small private galleries that sold paintings to decorate the homes of the well-to-do. From the 1890s sales to the Art Gallery of New South Wales and commissions by the colonial and later the federal government increased, providing a further source of income and exhibition space for painters.

But with dependence on governments and wealthy customers came complaints. Visual artists grizzled about the power of non-artists who controlled public gallery purchases and criticism, the tastes of moneyed philistines who bought pictures and the need to do press illustration to pay the bills. 'Art was becoming Queen of Commerce,' complained illustrator George Taylor, because 'idealistic art didn't pay'.[23] Young artists in Sydney, recalled Jose, 'devoted [themselves] for the most part to more black and white' for the practical reason that 'black-and-white work was saleable, and very few students had incomes that did not need working for'.[24]

The alienating effects of the market on art should not be exaggerated to the exclusion of the liberating opportunities it unleashed and the agency that bohemia gave cultural producers to explore new possibilities. As historian Richard White has shown, bohemianism was a weapon wielded by various kinds of artists in their bid to be recognised as professionals and to protect their livelihood from the contributions and critical judgement of amateurs who dominated galleries and prizes.[25] It was also an important cultural marker of distinction above and beyond new professional associations such as the Institute of Journalists and the Australian Artists' Association, especially as the occupations of journalist, writer and visual artist were still vague about credentialling.

PRINT MEDIA BOHEMIA AND THE LARRIKIN CARNIVALESQUE

The writers, journalists, poets and editors who made up literary bohemia continued to favour the carnivalesque bohemia inaugurated by the press men of the 1860s and 70s. The spirit of 'topsy-turvy' and 'misrule' underpinned the *Bulletin*'s cheeky larrikinism and its embrace of the rural working class and the Rabelaisian spirit of Norman Lindsay's nymphs and satyrs. But the carnivalesque was most explicit in a bohemian style of public and personal performance that accentuated feasting, inebriation, spirited talk, earthy humour, sexual licence, wit, practical jokes, fancy dress and dancing, which was staged in a succession of mock clubs, blokey pubs, cosmopolitan cafés and masquerade balls.

A succession of overtly bohemian clubs began in Sydney with the Century, founded in 1888 by former prospector and touring actor Fred Broomfield – now sub-editor of the *Bulletin* and a long-term contributor to *Melbourne Punch* – and conceived of as a broad church, 'a Club of pressmen, artists, actors, in short, of all varieties of men having literary, artistic & Bohemian tastes and callings'.[26] Wearing a broad-brimmed hat and brandishing a walking stick like a rapier, the theatrical Broomfield played the part of a swashbuckling cavalier in the streets of Sydney, parrying with fellow bohemians and even fighting a mock pistol duel in Centennial Park. Bohemian clubs multiplied in Sydney with the Dawn and Dusk Club, the Supper Club of the Artists' Society of New South Wales, the Brother Brushes, the Casuals and les Compliqués. Notable Melbourne clubs were the Buonarotti Society, the Cannibal Club, Boobooks, the Savage Club, the Ishmael and the Smoke Nights of the Victorian Artists' Society.

The most famous Sydney bohemian club was the Dawn and Dusk Club, founded by Victor Daley in 1898 as the rightful successor to the Cave of Adullam. Named in homage to an Adam Lindsay Gordon poem, Daley's own book of verse, *At Dawn and Dusk*, furnished its title. Described by John Le Gay Brereton as 'a happy, carefree, gay-bohemian crowd ... they wrote, and sketched, and sang with infinite merriment just because they were in love with the joy of living'.[27] Meeting first at the home of Broomfield, and later at Giovanni's Wine Cellar, the club boasted a large and diverse membership that orbited around the *Bulletin* but extended far beyond it. Daley combined a 'dreamy' poetic vision with a humorous personality encouraging of the carnivalesque. In this spirit he penned a poem to bohemia that began:

> These brave Bohemians, heart in hand,
> March on their way with spirits free;
> They count not moments, sand by sand,
> But spill the hour-glass royally.
> With wine and jest and laughter long ...[28]

The Dawn and Dusk continued the Cave's tradition of silly rules, exotically named office bearers, mock rituals, practical jokes and absurd speeches from Clarke's heyday. Lawson provided the club motto: 'Roost high and crow low'.[29] The humour and fun of gatherings dedicated to 'wine and jest and laughter long' emerged from the witty subversion of faux formality, structured around parliamentary-style debates, toasts and the official meeting procedure of real gentlemen's clubs. Excessive consumption of alcohol, performances of poetry and song, pranks and general showing off were the chief entertainments. Daley was elected 'Symposiarch', with Fred Broomfield the 'Arch-Dusker'. Leading 'Duskers' were titled 'Heptarchs' and included: 'Bard of the Tribe' Henry Lawson; James Philp, proprietor of the *Chinese Australian Herald* and thus 'celestial interpreter' and intermediary between the Duskers and Confucius; George Taylor, an aviation advocate who became 'a high commissioner, entrusted with the discovery of a North-west passage to Mars'; and editor Bertram Stevens, who was club archivist. Poet E.J. Brady and labour journalist and future premier William Holman were occasional Heptarchs. As well as writers, club members included the painters Tom Roberts and Frank Mahony, sculptor Nelson Illingworth, composer Nicholas Gehde and solicitor William Bruton, styled the 'Devil's Advocate'.

The group also elected 'spiritual' Duskers, who included Clarke's hero Balzac, joined by Shakespeare, Montaigne, Rabelais, Thackeray and Aristophanes. While amusing, the Duskers were laying claim for colonial artists to a place among equals in a particular western literary tradition. They also mocked in equal measure their country's lack of white antiquity and the alienness of European romantic models in Australia, with their objective 'to establish a society for the erection of ancient ruins in Australia'. The club rules were printed in Chinese 'so as not to give offence to members', a joke betraying the racial prejudice prevalent at the time.[30]

Humour, hoaxes and practical jokes were also seen as intrinsically bohemian. Henry Lawson leavened the pathos of his fiction about human dignity in adversity with a comedy about human foibles that flavoured not just his work but also his bohemian self. 'That humour', observed his close friend John Le Gay Brereton, 'was no superficial quality; it ran deep, and therefore was his chief characteristic'.[31] Lawson liked to hoodwink his hapless mates, such as the occasion he arranged for the police to pretend to arrest and fine his friend Jack Moses for carrying a rooster through the Strand Arcade.

Apart from its dedication promoting 'the good fellowship', the Dawn and Dusk Club had the more serious objective of criticising members' work 'with bracing candour and chastening conceit', free from the pressure of deadlines and editorial authority. But the club folded after a couple of years and the energy and core of people moved on.

EXCLUSIVE IN TOUGH TIMES

Whereas the first generation of bohemians went out of their way to find common ground with all sorts of people engaged in cultural pursuits, the second-generation clubs were much fussier, less likely to welcome civil servants, doctors and solicitors into their ranks. The 'Bohemian hatred of the Philistine' asserted by the first generation of bohemians became far more shrill and now applied to the type of cultured professionals who had been welcome in Clarke's bohemia. Thanks to the expansion of the press it was not difficult for clubs to attain a critical mass of gainfully employed media workers and to dispense with those who made amateur forays into writing.

But greater exclusivity had its problems. George Taylor, a capitalist himself, reasoned that it was the prohibition of the 'philistine' businessman that deprived bohemian clubs of 'the needful £ s.d., that cursed so many clubs to close after only "a brief and merry life"'.[32] While men of business such as himself clearly did gain entry if they had paid their dues in a creative profession, these clubs were not open to a large fee-paying membership in the manner of the long-lived Yorick, but pushed further the Cave of Adullam's model of exclusive coteries of friends and colleagues who derived their livelihoods from writing, editing and illustration. 'Bohemian clubs,' observed Jose, were started 'in order that soul may commune with soul alone, the Philistine is always debarred'.[33]

The discourse against respectability was heightened by a greater hostility to religion. There was also an increasingly virulent misogyny, evident in the journalism of the *Bulletin* and *Truth*. Unlike the more female-friendly cosmopolitanism to be found in café bohemia, the Dawn and Dusk – like so many other bohemian gatherings before the First World War – remained a boys club. Memoirs emphasise terms evocative of male group bonding, such as 'kinship', 'fellowship', 'brothers', 'comrades', 'boys' and, of course, 'mates' and 'mateship', reflecting the near absence of women on the staff of newspapers, and a prejudice against women artists who were unfairly dismissed as dabblers and hobbyists. Female writers did not have the option of working as career journalists and so had difficulty sharing in the male camaraderie of the press office that was the common currency of literary bohemia. Despite the success of *My Brilliant Career*, Miles Franklin could only contribute freelance journalism under a nom de plume, and tried careers in nursing and domestic service before committing herself to political activism. Author and poet Mary Gilmore earned her income as a teacher, submitting freelance contributions under assumed names in the 1890s. These talented writers remained outside the collegiate workplaces from which bohemian groups sprang. The result, as revealed by historian Marilyn Lake, was that male press bohemians at this time promoted a 'masculinist' discourse that accentuated men's right to pleasure in opposition to domesticity, women's support for temperance campaigns and the early feminist arguments for equality in marriage, work and suffrage.[34]

While most bohemian clubbists were from bourgeois or petit bourgeois families, membership became wider in class terms following increased mobility into journalism of young people from working class and provincial backgrounds. Archibald began as a compositor on the *Warrnambool Examiner*, moving into reporting and then to Melbourne as a journalist on the *Evening Herald* and *Telegraph*. Lawson's entry into the print media was through Archibald's policy of outreach among its readership and via an apprenticeship in the radical and labour press, which offered him the gamut of experience in journalism, editing and propaganda. Despite the gloss of an English grammar school education, Tom Roberts' widowed mother was without means on the family's arrival in Geelong in 1869 when he was fourteen and her subsequent marriage to a carpenter marked the aspiring illustrator as 'trade'.[35]

The social mobility experienced in the 1880s suffered a reversal in the next decade. Many bohemians who thought themselves financially secure found themselves struggling during the depression of the 1890s which stripped even well-established and connected writers, journalists and artists of their livelihoods. Many writers and illustrators from humble backgrounds simply lacked the fallback of wealthy family for borrowing money and resources. In such hard times, bohemia could serve as a safety-net. Henry Lawson's wife Bertha later remembered that the members of the Dawn and Dusk Club were 'all poor' but richer for their association because '[i]f they had money they shared it. If they had none, they would hold their meetings in a bar where they'd collect enough between them for a drink all round, and have a free counter lunch'.[36]

George Taylor tells of one painter who, unable to sell his paintings at the Annual Exhibition of the Royal Art Society, scraped the paint from the canvases in order to recycle them, apparently a common practice in hard times. Norman Lindsay claimed that the bohemian passion for smoking tobacco was in part because it was an antidote to hunger, explaining that 'as we never had breakfast, after a couple of pipefuls one's belly becomes a torpid void and one was able to endure the interval before the midday meal at a sixpenny restaurant'.[37] Brady complained that to 'live by literature alone has entailed self-denials, privations, shortages, sufficient to destroy the joy of living in some of us, and to breed despair in others'.[38] But Taylor observed that poets and artists were 'ever in a state of insolvency', yet 'could sing and sketch as if life were one great joke'.[39] The paradox of bohemia during this harsh depression was the display of a wealth of cultural capital even while actual monetary capital was lacking. Daley rendered this familiar contradiction in his poem 'The Old Bohemian':

> And though his purse was lean,
> And though his coat was dyed,
> He had a lordly mien
> And air of ancient pride.

• • •

Despite the acceptance of men from modest backgrounds, the clubs of literary bohemia continued to demonstrate rejection of the bourgeoisie by overtures to the gentry. This was best exemplified by Daley's cultivation of the British Governor of New South Wales, Lord Beauchamp. The young viceroy was known for liberal views. His homosexuality and Anglo-Catholicism are said to have later inspired Evelyn Waugh's *Brideshead Revisited*. A passionate art lover, the aristocrat attended some of the club's functions, and undertook the unprecedented public gesture of organising a bohemian ball at Government House with Daley. This 'society' trend in literary bohemia relied on the formal structure and rituals of the bohemian clubs, but was greatly enhanced by mixing with visual artists within and outside the clubs.

WHEN WRITERS AND PAINTERS MIXED

The older literary bohemia was changed from the 1880s by the movement of visual artists into the bohemian clubs. Artists had their own unique painters' groups but as illustrators Roberts, Streeton, George Lambert and the Lindsays were part of the print media community and active participants in many of the same bohemian clubs, circles and events as *Bulletin* writers. The writers were welcome in bohemian clubs in which illustrators and painters dominated, so when the Dawn and Dusk folded most of its members happily transferred their attentions to the Supper Club of the New South Wales Society of Artists that convened monthly at the Café François in George Street, Sydney. Founded and presided over by Tom Roberts, it was established for professional painters and illustrators, as opposed to the older Arts Society, which was dominated by enthusiastic laymen. Described by George Taylor as a 'glorious, wonderful feast of song, sketch and story that would follow the feast of beefsteak', the club introduced the innovation of visual dialogue to after-dinner shenanigans, with the illustrators competing to caricature 'friends and enemies'.[40] Archibald and most other editors of Sydney papers joined, reflecting the fact that many members of the Society of Artists depended on these men for illustration work. Chairman Tom Roberts became a crucial bridge builder between artists' and journalists' bohemias.

Visual artists' clubs had their origins in Melbourne, beginning with the Buonarotti Society, launched in 1883 by Cyrus
Mason, a British engraver and illustrator who understood the
need for the city's visual artists to come together in a community where they could exchange ideas, skills and bonhomie. The
club was named in honour of perhaps the greatest artist hero,
Michelangelo di Lodovico Buonarrotti Simoni, then enjoying
something of a revival in Britain and Europe. An enthusiast
for the English Pre-Raphaelite movement, Marcus Clarke had
taken a leading role in expanding the collection of more modern
paintings exhibited by the Public Library as a nascent National
Gallery, and in his clubs, as illustrators on his magazines, and
especially in the short story 'The Poor Artist' embraced visual
artists as part of his concept of bohemia.[41] The Buonarotti Society
sought to fill the bohemian space in Melbourne left by Clarke's
demise, but had the larger ambition of advancing the status and
income of artists by providing vital exhibition space, holding
soirees known as 'Conversaziones' and promoting experimental
techniques. The Society's first headquarters was the Prince's
Bridge Hotel on the corner of Flinders and Swanston Street,
owned by Henry Young and Thomas Jackson. The former was
an avid art collector and he adorned the labyrinthine spaces
of the newly renovated pub with works by overseas and local
painters, together with Pacific Islands artefacts and curios reminiscent of the Yorick Club.[42]

It was the Buonarotti Society that brought together the
young jobbing illustrators who would later be identified as the
'Heidelberg School' – Roberts, McCubbin, John Longstaff and
Louis Abrahams – and enabled these National Gallery School
students to mix with an older generation of émigré painters and
exposed them to plein-air camps. For a bohemian role model the
Buonarotti members looked to Adam Lindsay Gordon, whose
passionate poetry they found evocative of the Australian landscape. A revolutionary move for the 1880s was the Buonarotti's
insistence that women artists be admitted as members, participating in all the activities of the group, including life-drawing
classes.

The Victorian Artists' Society was the precursor to the
New South Wales Society of Artists, and established in 1888

with Tom Roberts on the executive before he and Streeton decamped to Sydney in 1891 as the depression tightened its grip on Melbourne. It held regular Smoke Nights in East Melbourne, usually run by Theodore Fink, who would open proceedings with the stock joke: 'Gentlemen, the bar is open and the drinks are free. The proceeds will be devoted to the building fund.'[43] Member William Moore described these nights as a heterogeneous collection of 'well-known citizens of Bohemia' where 'bards gave the glad-hand to painters, and journalists smoke in harmony with soulful musicians' and a 'caricaturist is seen haughtily arguing with a prominent merchant who has strayed in'.[44] It enjoyed a lively format of impromptu performances, jokes and sketches.

The Savage Club, established in 1894, was inspired by London's bohemian club of the same name, and sought to blur the line between a bohemian and a bourgeois gentleman's club by prioritising cultural and intellectual pursuits and welcoming (male) writers, artists and journalists such as Randolph Bedford and Roberts as esteemed members. The illustrators soon festooned the walls with caricatures and other images. The long-lived club continued to attract creative characters along with the professional and business elite through the twentieth century and indeed still thrives today, thanks to a spirit of tongue-in-cheek bonhomie and opportunities for networking with the city's power brokers. The Savage absorbed the Yorick Club in 1966, and can thus claim inheritance from Melbourne's first bohemian club and lineage back to Marcus Clarke.

The Lindsay brothers Lionel, Percy and Norman played a leading role in the Ishmael, a bohemian club notable for marrying Marcus Clarke's spirit of play with aesthetic flamboyance and a new embrace of sexual freedom. Founded in Melbourne in the late 1890s by Bedford, many of its members were *Bull-Ant* magazine regulars, including Bedford, Herman Kuhr, cartoonists Will and Ted Dyson, and Ray Parkinson. The group met in a private room above Fasoli's Café in Lonsdale Street and members adopted nonsense titles such as 'Comptroller of the Garlic', 'Medicine Man' or 'Lord of the Wine' and engaged in mock rituals. Lionel mixed a 'sacred' drink, a 'German student concoction' called 'Crambambuli', consisting of 'a dozen bottles of beer, mulled, into which two bottles of rum, a dozen eggs, and sugar to taste, were poured and whipped at the right moment'.[45] Like the Duskers, the Ishmaelites (named after the outcast wanderer of the Old Testament) drunkenly debated the membership credentials of luminaries such as the Devil, Petronius and Ben Jonson. Jesus Christ was blackballed. A decisive move into visual performance was signified by Norman carving a wooden idol of a Maori chieftain sporting a top hat, called 'The Joss', before which the members chanted.

Ishmael Club members met above Fasoli's Café, in Lonsdale Street, Melbourne. Here, gathered around their mascot the Joss are: Percy Lindsay, Will Dyson, Norman and Lionel Lindsay and Ray Parkinson; Godfrey and John Elkington, Randolph Bedford and Edward Dyson; seated: John Tremerne and Herman Kuhr.

The group of young tearaways had a far bawdier style than the Duskers, reflecting the Lindsays' Rabelaisian tastes. Evenings ended with the toast 'Let us be iconoclasts – idol breakers, remembering only the present in life … it remains for us to love wine, woman and art … and live for the moment'.[46] Although an all-male club like those of the earlier period, the evocation of 'woman' and 'love' signified a shift to a more Dionysian, libertine sensibility celebrating sex, which Norman in particular made integral to his aesthetic project. Lionel

A black and white poster by Percy Lindsay in 1906 promoting the good cheer to be had at the Smoke Nights of the Victorian Artists Society. The central figure is Percy, and artists Frederick McCubbin and William Moore are among members portrayed.

thought of brothel creeping as a cleansing tonic, casually noting in his memoir that '[o]n Wednesday I took the night off, and made oblation to Aphrodite, which cleaned my soul of Carey's [his editor] very nice, narrow, exasperating Puritanism'.[47] The fraternisation of visual artists with female models, including those participating in nude life-drawing classes, encouraged a

familiarity with the body and the 'beauty' of the female form
not so apparent in the mid-Victorian literary bohemian discourse. In George Taylor's memoir 'bohemian girls' are artist's
models who pose naked in a private studio for a select group of
artists he calls 'the sacred six' to draw. Despite his protestations
that there were 'no feelings of sex', he describes the scene with
eroticism, as into 'the dimly lit room' 'draped with dark velvet'
stands 'a beautiful woman', 'a high priestess' in a 'brilliant spotlight', 'her flesh glistening'.[48]

Norman Lindsay left Melbourne for Sydney in 1901 to take
up work with the *Bulletin*, and later joined by Lionel, they fused
the spirit of the Ishmael Club with Sydney bohemian networks
in a new club called Brother Brushes. It was headed up by *Bulletin*
manager and black-and-white illustrator William McLeod.
Brother Brushes were largely painters who worked as graphic
artists for magazines, including David Souter, George Taylor
and the Italian immigrant Anthony Dattilo Rubbo. Sporting a
pointed Van Dyke beard, Rubbo cut a romantic figure on the
streets of Sydney, and reportedly fought that city's last duel. One
of his models, Norman's Lindsay's second wife Rose, recalled
that Rubbo 'took fencing lessons [in his studio] with an expert,
a tall thin Italian with sad eyes, a greying beard so sharpened
to a point that it looked dangerous, and moustache-ends waxed
and curled to a rapier'.[49] The Brother Brushes' mascot was a
skull and meetings would kick off with each member presenting
for ridicule a sketch on that night's theme. The prominence
of the tough, commercially minded employer McLeod amid
a younger breed of illustrators suggests that paternalism and
office politicking may have dominated the atmosphere, but the
Lindsays ensured that the Sydney club continued the important
work of sketching nude models.

• • •

Even without the Lindsays, Fasoli's Café remained the centre of
Melbourne bohemia for artists and writers well into the twentieth century, perhaps because it offered very cheap 'Continental'
meals. 'At Fasoli's,' declared left-wing writer E.J. Brady, 'for a
few hours a day, any day, people could live the life of the mind!'
There with wine in hand 'groups of the elect would smoke under

a summer green canopy of willow and discuss subjects ranging from the art of Conder to the supposed canals of Mars'.[50] The café published its own mock newspaper, *The Waddy*, and had its legend rendered in poetry by Louis Esson:

> The Temple of Bohemia, it boasts no golden gate
> It flaunts no marble corridor to lure folk on to fate;
> But down the pavements dreary, towards one dim
>   lamp's glow
> Fasoli's draws the pilgrims where the good
>   Bohemians go.[51]

It had competition. Melbourne and Sydney writers and painters patronised European style cafes with exotic-sounding names like Café Française, Paris House and Café Barbizon. According to the *Australasian Art Review* of 1899, Café Barbizon was 'frequented between the hours of 1 and 2 by all the artistic, musical, and literary people who happen to be about', including McCubbin, Longstaff and George Marshall-Hall.[52]

Cafés were open to both sexes, allowing women to participate in bohemian gatherings, as they did in Paris. The painting *A Sydney Café* depicting members of the Art Society of New South Wales captures the Renoiresque mood of turn-of-the-century café bohemia. For Archibald, outdoor cafés represented a way of being cosmopolitan and were suited to the Australian climate. In an article on painters of Sydney, *Argus* journalist Florence Blair observed that there was something 'very continental in the way that Bohemia spreads itself about different cafés, and takes up new fads'.[53]

• • •

A more modernist flavour was emerging in Sydney towards the end of the century, associated with a younger generation, who were especially interested in new international trends in writing and visual art. Disparagingly dubbed the 'Boy Authors' by some of the old hands at the *Bulletin*, this group would coalesce in 1906 as the 'Casuals'. The luminary was Christopher Brennan, a brilliant scholar at the University of Sydney who, with university colleague John Le Gay Brereton, gave an academic feel to the group. Brennan, the child of Irish Catholic immigrants, had a vocation for the priesthood until literature and the scholarly life claimed his soul. Among the bohemians, Brennan's learning and intelligence earned him the nickname 'Encyclopedia Titanicus', and according to legend he 'once recited the first four books of *Paradise Lost* from memory'.[54]

Other Casuals included the future giant of literary criticism H.M. Green, Lionel Lindsay, editors of the *Bulletin* David McKee Wright and Arthur Adams, painters Sydney Long and Julian Ashton, and rising Labor Party activist William Holman. This group composed a particularly exclusive, if pretentious, aristocracy of the mind. With Brennan's Johnsonian intellect at the helm, the group dynamics were more freewheeling and Socratic, in contrast to the speeches, theatrics and mock formality of the other clubs. His appreciation of French literature in particular helped pitch the Casuals towards avant-garde developments in poetry and aesthetics, especially symbolism.

Women were also beginning to make inroads into clubland. Illustrator Thea Proctor and writers Amy Absell and Louise Mack joined the inner sanctum of the Casuals, reflecting a younger generation's more inclusive attitude towards women and the social trend towards greater equality for females in the new century.

PARTYING

Visual artists in Sydney invited writers and other creative workers to join with them in a completely new public performance of bohemianism, the mass party. The growth in the cultural community made it feasible to organise larger public events, ranging from Artist Society Smoke Nights, to the annual masquerade Artists' Balls that were held regularly from the late 1890s. The first such 'Night in Bohemia' at Sydney Town Hall was a collaboration between cartoonists organised as an 'Art Union' and the Duskers, followed by a much grander Artists' Ball in the same location to raise money for the Children's Hospital.[55]

Fancy dress was a feature reflecting the visual flamboyance of the artists and a trend in fin-de-siècle English bohemia reviving the tradition of the masked ball. The Lindsay brothers had played with fancy dress when living in Melbourne,

The young Lindsay brothers and sisters with friends from Melbourne's Ishmael Club performing fancy dress theatricals – directed by Norman and photographed by Lionel at the Creswick family home, c. 1901. Back: Pearl Lindsay, Percy Lindsay, Will Dyson and Mary Lindsay; front: Edwin Field and Norman Lindsay.

decorating their Little Lonsdale Street cottage like a pirate ship and cavorting around dressed as buccaneers. They would invite artist friends like Will and Ted Dyson to the family home in Creswick to perform and photograph historical theatricals and tableaux distinctive for outrageous fancy dress and a preference for Roman, Greek and mythical themes. This sensibility was on display at a Sydney Artists' Ball in the early years of the new century when Norman festooned the town hall in nursery rhyme-themed decorations and came costumed as a tube of paint![56] The highlight was a procession in honour of the 'Queen of Arts', sat upon a throne made of gum leaves.

Victor Daley reasoned that the 'public having heard a good deal of Bohemia, would naturally be anxious to see what it looks like'.[57] Parties and balls were an opportunity to show off to a larger audience and disrupt conventions and public order – if only for a night. Balls became much-anticipated events on the bohemian calendar, bringing together an increasingly diverse creative arts community. Unlike the insular, boys'-own in-jokes

of the club and pub, the Artists' Balls and other public parties
enabled male bohemia to perform for both women and the upper
echelons of colonial society. The balls were an expression of the
move of mid-Victorian bohemia into what Richard Waterhouse
calls 'heterosexual modernity' – a more open and permissive
fraternisation between the sexes in sites of recreation.[58]

Parties also attracted wealthy art consumers from business
and the professions – the men who controlled cultural institutions, politicians and even the vice-regal set. So popular did
bohemian parties become that the respectable council of the
Royal Art Society of New South Wales inaugurated an 'annual
Smoke' to which many bohemian artists were invited, including
the Duskers. It was here that Earl Beauchamp first encountered
Sydney's bohemia through Daley and resolved to forge closer
links with it to the extent of throwing his own bohemian
ball. He summoned the artists and poets of Sydney to a special
reception held in their honour at Government House but also
invited many from Sydney 'society', thus mischievously mixing
the bohemians and the upper crust. The chief amusement was
in condescending to the society guests 'who came in with grave
solemnity and stiff dignity', providing the bohemians, many in
ill-fitting second-hand formal attire, 'with choice subjects for
their sarcastic remarks'.[59]

Where artists and literary bohemians mixed, the influence of the artists was felt in the introduction of visual flair, as
well as the opening up of the bohemian club to the Dionysian
and the cosmopolitan – elements that were finessed and exaggerated in painters' own gatherings. By sharing their talents
with journalist and writer colleagues in the carnival of the
Artists' Ball, the visual artists enabled a more spectacular
form of celebration than bohemia had hitherto been able to
produce, and provided an avenue for Australian bohemia to
journey upmarket past the disapproving bourgeoisie towards
upper-class frivolity and even decadence.

PUB, PUSH AND BUSH

At the same time that literary bohemia was making a show of
its connections with artists and the gentry, it took an entirely
new direction towards the knockabout Australians of the push

and the bush. Many of the journalists, poets, short-story writers and cartoonists of the late nineteenth century were mindful to express a bohemianism that could be read as authentic by working-class and middle-class readers, by the bush as well as the city. Archibald had admired the satire and reportage of Marcus Clarke since his days as a young journalist on the *Evening Herald*. But where Clarke invited bourgeois readers to 'descend an octave in the social scale', Archibald sought a mass readership who were themselves down the social scale. His editorial bias was democratic, manifest in the *Bulletin*'s appeal to what I term a 'larrikin carnivalesque', more rooted in both the folk culture of the bush and urban popular culture.

By the 1890s many bohemian gatherings had relocated from the more exclusive restaurants and private clubhouses of Marcus Clarke's time to the traditional Anglo-Celtic public house. A site of working-class recreation, the 'pub' became attractive to journalists with offices near a particular watering hole – and in these days there were plenty. Beer was cheap relative to journalists' wages and the custom of Sydney pubs of providing free counter lunches to drinkers was attractive to men whose lifestyle left little time for regular meals. The proximity of pubs to one another led to a reworking of bohemian urban nomadism in the custom of the 'pub crawl', whereby drinkers journeyed from pub to pub, collecting comrades and becoming progressively inebriated. For example, on the day of sailing for England, Henry Lawson's farewell drinks took in the pubs of The Rocks and Circular Quay.

As well as being a place of relaxation where busy media staff could escape office politics and pressures, the pub gave people's poets such as Lawson, Victor Daley, E.J. Brady, Claude McKay and Roderic Quinn a stage on which to perform their common touch, in gregarious breasting of the bar. Drinking beer and participating in the blokey camaraderie of the pub was an easy way for bohemian writers to display an affinity with the workers they wrote about. Adjourning to the saloon was also a way a journalist might (temporarily) feel the equal of his boss, especially where pub protocols required editors and managers and even proprietors to participate in the egalitarianism of the public bar and its rituals.

Such cross-class fraternisation would have been rare in Marcus Clarke's day, except in the vicarious journeys into 'lower bohemia'. But by the 1890s pub bohemia was social, gregarious and on public display. By this time pubs had become a multi-use gathering place for public meetings and voluntary association dinners, for dancing and for gambling and sports like boxing. In a period where class demarcation was being weakened by social mobility, popular culture and the proletarianisation of journalism itself, the pub was a place where mass-market writers could imbibe egalitarianism for the cost of a shout.

Some bohemians were keen to romanticise the public house as a place of creative inspiration. Henry Lawson, a habitual barfly, relished the companionship of drinking mates and called this unity of bohemian and beverage 'beerhemia'.[60] Norman Lindsay believed that the best 'apprenticeship to poetry' was to be found in 'drinking and drabbing and consorting with all sorts and conditions of men, notably those who make up its disorderly and disreputable rabble'.[61] Although not a big drinker himself, he understood the rich linguistic pickings to be harvested at the bar. Lawson, Brennan and Hugh McCrae were said to compose poems while at the pub, and editor extraordinaire Adam McCay was rumoured to have led bohemians at the Assembly Hotel, Sydney, in the spontaneous collective composition of a bawdy ballad about 'the loveliest whore in Darlinghurst'.[62] Many literary bohemians believed in the connection of inebriated fellowship to creativity. 'Henry would have a pint,' E.J. Brady reasoned, 'and the only resulting injury to the community would be the following publication of some fine ballad or story.'[63] (Norman Lindsay later offered the commonsense view that writers and illustrators of this era could not have accomplished the work they did if they were perennially drunk.[64] Even Lawson achieved most of his literary output through hard work while sober.)

The move to the pub signalled a self-conscious imitation of the literary alehouse gatherings of Restoration London, and Norman Lindsay wrote fondly in his *Bulletin* memoir of 'those fraternities which foregather in pubs, which from Shakespeare's day to ours are the academies for a free exchange of ideas, and the conflict of opinion on life, art, and the profundities of human destiny on this planet.'[65]

Veneration of beer and the pub as a creative, if knockabout, muse was also the bohemian's answer to the campaigners for abstinence and restrictions such as Sunday closing, especially rife in Melbourne. By identifying themselves with pub life, some writers and journalists were living out the anti-wowser campaign they waged in the *Bulletin* and other publications, an editorial position that boosted circulation with a large number of male working-class readers who enjoyed alcohol and a punt.

• • •

There were other imaginative ways that authors of articles, stories, light verse, jokes and cartoons identified with the culture of town and country workers. Both the urban larrikin and the itinerant bush labourer provided writers with models of a freewheeling, independent working-class masculinity from which they selectively appropriated recreational idiosyncrasies and the patois of 'mateship' into their bohemianism.

The tendency of print media bohemians to associate themselves symbolically with larrikinism should be read as an attempt to garner some of the danger and spirit of non-conformity associated with the 'larrikin push', a deviant inner-urban working-class youth subculture. The larrikins were delinquents, often racialised as 'Irish', who disturbed the peace of city streets from the 1870s into the early decades of the twentieth century. They fought hard, dressed 'flash' and enjoyed 'snogging' in public. Sporting a uniform of flared black corduroy trousers, pointy shoes and wide black hats they made an unmistakable impression en masse, especially when they knocked the top hats off toffs trying to look the other way. As spectacular, mobile, outlaw tribes of the metropolis, the pushes could perform a role for Australian literary bohemians analogous to the free-spirited, exotic gypsies in Paris.

Clarke had mocked larrikins as blackguards or undertook reportage exposing their deviancy but from the 1890s bohemian writers began romanticising them in poems, novels and cartoons such as Lawson's 'Two Larrikins' and C.J. Dennis's *Sentimental Bloke* series. The larrikin's habits of drinking, fighting, sexual permissiveness and hostility to authority made him an effective symbol for writers seeking to express opposition to respectable society. That larrikins belonged to tight gangs or 'pushes' struck a chord with the group-minded bohemians. Like the larrikin, male bohemians down the pub or out on the town could be rowdy, drunken, permissive, ribald, even riotous. Norman Lindsay fancied his group of raffish, street-strolling student artists were taken to be another push by the Little Bourke Street larrikins.[66] Identification with larrikins was a dramatic way for bohemians to perform their separation from bourgeois life despite many being of that class. The association stuck and in the new century bohemian journalists, writers and cartoonists would be complimented for their so-called larrikin streak, though shorn of its criminal and deviant connotations by this artistic makeover. By the First World War 'larrikin' had become a cosy term for a devil-may-care working-class *joie de vivre* whether practised by 'diggers' or by someone who was manifestly not of that class, like a journalist or politician.

● ● ●

Most famously, the bohemians of the late nineteenth century performed what they imagined to be habits of the rural worker. Some of these habits – notably hard drinking, gambling and the creative use of Australian slang – were shared with larrikinism, but the bushman ideal allowed bohemians to extol his assumed virtues of stoicism, freedom and male mateship. In the short stories of Lawson the bushman met adversity with sardonic humour, displayed dignity in failure and found life's purpose in coming together to endure a harsh environment. The noble qualities of the bush battler were romanticised in a stream of poetry, short stories, articles, cartoons and illustration. The *Bulletin*, in particular, raised the Bush (with a capital B) and the mateship of the shearing shed and diggings into national ideals to distinguish both the magazine and what its editors and writers discerned to be an emerging Australian identity. However, among scholars interested in bohemia, there is conjecture as to whether the bush culture imposed itself on urban bohemians, or whether they, in fact, extrapolated their own bohemian values, such as male camaraderie, onto the bush workers.[67]

A significant body of ballads, short stories, humorous sketches and journalism in the 1880s, 90s and early twentieth century borrowed liberally from the slang, songs and especially humour of the common man of the bush. Likewise, artists were kept busy providing black-and-white images of bush life and scenery for the press, on postcards and in lavish pictorial books. Some bohemians, such as Archibald, Lawson and the Lindsay brothers, had a genuine affinity with the bush, having grown up in regional towns or spent time working on country newspapers. Lawson, Brady and Brereton were genuine in their incorporation of a bushman's idiom and interests into their identity, becoming keen bushwalkers and campers, finding the landscape and characters an inspiration and escape from city life. Most others undertook research at a distance, supplemented by an occasional foray. George Taylor recounts an amusing tale of an odyssey into the bush by city slicker bohemians hunting 'local color [sic]' who, after a day's exposure to the great outdoors, abort the trip exhausted, hot and thirsty and repair back to the comforts of their inner-city pub.[68]

• • •

By the early years of the twentieth century a new repertoire of bohemian activities and rituals had developed that evoked a sense of topsy-turvy via familiarity with urban working-class lifestyle and entertainment and a romanticisation of 'mateship', the folkways of the bush and Australianness. Unlike Marcus Clarke's condescending use of lower-class vernacular to mock those who used it, the *Bulletin*, *Bull-Ant*, *Lone Hand* and many labour papers used the language of the streets and the shearing sheds to mock those in authority, from squatters, parsons, 'wowsers' and magistrates to plutocrats, governors and the Crown. Instead of drawing on the cultural capital of the gentry and gentleman to poke fun at crass colonial materialism, as Clarke did, the literary bohemians of the 1880s and 90s became skilled at using a stylised working-class idiom, partly to subvert those 'others' they did not like by letting the lower classes in on the joke and partly to sell back to popular audiences. Sales and the bounty of material indicate that both the rural and city markets had a boundless interest in this romanticised bush life.[69]

PAINTERS AND THE RISE OF THE ARTIST HERO

Painters now had the critical mass to also cultivate their own distinctive bohemian groups relevant to their artistic practice. They had different expectations of the identity, related to the unique economics of their art. Whereas print media texts are mechanically reproduced and mass distributed at a low price, paintings are unique and sold individually to a single buyer. Painters had to cultivate a wealthier audience than the writers, playing more personal politics to sell a work or get a portrait commission, which involved exhibiting, networking, references, reputation, reviews, criticism and getting to know the buyer. That meant lobbying not just art connoisseurs but also the dreaded philistines who were privately derided by artists.[70]

Conder and his friends attracted a wealthy clientele by seeming to disown the market altogether, in a new bohemi-anism of the artist hero. To 'duffers like myself, art [is] almost a religion', the young Conder explained to relatives about his decision to abandon his apprenticeship as a surveyor to take up painting as a career.[71] In the 1880s young painters, especially those who travelled abroad like Roberts, were influenced by current European trends such as the Aesthetic Movement, which popularised the slogan 'art for art's sake'. It argued for the liberation of art from bourgeois morality and all imperatives other than the aesthetic, and insisted that only artists were fit to judge on matters artistic. In Australia the movement won adherents such as Julian Ashton, who argued that the artist 'must be content to live for art and for art's sake only; and unmoved by the praise or blame of the amateur or the dilettante, accept for critics none but those whose claim to be heard rests on the safe basis of personal knowledge and experience'.[72]

Aestheticism amounted to a declaration of independence by the artists from the enthralment to literary values, seeking to liberate painting and shift focus to the visual qualities and the mood evoked in the observer. The Buonarotti Society was a strong promoter of the Aesthetic Movement in Melbourne and members such as Roberts, McCubbin and occasional guest Streeton incorporated aspects of it into their bohemian style and personas. Ada Cherry recalled Buonarotti bohemian Tudor St George Tucker, 'at the height of Oscar Wilde's "aesthetic craze" "sauntering" down "The Block" with a lily or sunflower in his hand, and with hair combed out in beautiful fair curls'.[73]

From the 1880s a bohemianism influenced by what was lamented by art historian Bernard Smith as 'aesthetic fundamentalism' took hold among teachers and students in newly established art schools, entrenching the idea that artists were an innately talented elite, even geniuses.[74] George Lambert later confessed with sarcasm that 'the art student ... of my youth ... used to believe they were a race apart ... It was only natural that we should treat with contempt people who were so stupid as not to recognise that we were geniuses.'[75]

Art for art's sake contributed to artists' professional self-assertion in the 1880s and 90s. They resisted institutional manoeuvres to assert control over their work by splitting with the amateur-controlled art societies and academies, establishing the independent Australian Artists Association (1886), followed by the Victorian Artists Society and New South Wales Society of Artists (1888 and 1895). Through these societies, painters organised their own exhibitions, art unions and media, provided training, attacked amateur critics and sought control of public institutions such as galleries.

Norman Lindsay and his circle found a different path to the artist hero via the philosophy of Friedrich Nietzsche and his pronouncement of the death of God and the concept of the Übermensch. By the early years of the twentieth century Nietzsche's ideas were having an impact in Australia, where they were vulgarised by Lindsay and other vitalists such as McCrae to proselytise an anti-Christian, libertine, life-affirming paganism and fantasies of the artist superman who had taken the place of God. Norman and his older brother Lionel believed that creative genius was the gift of only a small elite such as themselves, and styled their bohemianism accordingly.

STUDIO BOHEMIA

The studio in which Lionel and Norman Lindsay lived on first arriving in Melbourne from Creswick was dubbed 'Parnassus', after the home of the god Apollo and the muses in Greek mythology, and quickly became the meeting place for their growing circle of friends. One of the regulars, Hugh McCrae, described the style of its bohemia, three storeys above Collins Street: 'Smoke from clay pipes hazing the light of a hurricane lamp, everybody's rump grafted to the floor … smell of sweat, of rum and hot water … a chapter read of Rabelais … Norman, mug in hand, brush in the other and painting – [he] works all night.'[76]

This knockabout and carefree shared living came straight from the pages of *Scènes de la vie de Bohème*. In 1913 Norman Lindsay turned these experiences into the semi-autobiographical comedic novel *A Curate in Bohemia*, which synthesised Murger with Melbourne and became an Australian 'how to' manual to complement the European descriptions where scallywag artists bluffed creditors and cadged wine and sausages from each other and girlfriends.

Studio bohemia emerged from the habit of young, impoverished visual artists of combining workplace and cheap city lodgings to live and paint together in communal settings. Roberts and Streeton had lived together under similar circumstances in both Melbourne and Sydney in the 1880s and early 90s, and Conder shared Roberts' studio at 9 Collins Street when he came to Melbourne in 1888. The same year Roberts hit upon the idea of repackaging a sanitised version of this bohemia for the public through his 'Studio Afternoons'. Streeton and Conder joined him in these studio soirees that had a more earnest and educative ambience, with the intent of attracting bourgeois customers. Artistic 'conversaziones', a lecture and a demonstration were held, where a French journal might be discussed to give potential customers, patrons and critics an insight into the world of the artist.[77]

Where bohemian clubs in which writers predominated emphasised wordplay, jokes and the formal 'speech' as entertainment, gatherings in artist studios were stimulated by the visual. Tom Roberts' purpose-built studio, modelled on the Renaissance style of London's Grosvenor Gallery, was decorated with trendy Liberty silks, muslin draperies and Japanese screens. The *Argus* noted that the studio 'is artistically got up in terracotta, with many jars and art objects around, brightened with flowers and draperies'. Roberts' studio had become 'a pleasant meeting place on Thursday afternoons' and 'quite a haunt of

artists and literary figures'.[78] The studio bohemia combined
the European idea of the salon with the window display of the
department store, designed to seduce the more discriminating
consumers. This meant a style of bohemia at once challenging
and safe, exotic but neither offensive nor revolutionary.

The studio tone was more serious, more refined, and more
elite in the 'society' sense than the boozy literary clubs and pubs.
Under the headline 'In Sydney Studios', an *Argus* journalist
described the artists as:

> very earnest and enthusiastic, and [they] don't put on any
> swaggering airs, but are sociable and form a kingdom of
> their own, a Bohemia of the true sort, which includes much
> meeting in studios reeking of paint and very dusty, much
> pipe-smoking, much drinking of tea (probably whisky,
> when ladies have been politely bowed out), many harbour
> excursions, meals at cafes, Tivoli parties, and much real
> hard work, which results in London exhibitions and gal-
> lery purchases.[79]

By the late 1880s this type of 'true' bohemia had come to
signify the successful 'artist' for the readers of the conservative
Argus.

SALONS, DANDIES AND THE 'SOCIETY BOHEMIAN'
Closely connected with the open studio was the salon proper,
where a 'society' patron invited artists into their home for regular gatherings. The salon had the advantage of bringing artists
with few means in direct social contact with potential customers
and also political patronage on neutral ground. This is how
salons had long operated in France, tying writers and artists to
'high society' and the state notables, but in the colonial city the
salon was a place where older aristocratic patronage was given
a nouveau riche makeover. To enter and make an impression in
this setting, Conder and Roberts, who became drawing-room
favourites, fussed over a more refined bohemianism. They were
particularly adept at Marcus Clarke's old game of playing the
dandy to move with ease between the saloon and the salon,
a flexibility necessary when they worked in both print media

and painting. Ashton noted that amid the bohemian chaos of
Conder's apartment the artist had a 'hallowed corner within
which were hanging from a nail a stylish frock coat, vest and
trousers. A top hat, gloves and a cane kept them in countenance.
When he walked abroad clothed in these garments, he looked
like the Man of Fashion, doing the Block and smiling on the
fair.'[80]

Conder was rehearsing how to be a dandy, a fine art of the
self he would make his life's true work. His biographer Ann
Galbally reveals that Conder was lucky in his mentors.[81] In
Sydney he was a regular at the salon of Constance Roth, who
invited guests to high tea at her Darlinghurst home. A wealthy
artist herself, trained in England and interested in the Aesthetic
Movement, Roth provided some financial assistance and, more
importantly, friends to buy his work and older mentors such as
Roberts, who first met Conder at one of Roth's 'at homes' in
1888.

In Melbourne Conder found a similar berth at the Brighton
home of wealthy doctor Stephen Mannington Caffyn and his
wife Kathleen, who commissioned portraits and gave him centre
stage in their lively eccentric salon that was dubbed 'Bohemia'.
In such environments painters came into contact with politicians, professionals, businessmen and their wives, who would
pay handsomely for their portraits. Highly educated 'modern'
writers, the Caffyns introduced Conder to older men of cultural
influence in Melbourne, including George McCrae, Theodore
Fink and James Smith. Journeying out to Brighton with his
father to visit the salon, Hugh McCrae observed, 'It was here, for
the first time, that I saw the coast-line of Bohemia, twinkling,
and dangerously beautiful.'[82] Ushered into a room by the doctor
he found 'Charles Conder, scraping down a corner-bit of canvas,
while Mrs Caffyn still kept her pose as a dryad [nymph]'.

The salon obscured the networking with a frisson of bohemian ambience but the artists could be more candid among
themselves. Mocked by his colleague D.H. Souter for playing
the 'society bohemian', Tom Roberts astutely observed that
'you don't as a rule sell your pictures to people who rent cottages
at 17/6d a week: business my dear boy, business'.[83] Likewise
Conder confessed to a close relative that 'if I had money I would

kill time in a really amusing way without any society rubbish',
and admitted that 'at homes', 'dinners' and 'conversaziones' were
necessary to pay the bills.[84] Roberts was especially successful
at cultivating wealthy customers, securing commissions in the
1890s to paint portraits of the who's who of the New South
Wales government and business elite. Souter concluded that the
suave Roberts 'represented the successful artists with the entrée
to Government House and was on the dining lists of most
people who had over a couple of thousand per year'.[85] According
to Souter, Roberts shared the limelight, tutoring his uncouth
friends who 'possessed no society clothes and were criminally
indifferent to the nice distinctions or the etiquette of social
functions. Tom Roberts showed us the error of all that. "There
is no occasion, dear boy," said he, "for an artist to be a boor. A
man may be able to paint decently well and also know how to
comport himself in good society."'

Frustratingly, the spending required of the society bohemian
frequently exceeded the income available from commissions and
freelance illustration, with Conder complaining to his cousin
that 'the fashionable existence … I lead under Mrs Caffyngton's
[sic] kind patronage … took too much money and left no time
for me to work, ain't I moral?'[86]

It may seem strange that artists professing to be bohemian
could get away with indulging such fashionable recreation, but
devices of irony and parody were used to distance themselves
from the bourgeois life they were recording. In the paintings
A Holiday at Mentone and *Allegro con brio, Bourke Street West*
Conder and Roberts had become flâneurs in the visual medium,
observing and interpreting the new urban hustle and bustle –
and its corollary: new ways of taking pleasure and spending – in
the manner of French impressionists Manet and Monet. By
stripping painting of moral lessons and substituting sensation
and flamboyance, the young Heidelberg artists were subverting
Victorian art orthodoxy while winning commissions from a
discerning clientele. Conder went further, with his work containing transgressive proto-modernist meanings in the emerging
symbolist manner for those who looked. For example, *Holiday
at Mentone* has mixed-sex recreation on the beach when this was
not allowed under the Vagrant Act. Both the fashionable seated

woman and the man are reading the *Bulletin*, designated by the red cover.[87]

Most importantly the artistic lifestyle itself was *aestheticised* in the painters' bohemia by the style-obsessed aesthete. Conder's biographer notes his perfection of the 'cult of self' implicit in bohemianism by 'leaving no detail of one's ordinary life, dress and behaviour to chance'.[88] Conder was to take his aesthete identity to extremes in France and Britain, where it meshed in well with the fin-de-siècle decadence favoured by his friends Toulouse-Lautrec, Oscar Wilde and Aubrey Beardsley.

HAPPY CAMPERS

The artists' camps of the 1880s and 90s were a consequence of the arrival in Australia of the overseas fashion for painting landscapes out of doors, first promoted in Melbourne by Louis Buvelot and in Sydney by Julian Ashton in the early 1880s and becoming a fixture of art school training in both cities and the Buonarotti Club. During the mid-1880s Streeton, Longstaff, McCubbin, Louis Abrahams, Emanuel Phillips Fox and many of their colleagues from the National Gallery Art School in Melbourne began painting in the bush around Templestowe. They were joined by Tom Roberts, who brought both his experience of English aestheticism and his Sydney friend Conder to artists' camps at Box Hill, Mentone and then Eaglemont, near Heidelberg. It is from their association with this bushland that this group of quasi-impressionists later became known as the 'Heidelberg School'.

The deepening economic depression and the 1893 Land Crash meant that the personnel and energy in visual art moved from Melbourne to Sydney and so too did the artists' camps, with Roberts and Streeton establishing the (rent-free) Curlew camp at Little Sirius Cove. Such was their reputation that the camp quickly became a magnet for other painters, illustrators and even literary and music people keen to share the experience.

There was a touch of the Dionysian as well. At the Heidelberg shack where they stayed, Conder, ever the ladies man, delighted that '[w]e have dances there too and invite all the girls in the country up to them'.[89] Unlike the male-only club and pub fraternities, women painters and friends in both cities attended and prepared feasts and joined the men in 'gypsie teas', songs and dance.[90]

The artists' camp was a form of bohemia distinctive for its focus on producing rather than selling. The emphasis was on the production of new works and establishing a temporary environment conducive to creative freedom away from commissions and media illustration, affording reflective time for the study of light, experimentation in colour and brushwork and discussions of technique. Camping together gave the painters a discursive community comparable with the press office and established the social conditions they believed were necessary for stimulating aesthetic vision and new skills.

Art historian Ann Galbally has argued for the importance to these artists of cultivating a 'reverie' of nature, in keeping with the Aesthetic Movement's stress on the mood that a picture could create through the viewer's gaze.[91] Streeton expressed his reverie thus:

> The enjoyment of 'the last summer at Eaglemont' was to me more intense than anything I have up to the present felt. Its suggestion is large harmony, musical rosy – fancy if you could grasp all you thought into a scheme which would embrace sweet sound, great colour and all the slow soft movement sometimes quick with games and through all the strength of the great warm loving sun.[92]

The aesthetic ambience of the camps produced an idealised tourist's image of the bush quite different from the harsh realism and levelling comedy that Lawson and the *Bulletin* writers captured. Far from the parched gullies of Lawson's selectors, Streeton, Roberts and Conder would slum it in Heidelberg with 'a bottle of claret, a tallow candle, a plug of tobacco' and 'beds we made of cornsacks nailed to two saplings'.[93] Art historian Leigh Astbury dubbed these urban sophisticates 'City Bushmen'. They were sufficiently removed from the hardships of the environment to romanticise the landscape.

While inspired by international trends and attracted to the European ambience of this part of Melbourne, the embrace by painters of Australian landscape, publicly performed through the camps, promoted their Australianness at a time when the National Gallery of Victoria continued to favour overseas work. By engaging so spectacularly with the local in a period of rising postcolonial nationalism, the Heidelberg artists were playing the same game of distinction as many writers – a game made explicit in the first major exhibition of pictures emanating from the Heidelberg camps.

EXHIBITIONISTS

The main purpose of exhibitions was to sell paintings and create publicity for the artists. In August 1889 the Heidelberg painters declared their arrival as a new generation of artists with the precocious *9 x 5* Exhibition at Buxton's Gallery, Melbourne, featuring much of their *plein air* 'impressions' controversially rendered on cigar-box lids. If the aim of the exhibition was to attract attention to the young painters and confront critics with the shock of the new, it succeeded. Critic James Smith was hostile to impressionism, and predictably condemned the paintings as 'incoherent', like 'primeval chaos' and 'a pain to the eye'.[94] These views were an antipodean echo of John Ruskin's withering description of James McNeil Whistler's 1877 London exhibition as 'flinging a pot of paint in the public's face'. But where Whistler unwisely sought remedy in the courts, the Australian painters revelled in the bad reviews, and displayed the criticisms at the entrance to the exhibition as an advertisement. By attacking the 'impressionists' so venomously the established critic rich in cultural capital helped confer legitimacy on the young painters, and brought them further into the media spotlight.

'[T]he promoters feel justified in making it an artistic event,' trumpeted *Table Talk*, 'seeing that it is the first exhibition of its kind that has ever been held in Australia.'[95] In fact the *9 x 5* Exhibition was the first French- and British-style proto-avant-gardist event in Australia. Like their personal studio 'afternoons', the gallery was decked with Japanese umbrellas, red Liberty silks, knowingly placing the small pictures into a total decorative ambience for a discerning home, topped off with piano recitals and high teas in the manner of salons. The artists exhibited in a private rather than public gallery, where they could avoid institutional politics and prejudices, maximise sales and exert control over the space. They hired a publicist in advance to raise anticipation and coordinate the response, and they took care to reference the latest French and English aesthetic ideas and styles in their pre-exhibition media notices and catalogue. The artists self-consciously identified with a new art movement by calling the paintings 'Impressions'. It worked, with a journalist explaining to readers ahead of the opening that Roberts, Conder, Streeton and McCubbin 'are generally considered the leaders of impressionism here'.[96] They came together in a carefully packaged group and, in the wake of Smith's attack, produced a manifesto appealing to artistic freedom and local identity, calling this collective reality a new 'school of Australian painting' – a label that stuck.[97] The exhibition was a social and commercial success; opened in the presence of the governor's wife, it attracted a large number of visitors and all the pictures sold. But its greatest achievement was attaching a 'buzz' to this younger group of painters, who were henceforth known as 'Australian Impressionists'.

However, the hybrid of bourgeois consumer décor and the rhetoric of French art vanguards confused and offended an older generation of cultural improvers who could not read the aesthetic and found 'grotesque and meaningless' the separation from morality of art that has 'no *raison d'être*'.[98] The painters used the conflict as evidence that amateur critics were unqualified to judge the work of artists and to illustrate the chasm in taste between older critics and young artists. By calling themselves 'a new Australian school' they were able to cast doubt on the taste of an older generation of immigrants in charge of the National Gallery of Victoria, which in 1888 had still not purchased a painting by a native-born Australian artist. By condemning the older generation as unable to appreciate Australian ways of seeing, these visual artists were drawing on the same mark of distinction deployed by their native-born literary peers. Like them, the artists hoped to advantage themselves in a market dominated by European imports and older immigrants. But they also depicted their critics as parochial and out of touch with the French and English vogues of impressionism and aestheticism, thus marshalling the art market's cultural cringe to their cause.

Exhibitions would continue to be events merging bohemian performance, public relations and commerce, although once secure in his own ascendancy in the art market Roberts settled in to a less confrontational style. As founding chairman of the New South Wales Society of Artists in 1895, he introduced showmanship into its exhibitions, which included special afternoon entertainments where artists played up their unconventionality for different professional groups such as doctors, lawyers, academics, the military and journalists, as well as for ladies and even French expatriates. Sydney Long observed that Roberts 'started a movement which gave the society's exhibitions a certain social attraction'.[99] This was an extension into a wider public of the consumer-friendly studio bohemia of his hungry youth. What needs to be appreciated is the crucial role of the artists' bohemianism in disguising the hustle, by creating the masquerade of freedom from commerce.

VISUAL ARTISTS' QUEST FOR AUTONOMY

Paradoxically, as art's sales pitch accelerated in the late nineteenth century, the bohemian discourse became more assertive in claiming artists' autonomy from commerce. Within Parisian bohemia it was often the artist most directly 'subject' to the market who felt obliged to make a show of independence from it. Bourdieu argued that to succeed in the literary field, writers 'had to demonstrate their independence vis-à-vis economic and political power', and this was bohemia's purpose whatever the art form.[100] The desire of connoisseurs to deny the commercial imperative in the transaction was crucial. The artist hero's romantic performance of revolt against the art market, though usually illusionary or quixotic, was the heroic gesture that came to signify 'artist' for cultural producer and consumer alike. Tom Roberts, Charles Conder and Norman Lindsay were very aware of their dependence on the market. Roberts remained dependent on portrait painting and, later, government commissions for much of his career while Conder juggled surveying, then lithography and illustrating greeting cards with painting until marrying into wealth. Lindsay's first jobs were illustrating scandal sheets, religious books and food labels. While proselytising the idea of an artistic elect he also churned out the weekly cartoons for the *Bulletin* on which his livelihood relied from 1901 until 1958.

The painters also wanted to be free of the older amateur critics who inappropriately brought benchmarks from literature to judge art. Aesthetic bohemia's public insistence that artists were born with the talent, 'taste' and 'a good eye' naturalised their claim to define art. Their experiments with a new 'aesthetic' style of bohemianism should be seen as an attempt by artists to liberate themselves from middle-class standards. But far from a rejection of the market, aesthetic bohemianism was about leading it.

CONSUMING AUTHENTICITY

Whether writer or visual artist, 'authenticity' or 'street cred' helped to make even mass-produced cultural commodities such as a magazine or a cartoon appear to be about more than making money, validating the consumer as much as the producer. The larrikin carnivalesque of Henry Lawson's 'beerhemia' suggested the poet of the common man was one himself. Aesthetic bohemianism flattered the discriminating consumer of paintings, forging an elitist bond between the 'naturally talented' painter and 'naturally tasteful' customer. The rough, rustic simplicity fetishised by the Heidelberg painters at their camps and promoted in their exhibition publicity and reminiscences authenticated them as both artists in the manner of French *plein air* impressionists and as Australian artists at home in the landscape.

Table Talk magazine explained to its readers that an actor-writer sitting on his studio floor 'was simply living up to his profession' and we should admire 'his freedom from conventionality'.[101] The bohemian identity itself became a commodity to sell. The popularity of Murger's book, other bohemian texts and Puccini's opera *La Bohème*, which toured in the 1890s, reinforced the public's view of a bohemian artist as a glamorous and troubled modern hero. A merchandising bonanza followed in the wake of the hit bohemian novel *Trilby* by George du Maurier. The *Free-Lance* reported that '[t]he Trilby craze is taking root … Already we have come across Trilby shirts, Trilby pies, Trilby chewing gum [and] Trilby tooth-wash'.[102] For the emerging writer or artist bohemianism was great PR.

Yet artists could resent this necessary compromise with the customer. Streeton complained that at a smoke night of the Victorian Artists' Society, he had to push 'through the crowd of philistines' to Longstaff's table where: 'the artists were no-where that evening – all the philistines had the seats and the artists [were] standing in the cold'.[103] Among writers, the caricature of the bourgeois philistine that drew on the gentry prejudice against trade was even joined to the stereotype of the capitalist 'fat man' promoted by the labour press in which many bohemian writers and illustrators worked.

The strident othering of businessmen as philistines helped police the borders of bohemia but it obscured the reality that many journalists and editors became proprietors and share-holders in cultural businesses, for example Archibald and Fink. George Taylor continued to attend the Brother Brushes despite his success in the construction and publishing industry, out of respect for 'what bohemia was left in him.' Aware of the tension in his position, he wryly observed in defence of the businessmen whose ranks he joined that the 'poetic ones are so impractical as to forget it is the "soulless Philistine" who keeps poetry and art alive by his purse'. Of course, the best way for a businessman to demonstrate he was not a philistine was to buy the work of those who asserted that he was. Thus bohemia's 'staged authenticity' had the capacity to confer distinction on the customer too.

Conder's biographer Ann Galbally views him as a man divided between success and bohemianism but the two were complementary.[104] For an artist of few means blessed with considerable charm and talent, aesthetic bohemianism was his entrée to 'society rubbish' that he pursued with a vengeance, an identity that gave him status outside conventional class markers of wealth and position, and also allowed him some subversive play. Far from making the Heildelberg painters' bohemianism unviable, commerce was an environment in which it thrived.

GENERATION GAP

Cave of Adullam stalwart Arthur Patchett Martin referred to bohemia's social fluidity when he wrote (paraphrasing Murger) that a bohemian

though poor, he is still one of those
Who with comfort and luxury seems to exist;
For whatever he does, or wherever he goes,
His expenses are paid, or he's on the free-list.[105]

More so than in the first generation, bohemian groups of
the late nineteenth century were open to people from working-
class and lower middle-class backgrounds, who found within
bohemia the freedom to play on their connection to larrikins
and bushmen, or use bohemia's social fluidity to climb higher,
either way escaping middle-class life.

Many more bohemians in the second generation were
Australian born and raised rather than immigrants, and this
influenced their relationship with local landscape, custom and
idiom. A significant number of these 'natives' originated in
small regional towns and were mobile across colonial borders,
encouraging a national rather than a metropolitan imaginary.
There was also a marked geographic shift of cultural energy
from Melbourne to Sydney that had begun with writers,
journalists and black-and-white illustrators flocking to
the *Bulletin* in the 1880s, and was accelerated by the 1890s
depression. Sydney's advantage was compounded when
the New South Wales Art Gallery trustees, under the
influence of chairman Julian Ashton, adopted a policy of
buying pictures from local artists on local themes, including
impressionist styles. Painters who had cut their teeth in
Melbourne's studios and bushland joined the exodus to
the more receptive marketplace in the north. This demographic
exodus underpinned the ascendancy of a younger generation in
Sydney over an older Melbourne cultural establishment.

The young bohemians who made their mark in the nineties
would dominate Australian arts and letters for many years to
come. In their novels, poems, memoirs and autobiographies they
forged the definitive Australian bohemian myth against which
successors would be measured. We should not be surprised
that, looking back from middle and old age, memoirists such as
Taylor, Jose and Lindsay would later deploy nostalgia to fend off
challenges from new generations after the Great War.

By the turn of the century even younger artists who were moving through media workplaces shared in a broad late-Victorian 'structure of feeling' with bohemians who made their mark in the 1880s and 90s, but they also came to feel different from them. While grateful to mentors Archibald and Ashton, Norman Lindsay came to resent their generation's incumbency, and complained of the old-fashioned Catholic prudery of Victor Daley and the pomposity of A.G. Stephens.[106] In their own ways both Lindsay and Brennan were bored with the literary straitjacket of bush realism and formed new groups to supplant the men of the 80s and 90s in the new century. Brennan's 'Boy Authors', resentful of the *Bulletin* for rejecting what they considered their best work, published the short-lived *Australian Magazine*, in a spirit of youthful independence from the mainstream. Brennan and Lindsay made their marks in the first two decades of the twentieth century and had careers spanning the late-Victorian and interwar generations of bohemians, but due to their age never quite belonged to either. Despite some inter-generational antagonism, this younger group of bohemians would be bound to the older group by a shared bohemia and, more profoundly, through their establishment of adult careers in the period prior to the First World War, and reactions to war that cast a new generational divide.

For the writers, riffing on emerging postcolonial themes of Australian difference, larrikin bohemianism was no antidote for imperial condescension. Lawson, who by the turn of the century despaired of receiving financial reward or recognition in Australia, believed:

> Talent goes for little here. To be aided, to be
>   known,
> You must fly to Northern cities who are juster than
>   our own.[107]

Lawson was, however, far from adept at the cosmopolitan aspects of bohemianism, and failed to make the impression he craved on his trip to Britain. Confronted with what he felt was metropolitan pretension, Lawson, like visiting colonials before him, reverted to the performance of parochial Australianness and mocking humour. While Lawson's bush authenticity and larrikinism was bankable cultural capital in the Australian market, it did not hold its value across borders. Disorientated and uncomfortable in British literary circles, Lawson became distracted in London's expatriate Australian bohemia and its pubs, sickened, and the hoped-for success eluded him.

It was easier for the painters. To be a really good artist it was felt that some training in France or Britain was essential – if only to see original pictures in an age of poor reproduction. Roberts, Streeton, Conder and Max Meldrum all spend considerable time in Paris and London, virtually abandoning Australia in the early years of the new century. This diaspora was mocked in the *Bulletin* by Victor Daley in the satirical poems 'When London Calls' and 'Corregio Jones'. As with Lawson, Daley's work had failed to set London's literary world alight, despite the praise of his work among his Australian peers. Imported from Europe in the first place, the painters' aesthetic style was exportable back to the metropolis. 'Society' bohemians like Roberts and Conder had the advantage of British childhoods and, in the latter's case, experience of India, enabling them to project an imperial exotic that allowed their work and personas to be accepted in London.

More than the other painters, Charles Conder's aesthetic bohemianism swam against the nationalist bush current and tested the limits of an alternative. One of the leading proponents of the English decadent mood that bridged the Aesthetic Movement and art nouveau in fin-de-siècle Europe, he experimented with decoration and symbolic meaning and evinced interest in urban modernity and recreation. Conder forged his aesthete style and identity in Sydney and then Melbourne, but did not find fertile ground for his brand of bohemianism. He left Australia in 1889 to live the rest of his life in Paris and London. English artist John Rothenstein described his friend in the thick of Parisian bohemia:

> Night after night he went to the Moulin Rouge and other places of the same kind, and watched enthralled the crowds who, animated by that curiously Parisian gaiety, bustled confusedly in the gaslight and smoke, and the

exotic evolutions of La Goulue, Nini-Pattenaire, and
Jeanne la Folle as they danced the Can-Can.[108]

By playing the English Aesthete, Conder moved within a
wide stratum spanning the sexually permissive entertainments
of the Moulin Rouge (from which he drew inspiration) to the
British aristocracy (into which he married). Yet, like Lawson,
he was committed to a bohemian way of life that in middle age
resulted in alcohol dependence and the squandering of talent.
He passed away in 1909 from the effects of the syphilis he had
contracted as a youth.

Victor Daley's death from consumption in 1905 marked the
end of the nineteenth-century style of bohemianism that had
been forged by Marcus Clarke in the 1870s. Keeping a deathbed
vigil were bohemian veterans grown old. Bohemia was a phase
in these men's lives that was coming to an end, retreating into
a defensive nostalgia for 'golden days' as they entrenched themselves as the new cultural establishment. As they cemented their
control of the new nation's cultural institutions the successful
Bulletin stalwarts and returning prodigal painters imposed on
the new Federation a monolithic national aesthetic of gum trees
and bush yarns. For those who lived long into the new century
past the Great War, some with knighthoods and the patronage
of prime ministers, the memory of their bohemian youth would
be paraded to mythologise the artistic achievements of the legendary 90s and to legitimise their dominance. Even as nostalgia,
bohemia remained potent enough to still add a touch of excitement and air of subversion to men who had long since ceased to
rattle the cage of Australian culture.

'IF BLOOD SHOULD STAIN THE WATTLE': REBELS, RADICALS AND ROMANTIC NATIONALISTS

1890–1920

John Le Gay Brereton, literary academic and member of the Sydney bohemian Casuals club, once recalled his discomfort on first meeting Henry Lawson over tea in the sober environs of poet Mary Cameron's Enmore home in 1894. Leaving their host early, the two men immediately repaired to 'the nearest bar' where they 'drank each other's health' more than once, then 'walked down to Circular Quay, happy in new comradeship'.[1] Lawson and Cameron (later Gilmore) were young writers and committed socialists from humble provincial backgrounds who had found their identities in Sydney's radical intelligentsia. Was it the earnest political discourse, Cameron's feminine fastidiousness, or Lawson's lower-class awkwardness (he spilt his tea) that discomfited the urbane, bourgeois Brereton? Editor of the University of Sydney's literary magazine, *Hermes*, the undergraduate Brereton was in awe of Lawson's reputation and gushed that his verse had converted him to 'democracy and the future that the workers were about to win for us all'. But walking down George Street the beer-fuelled Lawson confessed, 'I couldn't say it in public because my living depends partly on what I'm writing for the *Worker*; but you can take it from me Jack, the Australian worker is a brute and nothing else.'[2]

Lawson's 'youthful disillusion' proved infectious, and Brereton traded political idealism for the cult of the poet hero and communion with Lawson in 'Bohemian Adventures'. Yet

Lawson continued to write rallying words for the labour press, and for much of his career struggled to balance the bohemian and political parts of his life.

Lawson was one of many in this second generation of Australian bohemians who became 'radical bohemians', contributing their talents to progressive reform groups and the wider labour movement as cultural activists. Identification with socialist politics and the labour movement was one way for bohemians to transgress bourgeois society and assert their autonomy from markets. Yet the carnivalesque and Dionysian aspects of bohemian transgression could come into conflict with the discipline and self-improving respectability demanded by radical intelligentsia and the labour movement.

BOHEMIAN POLITICS

It is important to acknowledge the limitations of bohemia's radical rhetoric. Bohemianism is a rebellion undertaken mainly by the young bourgeois in a period of their career when they feel free from the restrictions of the social class they were born into or in which they might end up. Rather than overturning the bourgeoisie they claim to despise, bohemians settle for selling them their books, pictures, plays and songs. But within this market reality their revolution is to push to the extreme the individualism, hedonism and libertarian potential of capitalism that is routinely suppressed by the economy's need to keep the show on the road through bureaucratic order, the work ethic and stable family life.

Australian bohemians have attracted criticism for favouring the subtle symbolic subversion of the carnivalesque and making a show of outraging the bourgeoisie rather than taking a real fight up to the capitalists they claimed to despise. But in Australia a significant phalanx of bohemians did march beyond the carnivalesque to man the barricades as activists in the labour and socialist movements, the Communist Party and other radical groups. During the 1890s, a period of bitter industrial unrest culminating in the foundation of the Australian Labor Party, explicit socialist and working-class politics flavoured the work and identity of many leading literary bohemians. Writers and journalists who participated in socialist or labour politics included men at the very centre of bohemian life in Sydney and Melbourne, such as Henry Lawson, Victor Daley, E.J. Brady, Randolph Bedford, Fred Broomfield, Tom Mutch, Bertram Stevens, Will Dyson, Sam Rosa and a young Lionel Lindsay. Political activism for them meant producing poems, books, newspapers, pamphlets, posters, cartoons and articles and speeches advocating either revolutionary or reformist action against the owning class in order to improve the condition of ordinary people. Some were so driven by the cause they forsook the creative sphere entirely to make politics their vocation.

The engagement of artists in political causes and movements occurred in many western nations in the nineteenth century, including Britain, Germany, Russia, France and the United States, and countries that were subject to imperial power, such as Poland and Ireland. Western painting, music and literature had long served values beyond the aesthetic, reflecting the interest of a religion, a secular ruler or a wealthy patron. However the relationship of art to morality and other non-aesthetic values became the subject of passionate debate in Europe in the second half of the nineteenth century as romanticism pro- duced contrary strains arguing for 'moral art' and 'art for art's sake'. Baudelaire supported revolution in 1848 and sided with socialists, but quickly came to find political art too limiting. In Britain, the Victorian ideal proselytised by Matthew Arnold and Ruskin – that art should be directed to moral and social improvement – had acquired a radical edge in the 1880s and 90s in the hands of a new generation of artist-socialists such as William Morris, H.G. Wells and George Bernard Shaw. The last, a reformist and bohemian in his early career, was one of many dramatists, writers and journalists who sought to conscript their art to proselytise the goals of the Fabian Society and the Labour Party. There was also a strong anti-political expression among explicitly bohemian artists in Britain from the 1870s, exemplified by first the aesthetic, then decadent movements. Yet as prominent an aesthete as Oscar Wilde for a time flirted with socialism before losing interest because it 'took up too many evenings'.

In a country still composed of disparate colonies, rather than constituting an independent nation, any rallying by writers and journalists to radical politics had to contend with the problem of the imperial connection to Great Britain and their own role in creating a new Australian literary nationalism. The left-of-centre politics in which Australian bohemians participated took two broad forms: a labour movement based on working-class trade unions, and more disparate radical groups and causes grounded in the educated urban intelligentsia. The bridge connecting bohemians to both types of politics was the radical press.

A RADICAL INTELLIGENTSIA MEETS BOHEMIA
A rhetoric of revolutionary change entered Australian politics amid the economic collapse of the depression of 1890 and class conflict of the shearers' and maritime strikes that began that year. Working-class activists garnered support from, and exchanged ideas with, a small but articulate section of cultural producers working as journalists, writers and pamphleteers – sometimes termed 'middle-class radicals' or the 'radical intelligentsia' by historians – which included a subset of self-styled bohemians focused on print media.[3] Among radicals, core beliefs centred on humanism, secularism, socialism, unionism, republicanism and feminism's questioning of unequal gender relations. This was a diverse and feisty sphere, where protean cells debated and jostled to shape political progress. To the Australian Socialist League, and smaller anarchist clubs, we can add Christian socialists, Fabians, mutualism, free thought, spiritualists, theosophists and female suffrage.

The radical intelligentsia was concentrated in the main urban centres and based around popular bohemian haunts – newspapers, art galleries, cafés and especially bookshops, notably William and Matilda McNamara's in Sydney and Andrade's Anarchist Bookery in Melbourne. Radical activists and theoreticians also gathered in spaces associated with self-improvement and adult education, notably mechanics institutes, trades halls and schools of arts, to debate and discuss a variety of issues such as women's suffrage and temperance.[4] Within this milieu bohemian journalists such as Daley and Brady contributed to what historian Bruce Scates called an infectious celebration of reading, and became a valuable resource for radical groups and their media.[5] Daley joined the Socialist League; his friend

Bulletin literary editor Bertram Stevens became a devotee of the Single Tax movement; and journalist and novelist Sam Rosa started the Melbourne branch of the Socialist League, although he was at heart an anarchist. Brady became secretary of the Australian Socialist League, edited the *Australian Workman*, and was a founding Labor Party member.

Although described by the visiting British Fabian socialist Beatrice Webb as being of 'no particular class', the radical intelligentsia drew its leaders overwhelmingly from the educated knowledge professions such as journalists, teachers, administrators and even doctors, architects and lawyers, as well as cultural business people like bookshop proprietors and publishers.[6] However, heterogeneity was enhanced by non-British émigrés and increasingly self-educated working-class leaders from the labour movement with skills in journalism and pamphleteering. Men who would be future Labor ministers, premiers and prime ministers such as Tom Mutch, W.G. Spence, William Holman, John Christian Watson and W.M. Hughes are examples of 'organic' working-class intellectuals. They were propelled from humble backgrounds and occupations by a political calling to become union organisers, propagandists and journalists, finding common cause with many radical bourgeois reformers and cooperating in campaigns and periodicals. It was through journalism that some began fraternising with bohemians.

Not all organic intellectuals focused on the unions though. Louisa Lawson, the daughter of an itinerant gold prospector and estranged wife of a struggling immigrant selector, devoted her self-taught publishing and journalistic skills to improving the lot of women, which she connected to a vision of a socialist republic. At the age of twenty her son Henry followed Louisa into the radical circles that met at her Sydney home and McNamara's Bookshop. He joined the Australian Socialist League and wrote his first political poem in 1887, a call to arms entitled 'The Song of the Republic', published in the *Bulletin*.[7]

JOURNALISTS OF THE WORLD UNITE!

Radical journalism brought together political activists with bohemian journalists and illustrators who worked on commercial publications such as the *Bulletin*, *Truth* or the daily newspapers.

Between 1870 and 1899 an astounding 107 labour and radical newspapers began publication in Australia, many lasting only a short while but some enduring.[8] Colourful titles redolent of end-of-century optimism and proletarian assertion included the *Worker, Socialist, Revolt*, the *Shearers' Record, Trades Hall Gazette*, the *Liberator, Patriot*, the *Cooperator*, the *Transmitter* and the *Dawn*. Tom Mutch, a *Bulletin* literary editor and a leader in the Australian Journalists Association, found the union-controlled Sydney-based *Worker*, 'a common meeting place for many of the more prominent writers and artists in those days'.[9] J.S. Noonan even compared the *Worker* to the *Bulletin* as a significant 'rendezvous for the foremost writers and artists of the day, a careless, generous, good lot of fellows'.[10] Afforded a lavish production budget, Bedford's *Clarion*, launched in 1896, was a magnet for Melbourne's visual bohemians, marrying radical politics with excellence in design and production values. Bedford fused bohemianism, literature, mining and Labor politics in his career and the journal. It attracted the innovative young illustrators Ambrose and Will Dyson, three of the Lindsay brothers and poet Hugh McCrae, all members of the Ishmael Club. In the early 1890s *Bulletin* stalwart E.J. Brady edited the important labour weekly *Australian Workman*, enjoying the experience of 'a super-radical newspaper office'.[11] He was assisted in sub-editing by fellow bohemian and *Bulletin* journalist Roderic Quinn. Sam Rosa wrote for the *Labor Daily* and *Common Cause* but also the commercial weekly *Truth*.

Journalists from the capitalist *Bulletin* and *Truth* were welcomed in the radical press because they possessed necessary skills not just in communicating with, but also in entertaining, working-class readers, including tabloid design and storytelling techniques typical of the new journalism. Union official Ted Grayndler boasted to Randolph Bedford that New South Wales labour papers were superior because 'we run our papers with journalists' rather than 'comrades'.[12] From the perspective of professional journalists and illustrators, radical publications offered an outlet for work unacceptable to the commercial press and a further source of income.

Paradoxically, radical journalism provided an avenue for talented working-class writers to move into the commercial press and bohemia. Before gaining acceptance as a mainstream writer, Lawson recalled proudly, he 'helped write, machine, and publish … the *Republican*', owned and edited by his mother, and wrote for the Brisbane *Boomerang* and the *Worker*. He later assisted Louisa with her pioneering socialist feminist magazine *Dawn*, which she described as 'a phonograph to wind out audibly the whispers, pleadings and demands of the sisterhood'.[13] Reminiscing about his youthful idealism Lawson claimed he 'dreamed of dying on the barricades to the roar of the "Marseillaise" – for the Young Australian Republic.' Daley described him as 'a tribal poet – the poet of the great tribe of the Down-and-out'.[14] In this same spirit Lawson's poetic intervention in the shearers' strike threatened:

> We'll make the tyrants feel the sting
> Of those that they would throttle;
> They needn't say the fault is ours
> If blood should stain the wattle.[15]

The themes of extreme poverty, exploitation by bosses and landlords, class conflict, the solidarity of mates, the threat of a bloody proletarian revolution led by organised labour and a coming socialist republic were repeated in Lawson's early political poems such as 'Faces in the Street' and 'The Army of the Rear' and in poems and prose by Daley, Brady, Quinn, Rosa and Bernard O'Dowd.

The *Bulletin* may have been a commercial proposition committed to making a profit but editor J.F. Archibald was also a committed republican and democratic socialist, leading the magazine to became a magnet for writers, journalists and illustrators who had radical sympathies as well as bohemian tendencies. The fertile crossover between the commercial and proletarian public spheres via journalism broadened out the activities of political writers and the radical press from mere pamphleteering and propaganda to a portfolio of creative writing and media work – journalism, cartoons, poems and ballads, songs, plays – that is better understood as 'cultural activism'.

Radical publications assumed that working-class readers were interested in poetry, fiction and cultural issues in general.

Fabian Society founder Harry Champion's eponymous publication the *Champion* boasted theatre, book, concert and art
exhibition reviews.[16] While a militant trade unionist, Champion
proved to be an erudite, cosmopolitan editor and publisher,
who so approved of bohemia that he translated and published
an Australian edition of Murger's classic. *Free-Lance*, published
weekly in 1896, merged a strong bohemian and Fabian socialist
flavour, took aim at an increasingly utilitarian Labor for being
'a foe of the Intellect', and called for a new party for the 'many
Democrats who do not toil with their hands' but who 'are
sympathetic, and by many associations, have common cause
with manual workers'.[17] In 1897 *Free-Lance*'s editors, journalist
J.B. Castieau, and illustrator Lionel Lindsay joined forces with
poet Bernard O'Dowd to launch Melbourne socialist weekly the
Tocsin, which emphasised a free and eclectic approach to politics.
In his study of the Victorian radical press, labour historian Frank
Bongiorno considered *Tocsin* an exemplar of 1890s 'bohemian
socialism'.[18] The paper's name derived from a particular type of
alarm bell and was intended as a wake-up call to Australia. Victor
Daley contributed and Dr William Maloney, who had toured
France and Spain with Tom Roberts, was a *Tocsin* regular who
made an impression on the young people 'by wearing an outsize
Cavalier hat, a Van Dyke beard and an up-brushed moustache,
and who bore himself with the cloak-and-dagger air of a hero
of melodrama, constantly throwing back an imaginary cape and
flourishing an imaginary rapier, and shouting trenchantly, "We
MUST have a revolution!"'[19]

Bernard O'Dowd was a poor scholarship boy from Ballarat
who had graduated with honours from Melbourne University.
He went on to juggle political radicalism, a career in the civil
service and a talent for poetry in the tradition of American Walt
Whitman. He wore his unkempt hair long and had a Christ-like
beard that gave him a messianic air. A founding member of the
Victorian Socialist Party, O'Dowd argued that the achievement
of socialism required its own 'social atmosphere', encouraging
a community beyond the formalities of unions and the Labor
Party. Not all bohemians were impressed. Lionel's brother
Norman, while happy to sell drawings to *Tocsin*, didn't give a
fig for its politics, insisting that 'the working classes could stay

in the mud'. Norman Lindsay reflected a common libertarian prejudice of bohemian artists when he described all politicians as 'authorized bandits' who are 'more or less open in pilfering from the public coffers'.[20]

Sound strategy attracted labour press editors to literature and art. The puritanical British immigrant William Lane, who established labour weekly the *Boomerang* in Brisbane in 1887, was no bohemian but keen to recruit them to his cause. Indeed, he believed cosmopolitan writers and artists had the potential to move from individualism to collective, and even revolutionary, action. His appreciation of art's value to socialism was apparent in his influential novel *The Workingman's Paradise*, which focused on a Sydney bohemian group, the 'Stratton circle', whose members voice opinions on the importance of art in raising political awareness.[21] Lane had members of this fictitious group write and illustrate political material for the *Scrutineer*, a radical-leaning but commercial publication comparable to the *Bulletin*. Lane asked socialist bohemian Fred Broomfield to pen a poem for inclusion in his novel and clearly appreciated that people could be won to the socialist cause through art and in actual lived communities. He astutely enlisted the young Henry Lawson, whose poems did much to authenticate the labour movement in the eyes of workers.

ROMANTIC RADICALS

Socialism and labour politics appealed to late nineteenth-century bohemian writers on a number of levels. First, there were differences in the relationship of this generation of writers and their media to a working-class readership that took them beyond the flâneurism and slum journalism of Marcus Clarke, which had been designed to titillate the conscience of the bourgeoisie of the 1860s and 70s. By the 1880s the working-class market was a larger proportion of potential readers in Australia than in Britain, thanks to increased literacy and higher wages. It was shrewd for a new generation of writers in this market to appeal to the interests of working-class readers through political populism, while simultaneously cultivating the bourgeois intelligentsia. This was the *Bulletin*'s cross-class audience. Second, the proletarianisation of commercial journalism, especially on the bigger newspapers such as the *Melbourne Herald* or Sydney's *Daily Telegraph*, encouraged some journalists to identify with the union cause. At this time the socialist movement began to use the term 'brain workers' to encourage cross-class alliances between journalists and manual workers, with editors and writers such as E.J. Brady taking a lead in trying to unionise journalists.[22]

The 1890s depression hit harder in Australia than Britain and its vicissitudes created a commonality of interest between cultural and manual workers. Both groups experienced hard times due to unemployment, reduced freelance work and sales, and lower incomes. One in three Australians lost their job and eviction, job uncertainty and poverty disturbed the family life of intellectual and manual worker alike. Sam Rosa became a leader of the Sydney unemployed. Shortage of work combined with an intemperate lifestyle reduced Daley to temporary homelessness and Lawson to manual jobs to top up his freelance income. Such experiences created empathy with the plight of working people.

Most importantly, bohemia and socialism shared synergies as romantic ideas: a sense of alienation from capitalist society; a desire for freedom from the market; an enthusiasm to *épater les bourgeois* ('shock the bourgeois'), especially that philistine fraction that owned and managed business; an oppositional, rebellious outlook; and a vanguardist belief that they were seers of the future. The self-image of bohemians as classless fits with the socialist goal of eliminating class inequality and exploitation. At their roots, bohemia and socialist politics in the nineteenth century were both influenced by romanticism's critique of capitalist modernity that looked back with a sense of loss to pre-capitalist, pre-industrial, supposedly less-alienated communities. The socialist romanticism promoted by the bohemian radicals had several themes. One was a pastoral nostalgia based on the itinerant bush worker and selector as symbols of a way of life threatened by capitalist mechanisation and urbanisation. The second was the related but forward-looking belief that a new national type created by the Australian environment could renew society. Both engaged with an emerging nationalism.

Whereas Clarke had longed for the metropolis of Europe and imagined Australia's brutal convict past, the mainly native-born literary bohemians of the next generation were nostalgic for the imagined rough-and-ready colonial country life of their childhoods that was already disappearing. Lawson's poems collected in *In the Days When the World Was Wide* and *The Roaring Days* and his short-story collection *Joe Wilson and His Mates* mourn a lost community and freedom of movement that was being displaced by the capitalisation of agriculture, pastoralism, mining and rail transport, as well as urbanisation and improved communications. He recalled with longing the haphazard tent towns amongst the diggings of his childhood, where 'jests were driven' and 'good old songs were sung'. 'But Golden days are vanished' he lamented, because 'the mighty Bush with Iron rails/Is tethered to the world'.[23] Likewise Archibald's idealisation of the 'lone hand' and Edward Dyson's mining stories were created at a time when the enterprising prospector had given way to employees working for large-scale operations such as the Broken Hill Proprietary Company (today BHP).

Cultural radicals such as Lawson, Brady and Archibald also looked to a brighter future. There had been successive Australian identities in the colonies, but late nineteenth-century Australian nationalism was distinguished by the discourse of the 'Coming Man', personified in the nomadic workers of the bush who, to quote Lawson, 'call no biped lord or sir, and touch their hats to no man!' This man was an exemplar of the Anglo-Saxon race tempered by the Australian environment to produce an egalitarian spirit and a casual collectivism in work and play. Historian Graeme Davison argued that many of the characteristics attributed to the native-born rural working class by radical nationalist historians Russel Ward and Vance Palmer actually emerged within urban bohemia.[24] Not surprisingly, the Australian 'type' was exclusively male and possessed independence, disrespect for authority, irreverence, unease with respectability, freedom and, especially, loyalty to mates — traits that were also valued and practised within literary bohemia.

In couching the case for a socialist future in an appeal to an imagined rural idyll, Australian bohemian radicals were drawing on a pastoral aesthetic reminiscent of the English romantic socialists of the first half of the nineteenth century. This was a moral, even transcendental, argument against industrial capitalism and alienation, a longing for the bonds of a pastoral community that had been lost, and a dream of a future utopia, encapsulated in biblical metaphors of paradise such as 'millennial Eden', 'New Jerusalem' and 'the light on the hill'. Socialism, it was argued, required a 'revolution', in the sense of a turning back to an earlier, purer way of living.

Mining and shearing were on the frontline of struggles over modernisation, innovation and efficiency in primary industry that erupted in strikes in the early 1890s. Nostalgia was used to rally workers in these sectors to 'fight till the world grows wide' and became politically potent.[25] The coming man's character traits were mobilised against the local ship owners, squatters and manufacturers, now caricatured as 'the Fatman in his mansion fine'.[26] Mateship was celebrated by bohemians as the glue that bound them in work and play, but for those interested in radical politics, it was reinterpreted as the local version of socialism's brotherhood of man and exemplified the solidarity needed to wage strikes and build a political party. Lawson's view was that 'socialism is just being mates' and his credo of mateship proved elastic enough to incorporate the bond between isolated bush workers, the solidarity of the new militant unions, the loyalty between soldiers fighting in a common cause and the mutual support and collective recreation enjoyed in bohemia.[27] Larrikin humour and earthy slang were used to prick pretension and demystify authority while the use of colloquial working-class language expressed the empowering injunction that workers could govern themselves in workplaces and in parliaments.

What bohemians did for the cause of reform was to naturalise political aspirations such as community, solidarity and the 'fair go' as characteristics of ordinary Australians, in journalism, literature and black-and-white art. Folk nationalism united bohemian writers and the labour activists because it appealed to the mass audience that both needed to address. Lawson, Brady and others associated with the *Bulletin*, accomplished at invoking grassroots Australianness to authenticate their local product over foreign imports, could help legitimise union rights and Labor's claim to parliamentary representation and government.

There was an anti-colonial dimension as well, manifest in the *Bulletin*'s call for a republic. Radical and egalitarian policies and governing styles could be portrayed as 'racy of the soil', while imperial capitalism, especially 'free' trade, 'free' labour, and unrestricted immigration, could be criticised as an external imposition from the old country that benefited the English ruling class – the 'Old Dead Tree' contrasted with the 'Young Tree Green', as Lawson had it.[28] While shaped by a romance of the colonial frontiersman that was popular in the mother country too, in Australia egalitarian folk nationalism helped to weaken British imperial authority in the lead-up to Federation by contributing to a cultural shift Lawson characterised as 'a spirit totally at variance with Australian groveldom'.[29] It gave organised labour a counter-story of national interest identified with youth, progress and native birth to compete with the imperial belonging of the colonial ruling class. But this narrative had no place for women or non-Europeans, including Aborigines.

The political writing of the radical bohemians of the 1890s addressed working-class readers assumed to have the agency to change conditions for themselves. In contrast to Clarke's liberalism, young Lawson anticipated Sydney's Mammon falling to 'Red Revolution's feet'.[30] Where Clarke was cynical about the elitist hypocrisy of republican agitators, some bohemian journalists of the second generation became Labor Party politicians themselves. In place of the flâneur as curious spectator of the colonial city, the next generation of literary bohemians despaired of the city as a site of slums, poverty and exploitation. Clarke was not shy of slum journalism but the dominant tone of his urban writing is amusement and wonder at its speed, spectacle, commerce and technology. The next generation folded the city's modernity into their critique of capitalism and contrasted the exploited, underfed 'faces in the street' with the free and independent workers of the bush. For Lawson

> The city grinds the owners of the faces in the street –
> Grinding body, grinding soul,
> Yielding scarce enough to eat –
> Oh! I sorrow for the owners of the faces in the
>   street.

The marriage of bohemia with socialism was integral to this rejection of urban modernity in favour of the authenticity of the rural workers and the bush. The irony is that the bohemians of the 1890s project their own bohemian qualities onto the bush from the safety of Sydney and Melbourne. The urbane Irish-born Daley wryly conceded that 'I long for Sydney and its narrow streets' and while 'the country's free' it's 'the town for me'.[31] Archibald, who more than any other insisted on the Bush with capital B, nonetheless favoured the café-eye view himself. Even Lawson, sparring with Banjo Paterson in the *Bulletin*, declared his preference for the city pleasures of 'beer and lemon squashes, taking baths and cooling down' over the 'Desolation' and 'everlasting fences' of the country.[32]

The sense of belonging of the immigrant bohemians of the 1860s remained imperial – Clarke was an English gentleman in exile but still part of a cosmopolitan world and the empire that his relatives helped manage. The folk nationalist writers of the 1890s sought to make a virtue of provincialism, and make the artist feel at home in an Australia identified with the land and the people. The *Bulletin* circle did not abandon cosmopolitan and imperial interests and did not see these as unAustralian. Lawson wrote of being 'free from the wrongs of the North and Past', but he later acknowledged his debt to 'Yankee free-thought', Irish rebels, and nationalists from 'the fair land of Poland'.[33] Archibald admired Gallic republicanism and, like his colleagues Fred Broomfield and A.G. Stephens, was far more accomplished at achieving a balance between bohemia's cosmopolitanism and egalitarian nationalism than Lawson. Despite the important role of painters like Tom Roberts and others associated with the Heidelberg School in lovingly depicting the Australian landscape, ennobling rural working life in paintings like *Shearing the Rams* and later undertaking national commissions, the artists struck a genuine cosmopolitan counter-note. Unbounded by language or political institutions they were more easily international in their modus operandi, and looked forward to training and exhibiting in Europe, in the metropolitan centre. But *Bulletin* bohemianism stressed Australian distinctiveness defined against the metropolitan longing of Clarke's founding generation and opposition to what *Bulletin*'s literary gatekeeper A.G. Stephens (somewhat unfairly) considered their 'grotesque English prejudice against things Australian'.[34]

A CULTURAL REVOLUTION?

There were hopes for a cultural revolution, too. According to Brady the 'radical Bohemians', like Roderic Quinn and he, 'dreamed the establishment of a new Hellenic democracy' where 'Literature and the fine arts would be a permanent policy of the Administration'. Through state patronage of artists and philosophers, Brady predicted, 'Australia was to become the intellectual leader of the nations, and a signpost to the freedom and prosperity of the world.'[35] Having 'learned the rights of labour', Lawson argued in rhyme, 'Let the Southern writers start/Agitating, too, for letters and for music and for art'.[36] Their agitations were rewarded when the Liberal government of Deakin introduced a Commonwealth Literary Fund in 1908 of which Lawson became a recipient.

A more sophisticated idea of a socialist cultural transformation than Brady's was available at this time in the writings of William Morris, which were published in papers such as Brady's *Workman*. Morris grounded socialist transformation in the assertion of democratic crafts over elitist art. Where bohemians tended to view the artist as a heroic figure separate from ordinary mortals due to innate qualities, Morris believed all people could be creative producers. His ideas were well-known in Australia, where his disciples included journalist Sam Rosa, Melbourne poet Bernard O'Dowd and socialist Frank Wilmot. Brady also claimed he was converted to socialism by reading Morris's utopian novel *News from Nowhere*.

William Morris's view that all people were creative was not too far from the *Bulletin*'s revolutionary credo that 'Every man can write at least one good book; every man with brains has at least one good story to tell ... Mail your work to the *Bulletin*, which pays for accepted matter.'[37] Archibald's democratic cultural policy was to tap the talents of the pubs and shearing sheds and literary editor A.G. Stephens claimed to receive a thousand contributions a week. For Archiabld biographer Sylvia Lawson the *Bulletin*'s topsy-turvy culture of participation was its truly radical innovation.[38] The editorial outreach paid dividends, sourcing talent Australia-wide, and allowing the readers to communicate with each other via the letters page. A community was created in which the consumers had a sense of ownership of the magazine – not unlike some of today's online forums. Archibald's socialism was not simply unionism, public owner-ship and wealth distribution but also imagined the good society as one extending bohemian pleasures and sensibilities – such as enjoying the spectacle of city-life from a street-side café – to everyone. For this synthesis he has been dubbed 'a man for the barricades and the boulevards'.

For most radical writers and illustrators, it was one thing to call for the socialisation of money capital, but to democratise the cultural capital of the artist defeated the purpose of being a bohemian. So the elitist view of artists as special people to be supported by public patronage remained the policy of most left-leaning bohemians and, in the new century, exerted an influence over public arts bodies, while popular culture was catered to by commercial interests.

AGITATORS OR ARTISTS?

Pierre Bourdieu called bohemians who place their journalistic skills in the service of radical political causes, writing and pub-lishing in pamphlets, tracts, or types of realist fiction, 'social artists', and argued that in France they had less cultural capital than those artists who kept their art free of material and moral constraints. They were 'inferior' bohemians because their work was governed by non-aesthetic values, such as a party line, limiting their artistic freedom of action.[39]

In Australia political bohemians were more esteemed. Unlike France, the literary market in the Australian colonies was not large enough to accommodate a 'high' market for literature separate from journalism. Daley's lyric poetry took second place to his career as a journalist and it was journalism, rather than poetry, that organised his bohemian milieu. Australian writers of prose fiction for the most part eschewed the experimental modernism of a Flaubert and the idea of art for art's sake. In late nineteenth-century Australia the market for literature was more popular and cross-class than bourgeois, so the critique of political writing carried less weight in literary bohemia than in its French counterpart. Given the critical and popular ascendancy of realism as a literary style, writing for the labour and radical press might even enhance the skills, credibility and authenticity of a writer committed to this genre. Henry Lawson's trajectory, for example, reveals how 'social art' could elevate a talented young man from working-class life and manual occupations into the ranks of the radical intelligentsia and on to bohemia and literary acclaim.

While art and politics were entwined for Lawson in this first stage as a poet, political verse had the upper hand, and earned him the income and reputation that allowed him to be less dependent on manual work, setting him on the road to being a working-class intellectual. Brereton's memoir of his friend dismissed this phase as the 'natural impulses of impatient and ill-informed youth', reflecting 'enthusiasm for a class' and 'revolutionary zeal'.[40] Rather than a bohemian, at this stage he considered himself a volunteer to the cause of 'unionism and Democracy', a type of revolutionary amateur who 'hadn't dreamed of receiving payment for literary work', in contrast to the literary professionals who were attracted to bohemianism.[41] Lawson had few options. By his own admission 'a shy ignorant lad from the Bush, under every disadvantage arising from poverty and lack of education', Lawson simply didn't have the cultural capital when he first commenced writing to assemble a bohemian identity, let alone carve out a niche for himself in its competitive groups. Background, experience and his mother's connections led him to the fellowship of the labour movement and the drawing rooms of radical politics, an environment in which his talent with language and observation flourished. But far from the ghetto described by Bourdieu, radical journalism provided a bridge for Lawson into the literary bohemia that circled around the *Bulletin* and, by 1898, he was a founding member of the Dawn and Dusk Club. Lawson's growing sense of himself as a bohemian mirrored his sense of himself as a professional writer, apparent in a growing concern for fair payment for his poems and copy. The short stories he began to write from 1888, with their insight into character, ear for the Australian vernacular, sardonic voice and use of pathos and comedy, raised his stocks among those bohemians such as Brereton, Norman Lindsay, and even A.G. Stephens who looked to literary values and compensated for his inadequate education and commitment to political writing. Rather than dividing Lawson from the labour movement, literary bohemia welcomed such men as journalists on labour papers with interesting ideas and wit.

While conceding that by the mid 1890s '"the cause" didn't loom so big in my eyes as it used to', he still wrote and edited for the *Worker* and penned 'red hot socialistic and libellous political rhymes' for the populist *Truth* in a precarious market where every penny counted.[42] He maintained close links with the unions and the Labor Party through personal friends. (Lawson's sister-in-law married future New South Wales Labor premier Jack Lang, who on occasion socialised with his brother-in-law at the Dawn and Dusk Club.)

TENSIONS AND DISILLUSIONMENT

Political activism was not without serious problems for bohemians, who had to negotiate tensions between respectability and the Dionysian, individualism and solidarity, carnivalesque transgression and collective discipline, cosmopolitanism and nationalism, liberty and cooption by a party or the state. Just as Lawson's career demonstrates the possibilities opened up by the combination of politics, art and bohemia, it also highlights the limitations of this hybrid.

Bohemian drinking, laziness and hedonistic consumption, indulged from a position of superior cultural capital, could appear decadent to working-class improvers, many with Methodist or Calvinist convictions, who valued the rewards of sobriety, hard work, self-discipline, thrift, home ownership and stable family life. Likewise, feminists such as Rose Scott supported reforms such as temperance, as well as the sanctity of home life, fidelity in marriage and female sexual autonomy as protection for women from abusive male power. This provoked a virulent campaign waged by bohemian journalists against 'respectability', 'wowserism' and 'blue stockings' that took particular umbrage at feminist calls to restrict men's right of sexual access.[43]

Henry Lawson's alcohol abuse and treatment of his wife brought these tensions to a head in the Sydney radical community. Initially feted by his mother's radical coterie as the boy poet of the revolution, aspects of Lawson's bohemianism, especially his carousing with Brady and Stevens, were seen as socially irresponsible and a waste of his talents. Wed to William McNamara's

stepdaughter in 1896, Lawson complained to Brereton that marriage played 'hell with a man's notions of duty to his chums',
and that he remained devoted to 'the creed of the chaps, the
coves, and fellows'.[44] Lawson was stung by the criticism of Rose
Scott, an associate of his mother, who accused him of wrecking
his marriage through drinking and bohemianism, firing back
through his fictional character Mitchell, who accused 'advanced
idealist fools' from 'middle class shabby-genteel families that
catch Spiritualism and Theosophy' of being 'parasites or hangers
on' of genuine causes like socialism and unionism.[45] To be fair,
Lawson himself did support equal pay and suffrage for women.
He maintained close friendships with writers Mary Gilmore and
Miles Franklin, who moved in feminist circles.

Creative, brain-working bohemians might also find disagreement with actual manual workers who could exhibit traits
such as anti-intellectualism, materialism, social conformity, or
even violence. By 1894, after his trip to Bourke, Lawson was
alternating between stories of the solidarity of a union burial and
depictions of workers as drunks who would rather "ave a pint o'
beer' than a revolution.[46] Tiring of 'pander[ing] to the people',
his poems reveal resentment of Australia as the 'land where sport
is sacred' and 'where the labourer is a god'.[47]

Brereton came to lament that Lawson 'had not easily
found the great fellowship which he seems to have expected'
among workers whose 'rough and ready ways abashed him,
careless brutalities jarred a sensitive heart ... and when he found
evidence of gross selfishness he was angry.[48] Lawson did not
renounce labour's cause, but he conceded that the workers and
bush people who 'make a hero of a clod' were just as philistine
as the bourgeoisie. The stand-off between the uncouth working
class and artistic bohemians would prove enduring. This is how
Norman Lindsay depicted life in a mining bush town in the late
nineteenth century in his semi-autobiographical *Redheap*, and
the struggle of the sensitive young artist against conformist provincial yahoos became a common theme in twentieth-century
bohemian memoirs.

While the strikes of the early 1890s were romanticised from
afar, up close the discipline and tactics of collective bargaining
could offend the bohemian's sense of individualism. Lawson

was repelled by unionists' treatment of 'scabs', declaring: '[i]t is a great pity that the word "scab" ever dirtied the pages of a workman's newspaper ... few men, except bullies who have the brute strength to back them, would call a man so to his face.'[49]

He wrote this in the *Worker*, to the annoyance of its trustees, testing the limits of editorial freedom in the labour press. As they do today, unions and later the ALP demanded loyalty and extracted conformity through binding votes, decisions and pledges. This was a far cry from the 'freedom' the young Lawson had imagined the labour movement would deliver.

• • •

Colonial governments were not to be intimidated by industrial militancy, firing Gatling guns at picketing strikers and imprisoning the ringleaders, curbing the revolutionary enthusiasms of young idealists. The differences between labour and bohemians came into sharper focus as unions regrouped in the face of defeat and formed the new Labor Party to contest parliamentary and municipal elections. By the turn of the century party union 'machines' were controlling purse strings and purging diverse tendencies within journals in favour of a plodding labourist pragmatism and the party line, exemplified by the fate of the libertarian and pluralist *Tocsin*. Amidst union objections to the publication of 'offensive matter' and approach to 'politico-religious subjects', Trades Hall became a shareholder, and in 1906, *Tocsin* was renamed *Labor Call*.[50] As the remaining bohemian contributors drifted away, it was transformed into a stolid, predictable party journal – occasionally radical but not bohemian.

The spirit of topsy-turvydom apparent in clubs such as the Dawn and Dusk, journals like the *Tocsin* and the *Bulletin*, and many of the antics of literary bohemians were mocking of wider authority and social custom. The labour movement, on the other hand, took its own authority and rules very seriously indeed, and its leaders were suspicious of frivolity and disrespect that undermined the solidarity and hierarchy deemed necessary for fighting class war. This tension was not so apparent in the late 1880s and early 90s, when the labour movement was a loose rambunctious affiliation of unionists, middle-class radicals, populist agitators and cultural activists; a period that Lawson remembered nostalgically as 'The Carnival of labour'.[51] However, artists' and intellectuals' hopes for Labor were being frustrated by its narrow utilitarian conception of social progress limited to improving wages, conditions, job growth and increasing state intervention in the economy. In a general atmosphere of retreat from their earlier hopes, many writers and illustrators diluted their socialism, abandoned republicanism for the compromises of Federation and withdrew into a bohemia of nationalism, nostalgia and play.

THE LIMITS OF NATIONALISM

Once invoked as part of bohemia's identity, Australian nationalism could be overwhelming. In the decade after Federation it was difficult for writers so strongly associated with egalitarian nationalism to resist the claims on loyalty of the new Australian nation that, although constitutionally committed to a bourgeois economy and empire, had protected the living standards of workers through the Immigration Restriction Act, tariff protection and arbitration. By the time of the Boer War, Henry Lawson was able to cheer New South Wales troops making their way to South Africa. The *Bulletin* quietly dropped its calls for a republic and socialism in the years after Federation, while cranking up its campaign against 'coloured' immigration. The prejudice against non-British races evident in immigration policies was also expressed by bohemian writers and, from 1908, the *Bulletin*'s banner read 'Australia for the White Man'. The next year Bedford wrote the play *White Australia or the Empty North* and O'Dowd warned his 'chosen race' to 'guard the future from exotic blight', namely the 'Asian throng or island brown'.[52] The internationalism and pluralism that was to be found in both bohemianism and socialism succumbed to the imperatives of nation-building and a brand of egalitarian yet racially defined nationalism that both bohemian writers and Labor politicians had helped to create through the romance of the 'coming man'. While recognising the 'national capital' of locally born Anglo-Celts no matter their class or circumstances, the new belonging was restrictive in terms of race and reduced, but did not remove, the capital of being cosmopolitan or upper-class English.[53] In again cheering for the troops in 1914, Henry Lawson joined his old comrades Taylor, Stevens, Brady, Will Dyson and Archibald in the logic of colonial nationalism.

• • •

The growing electoral support garnered by the new Labor Party in the first decade of the new century owed something to the communication skills and energy of the bohemian radicals. Randolph Bedford, William Maloney and Tom Mutch even became Labor politicians. Holman and Hughes maintained friendships with writers and journalists as they climbed the greasy pole of politics. Arthur Parker, a friend of Lawson's from his socialist days, acknowledged in the 1930s that 'he inspired in the hearts of many of the Labor pioneers of 1890 great hopes which to-day have been realised'.[54] But more radical visions such as a socialist republic failed to materialise.

Disillusionment may have led to dissolution in Lawson's later years, as he stumbled down that other bohemian path of drink, divorce, poverty, melancholy and the asylum. Brady argued it was the decline of revolutionary potential in Australia that led to Lawson's personal decline. The poets were discarded by a compromised party they had helped popularise because '[t]he labour Movement was advancing on constitutional lines and revolutionary genius was rather embarrassment than asset to a leadership which aimed at establishing the Kingdom of God on earth by means of universal franchise and the basic wage.'[55]

Lawson's decline owed far more to his abuse of alcohol and growing mental turbulence, and it is more likely that his old Labor associates were wary of his mercurial eccentricities rather than his faded reputation as a revolutionary. Bouts of depression and mental instability meant spells in Callan Park psychiatric hospital and even Darlinghurst jail when he failed to make maintenance payments for his estranged family. Australia's great national poet ended his days a fixture at Circular Quay cadging threepences (the price of a schooner of beer) to quench his thirst at the nearby Plasto's pub. Yet in the dark days of the First World War, when England was demanding ever more diggers for the slaughter of the western front, Lawson could still be called to service by his old mate and now prime minister Billy Hughes, this time to support military conscription and the cause of empire over Labor.

By the time of the split in the ALP over conscription and the 1917 general strike, a younger generation of bohemian radicals were drawing inspiration from the revolution in Russia and the anti-war Industrial Workers of the World (colloquially known as the 'wobblies'), an American-inspired revolutionary socialist movement that was influenced by anarchist rather than statist ideas. The 'wobblies' placed culture at the heart of their activism, communicating with workers via specially penned songs, traditional folk music and graphic art. Veteran radical Sam Rosa resigned from the ALP and joined the IWW but it mainly attracted younger bohemians interested in its direct action among workers and anarchist streak. The 'wobblies' legend was only enhanced when it was declared illegal by Prime Minister and one-time Dusker Billy Hughes. For a number of 1920s and 30s bohemians the IWW, with its whiff of anarchist bomb plots and folksy protest songs, would be nostalgically invoked as a revolutionary touchstone in preference to a stolid Labor Party concerned with winning votes and civilising capitalism.

• • •

The experience of cultural radicalism among bohemian artists in the 1890s and the foundation decade of the new nation indicates the truth of the assertion by British cultural historian Raymond Williams that 'the dominant culture ... at once produces and limits its own forms of counter-culture'.[56] However hegemony is never monolithic, and Williams conceded that works and ideas are produced that, while affected by bourgeois society, 'are at least in part significant breaks beyond them'. First was the idea of a democratic, participatory, pluralist culture implicit in the project of the early *Bulletin* and in some labour papers, which drew spectacularly on bohemia's carnivalesque qualities. The *Bulletin*'s culture of participation, rather than its radical reform platform, was the truly revolutionary aspect. Second, bohemian writers working with the labour movement produced texts that ennobled the working-class culture of the bush by means of a new egalitarian nationalism that helped legitimate aspects of the labour agenda. The 1890s generation of radical bohemians provided dreams for the labour movement that could be mobilised to inspire even after the inevitable compromises of government threatened disillusionment. The blending of nationalism and egalitarianism was successfully harnessed by the Labor Party in its establishment decade and at other periods in the twentieth century. Some artists who had followed labour movement activists on their journey from rabble rousers to dominion nationalists earned veneration in the Australian nation, typified by Prime Minister Hughes, who granted Henry Lawson a state funeral in 1922. By contributing to this narrative the bohemian artist-radicals created a valuable legacy for the left, a romantic radical nationalist alternative that would be used well into the 1960s, although one increasingly challenged from the 1930s by modernist artists who would try to synthesise art and revolutionary politics through the idea of an Australian avant-garde.

'ANYTHING GOES':
SYDNEY'S JAZZ AGE CARNIVAL
1920S

It was indisputably the most spectacular dance that has taken place in the city … Jazz was the keynote in colouring and tone … and the spirit of Bohemia, which artists are credited with enjoying, permeated the atmosphere. There was dancing … fortune tellers … sculptors, crystal gazers, cartoonists, a 'movie' studio … a 'Poet's Corner', a picture gallery … Hundreds of people were in fancy dress … and altogether it was both weird and wonderful. Everyone wore masks, which were removed on the magic stroke of 12, revealing most of Sydney's best-known people.

Sydney Morning Herald, August 1922

The Artists' Balls of Sydney's 'Roaring Twenties' were the climax of a half-century long Australian bohemian carnival. But this ball was different, signalling the start of a decade of revelry in the harbour city. The ball had ceased during the war, but was spectacularly relaunched in 1922, with a modern makeover. Partygoers danced the Charleston to a jazz band, symbolic of the unstoppable global ascendancy of American popular culture with its dance crazes, Tin Pan Alley songs, Hollywood movies and comic books.

The next year's ball was even more daring. Romance writer and journalist Dulcie Deamer acquired instant notoriety by wearing a skimpy leopard-skin dress and a dog-tooth necklace, and was crowned 'Queen of Bohemia'. The First World War had loosened many nineteenth-century restrictions on women and some, like the talented and feisty Dulcie, were welcomed as journalists and into the heart of bohemia. She likened the end of the war to an 'out of school' feeling and the bohemian balls of the twenties to 'a sunburst announcing a *joie de vivre*'.[1]

Like Sydney's Gay and Lesbian Mardi Gras at the end of the twentieth century, the Artists' Balls were a steamy stage on which to exhibit new freedoms in sexuality and the body. Joan Lindsay, wife of Norman's son Ray, relished the fact that 'they were really sort of orgies I think, everyone was sick all over the place'.[2] She also remembered that the ball was a safe haven where homosexual men, many of whom worked in design, acting and fashion, could dress in 'drag' and avoid legal and moral repercussions. One newsreel story from the period, 'Bohemia's night out', highlighted the drunken, stumbling dancing as much as the imaginative costumes. Sex was joined by alcohol-fuelled violence at the 1924 ball, with police raiding the party and eleven casualties leaving by ambulance; there was a point at which the state's tolerance of bohemian revelry was withdrawn. Although the police presence increased after that debacle, Dulcie Deamer could happily report that by the 1927 party 'a glittering flood was threatening the dike that dammed it, and those in uniform … lost the battle. The gods of Spring – it was September – and Carnival were against them.'[3]

THOROUGHLY MODERN BOHEMIA IN SYDNEY'S 1920S

The question of a bohemian tradition becomes important in the interwar period as the founders of the 1860s and the second generation of the 1880s and 90s had either died or were in middle or old age. Would the baton be passed to a new generation in the 1920s and 30s? In fact, a lively print media-based Sydney bohemia of younger people came to the fore after the war to 'modernise' the identity. It emphasised a spirit of play, a celebration of modern living and a new romancing of the city. Women sporting flapper bobs and knee-high skirts became the toast of cafés, took a seat at bohemian clubs and in some cases even

A risqué 1924 promotion for the annual Sydney Artists' Ball held at the Town Hall. The balls represented a carnivalesque 'sunburst' of 'joi de vivre' and a thoroughly modern celebration of sex and the body.

tapdanced on the table tops. Some of the stars in this firmament were Dulcie Deamer, Jack Lindsay, journalist and poet Kenneth Slessor, cartoonists George Finey, Virgil Reilly and Joe Lynch, and sexual provocateur Anne Brennan. Likewise, older men and women who first made their mark in the early years of the century, such as Norman Lindsay, Hugh McCrae and Thea Proctor, also stepped into the limelight to influence the sensibilities of the interwar years. The light-hearted modernism of the 1920s took place in the realm of popular culture where bohemians plied their trade: in the new urban tabloid journalism, 'art deco' magazine cover art, cartooning, cinema, advertising or window dressing at David Jones. Bohemians were in the vanguard not only of new aesthetics, but also of new modern urban lifestyles associated with Americanisation. They lived in the new multi-storey apartment buildings, consumed 'mod cons', drove cars and danced to jazz.

This generation left a wealth of memoirs, including Deamer's then-unpublished *Golden Decade*, George Finey's *The Mangle Wheel*, Claude McKay's *This is the Life*, Norman Lindsay's *My Mask* and Jack Lindsay's *The Roaring Twenties*. The literary and visual arts groups of the interwar years have been the subject of several detailed histories, but only one of these has had bohemianism as its focus. Peter Kirkpatrick's *The Sea Coast of Bohemia* revealed the bohemianism that linked a variety of creative cultural milieus and projects in the 1920s and early 30s, and that also connected this generation of Sydney bohemians to their nineteenth-century predecessors. While making the case for bohemian continuities he also considered what made the twenties generation different, especially its celebration of modern times, its contribution to creating a 'Jazz Age' popular culture, and its moments of romantic ennui. In so doing Kirkpatrick rescued the 1920s from its depiction in earlier works as a cultural desert awaiting the modernist prophets of the depression and war years.[4]

Dulcie Deamer was convinced she and her friends in the 'Golden Decade' were the very first bohemians, explaining in her memoir that '[t]here was in Sydney a self-conscious seedbed. Lawsonian mateship and Hugh McCrae's ... gay paganism ... the spirit of the time ... burst into efflorescence. To alter the simile a long-laid egg ... cracked open and out came bohemia.'[5]

Everything that came before was but a sideshow to the main act of 1920s in which she would have a starring role. The refusal to acknowledge successors and heirs, to insist that the bohemia of your own youth is the only authentic one, is typical of the tradition as it developed in the twentieth century. Indeed, by the 1960s Deamer was at pains to tell interviewers that the beatniks cavorting around Sydney were not genuine bohemians like her mob, but mere 'poseurs' (which was a bit rich given her own youthful flamboyance).[6] But back in the 1920s, some of the nineteenth-century bohemians were not about to go gentle into that good night nor shut up about the bohemian inheritance they bequeathed the next generation.

The now classic nineteenth-century European bohemian works remained sources of inspiration, with *Scènes de la Vie de Bohème* being made into an American silent film in 1926 and the opera *La Bohème* in continuous revival. But by the 1920s the European texts had been joined by local bohemian accounts such as Norman Lindsay's comic novel of 1890s Melbourne bohemia, which, according to son Jack, had become an essential instruction manual on how to be an Australian bohemian (which would go through twenty-eight editions by the 1960s). He recalled that 'We now had Norman's *Curate in Bohemia* to supplement Murger as a text book on etiquette', and this led to him and his brother dodging Brisbane's larrikins offended by their crepe ties, before he decamped to a more tolerant Sydney.[7] Lindsay's novel was joined by George Taylor's bohemian memoir *Those Were the Days* in 1918 and would be followed by John Le Gay Brereton's autobiographical essays *Knocking Round* in 1930.

Family was important. Bohemian legacies were handed from fathers to children in the McCrae, Lindsay and Brennan dynasties. In the case of Norman's sons Jack, Ray and Philip Lindsay, Hugh McCrae and Anne Brennan, bohemia was a family business. The poets Christopher Brennan and Hugh McCrae, and the visual artist Norman Lindsay were frontline bohemians during the transition years from nineteenth-century romanticism to a more modernist sensibility in the 1920s. All three artists helped to move Australian art and bohemia beyond the bush, mateship and parochial socialism to explore more universal themes and imagery. McCrae and Lindsay sought to universalise their art through Graeco-Roman mythology, and the two collaborated as poet and illustrator respectively in the 1909 book *Satyrs and Sunlight*. Both men looked back to the west's classical pre-Christian past and the European renaissance to critique Australian modernity, and in doing so developed an antipodean equivalent to art nouveau that became a bridge to some modernist styles popular with bohemian designers, sculptors and painters in the 1920s.

Norman Lindsay was a driven, charismatic, amusing and gregarious man gathering interesting younger people around him at the end of the war, mentoring key interwar creative identities Kenneth Slessor, P.R. 'Inky' Stephensen, Brian Penton and Douglas Stewart. His influence on Australian and especially Sydney cultural life as a benchmark of unconventionality far exceeds his bawdy paintings of fauns, nymphs and Rubenesque women. His Rabelaisian play with sex and pagan challenge to Christian piety offended cultural conservatives, who tried to ban his anti-religious drawing *Crucified Venus* in 1913.

Lindsay was also a model for how a twentieth-century artist

Blue Mountains nymph. At his bush retreat at Springwood in the Blue Mountains, Norman Lindsay would celebrate his enthusiasm for the Dionysian through an art of female nudes, pagan motifs and the idea of sex as a life force. Photographed by Lionel Lindsay, model unknown.

Courtesy and collection Art Gallery of Ballarat.

could be both an elitist and popular, mixing genres, art forms and hierarchies of taste. While railing against 'the curse of the coin' that bound him to commercial work, he had an instinct for popular taste, penning the children's favourite *The Magic Pudding*, selling many oil paintings, etchings and watercolours, and keeping *Bulletin* readers amused for half a century.[8] The bohemian style Lindsay and his close associates cultivated from the late 1890s – libertine, earthy, humorous, immature, cheeky, sexual, anti-clerical – flavoured his creative work and struck a chord with mass audiences in the first three decades of the century. Lindsay's personal creative effort, the legend he popularised about his own bohemian youth and the ennoblement he attached to being an artist made the bohemian an appealing identity to young creative people in the postwar decade and beyond.

Young journalists and writers like Kenneth Slessor and Elizabeth Riddell absorbed bohemian folklore, were initiated into its rituals and argot, and picked up bad habits and hints in newspaper offices, in pubs and cafés and clubs, in small DIY publishing projects and events etched into the social fabric of the city like the annual Artists' Ball. All of these were sites where older journalists, illustrators and editors, such as Claude McKay, Lawson, Archibald and Sam Rosa inducted young people into the 'larrikin carnivalesque' bohemianism of the last century. Importantly, the writers and illustrators in Sydney still embraced the term 'bohemian' to describe themselves.[9]

The 'inky way' of journalism remained the principal institution economically sustaining and organising literary bohemia, especially in Sydney, from which a number of national weeklies were distributed. Young people flocked to the harbour city from all states to work in the press, with a disproportionate number of bohemian spirits coming from New Zealand, including George Finey, Joe Lynch, Dulcie Deamer and Elizabeth Riddell, accentuating Sydney's claim to be the 'Australasian' cultural capital. While the *Bulletin* and *Truth* continued to bring old hands such as Broomfield, Bedford, McCrae and Lindsay together with young journalists and cartoonists, bohemian hubs formed around new periodicals such as *Smith's Weekly*, the *Daily Guardian* and the upmarket *Home* and *Art in Australia*. *Smith's* journalist Elizabeth Riddell claimed that the paper encouraged a 'larrikin bohemianism ... it cut the powerful down to size, and crusaded for the battler': 'It sent up politicians much more than now. It had a knock down, drag out policy of let's be rude to everything. It took over from the *Bulletin*, which had become old-fashioned. It was irreverent and funny.'[10]

Smith's Weekly, owned by Sir Joynton Smith, Claude McKay and Robert Clyde Packer (the founder of this media dynasty), had some continuity with the *Bulletin*, enjoying initial editorial advice from veteran *Bulletin* editor J.F. Archibald. Editor Claude McKay and literary editor Adam McCay had experience of the pre-war press and inducted young journalists such as Kenneth Slessor and Elizabeth Riddell into both their trade and bohemian recreation. According to both Slessor and Norman Lindsay, McKay taught Slessor the art of pub-crawling within Sydney's journalistic bohemia amid an atmosphere of friendly intergen-erational rivalry and one-upmanship.[11] Jack Lindsay's memoir is peppered with encounters and friendships with bohemians of the late nineteenth century from whom he draws inspiration and learns bad habits. Deamer also recounted her exposure as an aspiring writer to the bonhomie of the *Bulletin* legends.

Smith's Weekly was a powerful influence for both conti-nuity and change. It was influenced by the new journalism, a style pioneered in Britain by Lord Northcliffe's *Daily Mail*, which eschewed middle-class manners and literary pretension to appeal to the tastes and emotions of the working class. But rather than drawing on rural romanticism and the bushman, it found inspiration and readers in the growing urban market and city living, as Marcus Clarke had done in the 1860s and 70s. While still appealing to 'battlers', it made a special cause of a new type of larrikin redeemed by war and suited to *Smith's* conservative masculinist politics: the 'digger'. Both *Smith's* and its associated bohemia of journalists and illustrators rekindled in a modern context the humour and sense of the larrikin carnivalesque that had made the early *Bulletin* popular, though with less irony and subversion and a philistine streak that belied the personal urbanity of contributors such as Kenneth Slessor, Elizabeth Riddell and McKay. The paper knew the value of a good stunt. Riddell remembers being made to take cocaine and write up the effects: 'I felt such an ass – that was a real Smith's

Weekly stunt!' *Smith's* also sold its own legend as it happened. McKay had worked with theatrical impresario J.C. Williamson, and understood the importance in a competitive environment of promoting 'stars' and their eccentricities.

Stories about *Smith's Weekly* personalites abound. Invited to address the New South Wales Police Association's annual dinner, editor Reg Moses began by saying: 'I have often wondered what becomes of the illegitimate children of barmaids. As I stand here tonight and look about me, I see the answer to my wonder. They become policemen, of course.'[12] The police loved it and invited him back repeatedly. Resident humorist Lennie Lower, described as 'a Chaplin of words', went too far and was sacked by Frank Packer over an encounter with Noel Coward in a Sydney hotel:

> Coward: Ah! The King of Australian humorists, one presumes!
> Lower: Ah! The Queen of the English stage, one presumes!

The wildest bohemian spirits were its cartoonists George Finey, Virgil Reilly, Stan Cross, Joe Johnson, Unk White, Cecil Hartt, Syd Miller and Frank and Joe Lynch. Finey was famed for his extraordinary caricatures. He wore his hair long, no hat, and favoured sandals. Once, after a particularly fierce Finey carica-ture of Archbishop Mannix had appeared in *Smith's*, a couple of burly priests turned up at its offices. The editor, Claude McKay, was a little worried, until one of the priests explained he'd like to buy the original. 'I collect caricatures of His Reverence, and the one you have today is the best that's been done of him.'

According to *Smith's* lore, Virgil Reilly's editor Frank Marien once locked him in a room to ensure that he made his deadline. Marien then went to have dinner, had a few drinks and forgot all about him. Reilly piled some tables up, climbed on top of them and put a light to a fire sprinkler, summoning the fire brigade and flooding much of *Smith's* offices.

Stan Cross kept a life-sized, anatomically correct male dummy, known as 'Dummy', in the attic where he worked at *Smith's*. It wore one of Cross's suits, a hat and shoes. One day

Henry Lawson wandered in looking to cadge sixpence, saw how much better dressed 'Dummy' was than him, and asked *it* for sixpence. 'Dummy' was carried through the streets to advertise Artists' Balls, and could often be seen propping up the bar with his fellow bohemians.

The male bohemian fraternity of the press continued to enjoy the larrikin customs of shouts and blarney in a rambunctious pub setting. This became even more intemperate when early closing was introduced in 1923, resulting in the urgent 'six o'clock swill', where men braced the bar to down as many schooners as they could before the doors shut. Finey remembers that 'the artists and the journalists were in full cry, and the bar of the Assembly Hotel ... was aglow from end to end with pink ten pound notes, punctuated by islands of silver piled on wads of notes, representing change from various shouts ... the air was blue with language and tobacco smoke'.[13] In his history of *Smith's Weekly*, George Blaikie insisted that his colleagues were 'the hardest drinking newspaper team in Australian, if not in Empire history'.[14] Bohemian pubs were concentrated around newspaper offices near Wynyard train station and Phillip, Bridge and Hunter streets, and included the Tudor, the Arcadia, the Star and the Victoria. The downtown business district of Sydney between Central Station and Circular Quay boasted over one hundred pubs.

Despite the male drinking rituals, by the 1920s bohemia had a 'queen' because in the interwar years women became reporters, painters and novelists in their own right. The irrepressible Dulcie Deamer's celebrity as a columnist and author of sensational romances exemplified the movement of women into the media industries. Still, the press remained a largely masculine environment, and most young female recruits, such as Elizabeth Riddell at *Smith's*, began work as 'sob sisters'. This was American slang for a woman reporter who used empathy to extract the human-interest angle of a news story from upset family members who had suffered a calamity or bereavement. By the late twenties Hollywood was also popularising wisecracking female journalists as heroines in films like *The Big News* (1929), *The Finger Points* (1931) and *Mr Deeds Goes to Town* (1936).

The public spaces of cities were more amenable to women

after the war. The growth in female-oriented consumption and the popularity of women's magazines from the 1920s provided creative women with sympathetic work environments and a connection to a female readership. They found work as writers, illustrators and cover artists, editors and designers on specialist women's magazines advertising new consumer goods to the women's market, such as the *Home*, and the more mass-market *Women's Mirror*, and (in the 1930s) *Women's Weekly* (Packer's female companion to the blokey *Smith's*), *Woman's Day* and *New Idea*. These working women had to be tough to survive, and they became bohemians in their own right, not just consigned to peripheral status as patrons, artists' models or lower-class women to be chatted up in pubs and red-light districts.

The most famous bohemian club in Sydney was the Noble Order of I Felici, Literati, Cognoscenti e Lunatici – the Happy, Literary, Wise and Mad – which convened at the Café la Bohème, and later the Roma Café. It was started by Sam Rosa, who was editor of the tabloid scandal sheet *Truth* at the time. He presided as Grand Master, with Deamer at his side as Grand Initiator – which meant she bestowed kisses on new recruits. While continuing the tradition of satirical rituals and faux formality, the participation of women changed the tone. Dulcie Deamer was officially crowned 'Queen of Bohemia' at a meeting in 1925 (later superseded by the title 'Empress of the Holy Bohemian Empire') and other women writers played leading roles. The group thrived right through the 1920s and 30s, and remnants continued to convene at a Greek restaurant into the late 1950s. Songs, mimes, chants, impromptu speeches and 'pints' of order represented the usual agenda. Deamer's nostalgic accounts of the Noble Order suggest a much more spontaneous and more sexually charged atmosphere (mixed drunken athletics contests!).[15] This bohemianism reflected the sexualised popular modernism to be found in the art deco magazine designs of artists such as Hera Roberts and Thea Proctor, or Deamer's sensual novels, which had exotic settings such as pagan Rome or a sheik's harem à la Hollywood's sizzling silent films. Bohemian heroines Dulcie Deamer, Anne Brennan, Margot Raphael and Dora Birtles were stars of café bohemia.

Slessor described Betsy Mathias's Café la Bohème as 'a

famous Sydney meeting place of artists and writers and actors and singers and pugilists and cat burglars'. He recalled: 'There was a music room on the upper floor, and up in the attic there were stretchers for patrons who had missed their last trains or lost the use of their legs.'[16] Christopher Brennan and his daughter Anne both lodged at the café when necessary. Norman's son Ray related the story of hanging out the window and vomiting on the head of Chris Brennan attempting the same from a window next flight down. Brennan hollered, 'Some filthy bastard has emptied the contents of his stomach on my cranium.'[17] Other cafés included Madame Pura's Latin Café, Theo's, Pakies, the Roma and 'the Greeks' in Castlereagh Street. Clearly these cafés sold sly grog, allowing women to drink with (and like) men, and to flout the law. More importantly, the café bohemia of this time allowed women pursuing careers in journalism or other branches of the arts and media to sharpen up their skills, knowledge and confidence through the mingling, the conversation, the transgressions and the showing off that male bohemians had long enjoyed in the pub or club. Anne Brennan tap-danced on tables, and Dulcie Deamer could always be relied upon for a performance of the splits!

As typified by Deamer, Sydney's 1920s accentuated a per- formative bohemia where making art was less important than the living of one's life as art. Deamer described bohemia as an 'artistic subsoil of people doing art or trying to – don't forget the trying to'.[18] Some committed bohemians who eschewed day jobs to concentrate on their lifestyle were Anne Brennan, who played the muse and sexual extrovert, and Les Robinson, a proto-environmentalist who intermittently lived in a cave. Another was Geoffrey Cumine, an eccentric freelance poet who claimed descent from Sir Walter Raleigh and attracted stares for his brightly coloured clothes, sandals, brass carrings and for having the words 'To let' tattooed across his forehead (to advertise his availability). Still others burned brightly for a brief period then self-destructed, like cartoonist Joe Lynch, or endured slow decline after a promising and productive youth, like Christopher Brennan, who succumbed to alcohol addiction.

Cafés like La Bohème, flat parties and spectacles like the Artists' Balls, where men and women freely consorted, gave

Australian bohemia a subversive sexual edge. Accounts agree that sexual promiscuity was an important part of bohemian transgression against suburban bourgeois morality at this time. Joan Lindsay stressed that 'the sex life was really rampant ... everybody had a very, very, very active sex life. They really did, including me.'[19] Even the cerebral Jack Lindsay engaged in extramarital affairs. The extroverted Ray made no secret of his many conquests, but later regretted having missed out on the most notorious of bohemia's sexual libertines, Anne Brennan, one of 'Those-Women-One-Could-Have-But-Never-Did-Fuck', revealing the double standards rife in this bohemia.[20]

Unlike Deamer, who had a permanent job and profile with a wider reading public, Anne Brennan's place in bohemia proved ambivalent as she was sexually exploited by male bohemians with tragic consequences. Daughter of the acclaimed poet, academic and pre-war bohemian Christopher Brennan, Anne drifted into delinquency and promiscuity in adolescence, culminating in her expulsion from the family home in 1917 at age nineteen. Contemporary observers and scholars speculate that her aberrant behaviour was brought on by an incestuous relationship with her father. Brennan certainly terrorised the family on drunken rampages, and fellow bohemians claim to have witnessed inappropriate sexual behaviour between father and daughter in the midst of parties at Café la Bohème and elsewhere. Making her way to Darlinghurst, Anne earned her living as a street prostitute and then, as her stature within bohemia grew, as a companion and vexing muse to male artists who financially supported her. Anne's intelligence, beauty, education and personality made her popular, but it was her sexual precociousness for which her peers remembered her. Kirkpatrick documents her sad de-personification as a sexual plaything by a series of for the most part intelligent men who could not escape the sexist assumptions of the mainstream society.[21] Despite their libertine rhetoric, even the younger Lindsays mocked Anne as a sexual plaything cheapened by her amorous adventures. But the various anecdotes also betray the sense of power and agency that Anne attained through her sexuality, swearing, alcohol consumption and erotic performance, all of which intimidated and attracted male bohemians. Ray Lindsay acknowledged that '(d)espite all her bitching ... she always retained an extraordinary and uncanny ability to arouse love'. Antics such as table-top dancing were Anne's artistic production, and became emblematic of the Dionysian spirit to which this bohemia aspired.

Within the bohemian tradition Anne fulfilled the female role of *grisette* and muse that Murger gave to the tragic Mimi, and like the doomed seamstress Anne died of consumption in 1929 at the onset of the depression. Her model of the female bohemian contrasts with that of the career girls like Dulcie Deamer, Elizabeth Riddell, Thea Proctor and Hera Roberts who, while they may have used sexuality, fell back on their jobs for an identity and stability beyond bohemia. Bohemia itself was Anne's life's work to the exclusion of much else. She took its riskier behaviour – sexual freedom, alcohol abuse, stubborn poverty – to the point where her sanity and health were undermined. In an age where bohemians were transgressing all manner of mainstream mores, Anne Brennan was spectacularly successful at breaking some of the strictest taboos and exposing the limits of her fellow bohemians' tolerance with regard to female sexuality and assertiveness. The animosity Anne aroused in her peers also suggests that, without a regular paid berth in the media or the arts, respect was elusive and bohemianism by itself cold comfort.

THE ALPS OF DARLINGHURST

By the 1920s Sydney literary bohemia was wearying of bush nostalgia in favour of a romance with the urban. Rather than seek escape in the countryside, inspiration was found in the timelessness of Sydney Harbour or apartment living in the clouds. This was partly a sensible reorientation of journalism to the growing urban reality of readers' lives, but also to the way bohemians lived. As in the nineteenth century, young media recruits lived close to the city until they married and moved to the suburbs, but these alternatives were made more extreme by changes in the city form. The growth in Sydney in all directions as a low-density city favouring free-standing houses resulted in the formation of specific bohemian precincts in inner-city villages, especially the Darlinghurst/Elizabeth Bay/Kings Cross precinct which was remade on the vertical by the erection of

high-rise apartment buildings, a contrast to the horizontal living
of the outer suburbs. Kenneth Slessor recounted his first visit to
Darlinghurst, where 'strata on strata of apartments hover over-
head, and in each layer of flats, men and women live their lives,
die and laugh and quarrel ... the queer suburb of Darlinghurst
has cropped and grown – not into waste land, like the expanding districts of realty agents, but into waste air – into the clouds
themselves.'[22]

Slessor's romanticised Darlinghurst has organic growth,
unlike the 'waste land' of the suburbs, increasingly criticised
by some bohemian writers as the homelands of domesticity,
respectability and conformity. From his rural eyrie in the Blue
Mountains, Slessor's mentor Norman Lindsay condemned the
suburbia stretching before him as a 'Kingdom of nothingness ...
a cloud of midges in a frenzied love dance above a manure heap.'[23]
Building on bohemian prejudices apparent since the 1890s, this
dichotomy disparaged the suburbs as bourgeois havens of family
life as opposed to the high-density city precincts that were connected in bohemian literature to a European and increasingly
American style of sophistication and modernity, and also to
crime, danger, sexuality and a liberating anonymity. Protesting
that 'Darlinghurst enveloped me and took me captive', Slessor
decided to take a flat there, and later lived in Tusculum, a
converted mansion at Potts Point.[24] Jack Lindsay moved into
a flat with younger brother Ray on William Street. Deamer
took a flat in Victoria Street and Christopher Brennan dossed in
nearby Woolloomooloo after leaving his wife. Elizabeth Riddell
remembers throwing parties on the roof terrace of her Potts
Point apartment block. Whereas writers of the 1880s and 90s
lamented the alienating aspects of city living, *Smith's Weekly* and
the *Home*, the poetry of Kenneth Slessor, and the cartoons of
George Finey, Virgil Reilly and Stan Cross typified a sensibility
that found authenticity in urban spectacle and comedy, reviving
the vision of the flâneur in preference to the bush nostalgia of
late nineteenth-century bohemians.

As a literary historian, Peter Kirkpatrick has argued for
the emergence of an 'urban pastoral' that reached its apotheosis in the light verse and poetry of Slessor. For Slessor,
'skyscrapers burst into lilac', 'fairies tap their sandals; On the

Alps of Darlinghurst', and 'the boulevards burst into bud'.[25] The dandyish Slessor himself embraced a flâneur-like identity in interwar Sydney, describing his relationship to bohemia as that of 'a very amused and detached observer'.[26] In the amusing, jaunty *Darlinghurst Nights* light verse published in *Smith's* from the late 1920s to the early 1930s he stepped into the shoes of Baudelaire to describe the sounds, sights, menace and comedy of inner Sydney, its flats, motor cars, eccentrics and villains. The idiosyncratic characters who people the verse – The Ice-Man, The Girl Who Has It, Backless Betty from Bondi, Cucumber Kitty – are heroes and heroines of the city, who triumph over its disorientating labyrinth. Whereas Henry Lawson had seen the wretched 'faces in the street', Slessor found the city intensity 'lovely'. Walking Sydney's sleazy would-be boulevard William Street, he observed:

> The red globe of light, the liquor green,
> The pulsing arrows and the running fire
> Spilt on the stones, go deeper than a stream;
> You find this ugly, I find it lovely ...

> Smells rich and rasping, smoke and fat and fish
> And puffs of paraffin that crimp the nose,
> Or grease that blesses onions with a hiss;
> You find it ugly, I find it lovely.

> The dips and molls, with flip and shiny gaze
> (Death at their elbows, hunger at their heels)
> Ranging the pavements of their pasturage;
> You find it ugly, I find it lovely.

Slessor has the ability to discern beauty and individuality within the mass of anonymity, to create meaning in the city.

The practice of journalism itself demanded that the bohemians engage with modern rhythms and issues – urban crime, dance crazes, new technology and sport. The interwar generation of journalists created a new literary and visual language to describe and appreciate the world of apartments, the rising Harbour Bridge, 'razor gangs', telephones, beach bathing, movies, typewriters and motorcycles. The newly liberated working girl, the flapper, becomes a symbol for modernity. In the *Home* covers of Thea Proctor and Hera Roberts elongated women tower over the city as stylised skyscrapers. The popularity of Slessor's *Darlinghurst Nights* poems derived partly from the black-and-white illustrations that accompanied them, largely of thoroughly modern and beautiful city girls working switchboards, sunbaking at Bondi, flying planes or falling into the clutches of the cocaine-peddling 'snowman'. The journalists and cartoonists of *Smith's Weekly* were so popular precisely because they tapped into many of the lunacies of modern city living.

A potent symbol of this urban comedy is the *Smith's* cartoon by Stan Cross of two guffawing workmen dangling off a skyscraper girder, one hanging precariously onto the other's trousers, which have fallen down. It is captioned: 'For gor'sake stop laughing, this is serious'.

POPULAR VISUAL MODERNISM

In the interwar period Melbourne had a reputation as the centre of visual art in Australia, while Sydney, owing to the centralisation of the press in that city, was the literary capital. Nevertheless, Sydney wasn't lacking the distinct visual arts bohemia that it had boasted in the 1890s. While some of the more innovative post-impressionist painters, such as Grace Cossington Smith and Margaret Preston, lived reasonably respectable bourgeois lives that did not allow for bohemianism, a distinct visual arts bohemia was still thriving in Sydney. This art-student bohemia, described by Meg Stewart in *Autobiography of My Mother*, her memoir of her mother Margaret Stewart, fed into the bohemianism that illustrators practised in the press and commercial artists undertook in the glossy magazines.[27] Older artists such as Julian Ashton and Dattilo Rubbo continued to teach rigorous draughtsmanship in their art schools, where they also imparted the romantic idea of the artist hero to students experimenting with post-impressionism, such as Roy de Maistre, Sydney Ure Smith, George Lambert, William Dobell and Donald Friend. Among Ashton's female students were painters who would find distinction in the 1920s and 30s, notably Grace Crowley and Thea Proctor. Women had been art students before the war but with the expansion in women's magazines with high production values in the 1920s, and advertising for new commodities in these publications, they found paid employment as commercial illustrators in magazines, advertising agencies such as Smith and Julius, and even in designing department store window displays.

A bohemia of younger female artists that included Hera Roberts and Thea Proctor formed around the lavishly designed publications of Sydney Ure Smith, notably the *Home* and *Art in Australia*. The strong connection in Sydney between painting, commercial art and media was underlined by Ure Smith being simultaneously an artist, an advertising executive, a magazine publisher and president of the New South Wales Society of Artists and trustee of the Art Gallery of New South Wales. Artists illustrating Ure Smith publications also included George Lambert, Margaret Preston and later Donald Friend. Unlike the male world of black-and-white cartooning, younger women – dubbed 'Sydney's girls' for their promotion by Ure Smith – were the leading illustrators in these publications, incorporating their personal 'flapper' style into popular modernist aesthetics, such as art deco, that graced magazine covers. Within print media this innovative work complemented the popular literary modernism of Kenneth Slessor and Kylie Tennant. Modernist aesthetics, resisted by male public gallery gatekeepers such as Lionel Lindsay and Julian Ashton throughout the interwar period, bloomed in the popular 'female' genres of illustration, design and decoration. While the Art Gallery of New South Wales remained resistant to even this accessible style of modernism, the private Macquarie Galleries exhibited and sold these women's paintings, helping to forge a community of painters that would compose the nucleus of the New South Wales branch of the Contemporary Art Society and the Sydney modernist alternative to the Melbourne avant-gardes in the 1930s and 40s.

The associations of American style with glamour, modernity, moral turpitude and the otherness of the 'Negro' made the jazz culture from across the Pacific subversive, exciting and relevant to writers and visual artists. These currents of American modernity, paradoxically chic and vulgar, surfaced in *Smith's* scams and skyscraper comedy capers, the *Home*'s jazzy geometric cover art, Deamer's racy romances and the bands at the Artists' Ball. The readers of the *Home* were told that the sensation of a jazz dance was like being 'caught in a vortex of exhilarating humanity … and immediately before you, on the shining floor, the great multitude pulses, shuffles, glides, to the wild infection of the most emancipated of syncopated bands.' Given that imported cinema and jazz were seen as corrupting of youth by Australia's moral guardians, American pop culture appealed to younger bohemians and their audiences as transgressive of Austral-British middle-class culture. This Americanisation of the carnivalesque blended with the *Bulletin* larrikin tradition reinvented at *Smith's Weekly*, and the local Dionysian style that had been developed by the Lindsays, Hugh McCrae and Christopher Brennan to create a unique bohemia in Sydney in the 1920s.

NOSTALGIA AND NEW TIMES

While Sydney offered a lively literary life in the commercial media and in Sydney's bohemia itself – its costumes, events, humour and stunts – many older pre-war bohemians rejected popular modernism as an affront to their romantic nostalgia. The 1920s witnessed the emergence of real tensions between the generation of the 1890s and younger bohemians over aesthetics, bohemian style and incumbency that would come into sharper contrast by the mid-1930s. Where Slessor's poems played with the tempo and possibility of the machine age, John Le Gay Brereton lamented the impact of the car on contemplative bushwalking and Lionel Lindsay came to fear technology was turning people into 'robots'.

Older editors remained influential mentors in mass-market publications, but there was a gradual changing of the guard in terms of ownership, management and editorial staff as magazines embraced new styles and content to entice the urban market. Slessor referred to the creative tension of this transition in his poem 'To a Friend' that recalled fondly the rivalry between the generations divided by the war. Dulcie Deamer responded to the older generation by accentuating the liberating, youthful aspects of the popular culture carnivalesque, which she characterised as

> entirely foreign to the rather sardonically cheerful descend-
> ants of our pioneers, the grin and bear it school, and to the

'Faces in the Street' socially embittered pessimists … it was, definitely, 'un-Australian' … For us a forced growing up, a stepping out of national kindergarten-hood … and the lovely, irrational … conviction that everything was going to be good-oh.[28]

In contrast to the new mixed-sex 'Jazz Age' parties and clubs, the older generation's creed of mateship, bush nationalism and 'grin and bear it' stoicism could be caricatured as dour and uncosmopolitan, and lost its hold in bohemia and with media audiences.

As a rearguard action, some cashed-up older bohemians used their cultural and financial capital to establish or control 'serious' but nostalgic literary magazines. The *Lone Hand*, *Triad*, *Bookfellow* and the *Bulletin*'s 'Red Page' were monopolised by surviving stalwarts of 1890s bohemia, such as Bertram Stevens, David McKee Wright, Frank Morton and A.G. Stephens, who looked back to the rural and nationalist themes of their youth.[29] While often lavishly produced, these magazines were self-referential, typical of an ageing artistic generation repeat-firing a rusty cannon to command the heights of the cultural field responsible for review, criticism and defining what constitutes literature. This incumbency began to evoke passionate resistance from the 1920s.

The young writers Jack Lindsay, an aspiring poet recently graduated from the University of Queensland, Kenneth Slessor and budding publisher Frank Johnson took on the old guard by starting a rival literary magazine, *Vision*. Their goal was to liberate Australian creative life from the grip of the bush nationalists and 'decadent' modern vogues sweeping Europe by their own notion of the Nietzschean artist hero and a vitalist literary aesthetic that was sexually permissive for the time. The younger men interpreted their mission in generational terms, arguing in their first foreword that 'to vindicate the possession of Youth, we must do so by responding to all other expressions of Youth, and by rejecting all that is hieroglyphic, weary or depressed'.[30] Nevertheless this resistance was enabled by the mentoring and assistance in kind of the older Norman Lindsay who bridged the two generations and shared the younger's disdain for the nationalism of the 1890s.

The middle-aged Lindsay, now living in the Blue Mountains, became the focus of a circle inspired by the Neo-Platonic idea he advocated in *Creative Effort* of an artist aristocracy. Like other, more modernist manifestos written near the end of the First World War, the essay arose out of Lindsay's personal struggle to find some meaning to life amid the senseless slaughter. His brother Reginald died at the Somme, evoking in him a profound grief. Lindsay's malaise is reflected in a stinging riposte to a patriotic remark by Bertram Stevens: 'do you know what you're talking about? The war isn't something over there, in Europe. It's here in this room. There's blood everywhere, all round us, on everything, on us. Can't you smell it?'[31]

For Lindsay, the post-impressionist paintings he had observed on a trip to Europe in 1909 were symptoms of the west's life-denying degeneracy that led to the slaughter. As was the case for many artists, the war shook Lindsay's conviction in the old bohemian romanticism, and drove him to rethink the place of the artist in a world he felt had gone mad. He sought to sanctify artists as the new gods to fill the void of modern existence. Lindsay arrived at a platonic duality between bodily 'Existence' (embracing the physical and the social) and an almost supernatural 'life force' pervading all living things, which has its purist expression in art. While bourgeois greed and machine-age science had robbed the west of its faith and plunged it into war, it was artistic 'Vision', not political revolution, that would reconnect the individual to 'Life'.

For the many young people influenced by Lindsay, *Creative Effort* reinvigorated bohemianism and its key notion of the artist hero in the interwar period, and provided a philosophical justification for the Dionysian. In opposition to the Christian 'wowser', Lindsay's new 'Vitalist' creed exalted sex as a means of briefly achieving the union of the body and the life force. The almost spiritual valuing of sex provided an intellectual excuse for bohemia's customary libertine attitude and Lindsay's own sexualised pagan aesthetic of nymphs and satyrs. Lindsay was not alone in paganism – Hugh McCrae had led the way with his collection of poems *Satyrs and Sunlight* in 1909, and it was republished in London by Jack and illustrated by Norman in 1928.

Traces of this aesthetic remain, as part of Sydney's creative sediment in the statues of cavorting nymphs and nudes at Lindsay's home in Springwood, the chance encounter with a bronze satyr in the Royal Botanic Gardens and the art nouveau style of the Sydney War Memorial completed in 1934. This sensual pagan celebration of the body and pleasure meshed with the balmy, pleasure-seeking harbour city, and its iconography resurfaces throughout the century in the arcadian countercultures of the late 1960s, in the sunbathing beauties of Brett Whiteley, and the neo-pagan motifs and mood of the Gay and Lesbian Mardi Gras.

Jack Lindsay characterised the bohemia around *Vision* as 'the gathering of a devoted company of poets, artists and musicians in Sydney, all pledged in the face of the stock exchange, the churches and the police force, to bring about a fresh Greco-Roman Renaissance'.[32] The magazine explicitly rejected the modernist movements of Europe, such as the Fauves, futurists, Dadaists and surrealists, as decadent, and looked back to classical, renaissance and early romantic art for touch points. Jack Lindsay explained: 'We wanted, not any sort of futurism, but a new grand art linked with Praxiteles and Rubens, Rembrandt and Turner, Aristophanes and Shakespeare, Catullus and Keats, Rabelais and Blake.'[33] Norman Lindsay had instilled in his protégés his own disdain for twentieth-century modernism in literature and art, and helped lead them to an aesthetic reminiscent of the fin-de-siècle English decadents such as Charles Conder and Aubrey Beardsley.

Despite a promising start in terms of circulation, design and as a focus for a small bohemia of contributors, *Vision* only lasted four issues. Too many contributors fell foul of restrictions on gum trees or free verse, and Jack's literary projects went off-shore. Still, the handful of contributors who made it through the sieve became leading players in Sydney bohemia in the 1920s, including Hugh McCrae, Dulcie Deamer, Les Robinson, Dorothea Mackellar, Ray and Philip Lindsay, R.D. FitzGerald and, from Melbourne, Adrian Lawlor.

Despite its overt anti-modernism, *Vision* writers employed some of the tactics used by modernist groups and also by the Heidelberg School. It sought to create a movement with its own manifesto and 'little magazine' pledged to nothing less than a cultural revolution – avant-garde posturing that anticipated the style of some of the periodical and aesthetic-based groups of the 1930s and 40s, like *Angry Penguins*. Jack Lindsay later recognised that his attitude of artistic revolt, more hostile to capitalism than his father's, was 'shared by large numbers of similarly placed young rebels in Europe', especially 'the surrealist inheritors of the dadaist repudiation of war and money'.[34]

STOP LAUGHING – THIS IS SERIOUS

Dulcie Deamer observed of the Noble Order that there was nothing 'IWW or Marxian' about its goings-on, and dismissed Sam Rosa's enthusiasm for leading the group in political songs and bayonet charges as ironic. She reckoned there were too many members from the comfortable 'boss class' (by which she meant editors and publishers) for Wobbly songs to stir them to action.[35] Peter Kirkpatrick's view that the 1920s bohemians' individualism, hedonism and ambition ultimately vanquished any romantic attachment to socialist rhetoric accords with the self-professed uninterest in politics of prominent bohemians such as Deamer, Slessor and Brennan, and the artist-hero elitism of the older McCrae and Norman Lindsay.[36] But the years following the war saw the emergence of both the Communist Party and committed right-wing radicals of the type D.H. Lawrence depicted in his Australian novel *Kangaroo*. Indeed, Francis de Groot, the New Guardsman who in 1932 made the dramatic gesture of cutting the ribbon to open the Sydney Harbour Bridge ahead of Labor premier Jack Lang, had been an organiser of the Artists' Balls in the 1920s. A counter-note to the Jazz Age bonhomie emerged in the anti-capitalist angst that pervaded Jack Lindsay's memoir, and the nihilism and self-destructive behaviour of the cartoonist Joe Lynch. The latter's drowning (and possible suicide) in Sydney Harbour is the key narrative device in Kenneth Slessor's important poem 'Five Bells', and signals the grim days of depression and war ahead. Lindsay and Lynch were influential bohemians, yet they were not the only ones driven by radical ideologies.

Sam Rosa, editor of the muck-raking tabloid *Truth*, had been a leading, if independently minded, socialist agitator in the 1890s, helping to establish the Australian Socialist League and Social Democratic League. He remained a committed left-winger at the *Labor Daily* in the 1920s, and was described by Jack Lindsay as still having 'violent anarchist ideas'.[37] Rosa, together with his friend Betsy Mathias, proprietor of Café la Bohème, had sympathised with the culturally radical Industrial Workers of the World in the war, suggesting that the Noble Order's choice of songs may have been less ironic than Deamer thought. Between 1920 and 1922 the IWW was absorbed into the new Communist Party of Australia (CPA), which in this decade encouraged links with radical free-thinking intellectuals, journalists and artists to the left of the ALP in both Sydney and Melbourne.

One of these 'fellow-travelling' socialist activists was the cartoonist and painter George Finey, who was at the centre of much of Sydney's 1920s bohemia. As well as being an irrepressible force for fun, Finey brought his radical edge to his newspaper cartoons, and was an active unionist who was famously sacked from Packer's *Daily Telegraph* in the depression by editor Brian Penton for refusing to produce an anti-Labor cartoon. One of Sydney's most eccentric bohemians, Geoffrey Cumine, was also a passionate anti-war poet and advocate of workers' revolution. Modernist designer and founder of the innovative Viking Press, Bessie Mitchell was an activist feminist and radical in the 1930s (and beyond) and, as Louise Poland has shown, was at the centre of Sydney's interwar bohemia as an organiser of Artists' Balls, publisher of Elizabeth Riddell and friend and lover to Dulcie Deamer for over forty years.[38] In Melbourne Guido Baracchi became an activist in the new CPA but did not surrender the bohemianism he had practised as a student radical and IWW supporter, living with a succession of lovers and valuing liberty as much as equality. Due to their zest for the larrikin carnivalesque, Rosa and Finey were never political bores within bohemia. Rather, in the case of Finey, union activism directed at protecting an artist's rights vis-a-vis management and press barons complemented bohemia's quest for creative freedom, and earned him admiration for standing up to Goliath.

An intellectual fellow traveller of communism was the University of Sydney's newly appointed Professor of Philosophy, John Anderson. Though no participant in downtown bohemia the young Scottish immigrant was an influence for non-conformity and cultural subversion in 1920s Sydney, where conservative politicians criticised him as the 'Red Professor'.[39] After a period as theorist to the CPA tested the limits of free thinking in the party, Anderson moved his support to the local Trotskyists in 1931 when they split from the Stalinist communists. His criticism of the Communist Party for being bureaucratic and opposed to spontaneity, and the CPA's suspicion of bourgeois academics, highlighted the difficulties facing an intellectual in 'proletarian' politics and prefigured the tensions that would confront radical artists in the 1940s.[40] Anderson remained committed to his own Freethought Society and journal on campus, where he was a focus and inspiration for dissenting students from the 1920s into the late 1950s. In the 1970s classic *Australia's Cultural Elites*, John Docker examined the continuities (and differences) linking the ideas of Brennan, Lindsay and Anderson into a Sydney 'intellectual' tradition, but did not explore his subjects' place in Sydney bohemia. In fact, Anderson's opposition to 'illusions' like religion and nationalism, censorship, social conventions and the authoritarian state, his enthusiasm for subversive aesthetics (especially the modernism of James Joyce's banned *Ulysses*) and the need for critical thinking and protest would provide an intellectual inspiration for a new generation of bohemian radicals in the 1950s and 60s known as the Sydney Push.

Norman Lindsay's aesthetic and philosophical views also had a political dimension. In keeping with bohemia's desire for autonomy, the *Vision* group were critical of capitalist mass culture, but they also wanted freedom from government and its bureaucracy and were critical of socialism as the levelling creed of the mediocre. Socialism, like Christianity, was a life-denying prescription, to be opposed by the individual artist exercising creative effort. Both suffered from a belief in the brotherhood of man and desire to restrain the will of genius. Through first the *Vision* project and then Jack Lindsay's Fanfrolico publishing venture in London's Bloomsbury, versions of Lindsay's artist-hero conservatism strongly influenced the poets McCrae, Slessor, Douglas Stewart, the flamboyant journalist Brian Penton and Rhodes Scholar cum publisher P.R. Stephensen, who founded the quasi-fascist Australia First Movement in the late 1930s.

Known by the nickname 'Inky', the brilliant and rebellious

Stephensen had joined the Communist Party in 1922 as an undergraduate at the University of Queensland, and after finishing his degree at Oxford joined with his old friend Jack in publishing the lavishly designed books of the Fanfrolico Press. Returning home, Stephensen drifted right via Australian nationalism, but Jack remained in Britain and moved leftward. In the midst of the Roaring Twenties, Jack Lindsay felt that 'the world had gone wrong' and blamed 'money-power'.[41] In the aftermath of the depression, Jack converted to Marxism and rejected his father's elitism, causing a rift between father and son that was never repaired. Establishing himself as a man of letters, politics and art in Britain, Jack tempered his socialism with a Nietzschean appreciation of individual agency and creative freedom, and championed William Morris's ideas of cultural democracy. While Jack Lindsay drew on his scholarship, skill with languages and political commitment to earn a living and respect as a full-time writer in England, back in Australia, Slessor and Penton became politically conservative editors of mass-market newspapers for Frank Packer. At the helm of Sydney's *Daily Telegraph* they found an environment encouraging of their opposition to left-wing do-gooders but, by the 1940s and 50s, not so stimulating of their art.

• • •

As modernity drifted into modernism in the 1930s, poets and painters came to grips with the darker elements of twentieth-century living. In Slessor's best remembered poem, 'Five Bells', written in 1939, he reaches back into his 1920s bohemian milieu, to the tragic death by drowning of *Smith's* cartoonist Joe Lynch. The two young men became friends while working on the Melbourne *Punch* and *Smith's*. Joe had established himself as a black-and-white artist of promise, and attracted attention in bohemia for his wild and reckless partying, perhaps fed by his nihilism. In many ways he typified the carnivalesque atmosphere of 1920s Sydney bohemia, and the 'roaring' boy is associated in 'Five Bells' with 'raging tales', '[s]lops of beer', the pubs of Darlinghurst and the possibility of 'blowing up the world'.

Observing the harbour at night, Slessor is moved to mediate on the life, drowning and dissolution of a friend whose body was never recovered. Out of the alienation of urban experience also came the emotional malaise we associate with modernism, the longing for past organic communities and intimate contact. The poem uses Joe Lynch's alienation and suicide to contemplate the nature of time and death. A particular episode in Australian bohemia, and the inner urban environment of Sydney, gives rise to universal themes. Lynch, like Slessor, had an aesthetic tie to Lindsay through the sculptural style of his brother Guy, epitomised in a still-standing statue of Joe as a leering satyr, staring out from Sydney's Royal Botanic Gardens to the spot where he disappeared. 'Five Bells' marks the end of the 1920s party and the darkening clouds of depression and war. A trailblazer of Australian modernist poetry, its themes echo many of the obsessions of the emerging avant-gardes of the southern cities, but the poet's vision was honed in Sydney's bohemian carnival.

THE ANGRY YEARS:
BOHEMIA VERSUS THE MODERNIST
AVANT-GARDE

1930–1950

'I am an Anarchist – So what?' snarled eighteen-year-old Max Harris with all the venom of an antipodean Johnny Rotten in the pages of *Bohemia*, the 'all Australian literary magazine'.[1] The year was 1939, just ahead of the outbreak of the Second World War. Harris declared the true Australian poet 'must put himself into relation with the general stream of European poetry and feeling ... sources external to his hopeless Australian heritage', which for him meant embracing modernist poets such as T.S. Eliot and Ezra Pound. Not for Harris the smokos and wine and cheese clubs, the 'life of literary pleasantry' of the older generation of foppish 'Bohemians'.[2] His identity would be based on an avant-garde assemblage of current international trends – surrealism, modish political causes like communism and anarchism – and his mission of cultural revolution.

Harris had grown up in the South Australian regional oasis of Mount Gambier, the brilliant son of Jewish émigrés who ran a successful smallgoods business. He had attended the exclusive St Peter's private school in Adelaide where he mixed with and out-raged the privileged sons of the South Australian establishment. At university he cut a controversial figure for his flamboyant bohemian dress, Communist Party sympathies and cheerleading for the 'New Apocalyptics', a movement of young writers who wanted a literary year zero. In 1939 the young firebrand outlined his 'Credo' to the scoffing dilettantes of *Bohemia*, declaring that

'intellectually Australian writers are bloody SLACKERS', and
the current crop of poetry 'reeks here of a half-decomposed
romanticism'. Harris sought to distance himself from the
magazine's editorial team of old bohemians and cultural
nationalists by claiming 'there is no Australian tradition in
poetry'. In reply, *Bohemia*'s editor indicated his impatience with
Harris's humourless zeal, swearing and Americanised slang.[3]
Harris would respond by launching his own 'little magazine',
Angry Penguins, to promote his particular brand of Australian
modernism. When the anti-modernists returned fire the shots
would come not from old bohemians but from a poet soldier
named Ern Malley.

• • •

In the aftermath of the Great Depression of 1929 and the gathering political polarisation in Europe and at home, the carnival
cheers gave way to 'passionate intensity' and artists began to
take sides. The hostility of the emerging generation of serious young modernists in the 1930s and 40s towards the jolly,
romantic bohemians of the preceding decades was an extreme
differentiation of two trends implicit in bohemia since it came
to Australia in the late 1860s – a carnivalesque play with popular
culture based on mass media, and a cult of the artist as a special
person determined to break through the taste barrier. There was
also a geographic division. Where the bohemia that persisted
in Sydney from the 1920s plied its trade in journalism and
commercial art, the modernists in Melbourne and Adelaide
were focused on creating unique paintings, and on poetry, prose
and criticism published in short-lived magazines with very small
print runs. In the avant-garde the new generation tried to find a
way to reconcile art and politics by harnessing radical communism to the cause of art itself. By the late 1930s the modernists
who came together in the Contemporary Art Society, the *Angry
Penguins* journal and creative communities like Heide appeared
to be on a collision course with the old guard bohemians like
the Lindsays and the promoters of the Heidelberg aesthetic. But
did the protagonists share more than they cared to admit? Did
the avant-gardes spanning the 1930s into the 1950s mean the
end of the Australian bohemian tradition or its renewal?

It is important to consider how leading art and literary historians have dealt with the troubled emergence of modernism in Australia, not least because of their contribution to how we retrospectively value artists and their works. The tumultuous years spanning the mid-1930s to the end of the Second World War are often depicted as an 'Angry Decade' when our art grew up, got serious, became modern.[4] With their focus on 'high' culture, literary and visual arts historians such as Geoffrey Serle, Richard Haese, Janine Burke and Michael Heyward have depicted the 1920s as a cultural backwater compared to the creative watershed that followed. In lively, original narratives they celebrate the emergence in the mid-1930s of self-consciously avant-garde painters, writers and publishers who pitch new forms of modernism such as social realism, expressionism and surrealism against the outmoded aesthetics of cultural 'conservatives'. Serle set the tone when he asked: 'can any of the arts in any decade rival the painting achievement of the 40s?'[5] Janine Burke wrote of 'a turbulent and momentous era' in which the Angry Penguins group 'participated in a renaissance in Australian art'.[6] For Richard Haese in the ground-breaking *Rebels and Precursors*, artists and writers such as Albert Tucker, Sidney Nolan, Noel Counihan, Max Harris, John Reed and Bernard Smith 'created a movement of revolt more volatile than anything hitherto seen in Australia', producing 'a revolution in Australia's cultural life'.[7] In different ways the historians of Australian modernism dismiss bohemianism as an old-fashioned artistic identity. Yet in accepting these artists' self-definition as 'revolutionaries' in conflict with 'conservatives' they have taken the rhetoric of generational rupture too much at face value and missed the strong continuities between these avant-gardes and the bohemia that preceded them.

BOHEMIANS AND PRECURSORS

'The original person has to do what they have all done in the past – appear as a total revolutionary and radical and has to make a statement against all odds and get it out and finally the day will come when it will be accepted. Not necessarily in his own time.'[8] So argued Albert Tucker in old age, recalling the idealistic passion that drove him to take on the art establishment when he started out as a painter in the 1930s. The Great Depression hit debt-laden Australia particularly hard, and did not spare a younger generation of writers and painters. The old Dionysian style of bohemian subversion was discredited for many younger artists confronting the social upheavals of mass unemployment and a looming war. It was altogether too twee, too predicated on privilege, too soft.

The crisis of the economic collapse, the threat of fascism abroad and at home, and the impact of total war sharpened bohemia's dissent and vague anti-bourgeois rhetoric into manifestos for cultural and social revolution. An embryonic Australian intelligentsia wrestled with the competing claims of communism and anarchism, the resurgent nationalism of *Meanjin*, and the Jindyworobak movement's attempt to reconcile English and Aboriginal traditions. After shopping around, some aspiring artists in Melbourne and Adelaide – like Max Harris – arrived at the model of the European modernist avant-garde as the best way to reconcile their notions of the individual artist genius with the collective urge to change society. The young modernists shied away from jobs in the commercial culture industries like journalism, cartooning, advertising and design. The revolution was to be waged in the domain of high art – serious writing and painting – which in Australia remained inward looking and wedded to the past.

Despite the Melbourne modernists' belief in their profound break with the past, there are deep continuities with the older bohemia. To begin with, twentieth-century modernism should not be cut off from the nineteenth-century romanticism that sustained bohemianism. Romanticism continued to exercise a profound influence over twentieth-century art, pop culture, politics and religion. Certain modernisms, especially surrealism, are but romanticism in modern guise. Romanticism and modernism shared an imagined autonomy from the market, the myth of the artist hero, a belief in the importance of tapping into the unconscious or irrational mind. Both harked back with nostalgia to an organic 'other', whether in the past, or an exotic ethnic group, or even the supernatural. The Australian modernists were themselves aware of their debt to romanticism. In 1939 Max Harris declared 'we are new romantics' and defined modernism as 'the tail of the best romantic sources', involving 'the use of imagination in the sense of Coleridge and Wordsworth', updated via surrealism and Freud's psycho-analysis.[9] In 1940 Tucker distinguished 'Romantic' art such as expressionism and surrealism, from 'inorganic' 'classical' art.[10]

These admissions accord with Bernard Smith's view that both the 'renaissance' promoted by Norman Lindsay's circle in the 1920s, and the local surrealism advocated by the Angry Penguins group in the 1940s, were high-water marks for Australian romanticism.[11] Smith argued that surrealism was the prime oppositional avant-garde of the twentieth century in terms of aesthetic and market influence, and in Australia it became influential within the Contemporary Art Society from the late 1930s.[12] However there were other branches of modernism active in Australia in the 1930s, including art nouveau, symbolism, expressionism and social realism. Modernism restored to romanticism a subversive edge, liberating writers from bush ballads and lyric verse, and turning younger interwar Australian painters from nostalgia for the Heidelberg aesthetic to curiosity about international trends in art.

Moreover, modernists emerged from interconnected bohemian communities of artists and writers that were already present in Melbourne and other cities, distinguished by lifestyles that were 'bohemian' compared to other Australians. It is to the credit of the histories of Heyward, Burke and Haese that their detailed research provides evidence of the modernists' debts to an older bohemia, a counter-narrative to the motif of cultural revolution. In Michael Heyward's study of the Ern Malley affair, Max Harris was 'a red, an artist and a bohemian', everything the establishment in his home city of Adelaide abhorred, and his two antagonists, James McAuley and Harold Stewart, were part of a bohemian group at Sydney University in the late 1930s.[13] As an undergraduate Harris breezed through the Adelaide University refectory wearing black tie and a cape, the creative dynamo among a group of English literature undergraduates that included would-be writers Geoffrey Dutton and Mary Martin. Harris's nemesis, the young poet James McAuley, entertained a beer-swilling budding literati at Sydney University parties by playing jazz piano.[14] In the tradition of Marcus Clarke, McAuley loved japes and stunts and had a gift for parody, and placed in this context the Ern Malley hoax can be interpreted as a supreme bohemian moment, but with the twist of being directed at other bohemian writers and artists of the same age. This reflects the fragmentation of so-called high culture into different genres and cliques. Harris graduated into Marxism, publishing the modernist *Angry Penguins* magazine, and in Melbourne moved into the orbit of John and Sunday Reed and the painters Nolan and Tucker. McAuley rejected his brush with the left to come under the influence of the older A.D. Hope, and went on to head up a group of young writers who mocked modernism as a passé fad in their own independent publishing projects. Heyward tells a tale of two bohemias as he depicts rival groups – the satirical, libertarian and more sceptical University of Sydney poets, and the earnest and politically radical modernists of the southern capitals – on a collision course.

Visual artists were at the forefront of Melbourne's bohemian life because of the impact of its art schools, and the plethora of small galleries and studio spaces to rent. These institutions and urban spaces were part of a visual arts infrastructure inherited from the 1880s and 90s when the Heidelberg School made its mark. The artist-hero bohemia of painters from the 1880s and 90s was nurtured by older artists teaching in the art schools, such as George Bell. While the National Gallery School taught old-fashioned academic aesthetics – frustrating students – its greater value was the extracurricular bohemian activity it encouraged among students. Janine Burke revealed the passionate and competitive networks forged between like-minded young artists such as Sidney Nolan, Noel Counihan, Arthur Boyd and Joy Hester.[15] In this way the Gallery School, Bell's more modernist private school and the Victorian Artists' Society (where Tucker studied) 'created' a bohemian identity for aspiring artists.

The European classics continued to inspire new bohemians in the 1930s and 40s. Writer Alistair Kershaw boasted that he'd 'read Murger and Du Maurier ... If anyone knew down to the last detail what an authentic art-for-art's-sake-and-to-hell-with-the-bourgeoisie studio ought to look like it was me.'[16]

French bohemian legends Rimbaud and Baudelaire enjoyed a modern reassessment in the pages of *Angry Penguins*, with

Sunday Reed and her lover Sidney Nolan translating Rimbaud's poetry together.[17] Bookshops and libraries were important sites for exposing young people not only to these classics, but also to reproductions of contemporary paintings by European artists such as Edvard Munch, Vincent Van Gogh, Pablo Picasso, and to international scholarship on the modern movement. The eclectic bookshop of Italian immigrant Gino Nibbi was an important cultural centre in Melbourne, providing an antidote to the aspiring artists' feeling of isolation from the wider world. Kershaw confirmed that:

> Initiates – Albert Tucker, say, or George Bell, or Adrian Lawlor – rarely let a week go by without visiting Gino at the Leonardo. They – we – went there to rifle through books in languages we couldn't read and to look at reproductions of painters we never heard of … We went there for the delight of Gino's urbane conversation. In fact the only thing we didn't go there for was to buy books.[18]

A cynical writer sceptical of both the left and modernist vogues, Kershaw was a self-deprecating and witty observer of the various warring factions and individuals that composed Melbourne bohemia, astutely emphasising the theme of conflict in his contemporary satirical poetry, and later in his memoir *Hey Days*. In a tone both nostalgic and patronising of provincial Melbourne, he described the 'bohemian enclave', 'our own antipodean Chelsea, our Greenwich Village, our St Germain des Prés', 'at the top of Melbourne's Little Collins Street where you could wear corduroy trousers without being taken for a poofter and where the sight of a beard didn't provoke a display of popular indignation.'[19]

Cafés and pubs were as important to this bohemia as in Sydney. They included Café Petrushka, Riste's coffee house, the Swanston Family Hotel, Richardson's, the Four Courts and the Mitre Tavern, close to the National Gallery School, which persisted as a bohemian haunt from the 1890s, with stalwarts Theodore Fink and Max Meldrum rubbing shoulders with young art students and writers. The bohemian quarter still offered the array of cheap lodgings and live-in studios described by Norman Lindsay in *A Curate in Bohemia* and romanticised by Kershaw as 'the genuine Vie de Bohème'.[20]

• • •

Before considering the avant-garde modernism that arose principally in Melbourne in the later 1930s it is worth stressing that a more traditional Australian bohemianism extended well into the 1950s in Sydney but also in Melbourne. The older style of larrikin bohemianism remained common among journalists, commercial illustrators and designers in both cities throughout the 1930s and 40s. Bohemians associated with the theatre, cinema and radio drama also eschewed avant-garde posturing. The continuing demand of Sydney's upmarket magazines for young visual artists as illustrators and designers ensured its painters had stronger connections to both commerce and high society, with implications for the city's visual arts bohemianism.

A loosely connected group of young Sydney modernist painters associated with Donald Friend, Justin O'Brien, David Strachan, F.A. Jessup and, for a time, William Dobell and Margaret Olley continued to practise a bohemianism that owed far more to the decadence of fin-de-siècle Paris and the aesthetic dandyism of Conder than to either the Heidelberg pastoral tradition or contemporary European vogues. In his impressionistic survey of Sydney innovation, Geoffrey Dutton discussed this alternative modernist art tradition that rejected the political engagement of Melbourne's avant-gardes in favour of a bohemianism of wit and pleasure. In Friend's case this extended to an exploration of homosexuality in lifestyle and art. Centred on the mansion 'Merioola' in Edgecliff, a group formed in the 1940s that included Friend, O'Brien, Loudon Sainthill, Jocelyn Rickards, Peter Kaiser and Arthur Fleischmann. They combined commercial work for publications such as the *Home* with their own projects and exhibitions, patronised by Warwick Fairfax. Friend described in 1984 how they came together 'drinking and dining and having parties' in 'the sort of Sydney Bohemia which did exist here right up into the 60s.'[21] Making allowances for nostalgia, Friend located his group in a bohemian tradition of 'Sydney extrovert sort of things, plenty of laughter and plenty of laughter in the paintings'.

Merioola was sexually permissive. Jocelyn Rickards lived 'in sin' with Alec Murray, while Harry Tatlock Miller and Loudon Sainthill openly enjoyed a homosexual relationship. This went beyond the late nineteenth-century bohemian boys'- own mockery of domesticity and built on the Dionysian party life of the 1920s. Rickards stressed that '[o]ur lifestyle was extremely radical and yet we were totally socially accepted'.[22] The acceptance had to do with the painters' exotic caché with chic members of the Sydney social set, who began purchasing their work after the war. Like the Heidelberg painters, especially Tom Roberts and Charles Conder, this bohemia favoured socialites over socialism as a way of achieving distance from philistine bourgeois life – and selling paintings. The Merioola painters became minor celebrities in the Sydney society pages of the 1950s, and were disparagingly dubbed the 'Charm School' by a later generation of abstract expressionist artists.

The 'Merioola' group of artists strike a pose in 1945. Favouring socialites over socialism, and commercial design over the avant-garde, it was later dubbed 'The Charm School'. Back: Loudon Sainthill, Jocelyn Rickards, and ballet dancer 'Miss Alison'; centre: Roland Strasser, Harry Tatlock Miller, Donald Friend, Arthur Fleischmann, Edgar Ritchard and Chica Lowe; front: Alec Murray (photographer), Justin O'Brien and Peter Kaiser (with guitar).

Alec Murray, *The Merioola Group 1940s*, 1945. Gelatin silver photograph. Courtesy National Portrait Gallery, Canberra.

While the cultivation of high society was neither so blatant nor so light-hearted in Melbourne, that city did have contemporary painters friendly with the 'Charm School', notably painters David Strachan (before moving to Sydney in 1941) and Wolfgang Cardamatis. Among writers, Alistair Kershaw at Melbourne University practised a satirical, carnivalesque bohemianism akin to that of McAuley's circle in Sydney. In this spirit he wrote the extended poem 'The Denunciad', satirising the various artists and writers of Melbourne, and was for a time suspected of being the Ern Malley hoaxer. The overtly radical modernist subjects of Kershaw's parody clearly emerged from within Melbourne's bohemian milieu, but their formation into a self-conscious avant-garde represents an important and timely reinvigoration of the tradition.

BOHEMIA BECOMES THE AVANT-GARDE

'The history of cultural development,' wrote Tucker in *Angry Penguins*, 'is a history of visionaries and innovators, who in their own day were regarded as cranks and mad-dog revolutionaries.'[23]

Despite the rhetoric of a revolutionary rupture, avant-gardes retained the principal elements of bohemianism. Avant-gardes should be defined as temporary, tight, militant groups of artists formed by newcomers within bohemia for the purposes of winning recognition, legitimacy, public space and, most elusively, autonomy. They emerged in the late nineteenth-century European art world to capture new positions in a competitive marketplace by disavowing any interest in making money, and by urging conflict with established competitors. The self-conscious modernists of the 1930s and 40s pushed still further the bohemian's traditional stress on autonomy, transgressive experience and authenticity by performing, theorising and debating these values and organising politically against established cultural institutions to promote and legitimate their own aesthetic. Despite the badging of groups of artists such as surrealists, 'New Apocalyptics' or 'Angry Penguins', it is difficult to understand the activities of avant-gardes if they are not analysed as practising variations on the artist-hero bohemianism that emerged among the Heidelberg painters in the 1880s (and poets such as Christopher Brennan).

Younger painters and poets still believed in the artist hero, but in an environment of genre and market fragmentation this shared creed alone could not confer distinction. The bohemianism of the artist hero could not deliver any sort of surprise, novelty or sense of danger to young artists given its association with older established artists such as Arthur Streeton, Hans Heysen or even the Lindsays, who were socially acceptable to the point of knighthoods and government commissions.

In Harris's case, the radical and cosmopolitan caché of the avant-garde was deployed to differentiate the young modernists from the 'half decomposed romanticism' of those who continued to imitate the *Bulletin* and the Heidelberg School. For these emerging painters, poets, novelists, patrons and publishers, 'bohemia' was transformed from being the dominant artistic *identity* into a *description* of the lifestyle of the artist, while identity was to be found in specific political and aesthetic positions that ranged from the Aboriginal-European fusion of the Jindyworobaks, the craft medievalism of the Montsalvat group and the Communist Party-supported social realist painters to the model of the post-impressionist European avant-gardes. Indeed, some individuals, like Max Harris, moved through a number of these movements in a quest for an identity.

Avant-garde practices refined older bohemian strategies that artists had used to stake their claims as artists. Heyward contended that the artists coming of age in the 1930s belonged to 'the first generation of Australians to feel truly modern' but this is an insufficient explanation for avant-garde formations at this time.[24] Certainly, international modernism found an echo in a generation raised in a world shaped by industry and technology – an urban world of cars, electricity, radio and cinema. However, the previous two generations of artists also experienced technological innovation and the excitement and dislocations of urban modernity, as did many artists and writers opposed to the avant-garde. More significant for the emergence of avant-gardist identities were new sources of support for artistic activity, especially the Communist Party, universities and public research bodies, 'little' magazines and, crucially, private patronage. These provided artists with space, time and intellectual justification and, in some cases, materials, income and distribution.

THE COMMUNIST PARTY AND THE POLITICISATION OF ART

In the 1930s and 40s many contemporary visual artists became socialists and either joined the Communist Party or became active fellow travellers supporting so-called 'front' organisations. 'Socialism emerged as the solution,' Tucker wrote of the mid-1930s in 1944. 'It became a panacea for all ills. We enthusiastically embraced it in its most militant form ... We were a little tired of waiting for history.'[25] That some painters came from lately impoverished petit-bourgeois and working-class backgrounds, such as Vic O'Connor, Noel Counihan, Tucker and Nolan, helped their identification with class struggle, just as background predisposed the young Lawson to take the underdog's perspective. However, communism also attracted (for a time) well-off undergraduates such as Harris and McAuley, and bourgeois professionals such as John Reed and his heiress wife Sunday. McAuley flirted with communism in the late 1930s, acting as musical director of the New Theatre's *I'd Rather Be Left*, before becoming disillusioned. The Reeds were fellow travellers who also contributed money to the CPA. Harris made no secret of his membership of the Communist Party, a banned organisation following the outbreak of war, and was thrown in the Torrens River by more patriotic students at Adelaide University. He was still a member in 1944.

For some painters socialism seemed to make sense of the economic crisis of the depression and the threat of fascism. 'Artists had to think about serious, serious issues,' recalled socialist realist painter O'Connor in 1996.

> The Depression years ... were a period of great suffering for people ... people were completely poverty-stricken and there were mass battles between the unemployed and the police. Union activities were very large and very rough ... Those things were overwhelming so you know when we were young and starting to paint these are the things we had in our mind.[26]

Yet the 1890s had seen an equally harsh economic collapse, and artists remained aloof. The difference in the 1930s was a socialist party that proactively engaged painters in politics *as painters*, and not merely as illustrators for writer's copy in the radical and labour press. The Communist Party (and some elements of the ALP, such as H.V. Evatt) made art itself a political cause, and supported modern painters in their professional struggle to judge what constituted art. Conservative politicians, especially United Australia Party attorney-general Robert Menzies, came out in defence of pastoral impressionism, making modernism a left-wing cause. Menzies revealed himself as a lover of the art of his own youth determined to use state power and patronage to protect his mates and 'quarantine' Australia against the shock of the new.[27]

The truly radical idea espoused by the communists and influential with the younger painters was that art itself was a political act. Following the Soviet-controlled Communist International's decision in 1934 to promote a popular front against fascism, the CPA found common ground with the many modernist painters who engaged critically with social themes. While the expressionist/surrealist painters would ultimately quarrel with the CPA's 'socialist realists', between 1938 and 1943 these groups were united as left modernists against those they defined as 'conservatives'.

The party established a Workers' Art Club (with Guido Baracchi in Melbourne and George Finey in Sydney), an artists' sub-branch and a union for commercial artists, they held exhibitions, and its members and supporters were active in the radical takeover of the Contemporary Art Society, established in opposition to Menzies' establishment of a Royal Academy. Opposed to the Anglo xenophobia implicit in the White Australia policy, the CPA welcomed Continental immigrant artists such as Harry de Hartog, Yosl Bergner and Danila Vassilieff. With the Soviet Union's entry into the war, the CPA became supporters of the war effort and helped establish an Artists' Advisory Panel in 1942, with the Labor government's approval, to find common cause with left, liberal and humanist artists, writers and intellectuals opposing fascism. The party tolerated eccentric behaviour as part of the artistic baggage, and welcomed as members explicit bohemians such as Harris and Counihan, who became the party mouthpiece in the Contemporary Art Society.[28]

The CPA and its cultural front organisations provided young writers and artists with the skills and the theory to fight for their professional and aesthetic niche, to politically buttress them against threats – whether from commercial art or conservative politicians. In *Australian Gothic* Janine Burke argued persuasively that for Tucker and other left artists without much formal education, the Communist Party was a university, and Marxism a unifying theory that made sense of a chaotic world.[29] Her research demonstrated how by actively engaging in the public speaking, debating, writing, campaigning and organising demanded by the artists' branch of the CPA, some young artists of the 1930s became 'public men' and organic intellectuals. Tucker, Counihan, O'Connor and Nolan brought these skills back into the wider art bohemia and the political battles of the Contemporary Art Society, issuing manifestos, writing polemics and theory, boycotting exhibitions and running leadership tickets.

Communism intensified bohemia's traditional antipathy to the market economy. Tucker gave up his commercial art activities to concentrate on his painting. He compensated for his low sales by living at home with his parents. When Keith Murdoch offered him a well-paid job as an illustrator on his newspaper, Tucker asked if the newspaper proprietor would consider employing him half the time for half the money. Murdoch showed him the door. Nolan, too, abandoned work in commercial illustration. Art of the marketplace, according to Tucker, was inherently conservative, because it 'slavishly confines itself to saleable, worn-out convention'.[30] Max Harris dismissed the work of 'journalist bards' who 'after rendering Sir Keith Murdoch his due eight hours, produce poetry from scraps'.[31]

The Angry Penguins group was also influenced by the British-based modernists Herbert Read, T.S. Eliot, F R. Leavis and Aldous Huxley, who believed 'mass culture' was debasing civilised and artistic values. Some were anti-Marxists but shared with the CPA a disdain for twentieth-century commercial popular entertainment industries. Swing music, vaudeville, Hollywood movies and sports got short shrift from Tucker, Nolan, Harris and John Reed, who argued these pastimes traded in 'phantasy-gratification' and cynically manipulated people's lower instincts for profit and American mass culture.[32] *Angry Penguins* had no interest in developing an Australian modernism in twentieth-century arts like cinema and radio. Harris likened going to the cinema to walking a dog on a very short leash, and dismissed Orson Welles as a 'charlatan'. There was no awareness of the popular manifestations of expressionism and surrealism in comic strips, animated cartoons, comedy and genre fiction. An exception was made for jazz music, which the group grew to appreciate through their close contact with American serviceman and poet Harry Roskolenko.

Tucker was appalled by the impact on Melbourne of American culture carried by US troops who descended on the city in the war, and portrayed what he saw as the people's moral degeneracy in paintings such as the *Images of Modern Evil* series. (Critics have pointed out the misanthropy and misogyny of these works that portray leering schoolgirl prostitutes waiting on street corners wearing miniskirts made out of American flags.) Even after his break with the communists, Tucker used Marxism to justify his elitism, rejecting the notion that art should be 'accessible to the widest mass of people' on the grounds that their 'aesthetic sense had been corrupted and stunted by decades of living under monopoly capitalism' – corruption a true artist like him could resist.[33]

The social conscience that underpinned the socialist and modernist opposition to 'mass culture' could become an elitist contempt for the 'philistine' tastes of ordinary people, as left humanist and postmodern critics have argued. Raymond Williams suggested the alternative view that there are not really any 'masses', 'only ways of seeing people as masses'.[34] The communist, conservative and modernist critique of 'mass' culture barely disguised a bourgeois prejudice against working-class cultural preferences dressed up as opposition to the capitalist media. But as we have seen, the *Bulletin* and *Smith's Weekly* explored modernity in creative, imaginative, often subversive ways, not least because of the sense of carnivalesque contributed by bohemian editors, writers and illustrators.

Given that paintings sold to a cashed-up elite, few of the modernists were ever really interested in proselytising to the workers. However the CPA had ambitions to lead a proletarian revolution, and its belief that art should be understandable to the working class would lead to conflict with the elitism of the Angry Penguins.

UNIVERSITY BOHEMIA

The growth of universities was the second change encouraging of avant-gardes. Some in this generation were lucky enough, through university study, sometimes through scholarships, to carve out a temporary space for a creative lifestyle free of commercial imperatives. The University of Sydney was a site hostile to bohemianism in the 1920s – expelling two bohemian students for writing sexually explicit poetry in *Hermes* in 1923, then academic Christopher Brennan for committing adultery and drunkenness – however by the 1930s both Sydney and the University of Adelaide were nurturing small campus bohemias centred on poetry and literary criticism. These were networks of arts undergraduates whose extracurricular activities made use of subsidised arts infrastructure.[35] They attracted the attention of fellow students by their eccentric dress, risqué or politically radical theatre revues, ribald songs and poetry, and japes and stunts.

Max Harris was the centre of such a group at Adelaide University while John Anderson was an iconoclastic force at the University of Sydney, teaching philosophy to McAuley and Donald Horne. His creeds of 'critical thinking' and 'obscenity, blasphemy, and sedition' had a profound impact on his students in the late 1930s.[36]

CIVIL SERVICE PATRONAGE

The increased intake into universities was related to a third change, the growth of graduate employment in the public service from the late 1930s that became much greater still with the war. This provided career paths for some student bohemians, especially those from working-class and lower middle-class backgrounds. 'Expert' bodies established within the public sector, such as the Council for Scientific and Industrial Research (later CSIRO), enabled a bohemian or an avant-garde consciousness. Dashing diplomat Ric Throssell was part of a Canberra-based bohemia that grew up among young recruits to the Department of External Affairs from the mid-1940s, and by the early 1960s the CSIRO in Sydney was revealed to harbour an unconventional and sexually permissive bohemian milieu. The shadowy 'Research Directorate', a wartime intelligence and planning unit of the army, sheltered a secret bohemia of young scholars handpicked by its eccentric commanding officer Alf Conlon, frequently Fort Street Boys' High School and University of Sydney old boys, including John Kerr (later the governor-general), James McAuley and Harold Stewart.[37]

Alf Conlon, described by radical historian Brian Fitzpatrick as 'the most entertaining and interesting' person he had ever met, was a high-profile left-of-centre student politician, elected to the University Senate and active in the embryonic National Union of Australian University Students, when he was made 'Head of the Prime Minister's Morale Committee and Director of Research'.[38] Philosopher John Passmore later reasoned that 'the war made a sudden demand for all kinds of expertness that were just not present in Australia' and Conlon and his circle of graduates 'stepped into the vacuum'.[39] As well as harvesting a coming intelligentsia, the Directorate, according to McAuley, 'had some elements of a Renaissance court, with Alf as the Medici Prince' and 'myself and Harold Stewart as court poets'.[40] At its headquarters in Victoria Barracks in Melbourne, Conlon promoted cloak-and-dagger esoterica marginal to the war effort, a climate encouraging Lieutenant McAuley and Corporal Stewart in the 'jape' of the Ern Malley hoax.

LITTLE MAGAZINES
A fourth important change encouraging the avant-garde was the 'little magazines' in the 1930s and 40s that in sheer number and diversity – nearly fifty published between 1920 and 1950 – represented an alternative to commercial publishing and the traditional labour press. They included *Bohemia*, a publication of Harris's despised Bread and Cheese Club, the Jindyworobak movement's *Venture*, edited by Rex Ingamells, *Comment*, edited by Cecily Crozier, the more overtly nationalist *Meanjin Papers*, edited by Clem Christesen, and *Southerly*. They were joined by a nameless journal only signified by its issue number, produced by McAuley's circle in Sydney, and Harris's *Angry Penguins*. Selling

mainly to other established or aspiring writers and artists, little magazines barely recovered their usually low editorial, production and printing costs, and were often assisted by universities in kind or through grants. In its first years *Angry Penguins* was published under the auspices of the University of Adelaide's English department, while *Meanjin* was supported by Melbourne University from 1945.

Together with universities, little magazines helped structure an Australian intelligentsia distinct from journalism and growing in confidence during the 1930s. Many of the same names circulated around these journals, including bohemian writers and some painters who were also polemicists and theorists. *Comment* and *Meanjin* allowed modernist polemicists such as Max Harris and James Gleeson to argue their positions, but also encouraged the satirical Kershaw. Adrian Lawlor, who contributed to *Vision* in the 1920s, was a prolific contributor to many of the magazines. Harris launched *Angry Penguins* in 1940 to encourage informed debate about modern cultural movements in Australia, especially surrealism, and on exposure to the Contemporary Art Society moved it from the purely literary focus of most little magazines to include visual arts.

PRIVATE PATRONAGE

Private patronage was crucial in freeing some young artists and writers from the necessity of market compromise. In the case of the Angry Penguins group of artists, the wealthy and politically radical Reeds granted Nolan, Tucker, Joy Hester, John Perceval and Harris temporary respite from having to earn a living by paying them modest stipends. John Reed was a prosperous Melbourne lawyer; his wife, Sunday, was born to immense privilege and social position as a member of the Baillieu family, one of the richest in Victoria. The Reeds' generosity underwrote a bohemian retreat at their farm Heide, the production of the *Angry Penguins* magazine (with greatly enhanced design values), and a prodigious output of paintings. Harris, who actively sought capital and partnership with the Melbourne modernist painters in the Contemporary Art Society, was impressed that the Reeds 'were trying to be relevant to the avant-garde over a variety of territories'.[41] Underwriting of the new 'Harris and Reed' publishing house meant that modernist writing could persist in the face of small readerships and financial losses. Kershaw related his surprise at being offered an advance by Harris, rather than having to pay for the privilege of being published! Patronage also led to a different bohemian style where haute bourgeois cultural and financial capital subsidised bohemian obsessions with 'authenticity' conveyed through genteel slumming on a farm coincidentally near Heidleberg.

Janine Burke's prolific art history is distinguished for its close attention to Heide and the place of women and their art and rituals within this communal environment.[42] This was a new bohemia of domesticity and intimacy in which women such as Sunday Reed, Joy Hester and later Mirka Mora could thrive. The artists' community at Heide, presided over by Sunday, whom Tucker called 'the magnetic centre', was an attempt to create the atmosphere of a female-friendly salon.[43] Whereas the entry of women into male-dominated journalism in the 1920s saw them participate in carnivalesque bohemia on men's terms, Heide cultivated a women's space. Artists visiting the rural property were invited to participate in the domestic rites of gardening, harvesting, food preparation, high teas, feasting and crafts such as doll-making. Certainly, artists such as Joy Hester, and from 1951 Jewish French immigrant Mirka Mora, felt comfortable about expressing themselves and painting there, though the work of the young male protégés, especially Nolan, was prioritised. The well-travelled Reeds favoured a French ambience in contrast to the male Anglo-Celtic pub culture of the Mitre Tavern and the Swanston Family Hotel, where women were still excluded.

On first meeting Sunday, the fashionably left-wing Hester asked if she believed in the equality of the classes. Sunday replied that she 'believed in love', anticipating the emotional ambience of Heide.[44] Tucker and Hester lived in a shed on Heide's grounds, while Sidney Nolan broke with his wife and came to live in the Reeds' home, eventually entering into a sexual relationship with Sunday. The evidence suggests a libertine acceptance of flexible sexual relations, a collapsing of moral taboos into an experimental permeation of the domestic borders of marriage and family – though not without bitterness and jealousy. As with the

Merioola group, bohemia's traditional critique of the family was transformed into an experimental way of living that transgressed respectable middle-class morality, and also the standards under which earlier generations of bohemians had lived publicly. This was exemplified by Sunday and Hester's exploration of sexual freedom, John Reed's stoic acceptance of a ménage à trois under his own roof, and the Reeds' adoption of Hester and Tucker's baby son Sweeney.

Heide nurtured a bohemianism that symbolically distanced its artists, writers and patrons from their mostly bourgeois origins by making a show of being rustics. Émigré social realist painter Yosl Bergner astutely wondered why the haute-bourgeoisie should affect the manner of peasants in order to demonstrate their solidarity with the downtrodden.[45] Burke, however, is more sympathetic to the romanticism apparent in the letters of Sunday Reed and Hester, and the recollections of Mora, arguing that through the Heide bohemianism of sexual freedom, cosmopolitanism and bucolic earthiness, Sunday Reed had escaped the limitations of the privileged bourgeois destiny to which she was born as a Baillieu. Other contemporaries found the mix of sophistication and rusticity – the red wine, high tea, free love and wearing old overalls – too derivative, try-hard and hypocritical. Dutton claimed that the Reeds looked to Bloomsbury as the model for their type of bohemia, and the atmosphere was 'very precious'.[46] The supercilious Kershaw claimed a pall of earnest pretension hung over Heide and 'gathered the aim was to achieve an amalgam of sophistication and the simple life, earnest conversations alternating with the philosophical milking of cows'.[47]

Cynicism aside, judged by output of paintings, Heide performed a role not dissimilar to the painters' camps at Heidelberg in the 1880s, removing the artists from the distractions of the city and creating an environment where work could be critically discussed and experimentation encouraged. Also activities associated with farm labouring and pre-industrial life disguised the Baillieu fortune that fertilised Sunday Reed's 'Heart Garden', as Burke metaphorically described the community. This performance of an 'organic life' endowed the Reeds and the avant-garde they patronised with the distinction of being above mere money-grubbing, potentially conferring greater value on their work.

• • •

Other artists cultivated their own retreats on Melbourne's outskirts from the mid-1930s, including the Boyds at Murrumbeena, Adrian Lawlor and Vassilieff at Warrandyte, and the craft community presided over by William Morris disciple and sexual libertine Justus Jorgensen at Eltham, centred on construction of a faux-medieval castle, Montsalvat.

The preference for romanticised arcadian retreats was the flipside of a critique of Melbourne as a site of hedonism, exploitation and alienation. Images of urban apocalypse, insanity and moral decay pervaded the wartime pictures of Boyd, Nolan and especially Tucker, whose Melbourne is a hell on earth, full of the grotesque and the fallen.[48] Its denizens bear traces of the

In the late 1930s and 40s Melbourne's modernist artists favoured creative retreats from the city to paint and cultivate a bohemia of reflection and intimacy as captured here in Arthur Boyd's studio, Open Country, Murrumbeena, c.1945, by Albert Tucker. From left: Matcham Skipper, Myra Skipper, Joy Hester, Yvonne Lennie, Arthur Boyd and David Boyd.

Albert Tucker, *Arthur Boyd's studio, Open Country, Murrumbeena*, c.1945. Gelatin silver photograph. Courtesy and collection Heide Museum of Modern Art, Melbourne, gift of Barbara Tucker 2001.

facial disfigurement he rendered as the medical artist in an army hospital. Far from the official images of the noble AFI, Tucker gives us drunken, oafish diggers brawling and vomiting in the streets. The rollercoasters of St Kilda's Luna Park streak through Tucker's Melbourne paintings, symbolising a city hurtling into the abyss.

This negative portrayal was in contrast to the optimistic if bemused embrace of the city evident in the writing and art of Sydney bohemia at the time. However, bohemians of the late nineteenth century also cast the city as degenerate compared with the bush. For both generations nostalgia for an imagined pre-industrial community led bohemians to deny their personal preference for metropolitan lifestyles. As with the country sojourns of the Bloomsbury set, the avant-garde's bohemianism of exaggerated rural simplicity was a way for these artists to perform a critical distance from the rush of urban modernity.

As discussed in the last chapter, Sydney's print-media bohemians took a different approach, romanticising, sensationalising or satirising the city's modernity and popular pastimes. However, both cities' bohemians shared an antipathy to the suburbs, and the hinterland art communities and permissive behaviour they condoned should also be read as a rejection of suburban petit-bourgeois respectability.

THE VALUE OF CONFLICT

For Tucker the modernists were disinterested agents of truth and social revolution, a 'cultural advance guard', akin to Marx's vanguard of the proletariat, in 'contradiction … with society itself', to create a 'higher form of society'.[49] The Australian modernist avant-gardes of the 1930s and 40s were vocal in their opposition to bourgeois art – but should we take them at their word?

In his study of the changing French cultural market over the nineteenth and twentieth centuries, Pierre Bourdieu showed how economic self-interest is as applicable to avant-gardes as to the more populist cultural producers in the mass media.[50] The formation of avant-gardes was a strategy by emerging artists to win attention and legitimacy at the expense of established artists, and to accumulate cultural capital and eventually real capital. In reality, the avant-garde was just another market, even if its invest-ment horizons were long term. While the avant-garde's rhetoric was revolutionary, and usually anti-capitalist, the stakes in this struggle between established art and avant-gardes were usually about securing bourgeois attention via orchestrated conflict, and ultimately acceptance through reviews, patronage, prizes, publicity and selection by galleries or publishers. Ironically, by playing this game the avant-garde gave legitimacy over time to the bourgeois art market they pretended to overturn. Its emphasis on novelty and fashion brought the high-art field in line with twentieth-century consumer capitalism's logic of built-in obsolescence and progress.

In Australia, the modernists criticised and abstained from working in the popular commercial media to appeal to discrimi-nating niche markets interested in experimentation – made up in large part of fellow artists in the Contemporary Art Society, art journalists such as the pro-modernist Basil Burdett who worked as critic for the Melbourne *Herald*, and a handful of wealthier art buyers and patrons such as the Evatts, Charles Lloyd Jones and Keith Murdoch. Despite the rhetoric, Harris and Reed proved to be less the cultural revolutionaries than cultural entrepreneurs, bringing talent and money together in projects for which they garnered maximum publicity. As would be expected from artists who believed change came from 'dialectical necessity', conflict is the common motif in the histories of the avant-gardes – conflict with the opponents of modernism, conflict with the state, and conflict amongst the radicals themselves.

In 1937 Robert Menzies, as attorney-general in the con-servative United Australia Party government, controversially launched the Academy of Australian Art in order 'to set standards of excellence and taste'.[51] In practice Menzies was trying to impose the critical judgments of art-loving amateurs, using the academy to prescribe and patronise a version of the Heidelberg pastoral aesthetic aged into orthodoxy by imitation and market popularity. By the 1930s Sir Arthur Streeton, who had become a critic with the *Argus* in 1929, was tireless in promoting nostalgia for 'Golden Summers' of the 1880s and a provincial pastoral patriotism. He was not alone. 'Never before, nor since, have we had such a wave of talent,' enthused minor artist Victor Cobb as he reminisced about Longstaff, Streeton, Roberts and Meldrum for *Bohemia*.[52] Tucker hit out in the press at 'amateur art critics', ridiculing the idea that a painting should be 'beautiful' and 'truthful', dismissing the former as 'a delightfully vague abstraction, a meaningless metaphysical term that can be used to describe anybody's erratic desires.'[53] Tucker transformed the art-for-art's-sake defence of Tom Roberts et al from half a century earlier, drawing on Marx and surrealism founder André Breton to declare modern art to be the outcome of the 'endeavour to realise the totality of the artist's relationship between himself and his time'.[54] Tucker's modernist theory gave the artist hero new justification and authority: artists were not just anybody, but prophets with the gift of seeing truths others could not. However, his idea also posited the artist, rather than party, as prophet, a declaration of creative independence that would eventually lead many modernists to split with their communist backers as well.

Two hundred of Melbourne's more modern painters attended a meeting in July 1938 and formed the Contemporary Art Society. It became the organisational hub of the emerging avant-garde groups, holding exhibitions and awarding prizes, and the institution in which the internal debates about the direction of the modern movement would be fought. Amounting to a boycott, the CAS struck at the Academy of Australian Art's credibility and established a rival source for credentialling, exhibiting and rewarding art. Starved of the best and brightest, the academy became a cul-de-sac, and its exhibitions flopped. The hardening of the cultural politics of the radical modernist painters grouped around Tucker, Reed, Nolan, Arthur Boyd and John Perceval, and social realist painters Counihan and Bergner, alienated the post-impressionists led by George Bell, who split from the CAS in 1940. In one sense this was a generational break, with the younger men taking the leadership positions, and represented the triumph of avant-garde formations – influenced by the CPA and taking shape around *Angry Penguins* – over the more broad-based bohemian community of artists that had existed from the nineteenth century. Max Harris declared that the 'humanist period of the world is at an end', and that a 'new non-romantic outlook will result in a self-imposed and communal ethical discipline that will restructure economic life along communist lines'.[55]

But predictions of romanticism's demise proved as premature as hopes for communism's triumph. The old guard hit back. For R.H. Croll the 'bright young things of the studios ... blaspheme the Olympians – the Streetons and the Lamberts, and sacrifice filth upon the altars of the new gods they serve'.[56] For the older men who controlled the galleries, modernism was primitive and decadent, indicative of Europe's moral decay in the aftermath of war. Lionel Lindsay, now a trustee of the Art Gallery of New South Wales, issued an anti-modernist polemic, *Addled Art*, ridiculing the last three decades of the modern movement.

The CAS modernists, on the other hand, looked to the present and themselves, and critically engaged contemporary urban society in a bohemia of radical politics, rowdy meetings, protests, polemics and opinionated publications. While modernists talked ideas, new international trends and the future, the defenders of the Heidelberg aesthetic made much of skill and a 'good eye', replaying the arguments James Smith had used in defending mid-Victorian painting against impressionism.[57] Just as the bohemianism of the artist hero and the dandy aesthete had legitimised the Heidelberg newcomers' status as professional artists in the late nineteenth century, so avant-garde bohemianism helped attract attention to, and later authenticate, the twentieth-century modernist artist.

As seen with Harris, debates about internationalism and how to be meaningful as an 'Australian' artist were enlisted in the conflict over modernism, with the younger writers and painters identifying with what they considered vogue movements within overseas metropolitan cultures to indict their opponents as 'provincial' and therefore out of touch. Australia's distance from Europe's interwar problems encouraged the view among anti-modernists who controlled public galleries and mainstream criticism that the country could be quarantined from troublesome influences, just as the Immigration Restriction Act kept out non-European people, and tariff walls protected local industries from cheap imports. Julian Ashton and critic James MacDonald linked Australian purity in race to a national preference for the pastoral painting of Heysen and Streeton. In the tract *Addled Art*, Lionel Lindsay indulged in anti-Semitism, claiming there was a nefarious conspiracy between Jewish art dealers and local press barons such as Keith Murdoch who, with his wife Elisabeth, supported the modern movement. The modernists, by contrast, shared with earlier generations of Australian bohemians a longing for the latest metropolitan cultures of the northern hemisphere, adding New York and Moscow to Paris and London, and identified with specific artists like Edvard Munch, and writers Dylan Thomas and T.S. Eliot. According to Kershaw, Russia rather than France fired the imagination of his generation of bohemians in Melbourne. For some, the appeal was the exotica of Petrushka café and the performance of a Lichine ballet. When the Ballets Russes toured in 1940 Sidney Nolan was commissioned to design the sets and costumes for its performance of *Icare*. The little magazine *Stream* translated poems, stories and essays from international periodicals and *Angry Penguins* had strong international content via the US magazine *New Directions*.

Australian painters had traditionally studied and exhibited in Europe, but impoverished by the depression and trapped in Australia by the war the modernists made the best of what was to hand. There was intense study of new quality colour reproductions in books that could be found in the State Library of Victoria, Nibbi's bookshop or at Heide. Then, in 1939, Melbourne artists had the excitement of seeing original paintings by Cezanne, Picasso and others courtesy of the *Herald* exhibition of international modern art. It fell to private benefactors Murdoch and, in Sydney, department store entrepreneur Charles Lloyd Jones to host the exhibitions because the great public galleries refused to sully their walls with modern art. Even after the outbreak of war against Germany, MacDonald, now Director of the National Gallery of Victoria, condemned the modern masters of allies France and Britain featured in the *Herald* exhibition as 'the product of degenerates and perverts', echoing the language of Hitler's campaign against modern art. When the works could not be returned to Nazi-occupied Europe, the Art Gallery of New South Wales, under Lionel Lindsay's influence, refused an offer to purchase them, instead locking them away in the gallery basement, with only ocassional viewings of these modern masterpieces for the duration of hostilities.[58]

Refugees from Europe played an influential part in the avant-garde, authenticating bohemia's traditional cosmopolitan performance. The Jewish Pole Yosl Bergner immigrated to Melbourne from the Warsaw ghetto in the late 1930s, settling in Carlton and participating in the bohemian community of the Swanston Family Hotel, and the Communist Party, where he fell in with Counihan and writer Judah Waten, whose Jewish parents had immigrated from Russia. Danila Vassilieff, a child of Cossacks, moved to Melbourne in 1937 and became a beacon to painters attracted to expressionism. Tucker explained to Janine Burke that the mere presence in their community of these cosmopolitan Europeans invigorated their work, as both 'were messengers from beyond, from the exotic, unbelievable, remote world'.[59]

After the war in the early 1950s French Jewish refugees Mirka and Georges Mora were welcomed into the Heide scene and Contemporary Art Society and opened the Mirka Café at 183 Exhibition Street. It became a mecca for artists and theatre people. Regulars included actor Leo McKern, Tucker, Hester, and John and Sunday Reed. Mirka Mora was a vivacious, eccentric and stylish young woman who had studied art in Paris and had eluded the Nazi occupiers for a time by living in the forest. The Moras became catalysts for Melbourne's postwar creative bohemia, taking a studio at 9 Collins Street (where, coincidentally, Roberts and McCubbin had shared a space in the 1880s and 1890s). Here she and Georges lived, worked and hosted parties for Melbourne's artists, writers, actors and photographers that would sometimes last 'for three days and three nights'.[60] The couple brought a dash of European chic and gaiety to the city just when postwar immigration was shaking up its Anglo-Celtic customs.

Geoffrey Serle suggested that some of the modernist painters and writers of this generation were the first to get the balance right, developing a cosmopolitan nationalism that avoided the problems of provincialism.[61] Yet the very extremism and shrill tones with which the cultural debate about modernism was conducted indicated provincial insecurity on the part of the young. In copying overseas trends they ceased to be original, and the distance

Post-war refugees Mirka and Georges Mora brought European chic and gaiety to Melbourne with the opening of the Mirka Café in Bourke Street, 1954.

Photographer unknown. Courtesy William Mora Galleries, Melbourne.

in space and time from the northern hemisphere metropoli meant the 'cutting edge kept moving out of reach'.[62] Heyward argued that it was provincialism, and fear of being left behind, that fired the Angry Penguins' yearning for an Australian T.S. Eliot (twenty years after *The Waste Land*'s publication), and the gullibility that made them vulnerable to the Ern Malley hoax.

• • •

Not all enemies of modernists were old bohemians. Tensions built in the war years between the Angry Penguins and the Sydney poets McAuley and Stewart, who believed that the modernism of the Angry Penguins was a cultural dead end, and naïve when it came to standards. They spent a jolly afternoon in their barracks concocting the complete works of the late unknown modernist poet Ern Malley, with the help of a dictionary, a book of quotations, a manual on swamp diseases and the collected works of Shakespeare. They sent a teaser poem to

Harris with a covering letter pretending to be from the poet's sister Ethel. This poem 'Durer: Innsbruck, 1495' concluded with the intriguing line 'I am still/ The black swan of trespass on alien waters', and an excited Harris wrote back to Ethel asking for more. Convinced he had discovered the Australian T.S. Eliot, Harris dedicated the Autumn 1944 number of *Angry Penguins* to Ern Malley's poems. In their statement revealing that Malley was an invention designed to expose the superficiality of surrealism, McAuley and Stewart accused the Penguins of being 'would-be *intellectuals* and *Bohemians*' (their italics) who fell for 'humourless nonsense'.[63] The implication was that the two soldier poets from Sydney University were *real* intellectuals and bohemians, in a position to judge genuine art from 'nonsense', and secure enough to enjoy a jape.

Despite this blow to their credibility, the Angry Penguins group were able to turn the conflict to their advantage, and the long-term benefit of Australian modernism. While humiliated by the Ern Malley hoax, the gullible Harris insisted that the poems had value and skilfully managed the publicity, gaining national notoriety during his subsequent obscenity trial brought by the conservative South Australian government because of lewd allusions in the fake poems. Emerging players have much to gain by culture wars as the publicity anoints them as worthy adversaries and brings their names before relevant people. Harris seems to have had the last laugh, as the Ern Malley poems became literary icons revered as either unintentional stream-of-consciousness masterpieces, enduring larrikin satire or even punkish performance art.

The war years also led to a bitter falling-out between the communist left and the Angry Penguins. Tucker wanted to be both a surrealist and a socialist, and originally hoped to synthesise the two. In his paper 'The Social Origins of Surrealism', given at a CAS exhibition in Sydney in 1940, he argued that surrealism was necessarily socially engaged. But by the 1940s socialist realism was firmly installed as the official line of the Soviet Union, and Australian communists joined with conservatives in denouncing surrealism as decadent. Despite the liberalised facade of the Communist Party after 1941, Harris, Tucker, Nolan and Reed were increasingly wary of its authoritarianism, and argued for a radical art based on democratic freedom as the best antidote to fascism. Harris insisted that 'a true artist must be free to be revolutionary, reactionary, traditional, innovator ... depending ... on his momentary relation to his environment'.[64] According to Dutton the Angry Penguins considered socialist realism 'just as bad as Menzies' Academy ... the most boring, stultifying, inhibiting bunch of rules.' In opposing political correctness by both the party and the wartime state, the Angry Penguins retreated from socialist activism to an assertion of artistic freedom more akin to the heroic bohemian individualism asserted by the Heidelberg painters.

Differences with the communist artists came to a head at the CAS Anti-fascist Art Exhibition in 1942. For Counihan and the communists behind the united front, Nolan and Tucker's obsession with the alienation of army life spread 'demoralisation, pacifism, defeatism', reflecting the 'fashionable viewpoint' of 'middle class intellectuals' suffering from 'narrow class arrogance and intellectual narcissism'.[65] Tucker attacked his communist critics in the essay 'Art, Myth and Society', arguing that 'conceptual cultural activity is ... autonomous and independent of society.' Political forces 'threatened with extinction' 'the carriers and creators of culture who do not conform to serving the immediate needs of decrepit "democracies", fascism, communism etc.'[66]

Tucker and Nolan's critique of the heavy hand of state control had its genesis in their own alienating experiences as conscript soldiers and the CPA's support of conscription to fight fascism. These two armchair socialists discovered that far from a panacea, 'public ownership' could be 'administered by a samurai of bureaucrats and deified politicians employing regimentation, coercion, violence and unfreedom as part of their program of socialisation.'[67] The Angry Penguins' criticism of the state at war echoed the Sydney Andersonians' critique of first the Curtin, then the Chifley government's centralisation of power and postwar construction of a welfare state, which they argued would breed servility. Both the Angry Penguins and Anderson opposed the state's banning of literature deemed seditious, blasphemous or obscene – a cause that would attain momentum in the 1960s. Anderson offered support to Harris during his trial for publishing the 'obscene' Malley poems, cautioning against government censorship in defence of the public good, arguing that 'attempts at suppression are ... not accidental, not something that we can turn off with a laugh' because 'wowserism is rooted in popular thinking and needs continual criticism'.[68]

By the 1940s the Angry Penguins' desire for autonomy meant jettisoning collectivist politics in favour of a liberal anarchism valuing individualism. Two competing ideas – the agit-prop political artist and the artist as autonomous visionary – jostled for legitimacy during the war, and this continued into the Cold War 1950s. What was more important to the bohemian artist: opposition to bourgeois society, or the quest for creative freedom? In 1945 John Anderson defended the elitist, avant-garde perception that

> an artist is not a person who can be put into a uniform; it is
> a condition of his work that he should reject the ordinary
> adherences and avoidances, that he should not be subject
> to the common standards ... There will of course, in any
> society, be a populace (or mob) demanding such sanctions
> and resenting the artist's independent judgement.[69]

The Melbourne modernists and the Sydney Andersonians, like Norman Lindsay and the *Vision* circle before them, had come to resist the idea of the state or party imposing a common good that limited the freedom of the artist, based on their assumed membership of an elect who need to be in protest against the 'mob'. This view would shape 1950s bohemia in both cities.

SELLING THE MYTH

Rather than revolutionaries, the Angry Penguins artists and writers were cultural entrepreneurs. Much of the value attached to the Heide paintings today is attributable to the myth of their creation in a bohemian paradise from which commercial values were banished by the wave of the magic wand of family wealth earned through commerce. However these artists remained part of a longer-term art market where the financial returns are usually realised by artists and authors, publishers and dealers much later, but the returns are often much higher than the field of mass production. Patronage by the Reeds, who claimed a portion of the works, proved a canny investment as the decades passed.

The commercial potential of avant-garde modernism was apparent in the role played by wealthy benefactors Keith Murdoch, James and Warwick Fairfax and Charles Lloyd Jones in creating an elite market for modernist art. Despite the opposition of the major public galleries, these well-travelled, cosmopolitan connoisseurs were prepared to spend money to educate the art-loving section of the public about modernism, and through their often bold leadership renovate the Australian art market in line with what they saw as international taste. In 1945 Bernard Smith, whose sympathies lay with the marginalised social realists, noted with irony, and some prescience for what was to unfold in Australia, that the international modernist movement, 'which maintained that it had a political and aesthetic recipe for a new and better order of society, has become the ... apologist for the very social system against which it has shadow-sparred so successfully to the diversion of the world's intellectuals for so many years'.[70]

Like bohemian painters before them, many of the modernists sought vindication overseas. Memoirs and reminiscences gave a strong sense of resentment at being stranded in Melbourne by war, the artists yearning to be part of London or Parisian bohemia beyond their reach. After the war Tucker, Kershaw, Nolan, Gleeson, Counihan, Dutton, Boyd and Strachan forsook Australia to sample the life of the expatriate artist. Despite commercial and critical success in Sydney after the war, most of the Merioola group also left for Europe in the late 1940s and early 50s, either to paint or to pursue careers in design.

The Reeds remained in Australia, reinforcing the embryonic institutions of the modern movement like the CAS and the Museum of Modern Art at Heide (MOMA), which they would nurture and manage into the late 1950s. After their deaths in 1981, MOMA was revived as part of the Reeds' bequest and played a large part in fostering the romantic myth of the avant-garde, as have retrospectives of the artists involved. Just as the Heidelberg painters were able to enhance the value of their early paintings through nostalgically recounting tales of their time in the camps creating them, so too sepia-toned recollections of Heide in the media gave the paintings of Nolan, Perceval, Tucker and eventually the work of Hester an aura of genteel bohemian inspiration.

After the war Tucker, Nolan and Boyd became convinced that Australia's history and landscape were ripe with new myths through which to explore the universal – Burke and Wills, and Ned Kelly. These ideas were criticised by Bernard Smith as early as 1945 when he noted that Tucker was using the jargon of 'science' and psychoanalysis to clothe myths of his choosing in a 'spurious authenticity' designed to appeal to bourgeois art buyers.[71] Perhaps the romantic idea of the 'artist' as seer was the greatest myth of all?

• • •

The cyclical nature of generational conflict was noted in 1939 when poet and writer J.A. Allan reminded the zealous young modernist Harris that

> [f]rom age to age the rebel arises ... whether he special-ises in pictorial art, writing or politics: he wants to be different! In every age he has his counterbalance ... the 'greybeards' ... Each section spends much time rating the other ... Ultimately the young rebel matures, 'adjusts' his outlook, slithers gracefully down the hill of time, and finally becomes a greybeard himself, full of fine scorn for the fresh crop of young whelps with nonsensical ideas.[72]

While Harris did indeed find a berth in middle age dis-pensing conservative contrarian opinion in the Murdoch press he had despised in his youth, generational conflict in bohemia is not merely a matter of revolutions in the life cycle, but one of the ways the cultural market changes through time. From the 1930s in Australia the avant-garde accelerated the process of continuous innovation introduced by nineteenth-century bohemians. The elitism of the avant-garde in the early 1940s became commonsense in the 1950s and 60s, dividing high art from popular culture in the leading cultural institutions until the consecration of new popular media arts, notably film, in the 1970s. The division of culture into hierarchies was always implicit in bohemianism, with its specialisation into press and painters' bohemias from the 1880s. The avant-garde artists, in their passionate assertion of autonomy from popular entertainments and political correctness, were introducing new hierarchies of distinction to the art market, and so it is not surprising that by the 1960s their aesthetic became the very definition of refined bourgeois taste.

COLD WAR ANARCHISTS: THE SYDNEY PUSH
1950S

Clive James recalled his first encounter with the Sydney Push as an undergraduate in the late 1950s at the raffish Royal George Hotel on the edge of that city's waterfront as a rite of passage:

> The noise, the smoke and the heterogeneity of physiognomy were too much to take in … Nothing feels more at home than a place where the homeless gather. Here was a paradise beyond the dreams of my mother or the Kogarah Presbyterian Church. Here was Bohemia. I had friends here … Happily I joined the circuit, forming a bad habit [drinking] I was not to conquer for many years.[1]

Typically in beer-toned bohemian memoirs like this, that have a provenance stretching back to the nineteenth century, a sensitive, creative and usually discontented youth leaves the suburbs of their childhood to start a new life of artistic endeavour in the city. Here the young romantic is initiated into the rites of sex, alcohol, love and knowledge and their brilliance is at last appreciated. What was different for young Clive was that he had stumbled into the lair of the Sydney Libertarians, an avowedly anti-romantic bohemia that cared little for art and a great deal about philosophy. It arose not from the press or painting, but among postwar students at the University of Sydney.

Pacing the musty sandstone lecture theatre in the old Quad, Professor John Anderson instructed his students in 'an urgent Glaswegian sing-song' that 'the life of thinking is only one way

John Anderson, the charismatic, free-thinking Professor of Philosophy at the University of Sydney, in the early 1950s. Anderson taught that 'the measure of freedom ... is the extent of opposition to the ruling order', influencing generations of students, including the Libertarians.

Philosophy conference at Newcastle, 1954. Including: Professor John Anderson; Albert Bussell; Emanual Roxon; Hector Munro; Ray Walters; J. Mackie; Tom Rose; B. Roxon; Harry Eddy; Ruth Walker. Reproduced with permission of University of Sydney Archives (Call no. G3_224_1767).

of living, but it is one way'.[2] While he himself preferred a life of thinking, it fell to a group of young 'Andersonians' in the early 1950s to turn their mentor's mantra of critical thinking into a whole way of life. They called themselves Libertarians, and the Cold War bohemia they created came to be known as the Sydney Push. In the university's student newspaper *Honi Soit*, David Ivison caricatured the Libertarian program in 1953 as concerned 'with the following activities, listed in order of importance: gambling, drinking, enquiry, discussing philosophy and fornicating.'[3] Out of a serious philosophical commitment to libertarianism grew a larrikin bohemianism of the pub and never-ending terrace house parties, encapsulated in the wry slogan 'critical drinking' and a subculture bonded by what they called 'free thinking' and 'free fucking'.[4]

From the late 1940s to the early 1970s several generations of students were inducted into an alternative 'libertarian line' that had more in common with traditional bohemian forms of dissidence than with the political radicalism of the old left. One of Henri Murger's original young bohemian quartet in *Scènes de la Vie de Bohème* was a philosopher and student, so the nexus between academia and bohemia had a pedigree. *People* magazine declared the Push 'the real Australian bohemians' in 1964 and approved that this 'loosely knit group of men and women … lack the artiness and pretension of their American counterpart, the Beatnik'. The journalist was surprised to discover that 'many [are] people educated to a high, professional, academic level. Some are advertising and market researchers, some are university and school teachers, scientists and students.'[5] Writing in the *Australian Humanist* in 1967 Ian Davison remembered the Push of the 1950s as 'a recognisable and characteristic Bohemia'.[6] The Push was influential beyond its size or public profile at the time because it operated as a clearinghouse through which generations of tertiary students moved on their way to developing intellectually and establishing careers. The inner core of the Libertarian Society focused on philosophy, but through the wider Push, libertarianism influenced several generations of students and graduates interested in creative arts, especially in film and television.

More so than earlier bohemian groups, the Libertarians came to act as a tight subculture, not unlike other more visible postwar youth subcultures. Cold War pessimists opposed to the left as much as the right, the Push sought personal liberation within a tight intimate subculture of the like-minded rather than through the institutional political activism of parties. But as countercultures emerged in the 1960s, the limits of the Libertarians' bar-stool anarchism and supposedly guilt-free sex became apparent.

GENESIS OF THE LIBERTARIAN SOCIETY

By the early 1950s John Anderson, the one-time Marxist, was intellectually defending the US against the greater threat of Soviet totalitarianism, dividing his students in the Freethought Society. Anderson supported Australian troops being sent to the Korean War, and when he continued his vehement opposition to the Communist Party in the midst of Prime Minister Menzies' campaign to have it banned, the Freethought Society split and effectively ceased. Early gatherings of what would become the Libertarians convened from 1950 at the Iron Workers' Hall in the cluttered union precinct of the city, rimmed by Central Station and China Town. Darcy Waters, who had been secretary of the Freethought Society, was elected to the same role for the Libertarians, but refused to serve with some of the conservatives in the committee, who objected to anarchism. The more left-wing and bohemian of Anderson's student followers then formed the Libertarian Society of the University of Sydney. They held their inaugural meeting on April Fool's Day 1952, dispensing with traditional bureaucratic rules and declaring all Libertarians to be part of the committee and decisions to be reached by 'unanimous consent'.[7] Under the headline 'Liberty for Loonies', *Honi Soit* reported that the Libertarians championed 'an empirical and objective investigation into all questions, and opposed censorship, authoritarianism and moralism.'[8] The more conservative Andersonians, such as Peter Coleman, David Armstrong and David Stove, ultimately based themselves around the new *Quadrant* magazine, first edited by James McAuley. However the new Libertarians symbolically deserted Anderson and the university for the city pubs, where they mixed with other bohemians and ordinary workers. Founding Libertarian Roelof Smilde explained that 'we wanted to go downtown ... We saw the university as an enclave, as elitist.'[9]

Standing out amid the large Push alumni were some well-known characters and high achievers spanning the 1950s, 60s and early 70s, including Paddy McGuinness, Margaret Fink (nee Elliott), Sylvia Lawson, Robert Hughes, Clive James, Lillian Roxon, Germaine Greer, Richard Neville, Frank Moorhouse and Wendy Bacon. But these are the people who made a mark through their later careers and cultural work, who were changed by the subculture, but ultimately outgrew it. As shown by Anne Coombs in her nuanced and lively history *Sex and Anarchy*, the heroes of the Push are those who focused inward and lived their lives through the subculture, virtually unknown to those outside. Transforming Anderson's ideas into a living libertarian subculture and credo was the work of an original hard core of philosophy students who began their studies in the late 1940s and early 50s. Men like Roelof Smilde, Darcy Waters, Jim

Baker, David Ivison and George Molnar are legends within the Push. Other student Libertarians in the early 1950s were Jack Gulley, Grahame Harrison, Ray Pinkerton, Ross Poole, Ian Bedford and Neal Hope.[10] Roelof Smilde and Darcy Waters were later dubbed 'Princes of the Push' because they were humorous, handsome, charismatic men especially attractive to the women of the Push. The lanky Waters had a cheeky and rebellious larrikin demeanour and a mane of long blond hair. He was nicknamed 'Horse' because he loved racing. Tall, fair and of Dutch descent, Smilde had a sharp intellect and was an intense conversationalist. He had a dry wit, a natural authority and an uncompromising conviction many described as 'hardness'.[11]

The Push was located within the central business district, or downtown as it was then called, and a ring of inner-urban villages near the university. The inner-eastern suburbs of Kings Cross, Darlinghurst and Elizabeth Bay that they drank in had been bohemian haunts since the First World War. Others, like Paddington, Surry Hills, Newtown, Glebe and Balmain, were traditional working-class and immigrant areas with cheap terraces built for families or dilapidated old mansions divided into flats that could be rented on a shared basis.

The Tudor Hotel in Phillip Street had a long history as a bohemian haunt and became the first Push pub. They later colonised the Assembly (another interwar bohemian haunt), the Newcastle, the Forest Lodge, the Royal George, the Vanity Fair, the United States and the Criterion hotels, and in the early 1970s pubs in Balmain. Alcohol was the Push's drug of choice, followed by amphetamines, with older members avoiding marijuana that was by the 1950s popular with American bohemian groups like the Beats and Beatniks. The Newcastle Hotel became the watering hole for the rival 'right-wing' Andersonians, including Donald Horne, David Armstrong and Peter Coleman, who practised a more gentlemanly bohemia. The two groups continued to mingle through the 1950s.

The chosen pub of the moment became the effective headquarters of the Push. In an era where women were excluded from the public bar and confined to ordering a 'shandy' in a hotel's 'Ladies Lounge', the Push came to a special arrangement with the adopted pub so that women could stand at the bar and buy drinks. The pub also became an eroticised zone, where casual sexual partners were chosen and bargains struck. Intrigued students could attend Libertarian Society meetings, but most curious people found and entered the Push through pubs like Clive James' Royal George encounter. As Margaret Fink recalls, 'It wasn't too difficult … in a city the size of present-day Adelaide … to find the social spots where the exciting people hung out.'[12]

Contrary to contemporary perceptions of this era, Sydney had a large and varied bohemia in the 1950s. Many of the bohemians encountered in downtown pubs were the veterans of interwar bohemian groups. The Push might converse with bohemian actors associated with theatre, radio and the occasional film. Performance bohemia attracted fresh companions from Sydney University's thespian societies, the Sydney University Dramatic Society, and the Players, known on campus as the 'Foyer Crowd'.

Painters, poets, journalists, cartoonists, science fiction fans and folk singers met at the Lincoln Coffee Lounge in Rowe Street, for a cappuccino and a chat. A sequence of candid photographs from this time show a cool mix of flannel suits, Gitanes-smoking waif-like girls and paperback-thumbing proto Beatniks. The better-heeled bohemians, especially journalists, would also eat (and be seen) at Vadim's at Kings Cross, where favoured regulars might also be served sly grog. The remnants of Dulcie Deamer's Noble Order were still meeting at 'the Greeks' in Castlereagh Street in the 1950s, and might have encountered young Push people who also appreciated its late-night Mediterranean cuisine. Lorenzini's was a wine bar where university poets mixed with older writers.

The Lincoln, Vadim's and the pubs were ecumenical sites where aspiring poets, cartoonists, musicians and painters moved in and out of the Push orbit. Jack Gulley remembers mingling with writers and artists of some accomplishment, but also 'riff raff' who came along to Push pubs 'because they were attracted to the Push ladies'.[13] Bohemian gadfly and budding student filmmaker Albie Thoms recalls a healthy cooperation between Libertarians and journalists, painters, jazz musicians and actors in the downtown milieu, and cites the The Lincoln Anthology, a

1951 book of poetry and songs by habitués of the famous coffee shop.[14] According to Clive James the focus for all the bohemia subgroups he moved in at university was the Royal George Hotel. He stressed that '[t]he Push was composed of several different elements', with the Libertarians dominating but 'the aesthetes' (Robert Hughes, himself and other *Honi Soit* contributors) coming a close second, followed by 'gamblers, traditional jazz fans and homosexual radio repair men who had science fiction as a religion'.[15] A bohemia centred around jazz was concentrated at Kings Cross. Unlike their American and British counterparts, Australian bohemians tended to prefer trad to the new bebop and later cool jazz. By the end of the 1950s the

The Lincoln Coffee Lounge in downtown Sydney's Rowe Street was a hub for the city's diverse and gregarious bohemians in the early 1950s.

'beatnik' would become the bohemian identity for younger jazz fans.

The Communist Party embraced bohemia through a handful of writers, the New Theatre, and through the Waterside Workers Federation Film Unit that produced documentaries on union issues and working-class life. Both the so-called old left and the Push enjoyed international cinema, and might also come together at university film nights and the Sydney Film Festival, which began in 1954. Like the Communist Party, the Push enjoyed protest songs, and might mix with the comrades at folk concerts. They indulged in group singalongs to old American protest songs, especially those written by the IWW and black American folk and bluesman Lead Belly. The early Push remained aloof from rock'n'roll, and even Bob Dylan, but this would change with the new generation who came into university during the late 1950s and early 1960s.

BOHEMIA BY DEGREES

Postwar Australia had experienced a massive expansion in tertiary education to provide skills needed in an industrialised economy. Between 1947 and 1968 the number of university students enrolled increased by nearly 400 per cent on the back of increased Commonwealth funding and state government teachers' scholarships.[16]

As part of postwar reconstruction the Curtin Labor government introduced the Commonwealth Financial Assistance Scheme in 1943, exempting students from fees and providing a means-tested living allowance, followed by the Commonwealth Reconstruction Training Scheme in 1944, which provided free university places to returned servicemen and women. Some of the first Libertarians were returned soldiers, confident and mature, yet open and curious after their wartime experiences. Jack Gulley remembers attending his first philosophy lecture still wearing his paratrooper's uniform: 'John Anderson had a great impact on me. Coming out of the army with the usual beliefs in God, King and Country, John was something of a culture shock.' These older men (and some women) were an influence for both radicalism and bohemianism on Australian campuses.

The Menzies government introduced the academically

competitive Commonwealth Scholarship Scheme in 1951 as part of a policy of expanding Australian tertiary education· and the number of students from state and Catholic schools and lower middle-class and working-class backgrounds to attend university greatly increased in the 1950s and 60s. Many of the Push students came from state selective high schools on scholarships, as did many of the students who entered other radical clubs and societies such as the labour club. Darcy Waters and Grahame Harrison were public school students from Casino and Newcastle, while fellow Novocastrian Jim Baker hailed from a Catholic school. Educated in Melbourne's bayside suburbia, Germaine Greer attended systemic Catholic schools and won a place at the selective Star of the Sea College. Scholarships provided a measure of independent living for qualifying students.

THE LIBERTARIAN CREED

The Libertarians loudly distinguished themselves from their former mentor Anderson, but retained his realist philosophy, opposition to illusions, defence of freedom, belief in social diversity and scepticism about the state and utopias.[17] Respect for rationality and evidence was contrasted with the romanticism of the left, especially its more utopian strains in communism, but also the utilitarian welfare state model advanced by the postwar Labor Party and Coalition, which was criticised for encouraging 'servility'. Creativity, democracy and culture itself came from the continuous clash of competing interests, not from unitary impositions like the nation or the common good. The Libertarians were confirmed pluralists and would cite Greek philosopher Heraclitus on the necessity of conflict. Anderson's emphasis on continuous struggle led to the Push conception of themselves as 'permanent protesters'.

Amid escalating tensions and anxieties of the Cold War stand-off between right and left, the Libertarians found fault with both sides of the ideological divide. As radicals opposed to both capitalism and communism, the Push were drawing from the same well of disillusionment and experience as the *Angry Penguins* writers and artists, who by war's end found solace in liberal anarchism. In Britain George Orwell had taken up his pen against Soviet communism, while remaining a democratic

socialist. Politically the Push philosophers were most comfortable with the label 'pessimistic anarchists', which implied their
scepticism that an anarchist utopia could be achieved. Despite
the best intentions of idealists, authoritarian oligarchies seemed
to take control of all systems, and would confound an anarchist
utopia as well. Jim Baker, the Libertarians' Anderson surrogate,
developed the idea of 'anarchism without ends' in which 'permanent protest' and critique in an anarchist direction would be
the best possible outcome.[18] Freedom was not an end, but existed
in the struggle against authority.

These beliefs conveniently allowed the Libertarians to
criticise capitalism and communism without having to put up
an alternative, and to seek freedom without responsibilities. The
longevity and influence of the Libertarians in Sydney meant that
dissident students from the 1950s into the 1970s had an alternative style of radicalism to the organised left of the Communist
Party and the ALP. Anarchism would surface again as the
favoured political position of bohemians, with the late 1960s
counter-cultures, the punks of the 1970s and the cyberpunk
hacker cells of the 80s and 90s.

Anderson had argued in 1941 (following Freud) that
'freedom in love is the condition for other freedoms', but it was
the Libertarians who put this maxim to the test, theorising and
practising promiscuity with enthusiasm. The Push theoreticians
were profoundly influenced by breakaway Freudian psychologist
Wilhelm Reich, who argued that the roots of the authoritarian
society were to be found in the family, and pleasure through
orgasm was liberating. They came to believe that sexual repression was the basis of servility and repression in society and
that sex between consenting adults should be uninhibited by
law, religion, guilt or morality. For the Push, marriage and
family life mirrored societal repression because they repressed
and regulated spontaneous sex, which was accordingly valued as
a barometer of freedom. Australian bohemians had long justified
promiscuity as a muse for creativity, but for the Push it was a
theorised article of faith and way of life.[19]

The Push developed and debated these ideas in regular semi-
nars where its philosopher-kings and aspiring sages gave papers
and pitted wits. During the 1950s these were held on campus,

in the Philosophy Room, and downtown at the Italo-Australian Club near Central Station. However the real discourse and development of ideas occurred away from scholarly strictures, in the downtown pubs where the Push's thirst for ideas and talk was quenched in the practice of 'critical drinking'.

PUSH BOHEMIANISM

It was the practice of these ideas as a new bohemianism that is the most lasting aspect of the Andersonian creed. McKenzie Wark conceptualised the Libertarian bohemianism as 'an ethical practice of living', a 'technique of the self', and this is where the Push's originality lies.[20]

The Libertarians argued that freedom is 'a character not of societies, as a whole, but of certain groups, institutions and people's ways of life within any society'.[21] To be free, Libertarians needed to divide off and experiment with living. Waters' ASIO file identifies him as one of the organisers of the Society for the Promotion of a Fantastic Way of Life – surely a joke on a hapless agent, but also an apt description of the Push and Darcy's role within it.[22]

For Ian Davison, the Push of the 1950s was distinguished as a bohemia by its 'regular drinking places ... a folk lore of anecdote, history and episode passed on from generation to generation, an inexhaustible repertoire of songs that were bawdy ... irreligious ... anti-authoritarian ... Irish Rebel, reflecting on the outsider tradition of all western Bohemias.' In 1971 Frank Moorhouse described the Push as 'bohemia' to *Bulletin* readers, and explained that 'counter culture' was now the fashionable term for the same thing.[23] In 1975 Jim Baker referred to the Libertarian's 'irreverent, downtown bohemianism'.[24]

While participants at the time called themselves 'Libertarian', or 'Push', today they reach for the word 'bohemian' to describe their group ethos. Paddy McGuinness referred to the Push as a 'bohemian movement of the 1950s', while Susan Varga distinguished the Libertarians as 'the intellectual arm of the Sydney Push', which was 'a bohemian and anarchist movement of the late '40s to the '70s. Moorhouse concurred, distinguishing the core of Libertarians from the wider 'Push', which included 'poets, journalists, and non-intellectual bohemia'.[25]

Most Australian bohemian groups had been loose networks that came together for regular occasions, like the bohemian clubs of the late nineteenth century or the payday round of shouts at a *Smith's Weekly* pub. Rarer have been bohemian subcultures that consumed people's lives as an alternative society. At its outer edge the Push behaved far more like a casual bohemian network, with part-timers who joined the throng in the pub on Friday nights identifying as 'Push' but mixing with other bohemian milieus, and going back into their weekday lives on Sundays. But at its inner Libertarian core the Push could be inward-looking, even cultist.

Most bohemian groups endured a few years before the original enthusiasm ebbed and its members formed other groups. Even avant-gardes like the Angry Penguins were short-lived, breaking up when their art ceased to be new or the artists became established. Not so the Libertarians and the Push, which lasted three decades. In reminiscing, the 1950s veterans tend to refer to their undergraduate years as the 'authentic' Push, with subsequent periods and splinters being hyphenated with a descriptor such 'Baby' or 'Balmain' Push. They also recognise that the Push was but one of a number of bohemian groups that intermingled in the small Sydney community of inner-city non-conformists.

Of all of Australia's bohemian groups, the Push was the most intense and demanding on a full-time basis, with its own unique rules, argot, style and pecking order. The postwar decades gave rise to a diversity of identifiable, often notorious, youth subcultures in Britain, the US and Australia in tandem with the invention of the teenager as consumer category and the growth of youth consciousness organised around schools, colleges, workplaces, sites of recreation and popular culture. Though much more discreet and secretive, the Push mirrored other new youth tribes like the teddy boys, mods and rockers of Britain and the bodgies, widgies and surfies in Australia. These new youth tribes shared rituals that projected resistance, often symbolic rather than overt, against mainstream society. But as educated children of the middle class, the Libertarians differed from the working-class youth subcultures through the subtlety of their style codes and occupation of public space, by evading the tag of delinquency, and embracing the 'Push' identity well into adulthood.

LARRIKIN REVIVAL

The Push embraced rituals of resistance that *People* magazine described as 'unmistakably Australian in character'. The journalist noted that despite its denizens living on the fringe, the most characteristic Push activities were drinking and gambling, 'Australia's most hallowed past-times'. While opposed to the Marxist belief in the historical mission of the working class, the Libertarians consciously exaggerated some elements of Australian male blue-collar recreational culture in their bohemianism. Cultural historian John Docker observed that while Melbourne cultural elites care more about an abstract working class, Sydney intellectuals and artists are more likely to adopt workers' mannerisms, even mix with them, while being less bothered about their 'improvement'.[26] It certainly is true that a succession of Sydney bohemians, especially writers and journalists, had combined their bohemianism with working-class pub culture – the bohemias of the *Bulletin*, Lawson and the labour papers, the Lindsays, *Smith's Weekly*. Like these forerunners the Push performed a stylised version of proletarian customs.

Even the term 'push' was rich with working-class, criminal, deviant and rebellious associations, and it already had a bohemian lineage, especially in Sydney. It appears that the term was first coined derisively by Anderson himself, who dismissed the off-campus defectors as the 'Proletarian' or 'Paddington Push'. Anderson would have been aware of these associations, and was likely mocking the mutinous cabal's pretensions to youthful rebellion.[27] The name 'push' was readily embraced by those students familiar with the history of the larrikin gangs known as 'pushes' that terrorised Australian cities in the late nineteenth and early twentieth centuries. Larrikins were delinquent working-class youths who gathered in tight gangs identified with particular locations, such as the Rocks Push or the Sussex Street Push. There was a tradition of bohemian writers and artists expressing their own marginality and non-conformity through identification with the larrikin pushes, admired for outraging wowsers and their sense of group loyalty.

Many Sydney Push members graduated into journalism, where they mixed with veterans of the interwar larrikin bohemianism. *Smith's Weekly* characters had happily described themselves as 'larrikins' and referred to their journalistic group as a 'push'. When the young Andersonians arrived at the Tudor Hotel the term 'push' would still have had currency among the older bohemians with whom they mingled, like George Finey and Harry Hooton. 'Push' was a good fit for the young Libertarians, resonating with their tight gang-like dynamics, disdain for bourgeois propriety, aggressive manner, self-perception as outsiders, anti-elitism, drinking, gambling and sexual promiscuity. For the Dutch-born Roelof Smilde, however, Push was an anglicisation of the German Putsch, which means uprising or rebellion, and reminded him of Hitler's aborted Beer Hall putsch in the 1920s.[28] For Smilde, 'Push' had a more overtly political intent as a signifier for protest and anarchy.

A community assembled around 'critical drinking' was semiconsciously staggering in the footsteps of Lawson and Brennan's well-lubricated Dionysian talkfests. Gulley recalled an atmosphere 'of a lot of discussion and politics and social and philosophical topics and a lot of beer ... quite a lot of beer.'[29] Context is everything. The wild social life of the Libertarians distinguished them from the respectable bourgeois temper of the universities and suburbs, whose assumed wowserism was now theorised as a cause of their 'servility' and conformity. It was the triumph of the carnivalesque over 'quietism', an Andersonian no-no.[30]

Yet the Libertarians were primarily intellectuals umbilically tied to the university. Whereas the bodgies and widgies tended to be genuinely working-class subcultures composed of people employed in, or destined for, blue-collar occupations, the Libertarians were largely composed of tertiary students, academics or quasi-professionals.

Not all Libertarians came from privilege. The incorrigibly working-class Darcy Waters was Push royalty, and over the years students from more humble backgrounds like Germaine Greer and Clive James made a mark on the basis of ability. It was a competitive meritocracy. Fink concedes that the major distinguishing factor of the Push, 'if one wants to be intellectually snobbish, [was] high IQ, most people woud have been pretty intelligent'.[31]

In the 1950s and early 1960s the gap between working-class culture and the white-collar environment of the university would have been particularly acute for the many scholarship students from humble backgrounds or war service, and the Push's play with blue-collar male pub behaviour would have soothed the culture shock. In a similar way male writers in the 1890s press accentuated aspects of working-class masculinity to deal with similar contradictions about their role as creative artists in a settler culture that valued physical, practical work. But the Push men only played with 'hardness' and 'toughness'. They drew the line at the violence that attended blue-collar pub culture, rejecting physical coercion on principle.

Gambling became a popular ritual of Push bohemianism. The element of risk appealed to the idea that life was unpredictable and deriving income through gambling was seen as unexploitative. Card games were enjoyed but the horse races were particularly popular, with regular Push outings led by Darcy and Roelof. *People* learned that 'there are a few in the Sydney Push who eat or starve on the performance of a horse or the fall of a card', and struggling Push expatriate in Spain Grahame Harrison recounts being saved from eviction by a timely cheque courtesy of Darcy's winnings on the track.[32] While both sexes were avid punters, including Margaret Fink, Lillian Roxon and Germaine Greer, the track allowed the men an association with an Australian masculine archetype contrasted with the feminised 'wowsers'. Resolving to live off the proceeds of gambling, Smilde eventually became a world bridge champion, representing Australia, as well as a fixture on the Sydney racing track.

Leading Libertarians demonstrated their rejection of 'bourgeois careerism' by 'dropping out'. Disgusted by the temptations of 'careerism', George Molnar gave up a promising career as a tenured university lecturer in 1970 to become involved in community development. *People* was surprised to meet an articled solicitor turned builder's labourer, who explained that 'the whole idea of building up a business and a reputation and acquiring a house and a wife in the right suburb made me feel slightly ill, so I just threw it in'. Dropping out was possible at a time of full employment, when well-paid unskilled work was abundant. However, anti-careerism was a Push standard honoured in the breach (as later achievements of alumni reveal) and had its critics at the time. Paddy McGuinness maintained his status in the group while becoming an economist, and is typical of the majority in his successful attempt to blend bohemia, youthful radicalism, academic achievement and a career, observing in 1997: 'A student radical who is a trouble maker is educating himself in many … valuable ways – but the right to be a student agitator carries the corresponding duty to be a serious student.'[33]

According to Judy Ogilvie, dropping out held little attraction for Push women at university, 'who were always conscious of how important it was to graduate': 'If they didn't seize the few opportunities open to them, if they did not become teachers or librarians, the future offered them no security at all.'

On pub closing time Push domiciles would host spontaneous parties hastily organised as drinkers spilled into the streets. Davison recalled that:

> Push houses were known to all initiates, and on a Friday or Saturday night a simple street name, meaningless to crasher and authorities alike, was sufficient to send a score of battered cars to the turn in question. Such parties frequently lasted for days, the party-goers flaking out on couches or vacant floor space when they tired, or picking up on amphetamines if they wanted to continue.[34]

It was not unusual for a Push phalanx to move en masse from party to party, often gatecrashing more formal celebrations to which only some of their number had been invited. 'The party,' observed *People*, 'is a melting-pot where relationships are made and broken, where those who are reserved ease the elastic of their minds and the cynical show a little feeling.'[35] Parties, spontaneous or otherwise, in shared houses provided the circumstances for 'flying fucks' between consenting inebriated couples. 'In these houses,' Davison noted, 'sex, like everything else, was generally regarded as communal.'[36]

THE PUSH AND THE PASSION

Interviewed in 1996, Paddy McGuinness described the Push's philosophy as 'fucking and free thinking', but cautioned that within bohemia the practice was not so new. What *was* new was the Libertarians' deployment of Freud and Reich to justify and regulate the practice. Sexual freedom was central to living as Libertarians. This meant that to be Push one had to enthusiastically jettison monogamy and forsake jealousy when partners inevitably and regularly had sex with others. The Libertarian line on sex was essayed in *Honi Soit*:

> what is important in free love is the absence of guilt feelings and compulsive tendencies … In an affair which is marked by the absence of guilt feelings, there will be an increase in sexual pleasure and satisfaction, leading to a lessening or disappearance of neurotic tensions … a relationship in which both partners have an objective, realistic approach. You would expect to see this sort of attitude carry over into other situations … free love, which includes seeing through sexual illusions, promotes … seeing through illusions in other fields.[37]

The Libertarians' antipathy to sentiment and romanticism meant that intimate relations were shorn of any pretence of love or tenderness – at least within earshot of others. Margaret Fink remembers 'Want a shag, Mag?' as typical of the level of romance to be found in a Push proposition.[38] Fink found such straight talk liberating, and blessedly free of the double standards that condemned sexually active women as 'sluts' and 'nymphos' in the wider society.

But the Push failed to live up to its ideals. In her memoir of her Push days Judy Ogilvie conceded bitterly that '[f]reedom in sexual relationships was only theoretical in the Push, in practice the leaders acted as censors over everyone's sexual behaviour.'[39] Disdain of monogamy meant that any relationships that formed were fair game for predation. Push love affairs were thus inherently unstable, which made for a highly charged emotional atmosphere, and some less than savoury conflicts and depression. Elwyn Morris, one of the early Libertarian female students, argued many years later: 'When Push men made women feel guilty about being "possessive", they were promoting their own interests ... free love was free, in that men didn't have to pay, or even take a girl out, or buy her a beer; for a few of them, it was a new and loveless way of exploiting women.'[40]

In this sexual roulette the male players had the odds stacked in their favour. Reich's emphasis on vaginal-penile sexual activity, and criticism of clitoral stimulation as neurotic steered the Push towards male sexual gratification. Condoms were rejected as a restriction on pleasure and abortions, known as 'scrapes', were commonplace despite their illegality. It was the Push custom for terminations to be funded communally, with a hat passed around the pub, but it was the woman's responsibility to arrange the clandestine operation. Children had no place in Push social life, which centred on pubs and parties, and a woman with children had little option but to drop out.

Male bonds of the sort that had underpinned nineteenth-century bohemia proved more enduring than fleeting 'free fucks'. Ogilvie claimed that: 'The men in the Push ... tended to remain there, mateship enduring as a stronger bond than sexual attraction. They stayed together, growing older, while the women were continually being replaced by younger ones.'

However, not all women in the Push felt exploited. The sexual appetites of women were acknowledged and women free to initiate sex. Fink found it liberating in the context of 1950s morality 'to find people who were actually getting off with each other ... That's what I was searching for – sexual freedom.' But it was not only sexual liberation that appealed to young Push women like Fink: 'One was magnetised towards these people because women had a better chance of not being treated conventionally – taken seriously as conversationalists and thinkers.'[41] This buoyed female graduates entering the labour market as teachers, journalists and academics. Push women like Fink, Lillian Roxon, Germaine Greer, Eva Cox, Liz Fell and Wendy Bacon enjoyed a creative freedom relative to the wider society – but ultimately, according to Anne Coombs, 'a woman gained her status in the Push from whom she was fucking'.[42] Ogilvie agreed that '[w]hom you slept with was of overwhelming importance ... in the early days a woman had sufficient prestige in the Push if she were attached to one of the really big men.'[43] Push women made their mark after graduating and moving away from its male embrace, though they took something of its libertarianism with them, together with an understanding of patriarchy's persistence whatever the ideology.

Still the Push was internally diverse and this could be liberating. *People* observed a mixed bunch in the Push – an economics honours student, a folk singer with a day job, a librarian, a lawyer, an ad man, a scientist, a painter, a Dutchman in shorts, thongs and sunglasses, and a bearded German giant called Adolph.' The Push was also open to immigrants, as long as they could argue well. They included Jewish 'Dunera Boy' Henry Mayer, Eva Cox and especially spiky, witty Hungarian Jewish refugee George Molnar, who deployed the tenacity of the Continental philosopher, to keep, what Susan Varga later called the 'Oh so Aussie larrikins' of the Push, on their toes.[44]

The Push had its own patois, distinctive for its original slang and 'a characteristic mode of speech which in its cadences, emphasis and energy is quite unmistakable.'[45] The Push males of the 1950s sought to be anti-fashion, in contrast with the aesthetically conscious beatniks of the jazz scene or theatrical bohemians. Trousers and plain white shirts, worn without a tie, were de rigueur for men. The aim was to signify substance over style, with attention directed to discourse and personality rather than clothes. Still, bohemianism was suggested by a general scruffiness, and a tendency for many men to wear beards.

By the early 1960s, however, younger Push people were wearing some of the fashion items associated with non-conformist students in Britain and the US and the monochrome chic of European new wave cinema – duffle coats, corduroy, woolly jumpers, desert boots, and slightly longer hair. Both men and women were more likely to wear black, in keeping with the international beatnik look. Some Push women also wore their hair long and straight, and wore white or pale lipstick and dark eyeliner.

To the outside world in the 1950s and early 60s, the Libertarians were barely noticeable, or a mystery. Whereas working-class subcultures were spectacular, seeking public notoriety in a quest to control public space, the Libertarians were private, even secretive, communicating with each other by more subtle codes. Margaret Fink doubted whether 'anarchists or Libertarians were considered to be in existence by the general populace in the fifties'. They were paid scant attention by a media obsessed with the communist threat and the American beatnik fad. Push people interviewed for the ABC's 'Inquiry into the Beats' in 1959 explained, 'we're mainly students. We all stick together more or less. I suppose it's all very cliquey. An outsider wouldn't have much fun.'

Nevertheless, 'critical drinking' implied a willingness to drink with those with whom you disagreed, explained Albie Thoms.[46] Push pluralism was about dialogue, tension and conflict, not about compromising one's principles into a bland social unity. This prickly intercourse occurred with the wider bohemian community who drank downtown, linking the Push network to other intellectuals, artists, radicals and assorted characters that influenced the Libertarians and were influenced by them. In the pub, Push people would also seek out suburban men, who they mocked as 'Alfs' 'fraternising with them and cultivating them for beer money in return for anecdote'.[47] But cross-class dialogue could be more genuine, with leading Push men like Waters and Smilde also fraternising with manual workers and trade unionists working on building sites, the wharves and at the races.

A brighter media light was shone on the parties, trysts and open marriages of the Push following the discovery of the dead, partially naked bodies of nurse Margaret Chandler and Dr Gilbert Bogle on the banks of the Lane Cove River on New Year's Day 1962. The couple met through the CSIRO, where both Margaret's husband Geoffrey Chandler and Bogle, a physicist, worked. Geoffrey had a Push girlfriend, Pam Logan, who was a secretary in the Department of Psychology at the University of Sydney, which involved him in the wider Push social life.[48] On the night of their death Mrs Chandler and Dr Bogle had left a New Year's Eve party on the upmarket north shore together, while her husband left to join his girlfriend at a Push party across the harbour in Balmain. When suspicion of murder briefly fell on Geoffrey Chandler the media pack descended on the bohemain milieu with which he drank at the Royal George.[49] Chandler was exonerated and theories about the couple's mysterious demise range from a bad dose of homemade LSD to sulphur dioxide fumes belching from the polluted river. But in the blaze of publicity and the court case that followed, even open-minded Sydneysiders were shocked to discover that educated professionals conducted such libertine love lives – though they were possibly somewhat proud to know bohemia was alive and dangerous in Sin City.

ANTI-ROMANTICS?

Smilde stressed to Coombs that the defining character-istic of the Push was the relationship between ideas and lifestyle, as exemplified in the principles of anti-authoritarianism and sexual freedom. In her biography of Germaine Greer, Christine Wallace agreed that what made the Push unique as an Australian 'bohemian enclave' was having core members who 'shared a passionate belief in the theories of an intellectual … Its key figures embraced and propagated an all encompassing and apparently rigorous theory – philosophical, political, social.'[50] The fusion of bohemian-ism with hard philosophic thinking about that lifestyle is a product of the Push's grounding in academia, and is of a different order to the nebulous romanticism and identity play of earlier bohemias. No one since Marcus Clarke had so self-consciously interrogated the bohemian lifestyle itself.

Push commentators have shown considerable awareness of their group's place in an Australian bohemian tradition. Ian Davison acknowledged as a predecessor 'the artistically creative bohemia at the turn of the century, to which gravitated Lawson, the Lindsays, and many others associated with Archibald's *Bulletin*'. What distinguished the Push from other bohemian groups was its avowed opposition to romanticism. Anderson once described himself as having the heart of a romantic and the head of a realist, and taught his students that romanticism was an illusion. Acknowled-ging that traditional anarchist theory became mired in romantic aspiration for a non-authoritarian society, the inaugural Libertarian journal declared: 'Libertarians oppose the state but they are not romantics, utopians seeking security of return to the womb, for they know that the world cannot be made safe for freedom' and requires permanent opposition.[51] If bohemianism is at root a romantic trope, how can anti-romantics be bohemians?

On closer inspection the Push was not as free of romanticism as its theorists claimed, and Anne Coombs noted that for anti-romantics the Push were good at romanticising themselves.[52] Albie Thoms described Smilde as 'a very romantic figure', especially for the women, and Germaine Greer's love of Byron was evidence of her falling 'for all the male romantic bullshit of the hero' which was present in the Push.[53] Christine Wallace argued that the Push philosophy was 'essentially romantic in nature' because '[w]hile aspiring to realism, they idealised a kind of spontaneous sexual combustion as the acme of human connection.'[54]

The Push also echoed the enthusiasm for Nietzschean ideas associated in interwar Sydney with Norman and Jack Lindsay, Kenneth Slessor, Brian Penton and P.R. Stephensen. The vitalism of Norman Lindsay, especially his obsession with sex as the life force, finds echoes in the Push's theory and practice of liberating the inner biologic core through spontaneous sex. Anderson and the Push also share Norman Lindsay's and the *Vision* group's passionate atheism, and disdain for Christian morality. The Libertarians would similarly find little to disagree with in Lindsay's proselytising for a carnivalesque bohemia of pubs, wine bars, parties, talk and boarding houses. But the continuities were unconscious.

For the Libertarians, Lindsay was a relic from another age, barely noticed, until academic and Push associate John Docker examined the continuities between Lindsay and the Andersonians in the influential work *Australia's Cultural Elites*, published in 1974. Docker argued that both Lindsay and Anderson opposed social improvement, whether at the hands of a coercive state or God-bothering missionaries and charities. They were pessimists about society, and found solace in acts of scepticism, personal dissent, the life of the mind and social conviviality.

THE ART OF THE PUSH

Like their mentor Anderson, the Libertarian Society remained
alert to attempts to censor culture, but had little passion for
art. But there were people on the outskirts of the Push who
were more interested in literature and visual art than philosophy. Margaret Fink (then Margaret Elliott) was one of these,
a young art teacher who found a soul mate in futurist poet
Harry Hooton, an older downtown bohemian who gravitated
towards the Push in the 1950s. Hooton was an anarchist and
futurist who predicted in his 'little magazine' *21st century* that
technology would liberate humans from drudgery. A passionate admirer of Lawson and the bush, he grafted an Australian
sense of place onto his anarcho-utopianism. This original poet
was something of a bohemian gadfly of the twentieth century,
moving through the IWW, contributing to *Bohemia*, *Comment*
and *Meanjin*, mixing with the Malley hoaxers and other
university litterateurs and even working for the Packer and
labour press. He hosted a small salon at his flat in Wylde Street,
Potts Point, attended largely by admiring young women – like
Margaret who shared his romantic optimism (in contrast to
Push pessimism) and became his lover. John Olsen was one of
a handful of painters who moved on the outskirts of the Push.
He lived in Paddington, within cooee of the galleries of the
eastern suburbs and East Sydney Technical College where he
was a student.

In the late 1950s and early 1960s a new intake of undergraduates brought into the Push milieu students primarily interested
in literature, fine art, theatre and music. While moving in
the wider Push rather than making a lifelong commitment,
bohemian artists like Albie Thoms, Robert Hughes, Clive
James, Germaine Greer, Bob Ellis, Frank Moorhouse and Barry
Humphries helped to invigorate the Push and were affected by
the Libertarians' way of thinking.

Albie Thoms was Push from his desert boots to his goatee. As
an undergraduate in 1959 he developed a passion for experimental
drama and cinema that challenged conventional storytelling
narrative, and ran the gauntlet of the prevailing obscenity laws.
In 1963 he directed an absurdist revue for the Sydney University
Dramatic Society, which featured 'The Song of Disembraining'

by Frenchman Alfred Jarry. The chorus 'Hooray! Arseholes to you' brought the vice squad to the stage and the performance to a close. Thoms was charged with 'aiding, abetting, counselling and procuring' an obscene ditty.[55]

Robert Hughes was an architecture student from a wealthy eastern suburbs family with strong Catholic Church and Liberal Party connections. While at university Hughes dabbled in painting and studied art history, theory and criticism, taking time off in 1962 to write *The Art of Australia* for the new Australian branch of Penguin. He socialised with the Push, and was accepted enough by its leaders to be allowed to paint a 'Push' mural on the wall of the Royal George.

Hughes' mate Clive James hailed from the other side of the tracks, a war widow's only son from Kogarah. Clive studied English literature and fancied himself a poet, sketch writer and critic. He threw himself into the student union revues and *Honi Soit* and was active in the film society. Thoms describes James performing amusing reviews of books and films for admirers over lunch that were well on the way to his trademark style and cadence. Never a subcultural Libertarian, James felt himself part of the Push as he drank at the Royal George with other aspiring aesthetes 'on the verge of writing, painting or composing something'.[56]

Germaine Greer enrolled at Sydney University as a postgraduate from Melbourne University around 1962 to complete a Master's thesis on Lord Byron, having already made a name for herself with the Push as a forceful, witty contrarian, intelligent theoretician and debater. Having socialised with the Push while in her honours year, she moved to Sydney in 1960 to immerse herself in it. The Push provided Greer, already an anarchist by inclination and lifestyle, with a theoretical foundation.

In 1960 Greer gave a paper on 'Libertarianism and Sex' which established some of the arguments she would develop in a most original direction in *The Female Eunuch*. She forged close friendships with the creative Push associates Harry Hooton, Margaret Elliott (introducing her to future husband Leon Fink) and Clive James. During her brief spell in Sydney Greer was welcomed into the Libertarians' inner sanctum, becoming Smilde's lover.

A self-made scholarship girl from a middle-class background, Greer combined academic rigour with an outrageous
style of bohemia, characterised by humour, intelligence, vulgar
language and an assertive sexual appetite that surprised even the
Push. The combination of this aggressive, sexualised bohemia
with postgraduate scholarship was a rare amalgam for a woman
at this time, as most Push females were undergraduates or
working, and were not as sexually assertive in public. Smilde
was impressed: 'She was vivacious, lively, a bundle of life …
thought she could do everything. Irrepressible. Women in those
days were inhibited, shy, hanging back. She was such a natural,
such a goer in herself — she just leapt in, wasn't inhibited or
intimidated by the men. Germaine couldn't be intimidated. I
thought Jesus Christ!'[57] Anderson had warned his students that
bohemianism threatened to undermine the scholarly life, but
Greer used her time with the Push to fashion a hybrid of the
two that set her on the path to becoming a celebrity intellectual
in the mass-media age.

Bob Ellis arrived at Sydney University from a working-class
Seventh Day Adventist household on the north coast of New
South Wales. Far too romantic in temperament and intellect for
the Libertarians, Ellis mixed with creative people on its edges, but
concentrated on forming his own idiosyncratic, arts-based bohemian group on campus, based around *Honi Soit* and the annual
Union Revue, which included Jim Coombs and his friends from
Lismore, Les Murray and Quentin Masters, resulting in them
being dubbed 'the Northern Rivers Push'. Ellis later described
the Push from the perspective of an up close outsider:

> To an outsider, and many of us were outside the Push,
> unable because of our tentative personalities to break
> through the strong royal curtain into their loving affec-
> tions, they loomed as Homeric giants, whose life was one
> long bland adventure, night after night, party after party,
> race meeting after poker session and tragic love after tragic
> love … delivering their papers on sex and death and Reich
> and Christ and Camus and Phar Lap, arguing and drinking
> far into the night, taking around the hat for incidental
> abortions … conducting their ritual contests, inventing

their savage games, and having their parties, parties, parties, all the parties I missed.[58]

Frank Moorhouse came to the University of Sydney in 1957 and was interested in journalism and writing fiction. Challenged by the Libertarians he sought acceptance by confronting its hardcore philosophers head on, presenting papers and, in the later 1960s, asking that the group re-examine some of its core attitudes and rituals. He lived the complete Push lifestyle, drinking at the Newcastle, the Royal George and the Vanity Fair, going to all the parties and living in a series of Push houses. In the late 1960s he participated in the so-called Balmain Push, where he shared a house with Albie Thoms and British expatriate academic Michael Wilding. Commencing with *Futility and Other Animals* and *The Americans, Baby*, Moorhouse's short stories chronicle the countercultural and political turbulence of the late 1960s and early 1970s from a broadly Libertarian perspective that engaged robustly with his bohemian milieu.

In 1957 the Libertarians undertook their first publishing venture, the *Broadsheet*, released bi-monthly. In the same year the first issue of a little magazine, *Libertarian*, rolled off the presses. While only three issues were produced by 1960, the periodical was distinguished by its breadth of topics and depth of analysis. Jim Baker wrote on Max Eastman, anarchism and Reich, George Molnar on the managerial revolution and David Ivison on futilitarianism and on the theory of orgasms. The best of the *Broadsheet* articles were published in 1963 as *The Sydney Line*, edited by Baker and Molnar. These journalistic ventures were a good training ground in writing opinion, reviews and essays for public consumption, and provided the Push with a sense of shared community.

That same year, new Push undergraduates Robert Hughes, Clive James and Paddy McGuinness toiled on the University of Sydney student newspaper, *Honi Soit*, learning how to edit, write and design for the print medium. Hughes drew cartoons and James composed amusing poems. Later *Honi* editors with Push connections included Bob Ellis and Richard Walsh. The downtown pubs at which the Push drank, like the Royal George and the Assembly, and cafés like the Lincoln and Vadim's brought talented young students into direct contact with editors and seasoned journalists from an older bohemia and some landed jobs.

Push femme fatale Lillian Roxon had grown up in Brisbane as a child refugee from Europe in an intellectual Jewish family. Interested in fashion, music and the arts, she worked on a teen magazine edited for the Packers by Donald Horne where she wrote about the latest trends in youth pop culture. Lillian

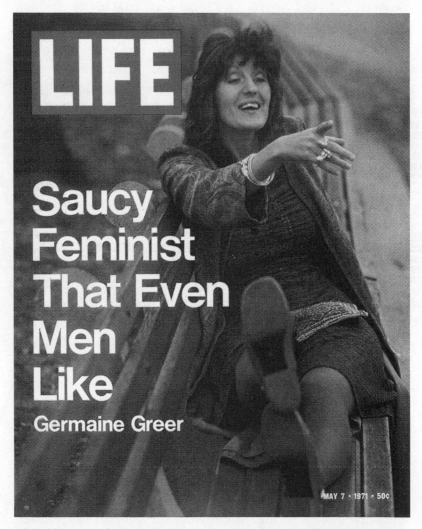

LIFE

Saucy
Feminist
That Even
Men
Like

Germaine Greer

MAY 7 • 1971 • 50¢

After publication of *The Female Eunuch*, Germaine Greer found kindred spirits in the Sydney Libertarians and went on to communicate radical ideas to millions as a multi-media public intellectual.

LIFE magazine, 7 May 1971. Photo by Vernon Merritt III. Courtesy Time & Life Pictures/Getty Images.

graduated to the *Sydney Morning Herald*, becoming its New York correspondent in the early 1960s, where she reported on the Kennedy presidency and the dissent provoked by racial discrimination and the Vietnam War. She understood the connection of these political upheavals to changes in youth culture and became an acclaimed chronicler of rock'n'roll's revolution into a force for change in the later 1960s in the bestselling *Encyclopedia of Rock*.[59]

Robert Hughes secured a job as art critic on the highbrow *Nation*. Albie Thoms reports that on his elevation to the prestigious journal, Hughes was literally elevated at Vadim's to dining in the exclusive mezzanine with other *Nation* journalists, looking down at the hoi polloi. Another Push tyro, George Munster, became an editor of the *Nation* and even Darcy Waters found a regular gig writing its racing column.

Bob Ellis moved from *Honi Soit* to the *Herald*, finding a berth on the shipping news. He later researched for the ABC, then become feature writer and columnist for *Review*. Moorhouse was employed as a journalist at ABC radio until 1969, when he left to concentrate on writing full time. Right-wing Andersonians were well established in the print media, with both Donald Horne and Peter Coleman each editing *Quadrant* and the *Bulletin*.

In the literary sphere the outstanding Push fiction writer was Moorhouse, but his housemate Michael Wilding also set his early short stories and novels within student and academic bohemia. In non-fiction many Push people have made a mark, either in scholarly publications, such as Sylvia Lawson's *The Archibald Paradox* and Jim Baker's work, or in the popular histories, criticism, literary memoirs and polemics, with which Hughes, Greer, James and Ellis have enjoyed commercial and critical success.

However, it was in film and television that Push creativity broke new ground. From the 1950s the Push was interested in cinema, and participated in emerging film societies, and organised their own film study groups. The first Push filmmaker was Albie Thoms, who reckons that cinema was the dominant Push art form. He was interested in challenging Hollywood conventions, and was also highly critical of the socialist realism of independent documentaries produced by the Waterside Workers Federation Film Unit and praised by the communists.

Thoms made a number of experimental films from the early 1960s, usually starring Push luminaries. In the surrealist ... *it droppeth as the gentle rain*, made in collaboration with Push fellow traveller Bruce Beresford, the cast, including Germaine Greer, are subjected to a shower of faeces. Thoms considered himself a filmic 'modernist' trying to break from nineteenth-century storytelling and to create a surrealist film language.

In 1970 a number of filmmakers associated with the Push founded the Sydney Filmmakers Cooperative to help fund experimental projects. One of the more accomplished features produced by the group in the 1960s include Michael Thornhill's *The American Poet's Visit*, based on Frank Moorhouse's short story set in and starring the Push. Thoms also founded Ubu Films to pursue more experimental techniques in cinema. Margaret Fink, immersed in film from her early Push days, also moved into film production in the 1960s, eventually producing important feature films during the 1970s, notably *My Brilliant Career*. Likewise later Push cinephile Richard Brennan surfed the new wave of Australian film, contributing to defining movies such as *The Removalists* and *Newsfront*.

The Push students understood the potential of the new medium of television. Introduced to Australia to coincide with the 1956 Olympics, its early pioneers came from radio and newsreel, and brought with them the conventions and limitations of those media. The younger Push generation, especially those graduating in the early 1960s, had some familiarity with TV and were sufficiently conversant with performance, cinema, literature and visual art to comprehend its potential. The televisual literacy of the Push generation is best exemplified by the aforementioned 1959 ABC program 'Inquiry into the Beats'. A motley group of bohemian students and Push stalwarts mistaken as local devotees of the American trend were brought into an ABC studio, decorated as a café, to be interrogated about the beatnik craze. The stiff and formal interviewer is taken aback when young interviewees Clive James and Robert Hughes commence criticising the beats with rigour and humour, turning the tables through their accomplished performances to become 'experts'.

Another bohemian who embraced television, along with

painting, writing, theatre and film, was Melbourne thespian and satirist Barry Humphries. Affecting the style of a Wildean dandy and aesthete, Humphries for a time moved and drank (unimpressed) in Push circles while living in Sydney en route to London, where the expatriate Australian became a true multimedia celebrity in the 1970s. Humphries began his career in the theatre and remained essentially a 'performer' but made his name through television, appearing on screen in its first year as Edna Everage to satirise Australia's hosting of the Olympic Games.

THE MELBOURNE DRIFT

While an undergraduate at Melbourne University and Dadaist about town, Barry Humphries was part of a bohemian network called the Drift, which included students and graduates Tim and Betty Burstall, Germaine Greer, Leon Fink and Beatrice Faust. In her biography of Greer, Christine Wallace describes the Drift gathering at favoured inner Melbourne pubs and restaurants, and in the creative milieu of Eltham and its artistic centre Montsalvat in the 1950s and early 60s. The chief pub remained the Swanston Family Hotel, popular with bohemians and radicals since the 1930s, and the Del Capri and Blue Grotto, Mirka Mora's cafés and Italian restaurants in Lygon Street, Carlton. Its leading lights were modernist artists and left intellectuals who had first come to prominence in the 1940s, including painters John Perceval, Clifton Pugh and Arthur Boyd, and writers Chris Wallace-Crabbe and Glen Tomasetti. Its recreations were more conventional than the Sydney Libertarians, but not constrained by a credo. Dinner at an Italian restaurant would be followed by spirited conversation at the Swanston, described by Humphries as containing the country's most interesting spirits: 'The noise was deafening, but the atmosphere was heady and as I stood in that packed throng of artists' models, academics, alkies, radio actors, poofs and ratbags, drinking large quantities of agonisingly cold beer, I felt as though my True Personality was coming into focus.'[60] Spontaneous late-night parties were held at a string of urban artists' studios, craft workshops, and houses in semi-rural Eltham.

Tim Burstall's recently published diary of the years 1953–55 offers glimpses of the permissive sexuality practised within the Drift.[61] To the young charismatic ABC apprentice Burstall, Eltham was 'like a madhouse, sexually' and he enjoyed affairs with young creative women while maintaining an 'open' marriage. Opposed to monogamy's possessiveness and restrictions on personal fulfilment, Tim and Betty, like some in the Push, could not escape the emotional angst and pangs of jealousy that attended their fluid infatuations and the supposedly guilt-free pursuit of pleasure.

The Drift practised casual sex in a far less theorised way than the Libertarians, with the young Greer at the forefront. A Drift contemporary recalled that on one occasion Greer walked into a Melbourne café and declared, 'I'd like to wrap my big juicy cunt around …', naming the male after whom she lusted. While shocking for the time, such language was acceptable within the Drift, just.[62]

The Drift, inspired by romantics like D.H. Lawrence and the surrealists, and building on Melbourne traditions from the previous decade, was far more self-consciously aesthetic than the Push. Literature, painting and especially performance were embraced by the younger generation. The romantic focus on art was one way in which the Drift distinguished itself from the Marxist radicals who dominated Melbourne's intelligentsia and the campus. Thoms acknowledged the Drift had an irreverent sense of humour, but criticises them for lacking 'strong ideas'.[63] Greer, with the benefit of comparison with the rigours of the Push, concurred, arguing that the Drift 'was a lifestyle, it represented a way of just hanging around ... I knew it was second rate.' She was critical of the Drift for being more conventionally bohemian, trapped in its myths like 'truth', 'beauty' and 'art', while the Push 'talked about only truth' and saw through such 'ideology' as 'bullshit'.[64]

Humphries admired and practised surrealism while in Melbourne, combining Dadaist elements of shock and absurdity into early performance art, such as expelling fake vomit into brown bags on train platforms. While attracted to the anarchistic elements of these aesthetics, he rejected their association with left politics in favour of the aestheticism and decadence of the fin-de-siècle, adopting aspects of the style of both Oscar

Wilde and especially Charles Conder, whose paintings he began collecting. Humphries demonstrated that the combination of cultural iconoclasm and political conservatism evident in the artist-hero bohemianism of Conder, Tom Roberts and Norman Lindsay was very much alive in the 1950s and 60s. Succesful bohemians like them made themselves a work of art, modifying their identities and performances to suit the audience and the medium, balancing the shocks with the familiar. Barry Humphries made this his career.

By the late 1950s Humphries had discovered the best art form in which to express his amused disdain was comedic character-sketch monologues rich in irony and bathos, with his first great character being the respectability-craving suburban housewife from Moonee Ponds, Edna Everage. While Humphies found artistic support for his creative iconoclasm in Melbourne, his nihilism, misanthropic delight in human foibles and pessimism about social progress sat uneasily with Melbourne's left liberalism. Greer found female outspokenness and sexual assertiveness more acceptable in Sydney, and was warmly embraced by the Push.[65] Not so Humphries.

Recalling his first visit to 'Sinni' in 1956, Humphries had nothing good to say about the Push: 'a fraternity of middle class desperates, journalists, drop out academics, gamblers and poets *manqués*, and their doxies … These latter were mostly suburban girls; primary-school teachers and art students, who each night after working hours exchanged their irksome respectability for a little liberating profanity, drunkenness and sex.'

Humphries' withering criticism of the Push reflects Melbourne–Sydney rivalry, and betrays the upper-middle-class snobbery he both enjoys and likes to send up. While drinking in Push pub the Assembly, Humphries may have kept his distance from these 'talentless tosspots', but recalls that the 'Push shunned me as well because I was actually doing something vaguely and peripherally artistic', anathema to their 'snobby philistinism and … distrust of success'.[66] Critical of what he saw as Push sloth, Humphries claims his ambition to achieve in theatre marked him out as careerist, and therefore beyond the pale. He had relationships with several Push women, such as Margaret Elliott, failed to impress a leagues club audience with his brand of avant-garde comedy, and drank far too much.

Drift members who came to Sydney invariably moved through the Push on their way to London. Some who remained in Melbourne embarked on artistic careers, like Tim and Betty Burstall, who joined with a later generation of students from the mid-1960s to create a theatre, film and music bohemia centred on the inner-city university precinct of Carlton.

Bohemianism in Australia is obsessed with the opposition of province and the metropolis, continually recycling a rite-of-passage motif in which young people leave rural or suburban backwaters for the city, provincial cities for Melbourne or Sydney, and the antipodes for the centres of metropolitan culture – London, Paris or New York. The contrast of the cosmopolitan inner city with dreadful suburban dullness which began in the 1890s is a strong and persistent characteristic of Australian bohemias through the Sydney Push and 1960s countercultures. The Push liked to mock ordinary suburbanites, and private jokes at the expense of 'Alfs and Daphnes' became popular and thought-provoking satire in the hands of a master like Humphries, beginning a variant on the larrikin carnivalesque that would climax in the ocker comedy fad of the 1970s that persists to the present.

PROTEST GOES MAINSTREAM

The Push's antipathy to what they saw as the muddle-headed romanticism of the left led them to avoid overt political protests and campaigning during the 1950s and most of the 1960s. Many Push luminaries, such as George Molnar, voted informal in opposition to the authoritarianism inherent in compulsory voting. There were rare political engagements, and these centred on issues of liberty. Consequently it was easy for first old-left and then new-left activists to caricature the Push radicals as 'armchair anarchists'.

One-time Andersonian and conservative philosopher David Stove argued in 1958 that Anderson's negativity about joining parties and institutions produced 'a sort of paralysis of the active and practical side' among his students that ultimately led to impotent nihilism. Alan Barcan supports this thesis from the left, arguing that the Libertarians' bohemianism was a symptom of their disengagement and a sign of radical defeatism in the face of the Cold War stand-off. The Libertarians had advised that if 'middle-class socialists' like him were to 'stop seeking a purpose in life and become somewhat more intellectual, they may come to see the futility of it all'.[67] Even the tabloid *People* magazine rounded on the Push for its lack of political engagement, lamenting as '[t]heir saddest characteristic … the fact that none of them believes he can use his abilities to improve anything for himself or for others'.[68]

Throughout the Vietnam demonstrations the hard core of the Push remained hostile to student protest, which they found too enamoured of fuzzy idealism and already failed socialist panaceas. But a younger generation of radicalised students came into the Push in the late 1960s and early 70s, changing its attitudes to activism, media culture and even to sex. Leading spirits in the new generation were the University of New South Wales women Wendy Bacon, Val Hodgson, Liz Fell and Sandra Levy, who rallied around the outlawed underground publications *Tharunka* and *Thorunka*, that would push the boundaries of transgression in an era when the oral contraceptive 'pill' was mainstreaming ideas like 'free fucking' into a 'sexual revolution' in the suburbs. Under their influence the older Push inner core were roused to atypical activism in the cause of urban preservation – the fight to preserve Victoria Street in Kings Cross from developers in solidarity with the far-left Builders Labourers Federation and its charismatic leader, Jack Mundey.

This was bohemia protecting its own backyard. Like their bohemian predecessors, the Push men and women were most at home in the pubs and terraces of Sydney's Victorian inner-city neighbourhoods. It was a David and Goliath struggle between big business, aided and abetted by gangsters and government, on the one side, and working-class residents and student squatters on the other. The BLF was showing a post-materialist, altruistic way forward past the bread-and-butter materialism of traditional left politics. Inspired by firebrands Bacon and Fell, Push stalwarts Smilde, Molnar and Waters took to the streets and manned the squats.

By the early 1970s the Push was fragmenting into different subcultures, as well as blending at the edges into the wider counterculture. The BLF green bans may have saved The Rocks, but in the wake of commercial development the 'downtown' area was becoming a central business district, its pubs knocked down for skyscrapers and its streets deserted after office hours. Push identities withdrew to the different villages circling the city, especially Balmain and Paddington. A number of more literary people living in Balmain became the Balmain Push, continuing a bohemian life of pubs and parties well into the late 1970s. Ultimately buying rather than renting, these largely tertiary-qualified journalists, writers and academics were a beachhead for the gentrification of inner-city suburbs. A number of the filmmakers bought homes around harbourside Mosman and the northern beaches, particularly Palm Beach, which had Push connections, and bohemian echoes back to the artist camps of the late nineteenth century. During the 1970s and 80s students who had moved through the Push began the long march through the institutions of media, politics and academia, and created quite a few new ones, and were now in a position to shape society, while themselves being shaped by the inevitable compromises of power and patronage.

In 1840 the French writer Balzac characterised Parisian bohemia as vast nursery for bourgeois ambition, 'made up of men between the ages of twenty and thirty, all of them men of genius in their way; little is known as yet, but to be known hereafter, when they are sure to be distinguished'.[69]

That the more driven and talented of the Libertarians shared this fate was summed up in the title of a 1996 *Sun Herald* story about the Sydney Push: 'How a Bunch of Bohemians Became the Rich and Famous.'[70]

LIBERTARIAN LEGACY

It was not in traditional politics, but in new fields such as the politics of the self, lifestyle experimentation and creative work that the Push's radical challenge to bourgeois society was to be found. Smilde acknowledged to Anne Coombs that 'in other times and other places we would have been revolutionaries – we had the same sort of political passion that would have made us revolutionaries … But in this particular time, and this kind of place, with the sort of philosophic influence that we had on us, we became pessimistic, non-revolutionary radicals who came to emphasise a way of life.'

In many ways the Push represented a vanguard of wider social change that would come in the late 1960s. Speaking of the 1950s Jack Gulley, who became head of ABC News and Current Affairs, recognised that 'the Push was a generation ahead of itself. In the sixties a lot of attitudes and views expressed in the Push became fairly normal for most young people of that time'. Another Push participant John Docker argued in the early 70s that Libertarianism had flourished in the 1950s when philistinism was the norm in Australian society, and an anti-intellectual authoritarian puritanism dominated the left, but 'once there was a greater degree of sexual permissiveness in society, and once the left became more counter-cultural ... Libertarianism began to falter".[71]

Certainly the Push was a genuine agent of pluralism relative to Australian society in the 1950s and early 60s. The idea of a society where differences are encouraged and rub against each other, long valued in bohemia, is as valid a measure of radicalism as the indices of wealth distribution or collectivism applied by the old left, and subsequently became a goal of mainstream small 'l' liberal politics from the 1970s.

The Libertarian Push remains a living tradition because the Push influenced people who influenced people. Andersonian thinking and the Libertarian line persevered into Australian countercultures, influencing the bohemias around the underground press, the film industry and identity movements. During the 1970s Libertarian ways of thinking and living were carried into academic institutions and courses, where they fed into postmodern intellectual culture and its youthful scene in the 1980s. It was the achievement of the Push to smuggle into Sydney's bohemia an intellectual rigour around long-held values like anarchism, promiscuity and cultural protest to in effect theorise a bohemian way of life.

7

REBEL SELL:
COUNTERCULTURES AND
CONSUMER CULTURE

1960–1980

In the late 1990s self-styled futurist Richard Neville was looking backward, reminding youngsters that: 'We revved up the
underground and a thousand nutters published ... We made
Australia safe for D.H. Lawrence, Nabokov and even the Sex
Pistols ... Our heroes defied odds, righted wrongs and retired
to communes.'[1]

With some justification, Neville locates himself on the barricades of a rebellious movement of young people that swept
western nations, including Australia, from the 1960s into the
1970s, popularly labelled 'hippies', 'flower children', the 'youth
quake' and the 'underground', and theorised as the 'counterculture' by the sociologist Theodore Roszak.[2] Neville shares
with other participants in sixties dissent the conceit that their
generation of rebels was unique, especially in conservative
Australia. Given that most of the self-appointed 'voices of a
generation' were writers, journalists, visual artists, musicians,
theatre performers and filmmakers who claimed to be opposed
to bourgeois society, it is important to consider how the local
countercultures of the 1960s and 70s related to the Australian
bohemian tradition. Consistent with earlier generations of bohemians, young participants in the countercultures asserted a very
explicit desire for creative autonomy to 'do their own thing',
while experiencing personal elevation within the mainstream
media market and the commodification of their work. Yet there

were differences, notably the ease with which countercultural artists moved back and forth from avant-garde to mass media. This chapter questions the generational claim about freedom from the market to be found in sixties countercultural myth-making to ask what was consistent with bohemia, and what was truly new and even revolutionary.

COUNTERCULTURES AND BOHEMIA

The term 'counterculture' was coined by Roszak in his impor-tant 1969 study, *The Making of a Counter Culture*, after which it entered popular usage to describe an array of dissenting youthful groups that spread across political, artistic, lifestyle and spiritual activities. In *Play Power, Oz* magazine editor Richard Neville used the overarching term 'the Movement' to embrace three divisions: the New Left, 'comprised largely of the alphabet soup of student protest'; the 'underground' of cultural radicals who rejected rigid political ideology or structures, such as 'hippies, beats, mystics, madmen, freaks, yippies'; and the 'militant poor', including those lower-class elements that were radical, such as black power and radical ethnic communities.[3] For Neville 'the Movement' was linked by its youth, opposition to the status quo and spirit of play.

Writer Frank Moorhouse, drawing on his experience of the Push, preferred Roszak's term 'counter-culture' and defined it as 'those who feel themselves apart from the wider society' and who 'live by … distinctly different mores – in their own subcultures'.[4] He then listed a long heterogeneity of identities that stretched back in time and included 'old-world bohemians', 'fifties beatniks', 'minstrels' and 'pranksters' alongside 'hippies', 'libertarians', 'sceptical anarchists', 'film makers' and 'déclassé academics', linked in their diversity as 'lumpen intelligentsia'.

Australian social commentator, journalist and Push fellow traveller Craig McGregor argued in 'What Counter-Culture?' that the idea of one homogeneous movement or totalising youth consciousness was the wrong way to think about what was happening amongst disgruntled young people. Rather, a diver-sity of dissenting groups was emerging in the west – including Australia – anticipating a new pluralism. 'Cultures', rather than 'culture', was appropriate.[5] For McGregor – a socialist who had absorbed elements of Anderson's philosophy and associated with the folk, blues and surfing scenes – the most important word was 'counter', as it accurately conveyed the sense of self-conscious opposition to capitalist society and the desire to experiment with, and demonstrate, alternatives. This oppositional stance connected what McGregor considered the main strands – bohemianism, New Left politics, protest, sexual liberation and a spirit of non-conformity – to the mainstream culture of the generation of the Second World War.

Rather than being one movement, the many smaller groups and networks were linked internationally in the west via media and travel, while marked by national and regional specificities. The plural 'countercultures' is a more appropriate description of the variety of groups based around media, philosophies and aesthetics. Sydney, for example, had the university-oriented Libertarian Push, independent publishers like *Oz* and *Tharunka*, the Ubu underground filmmaking network and the Yellow House artists, while Melbourne had the Carlton theatrical and filmmaking group based around the La Mama Theatre, *Nation Review* and Mushroom records.

McGregor, like Roszak and Neville, considered the countercultures to be unique social protest groups because of their oppositional character, and did not consider whether they shared features with earlier bohemias. This set the tone for memoirs and media reminiscences by counterculture participants, in which the 1960s (usually stretched into the early 1970s to include the period of the Whitlam government) was romanticised as a golden age of cultural renaissance and revolutionary change. Neville explained to young people in 1998 that the counterculture was no less than a 'complete rethink of western civilisation'.[6] With a sense of irony, La Mama theatre director and actor Graeme Blundell remembered how 'some of us … wandered the inner city streets bruised after talking all night, with empty pockets and big plans, or sat doodling plans in the new Italian cafes, sketching out … theatrical revolutions and film industries'.[7]

As well as conventional memoirs such as Richard Neville's *Hippie Hippie Shake*, Graeme Blundell's *The Naked Truth* and Robert Hughes' *Things I Didn't Know*, 1960s and 70s bohemians have produced edited collections of contemporary writings with memoir elements. Examples include *Days of Wine and Rage* by Frank Moorhouse, Peter Mudie's *Ubu Films*, Albie Thoms' *Polemics for a New Cinema*, Bob Ellis's *Letters to the Future* and *Goodbye Jerusalem* and Richard Walsh's annotated archive of the *Nation Review*, *Ferretabilia*. These memoirs and collections balance nostalgia with a confident assertion of the continued relevance of their cultural rebellion. A less romantic but nonetheless nostalgic tone can be found in Barry Humphries' autobiography *More Please* and Clive James' *Unreliable Memoirs* series, both of which mock fashionable left contemporary claims to cultural revolution from a perspective that looked back to earlier artists, while including themselves in the action.[8]

To these memoirs and collections must be added a variety of substantial interviews, articles, regular columns, television documentaries, feature films and exhibitions in which leading countercultural activists recalled and romanticised their experiences.[9] What is interesting in this popular media packaging of the sixties and early 1970s is the extent to which the bohemian and radical political experiences of the countercultures and a minority of mainly university-educated young people were generalised to be the common experiences of the decade. The 1890s was similarly recalled as an era of bohemians and radicals and that may have been because in both periods mass audiences consumed texts produced by bohemians, both at the time and as nostalgia later.

Alongside the theme of the golden age was the lament that its rebels fought for and achieved artistic and political freedoms that subsequent generations have failed to safeguard – the self-serving theme of a revolution betrayed. While Anne Summers berated the next generation of women for taking feminism for granted and expecting 'we pioneers' to 'let go', Neville lamented that '[o]nce we brooded in cafes, fashionably, about poetry, romance, revolution. Now we prattle on car phones about capital gains, digital cameras and software solutions.'[10]

However a number of scholarly studies have strongly critiqued the mythologising of the 1960s in Australia, arguing that 'nostalgia has emptied the age of its political reality'.[11] In *Gangland*, Mark Davis examined how individuals occupying influential positions in media and other cultural institutions in the late 1990s deployed war stories about their creative or radical exploits in the 1960s and 70s to legitimise their power as 'gatekeepers' and to exclude younger competitors. Davis did not consider whether the 1960s and 70s remembered by a new 'baby boomer establishment' conformed to a tradition of an older cultural generation deploying bohemian nostalgia to remain relevant and exclude newcomers. But as discussed previously, the 1890s and 1940s saw comparable mythologising by ageing artists who could also command an audience for their nostalgia.

The new countercultures asserted creative autonomy through the skilful building of independent media and cultural institutions such as *Oz* magazine, Ubu Films and the Pram Factory in Carlton, where artists could experiment, communicate with like-minded people and also influence, and perhaps change, the public sphere. The young Dadaist Barry Humphries stressed his autonomy from bourgeois society through his dramatic monologues mocking respectable suburbanites. Richard Neville, Martin Sharp, Richard Walsh, Frank Moorhouse and Wendy Bacon goaded the mainstream press and government obscenity laws through student and 'underground' publishing. Bruce Beresford, Albie Thoms, Clive James, Bob Ellis, Tim Burstall, Germaine Greer and Graeme Blundell parlayed student dramatics into experimental theatre and film. But this autonomy was continually contested by the state, which sought to regulate and censor freedom of expression, and more subtly by the simultaneous immersion of counterculture bohemians in mainstream media.

Countercultural groups shared with earlier bohemian groups a romanticism in their work and also their identities. There are echoes of the eighteenth-century English romantic movement's nostalgia for pre-industrial society, transcendence via the consolations of nature, and a utopian belief in escape to paradise. A resurgent romanticism in the west influenced alternative lifestyle experiments, altering consciousness through drug use, exotic travel, the upsurge in student radicalism on university campuses from 1968, and the dramatic changes in popular youth culture such as music, fashion and cinema. Late 1960s countercultures reinforced some of romanticism's original concerns about alienation, mechanisation, innocence, childhood, community, authenticity and revolution (in the sense of returning to simpler, organic times). As we have seen, romanticism had appeared again and again in Australian bohemia from the mid-nineteenth century – in Victorian gothic, the idealisation of the Bush and aestheticism, Lawsonian socialism and a variety of modernisms.

While heroic individuals were celebrated, art projects and transgressive countercultural lifestyles were usually expressed through groups, even to the extent of 'collectives', 'tribes' and 'communes' being celebrated as an alternative route to creativity and personal fulfilment. Many participants in countercultures were the young bourgeoisie, attending or just graduated from university, which became as important a site for skilling and grouping together young creative people and encouraging bohemianism as journalism and art schools were in earlier generations – though these persisted too. Just as the press had been a vehicle for social mobility into bohemia from the late nineteenth century, postwar universities opened up places to lower-class students – initially via scholarships and climaxing in the abolition of tuition fees – who gained access to counterculture groups on and off campus.

Rather than a break with the bohemian tradition, countercultures embraced elements of both the popular culture carnivalesque literary bohemia and the artist-hero bohemianism of the modernist avant-garde. Both play and the Dionysian pursuit of pleasure were fetishised by countercultural bohemians in theory and practice and made integral to their art.[12] The traditional bohemian emphasis on sexual freedom was emphasised, but was now theorised as linked to freedom of thought courtesy of both John Anderson and Wilhelm Reich. The bohemian interest in consciousness-altering drugs that in Australia began with Marcus Clarke was reinforced by the American Beat and jazz cultures, enthusiasm for marijuana and opiates and the promotion of hallucinogens by countercultural leaders Timothy Leary and London *Oz*. Bohemia's longstanding commitment to free expression was focused into political campaigns against the censorship of art and media.

The suburbs were caricatured as the home of philistine, lower middle-class domesticity à la Edna Everage, and a working-class paradise of yobbos, disparaged as 'Alfs' in *Oz*, popularisng the Push put down. The same rejection of the suburbs led some countercultural bohemians to romanticise the countryside and rural simplicity. In establishing retreats styled as communes in hinterland areas such as Nimbin and Byron Bay, they recalled the bush nostalgia and artists' camps of the late nineteenth century and bucolic avant-garde properties in Melbourne in the 1930s and 40s.

Older bohemians from the interwar period and the 1950s persisted in Sydney and Melbourne through the 1960s and 70s, and played a part in transmitting traditional bohemianism to the younger generation. The mythology of the 'Swinging Sixties' likes to portray the 1950s as a dull decade of suburban conformity. Typical was Graeme Blundell's journalistic memory that the ''60s were a welcome challenge to the rigidity and repression of the grey-flannelled '50s, a time so dull it was hard to breathe'.

Most 1960s student bohemians lived in the suburbs or regions as children, and would have been oblivious to artistic groups in precincts such as Kings Cross and Carlton, for example the milieu described in Tim Burstall's diary. In reality the 1950s had a diversity of bohemias, from the Push to showbiz, and these groups were not as distinct from the countercultures as sixties mythology suggests.

As always there were family connections as children raised in artistic bohemian families tried to keep the dream alive. Mirka Mora's son Philippe moved in Melbourne's creative Carlton scene and became a maker of avant-garde films with a satirical, larrikin bent. Sweeney, the child of Joy Hester and Albert Tucker adopted by the Reeds, grew into a handsome and popular young man who cut a dash as Heide's love child in the arts scene anchored at the Museum of Modern Art. In the 1960s and early 70s he came to imbibe all that the permissive countercultures offered, with tragic consequences when he committed suicide in 1979.

Bridges existed within media workplaces such as the mainstream press and small-scale publications such as the *Observer* and *Nation*, and in clubs and pubs that persisted from the 1940s, notably the cosmopolitan Lincoln Coffee Lounge and the rambunctious Tudor, Newcastle and Assembly hotels in Sydney and the Swanston Family Hotel in downtown Melbourne.

Recalling different times between the mid-1950s and mid-60s, Humphries, Hughes, James, Ellis and Neville report almost identical baptisms into an already-established bohemia in select inner-city pubs. Contrary to the popular association of the 1960s with baby boomers (born between 1946 and 1965), many of the artists and spokespeople associated with counterculture groups who came to public attention through their cultural work in the 1960s and 70s — such as Hughes, Margaret Fink, Humphries, Greer, Moorhouse, Albie Thoms, Neville and Martin Sharp — were born in the 1930s or early 1940s and had strong associations with the Libertarian Push in Sydney and the Drift in Melbourne. These groups were a key link between 1960s bohemianism, the older interwar bohemian traditions of Andersonianism and the visual arts avant-gardes in Melbourne such as the Angry Penguins, the Boyds and Jorgensen's community of artists at Montsalvat. Humphries recalled the latter group as 'liberated members of the middle class who built mudbrick houses and coyly indulged their taste for pottery, folk music and adultery'.[13] A writer interested in traditions and connections, Ellis observed that the 1960s Push's 'history stretched back to Lawson and beyond', and exposed a student such as himself to a 'group of lethargic, amorphous, comradely, passive … elitists that included professional gamblers, known crims, uni lecturers, slumming millionaires, drug peddlers, wan folk singers, fierce proud poets … cocktail hostesses and dosshouse tramps'.[14] Humphries even took personal art lessons from George Bell at his private art school. The Drift became the 'Carlton' scene of the late 1960s and the long-lived Push was strong into the mid-1970s, influencing new cohorts of 'baby boomer' undergraduates such as Wendy Bacon. As late as 1971 Frank Moorhouse described the Push as 'bohemia' to *Bulletin* readers, and explained that 'counter-culture' was now the fashionable term for the same thing.

Under different labels the countercultures of the 1960s were opposing the bourgeoisie just as bohemias always did, while still bound to capitalist culture. But there were differences, driven by career opportunities in a new phase of consumer capitalism and the ambition of the countercultures to use the media to

transform society. There was also angst about what commodification meant for their art. Germaine Greer worried that the
'Underground' is 'where life is, before the Establishment forms
as a crust on top, and changes vitality to money'.[15] Did this mean
they were selling out, or was something far more interesting
happening to popular culture?

CULTURE OVER THE COUNTER

In the late 1990s Neville delivered the 'home truth' to so-
called 'Gen Xers' that '[o]ur counter-culture was a complete
rethink of western civilisation, while your counter-culture
is the shopping counter'.[16] The idea of 1960s countercultures
escaping the market is sometimes argued by countercultural
veterans who use their media profile to defend their legacy. A
contrary approach on the left, recycling the Marxist suspicion of
bohemianism, began during the 1960s with historian Ian Turner
and ABC broadcaster Allan Ashbolt denouncing the counterculture's embrace of pop music and the media as capitulation
to shallow commercial values.[17] More subtly, cultural historian
Stephen Alomes argued how neatly countercultural values such
as 'Do your own thing' dovetailed with postwar consumerism.[18] Canadian sociologists Joseph Heath and Andrew Potter
argue that authenticity and altruism gave greater market value
to commodities associated with countercultures, from fashion
and music to organic foods and loft apartments. Claiming that
bohemianism was now an integral part of bourgeois life,
their book Nation of Rebels also showed how countercultural
production and consumption conferred distinction. Far from
threatening capitalism, '[i]ndividualistic sartorial and stylistic
rebellion ... simply feeds the flames, by creating a whole new set of
positional goods for these new "rebel consumers" to
compete for.'[19] Likewise Australian economist Clive Hamilton
condemned the counterculture's permissive hedonism that 'tilled
the ground' for the hyper-consumerism of 1980s and 90s.[20] In
denouncing countercultures as 'effortlessly coopted', Hamilton
failed to consider the creativity, freedom and even subversion
that can be present within commercial popular culture.

Arguably, countercultures' bohemian values became a mainstream bourgeois lifestyle choice in the later twentieth century.

In 1987, British academics Simon Frith and Howard Horne examined the symbiotic relationship between 1960s and 70s bohemian creative producers and the pop industries in Britain, emphasising the movement of artists from underground projects into popular music, film and fashion via the British art schools.[21] They allowed far more agency for the art school bohemians, who are not simply dupes of capitalism, but curious to probe and play with the consumerism all around them, and to shape, and in some instances subvert, commercial youth culture with bohemian values. As a young proselytiser Neville also argued in *Oz* and *Play Power* for the liberating qualities of youth culture, especially rock music and mass media such as television. Of course, literary and many visual arts bohemians in the 1890s and 1920s worked as both independent artists and in the commercial sector, suggesting that these practices were complementary, not antagonistic.

Traditionally, economic value in the avant-garde lay in the denial of concern for the immediate profit. Only occasionally and over time did the investment pay off as an artist or work became a 'classic' with larger commercial appeal. But by the mid-1960s something different was happening, as these distinctions between 'underground' and pop, avant-garde and commercial began to break down, with countercultural bohemians leading the charge across this barricade as both consumers and producers.

POP GO THE BOHEMIANS

Sixties bohemians were conspicuous, yet discriminating, consumers. Whether from socially mobile working-class or, more commonly, well-off bourgeois families, most of the 1960s radicals experienced a childhood in which an unprecedented range of toys, gadgets, comics, pre-packaged confections and other consumer goods and media were available to a greater number. As adolescents they were targeted as the new teenage market for youth-specific cultural merchandise (often American imports or locally produced versions), like rock'n'roll (on 45 and 33 rpm records), fashion, magazines, cinema, comics, paperbacks and the new cheap, mobile transistor radio. As students and relatively well-paid young workers this generation was accustomed to self-realisation through consuming – the background to the growth of both a more discriminating bohemian consumption, and an 'anti-materialist' romantic backlash.

'Mass media,' declared Neville in 1970, is 'partly responsible for today's extraordinary generational self-consciousness'.[22] Far from being an opiate of the masses, the popular culture that was being consumed by teenagers in the 1950s and early 60s had diverse, often subversive meanings. As a film critic, Clive James later paid tribute to the qualities of the Hollywood film noir gangster and western movies his generation enjoyed at the 'pictures', and both the Drift and Push made cinema an art form of choice. Blundell, who was a teenager in the first half of the 1960s, claimed TV was not just 'novel' and 'cool', but 'ingrained in us a generational collective sense of irony we shared with our American brothers and sisters'.

Richard Neville, who ironically confessed, 'my life is measured out with dusty 45s', paid tribute to the influence of rock'n'roll on his generation's sensibility, explaining that 'to account for the manners of the sixties generation, it should be remembered that we grew up in the shadow of the Beatles … the Rolling Stones, Animals, Manfred Mann, Kinks, The Who.'[23]

Many students entering university in the 1960s had enjoyed a teenage life exposed to rock'n'roll. Like jazz for an earlier generation, the new music may have been commercial and American, but it was also rebellious, implicitly black, and something many older Australians – conservative and liberal – despised. Rock'n'roll could be threatening – largely because of its association with delinquency and the moral panic about the working-class youth subculture, bodgies.

Pop music became a spur to bohemianism among some young people at Australian universities and art schools, as jazz and other popular art forms had been among musicians, writers and visual artists in the 1920s. An earlier phase of rock'n'roll distinguished by old-fashioned showmanship held little attraction for bohemian youth, which tended to focus on jazz, blues and increasingly folk in the 1950s. However the early to mid-1960s witnessed a hybridisation of rock with the more middle-class protest folk scene in the US via singer-songwriter Bob Dylan, and groups Peter, Paul and Mary, Simon & Garfunkel and the

Byrds. Neville remembers the radicalising impact on emerging Australian university students of Bob Dylan's anthemic call to arms 'The Times They Are A–changin'. Protest folk was in tune with bohemia because both valued authenticity and were critical of the middle-class status quo. But the *Oz* satire circle also went stomping to surf bands, intrigued by the semi-delinquent hedonistic 'surfie' culture emerging on the northern beaches of Sydney.

In consuming 1960s rock'n'roll, Australian bohemians were not just being drip fed by capitalism, but were being exposed to British bohemian traditions and subcultures then seeping into show business. British art students John Lennon and Stu Sutcliffe had smuggled elements of the bohemian art scenes of Liverpool and Hamburg into the style of the Beatles, from long hair and black skivvies to the Goons' absurdist humour. In their wake, UK 'art school' bohemians such as musicians Keith Richards, Pete Townshend, Eric Burdon, Ray Davies, Jimmy Page, Eric Clapton and fashion designer Mary Quant made their cultural mark in pop music. The bohemianisation of Australian pop music began at the same time, with the movement of young jazz musicians into Beat music, most notably Melbourne's the Loved Ones, Wild Cherries and the Cherokees, and Sydney's the Missing Links, who were popular with the *Oz* scene. Craig McGregor and Lillian Roxon were two Australian commentators to glimpse in the mid-1960s the fertile crossover between avant-garde and pop creation. In debate with Ashbolt and Turner, McGregor argued that contemporary pop culture – rock'n'roll, TV satire, cartoons, and films – had high artistic and even politically subversive values.[24]

Literary scholar Greer was converted from an elitist indifference to enthusiast by rock's interplay of newfound lyricism and its visceral sexuality, declaring that '[m]usic became commercial and creative, not only notes but words, not only sound but physical onslaught, sight, movement, total environment ... the revolutionary-poet calling all to witness the new order.'[25]

But how did Australian bohemians combine the 'commercial and creative'?

ART INTO POP

As well as the experience of pop culture, the 1960s countercultures arose from the combination of free time spent in
education and creative employment in the commercial culture
industries. Within the cracks between these experiences, groups
formed their own autonomous projects, such as *Oz*, La Mama
Theatre and Ubu Films. Moorhouse, Greer, Thoms, Beresford,
Humphries, Neville, James, Richard Walsh and Bob Ellis began
writing, editing publications, directing theatre and films and
acting as part of their extra-curricular activities while undergraduates or postgraduates.

While they gleaned practical lessons in Andersonian libertarianism and Reich's theory of sexual freedom by drinking
at the Royal George Hotel with the Push, each participated
in smaller bohemian circles based on extra-curricular projects.
James, Ellis and Walsh edited *Honi Soit* and wrote comedy revues,
Neville edited *Tharunka* at the University of New South Wales,
and Greer performed for Sydney University Dramatic Society.
Thoms, Beresford, Richard Brennan, Jim Sharman and Ellis
moved from screening art and classic cinema at the University
Film Club to making their own short films. Ellis wrote in 2006
that the university-funded extra-curricular activities were not
only an antidote to potential isolation, but taught his peers

> how good things come in clusters, in groups like the one
> we were in. And how, admixed with our team spirit, our
> esprit de corps, was a stirred competitiveness that moved us,
> rubbing up against each other, to do better than each other.
> We wrote reviews of each others' stage performances. We
> wrote and sang new songs. We gave speeches at Union
> Night defaming one another.[26]

Vocational art schools such East Sydney Technical College
and Royal Melbourne Institute of Technology continued to perform the role among visual arts and other design students they
had since the late nineteenth century: brokering an exchange
between the romantic idea of the artist and commercial art.
The expansion in the 1950s and 60s of cultural industries such
as advertising, television, off-the-rack fashion, magazines and

publicity had increased demand for trained commercial artists producing a popular modernism in design. Illustrator Martin Sharp and fashion designer Jenny Kee first rehearsed their bohemian 'mod' style and creative skills while studying at East Sydney Technical College.

In the 1960s the expanding music business, notably record labels Festival and Spin, engaged with alternative cultures and producers in their quest for profitable content, and found underground rebel styles within the counterculture or youth subcultures such as mods or surfies. Creative people from these subcultures were employed by or contracted to the mainstream industries as copywriters, talent scouts and producers, changing them a little, and being changed in turn. Greer observed that 'the Establishment has to draw nourishment from [the Underground] and so plunders and is plundered by the Underground'.[27]

Richard Neville learned the art of persuasion working in advertising, serving a two-year apprenticeship marketing consumer goods at Farmers department store while at university part time and then taking a copywriting position at Jackson Wain. Neville was as skinny as a mop with hair to match and an elfin face like the young Norman Lindsay. A born self-promoter and prankster, he once kidnapped Brian Henderson, host of the TV music program *Bandstand*, gaining great media coverage. Neville's more level-headed collaborator in *Oz*, Richard Walsh, had originally intended to become a medical doctor before being drawn into the world of the student and underground press, then placed the media skills gleaned in them at the service of advertising agency J. Walter Thompson. Ellis, Beresford and Jim Sharman worked at McCann Erikson. Short-story writer Peter Carey and Montsalvat attendee and former Communist Party member Phillip Adams were copywriters in major advertising firms and many aspiring filmmakers, including Tim Burstall and Peter Weir, honed their filmmaking skills directing advertisements. Neville and Walsh also wrote freelance scripts for commercial television's hit comedy, *The Mavis Bramston Show*. Regular *Oz* contributors and countercultural writers Hughes, Ellis and Moorhouse were all working journalists at the *Bulletin*, *Nation* and/or the ABC. *Oz* co-editor and artist Sharp produced cartoons for Horne's *Bulletin* and designed record covers and posters for bands such as Cream. Underground filmmaker and Ubu Films founder Albie Thoms trained at the ABC and made commercial television series such as *Skippy* and *Contrabandits*.

Robert Hughes would break new ground in delivering art education via television, writing and presenting a series of accessible documentaries such as *Art in Australia* and *The Shock of the New*. Bob Ellis secured the job of researcher on the innovative new ABC current affairs program, *This Day Tonight*, where the traditional stolid style of news reporting gave way to a deeper style of analysis combining intelligence and opinion with humour and irreverence. In Britain Germaine Greer and Clive James became 'talking heads' for television, sought after because they were skilful media performers. James would tackle the medium of TV itself, as television critic for the *Observer* and eventually transformed his insights and performance style into television programs mocking TV.

Neville attributed his bohemian awakening not to university but to the skills and ideas he picked up in advertising. 'Adland taught me the basics of printing, lay-out and come hither headlines,' he confessed in his memoir, *Hippie Hippie Shake*, but it also provided valuable insights into how consumerism worked, which turned up in the article 'The Crime of Big Business', written for *Tharunka*.

In the same vein Bob Ellis recounted the mentoring in skills, contacts and knowledge he received from the eccentric Francis James when employed editing *Anglican Year Book* while at *Honi Soit*. Humphries mastered musical performance while treading the boards as Fagin in the West End and Broadway productions of *Oliver!* in the mid-1960s, and song-and-dance routines were introduced into his one-man shows which made the leap from fringe venues such as London's Establishment Club to commercial hits. After slumming in the 'Alternative Press' in the late 1960s, Clive James paid tribute to the lessons in epigrammatic style he learned from Fleet Street editors such as the *Listener*'s Karl Miller and the *Times Literary Supplement*'s Ian Hamilton.

Some had difficulty conforming to work discipline, and missed the freer creative life they had enjoyed as students. Ellis was sacked from the *Sydney Morning Herald* for inattention to detail on the shipping news, and was almost dismissed from the ABC after describing its management as 'pickled pontiffs' in an *Oz* article.[28] James, relishing the role of the grub street hack in his memoir, reported frustration at having to produce formulaic material, 'scraps that added up to a pittance' in order to support his bohemian lifestyle and partner, and worried that '[e]ven the byline journalists tended to die poor'.[29]

Answering to a manager or editor as a jobbing journalist, TV producer or copywriter would never be enough for some, and it was precisely this quest for creative autonomy outside their day job that distinguished bohemian artists from the pack of media workers. The common pattern in the 1960s and 70s was for countercultural bohemians to enjoy regular if intermittent employment in the commercial and government media, while simultaneously working on 'do-it-yourself' projects in which they enjoyed greater creative freedom. Robert Hughes painted while writing for *Nation*, Clive James combined poetry and song writing with a job on Fleet Street and Albie Thoms directed the underground film *Blunderball* while at the ABC. Frank Moorhouse juggled teaching, a column at the *Bulletin* and a literary grant to survive while writing *The Americans, Baby*.

Of course they came up against commercial problems like production bills and distribution, and tough state government laws censoring content in media. In practice, young innovators faced the perennial bohemian challenge of establishing a community conducive to creativity and media for communicating with audiences, while earning enough to earn a living and reinvest in their projects. Fortunately for the generation coming of age in the 1960s and 70s, they had the advantage of new technologies that aided small-scale independent production such as offset printing and cheap hand-held movie cameras.

OZ AND THE UNDERGROUND PRESS

While Australia had a long tradition of little magazines and independent publishing ventures, the 1960s underground press emerged from experiments in student campus journalism. Ellis observed that the Sydney University paper *Honi Soit* 'got me writing, and from that sort of writing into the ABC, and screenwriting, and film direction, theatre owning, books on politics, plays. They taught me – and Clive, and Germaine – the variety of things we could possibly do with words and punctuation. They gave us a new dimension to work in.'

But first of all they wrote for *Oz*. While affording the editors, writers and designers far more creative licence than was experienced in the commercial sector, the student editors nevertheless had to answer to the Student Representative Councils and university authorities. Moreover, the harsh state obscenity laws that operated throughout the 1960s curtailed blasphemy, obscenity and especially sexual content. In 1964 *Oz* grew out of its editors' frustration as consumers and aspiring journalists at how out of touch the stories and aesthetics within the mainstream media of the early 1960s seemed with the ideas and style of young people. Neville recalled, 'We pooled our views on the seismic shifts in the cultural landscape: the new protest music, pop art, the Pill, sick humour, the stirrings of Aboriginal rights, and the growing revelation that it may not be necessary … to live the same lives as our fathers.'[30]

A company was formed with Neville, Sharp and Walsh as co-editors, a 'weekend office' found in a joinery workshop at The Rocks, and a team of volunteers assembled from student and professional journalism. Although *Oz* was an independent company, it enjoyed considerable symbiosis from the outset with the mainstream media outlets through its personnel. *Nation* correspondent Robert Hughes, ABC journalist Frank Moorhouse and Fairfax cadet Bob Ellis threw in their pens as freelance columnists. The attraction was that *Oz* allowed them a free space to experiment with stories and styles unacceptable in their day jobs.

Satire and absurdity marked the magazine out from other worthy avant-garde and radical publications, such as the Communist Party's *Tribune* and the intellectual journals *Meanjin* and *Nation*. It had more in common with the social satire of the university and the downtown Phillip Street revues and new television sketch comedy *The Mavis Bramston Show*. The first issue, published in April 1963, featured a 'Dear Diary' account of the accident-prone 1963 royal tour by the Queen, a photograph of a man in a chastity belt about to be unlocked by a woman and an interview with a backyard abortionist.

Subsequent issues took aim at less predictable targets, and went full throttle with the absurd. Robert Hughes wrote a parody of a 'Ban the Bomb' march that deployed an Andersonian critique of the infant peace movement's clichés and authoritarianism. In a self-reflexive vein Frank Moorhouse detected middle-class snobbery in the growing popularity of Humphries' Edna Everage. Patricia Rolfe conducted an interview with God, while Bob Ellis penned a Freudian analysis of the sexually frustrated Donald Duck. Other targets included Harry Siedler's modernist architecture, 'Alf' culture, Arthur Miller and an Underworld Top 20 profile of Sydney's gangsters.

Oz stands out in the history of Australian 'little magazines' by its comfortable blend of Andersonian libertarianism critical of 'authoritarian' governing institutions, a larrikin sense of humour cultivated within the Push, enjoyment of japes long tolerated in university students' celebrations, a visual literacy in pop art courtesy of Martin Sharp and a critical appreciation of popular culture and the mass media itself. *Angry Penguins*, by comparison, was concerned with 'high art', and was earnest in its radicalism. Not since the early *Bulletin* had an Australian publication had so much fun mocking the mediascape that surrounded it. *Oz* had populist ambitions beyond avant-garde 'little magazines', reflected in the circulation figures and its longevity for an independent publication. Thanks to a poster campaign around Sydney and a newsagent distribution deal, the first issue of *Oz* sold out all 6000 copies on the first day, and went to reprint. By 1964 circulation in Sydney was 10,000 and when the magazine went national in 1965 circulation approached 40,000.[31] Importantly, Neville drew on his advertising skills to ensure a revenue stream by selling space to department stores, theatres, pop concerts, surf wear, restaurants and bookshops.[32]

The limits of free speech were tested when the New South Wales police charged *Oz*'s editors for publishing obscenity in 1963 and 1964. During the 1960s and early 70s the state, rather than the market, was viewed as the main limiter of youth and bohemian freedom. In 1955 the New South Wales Labor government had introduced the Obscene and Indecent Publications Amendment Bill. Neville, Walsh and Sharp challenged the 1964 charge on the defence that *Oz* 'was of literary or artistic merit', but were jailed, bailed and appealed.[33] Taking on the strict state government laws against obscenity was also a way to attract publicity and aid circulation. By drawing media attention to the restriction of artistic freedom of expression – a longstanding bohemian cause – the editors attracted the support and bourgeois cultural capital of the older liberal anti-censorship movement, such as Anglican Church publisher Francis James, who had lent his press to print the offending issue. The controversy surrounding an initial verdict of guilty generated the 'buzz' that Pierre Bourdieu argued helped new artists make their mark in the cultural marketplace.[34] 'For the three of us,' Neville conceded in his memoir, 'it was a taste of celebrity. Students wanted our speeches, glossy mags wanted our portraits, girls wanted our good vibrations.'

The court's finding in 1965 that *Oz* had literary merit was a significant victory, encouraging other cultural activists to eschew the customary self-censorship. *Oz* continued under Richard Walsh until 1969 and much of its iconoclasm migrated to a new weekly which he edited from 1972, *Nation Review*. Meanwhile Neville and Sharp took the *Oz* franchise to 'Swinging' London in 1967. There in 1971 it provoked another obscenity trial, a period of jail, and a skilful mobilisation of publicity to the eventual benefit of the editors.[35]

Oz was the local trailblazer for an international and Australian revolution in 'underground' publishing, defined by Frank Moorhouse as 'a western-wide movement expressing a rebellion against censorship, especially sexual censorship', made possible by the spread of offset printing technology.[36] *Oz* was one of the first Australian magazines to use the new technology, finding it not only saved money and enhanced the visual design, but that its shorter set-up time was a boon to guerrilla-style publishing where speed and secrecy were paramount. The large hot-metal printing houses had traditionally acted as censors of independent publications for the authorities. Now lower unit costs meant runs of 10,000 could break even – a significant circulation. Offset printing also enhanced experimentation with the aesthetic of pastiche, in which *Oz*, for example, would take headlines and images from tabloid papers and reassemble them to create new meanings in the manner of Dada collage. As presses became cheaper and more plentiful the number of underground magazines doubled, from fifty in 1970 to over a hundred – including *Thorunka*, *High Times*, *Troll*, *Super Plague*, *Mejane*, *Cane Toad Times*, *Ubu News* and *Eyeball* – at the decade's end.

BOHEMIANS FOR SALE

Despite the headlines in some tabloids warning parents about sexual permissiveness and illicit drug use, consumer capitalism had an interest in countercultures challenging the state to free up what was morally acceptable to be worn on the street, heard on the radio, broadcast on television and seen in the cinema. Coalition and right-leaning Labor governments in the mid-1960s, on the other hand, were bewildered by the cultural excesses of an economic transformation that their own pro-business policies promoted. The younger tertiary-educated bohemians who had grown up as consumers were attuned to this new economy and tooled up to satisfy its hunger for fashion, music, media, even food and drink, with countercultural cachet.

Whereas working-class subcultures like bodgies or, in the seventies, sharpies offered escape from mundane occupations, 'hippy' and later 'punk' countercultures blurred distinctions between consumption and production. For a lucky few, such as Richard Branson in Britain and Michael Gudinski in Melbourne, this transformed DIY music, publishing or fashion into a business. In some cases, such as the alternative music magazine *Rolling Stone* and independent record labels Virgin and Gudinski's Mushroom (in the US, UK and Australia respectively), cottage industries became large commercial corporations. By nurturing a small business, the loyal countercultural market allowed the cultural entrepreneur to enjoy the bourgeois individualism of economic capitalism with the hip cover of providing 'authentic' and 'alternative' goods and services. But more commonly an independent project burns brightly for a brief moment until funds and enthusiasm ebb in the face of commercial realities, legal action, the exhaustion of the original idea or attraction to new projects. This occurred with Australian and London *Oz*, *Thorunka* and the Yellow House, but the ideas, aesthetics and personnel were embraced by mainstream cultural industries on the lookout for 'street cred' or the next big thing.

A Martin Sharp cover for London Oz, no. 12, May 1968, demonstrating the satirical publication's late 1960s move into the pop-surrealism of 'psychedelia', the new romanticism of the hippy movement and a more permissive sexuality.

THE REAL THING: PSYCHEDELIA FOR THE MASSES

The countercultures brought together the two strands of carnivalesque literary bohemia and the artist hero that had diverged even further under high modernism in the 1930s and 40s. Like the press-based literary bohemians, the countercultural creatives appealed to mass commercial audiences through journalism, television, rock music and film, and promoted a carnivalesque sense of play that emphasised fun, humour, mockery and vulgarity. Yet they also considered themselves romantic artists and visionaries in the manner of the avant-garde, and drew on modernism. One example of this synthesis, in which Australian artists at home and in Britain played a part, was the aesthetic of 'psychedelia'.

A multicoloured, trippy variant of surrealism, psychedelia spread rapidly from a small avant-grade practice into the heart of commercial youth culture, illuminating music, decoration, fashion and performance. The vector was artists working in both fields, notably Martin Sharp, whose experiments with the synthesised and yet-to-be-banned hallucinogenic drug LSD produced a new vividly coloured look for London *Oz*, and inspired a series of underground 'happenings', both confronting and carnivalesque, which combined music, theatre, dance and cinema with copious quantities of acid. Unconsciously, these artists were tripping along the same journey as Marcus Clarke's hash-inspired writing experiments of a century earlier. Albie Thoms found Ubu's surrealist quest to deconstruct and subvert film narrative was enhanced by LSD, and collaborated with Sharp in the staging of these avant-garde experiences in Europe and Australia.[37] This partnership culminated in the Yellow House of 1971, a live-in mix of artists' commune and multimedia gallery in Kings Cross 'for the people of Sydney to play in', featuring work by Sharp, Thoms, Brett Whiteley, George Gittoes and Marie Briebauer, among many others.[38] The social cachet and carnivalesque spirit was more akin to the hijinks of the 1920s Artists' Balls and the ambience of the Charm School of Sydney's late 1940s than the surrealist avant-garde of the Angry Penguins.

Yet alongside these rather exclusive underground events Sharp produced psychedelic posters of pop icons Dylan,

Donovan and Hendrix that sold worldwide through Big O posters. He happily lent his design flair to Atlantic Records, creating iconic psychedelic covers for the British band Cream's albums *Disraeli Gears* and *Wheels of Fire*, and even wrote a track with Eric Clapton. Back in Australia, the Loved Ones, the Masters Apprentices and Russell Morris made a similar leap from countercultural to mainstream commercial success via the pop surrealism of psychedelia.[39] Albie Thoms was able to introduce aspects of surrealism he experimented with in his films *Blunderball* (1966) and *Marinetti* (1969) into the ABC music television program he directed in the early seventies, *GTK* (which aired at 6.30 pm for 10 minutes before *Bellbird*), providing underground bands with experimental film clips, and contributing to the emerging art form of music video. At ABC radio's new youth station 2JJ from the mid 1970s, recently arrived English iconoclast Tony Barrell introduced avant-garde audio art experiments informed by Dada and surrealism such as montage 'cut ups' (from old movie soundtracks, comedies and dramas), and richly layered aural soundscapes, into new non-linear documentary series exploring society and culture such as *Watching the Radio with the TV Turned Off*. Surrealism was an important part of modernism and had resurfaced as an aesthetic among successive bohemias in Australia. But it took the pop psychedelia of counterculture artists working in music, design and broadcasting for surrealism to have a popular impact in Australia as well as in Britain and the United States.

Other countercultural ideas and styles moved from the underground to commercial youth culture. Sexual freedom and social libertarianism, ribald humour, appreciation of nature and bucolic communal retreats, transcendence through Third World travel, non-Christian 'New Age' spirituality (typified by the Aquarius Festival held in Nimbin in 1972), drugs and, from 1968, the politics of peace, protest, revolution and identity took hold in mainstream youth culture.

Romantic counterculture themes and iconography found their way into advertisements selling fashion, stationery, cigarettes and even petrol. Rebellion was commodified in jeans, TV shows and the ubiquitous Che Guevara posters. Countercultural slogans such as the 'real thing' were used by the Coca-Cola corporation to convince young consumers of the drink's authenticity when compared to Pepsi. In the early 1970s Lindeman's cask wine was presented as the tipple for hammock-swinging, laidback yet discerning hippy types who might have stepped out of a Renoir painting into a country hideaway. This ad was the brainchild of Peter Carey, who while writing short stories coined the slogan 'You make me smile, Dr Lindeman'. Likewise, Phillip Adams established his own advertising agency while making films and writing columns. These bohemian ad men (Bad Men?) knew how to deploy the cultural nuances necessary to appear genuine to a younger generation of consumers.

In 1970, London's conservative *Daily Mail* praised the influence of the 'Underground' on art, fashion, television, 'even the Beatles'.[40] The ingredients that mainstream youth industries and their consumers craved from the counterculture were the traditional bohemian values of authenticity and transgression. For example, 'rock' owed its post-'67 aura of authenticity as much to its bohemian idea (smuggled in through folk, psychedelia and other 'progressive' genres) of the rock star as visionary artist hero as to its black roots. A number of 'progressive' Australian bands on major labels identified explicitly with the counterculture and promoted its values while enjoying commercial success. These groups included the Masters Apprentices, Billy Thorpe and the Aztecs, and Carlton scene insiders Daddy Cool, the Captain Matchbox Whoopee Band, Spectrum, MacKenzie Theory and, most famously, Skyhooks, whose initial fan base was mainly drawn from the sharpie subculture. Mushroom also supported a local heavy blues scene featuring acts like Lobby Loyde and the Coloured Balls that attracted both countercultural and working-class aficionados of the genre. The crossover of the counterculture and commercial pop climaxed in Australia's answer to Woodstock, Sunbury. These four open-air rock festivals, held on the outskirts of Melbourne between 1972 and 1975, were organised by members of the commercial television industry and Mushroom entrepreneur Gudinski who produced a live album. The concerts drew fans from around the country.

From Dylan to Bowie, *Oz* to Sunbury, the countercultures had a much cheaper entrance fee than the avant-garde, who sold to haute-bourgeois fine-art buyers. What changed in the 1960s was that cultural commodities – a Martin Sharp poster, the 'live' *Sunbury* album – were constructed as works of art within the countercultural milieu, and then mass-produced and mass marketed. Blundell observed that '[t]he avant-garde, political and cultural, for the first time in its history, became the glass of fashion'.[41]

Australian bohemians beginning with Marcus Clarke and Charles Conder had created dandy styles to communicate identity to those who could read the codes. Clive James described the late 1960s as another era of dandies. Within countercultures it was important to wear the latest underground fashion, collect the right records, personalise your 'pad' with hip decoration, buy the right drugs. By arranging a cool ensemble of consumer items – such as a leather trench coat, an Afghan jacket and Indian beads, a paisley or army shirt – countercultural bohemians communicated distinction from the mainstream and their membership of a particular group. London *Oz* became a guide on how to dress. Expatriate art school graduate Jenny Kee began selling original 'flower child' clothing designs out of a stall at the Portobello Road markets and then opened her own boutique in Carnaby Street. Off-the-rack hippy gear was soon available in Pitt and Bourke streets, by which time the bohemian edge had moved on to new styles.

FROM CRITICS TO CELEBRITIES

The emphasis on popular culture and mass-media communication enabled countercultural artists such as Sharp, Neville, Hughes and Greer, together with the more traditional bohemians James and Humphries to distinguish themselves from the older established modernist avant-garde favourites of galleries, academics and critics who limited themselves to traditional media and the field of limited production. However, by the later 1960s, and credentialled with university degrees, Greer, Roxon, Neville, Ellis and James had joined slightly older academics such as Craig McGregor as critics capable of reviewing countercultural, popular and traditional arts, making a mark by their ability to collapse categories, 'transcend[ing] the self-imposed bounds of good taste', and did so in new and old media.[42] Without abandoning his literary ambitions James marvelled at his 'TV column's buzz-making prominence from week to week'.[43] They had the knack of being simultaneously highbrow and pop. James later described in his 2006 *Unreliable Memoirs* the approach he worked out in his *Listener* and *Observer* columns as a forerunner of a 'postmodern' approach that analysed popular culture, such as television comedy, as if it were as important as so-called high art, rather than dismissing it, but also doing so in a playful, entertaining manner.[44] A similar approach to criticism was demonstrated by Phillip Adams in the *Australian* newspaper, Ellis in the *Bulletin* and *Nation Review*, Hughes in his books and television documentaries of art history, and Neville and Greer in London *Oz*, the mainstream press and their controversial first books, *Play Power* and *The Female Eunuch* respectively.

Reflecting on their youth, James, Neville and Ellis were surprisingly candid about their drive to be famous, and talent for self-promotion. Clive James, an acute observer of literary and media markets in his memoirs, commented that the appearance of the *Oz* editors at the Old Bailey in 1970 'was a mere prelude to their appearance on television ... the trial was a stage: a stage on the road to institutionalised protest'.[45] In 1965, in the wake of the Sydney *Oz* trial, Neville was given his first regular column as a film reviewer for the *Sydney Morning Herald*, and as controversial editor of the London *Oz* he became a regular 'youth' commentator in the broadsheet press and on the BBC, eventually securing a column called 'Alternative Society' in the *Evening Standard* and hosting 'The Neville Report' on the BBC's *Eleventh Hour Show*, followed by another television show, *How It Is*.[46]

As a literature scholar at Melbourne, Sydney and Cambridge universities, Germaine Greer had been an enthusiastic disciple of F.R. Leavis – a harsh critic of commercial mass culture. An acclaimed comedic performance in the Cambridge Footlights Theatre tempted her from the ivory tower into the limelight, beginning with a provocative and amusing exposé for London *Oz*, 'In Bed With the English', in which Greer's sexually assertive and larrikin Australian bohemian persona was let loose on the English male. Greer embraced the new pop culture, especially rock'n'roll, sensing its liberating possibilities, while bemoaning that 'the capitalist system has the power to absorb and exploit all tendencies, including the tendencies towards its own over-throw'.[47] Never one for half-measures, she ambiguously satirised the 'rock groupie', confronting the sexuality of the music scene head on as *Oz* music critic, and rehearsing themes of female sexual agency she would explore in *The Female Eunuch*.[48] Greer was not above bodily exposure, appearing naked and crotch-first for *Suck* magazine and in an article on female sexuality bid women to embrace 'cunt-power'.[49] Greer's enthusiasm for the new gurus of rock'n'roll and gift for popularising complex, confronting ideas was a huge leap from Leavis's condemnation of modern mass media.

Intergenerational conflict was inevitable, even relished. Richard Walsh opened up the pages of *Nation Review* to several generations of critics and encouraged debate on aesthetics. Over a series of articles the formidable Max Harris debated Phillip Adams, Barry Humphries and Bob Ellis over the emergence of the 'ocker' trend in cinema, theatre and television, for him the betrayal of his generation's struggle for sophistication. Such attacks, which in this case spilled over into other media, had the effect of elevating the younger players through controversy. Clive James claimed that in retrospect he came to realise how attacks from journalists were 'boosting my stock in trade'.[50] *Review* was joined in the 1970s by other 'industry' publications that emerging artists established to help consecrate new approaches, including *Ubu News* and *Cinema Papers*. As with earlier artists' societies, new sanctifying institutions also had to be erected to strengthen counterculture networks. The Sydney Filmmakers Co-op was created to pool resources and staff so more experimental films could be made, and La Mama and the Australian Performance Group was founded in Melbourne by Betty Burstall to implement avant-garde ideas in theatre. In London, Push film luminary Bruce Beresford was put in charge of commissioning for the British Film Institute's experimental film initiative.

Eager to leap on the bandwagon, commercial companies could grant a degree of creative freedom to favoured artists. Russell Morris's number one hit of 1969 was called 'The Real Thing', and in a way it was. Morris and his producer, *Go-Set* magazine's editor Ian Meldrum, kept EMI executives out of the studio while they experimented with new techniques pioneered on the later Beatles' albums to produce a nine-minute, boundary-pushing psychedelic epic – a happy confluence of risk taking and popularity.[51] As an iconoclastic columnist, Phillip Adams was guaranteed rare freedom of expression in his contract by his employer Rupert Murdoch, who is on record as stating profitability was not his prime aim in establishing the *Australian* in 1964.[52]

Bohemian artists sought wealth and fame, but also wanted to maximise opportunities for creative expression. This was what Marcus Clarke achieved with his 'Peripatetic Philosopher' column in the *Argus*. In the 1960s and 70s some young people used the profile gained through underground publishing to leverage space within the mainstream media and entertainment industries to establish reputations as 'artists', and were eventually provided the material and contractual freedom to work independently. James explained how publishing a well-reviewed book of his collected columns so impressed the *Observer* that they placed him 'on a stipend that any unattached freelance would have recognised as top whack, and certainly no staff writer would be doing better'.[53] Likewise, on the strength of his *Oz* reputation, Richard Walsh was given a free hand by the owner of *Nation Review* to synthesise countercultural issues with a mainstream news agenda to produce an innovative paper of national significance. Gordon Barton, the eccentric proprietor, entrepreneur, and 'Liberal reform' campaigner had come through the Push a generation earlier, and was committed to editorial freedom on principle.[54] Indeed, when Barton was to have a media interview at *Nation Review* he had to call from a pay phone for directions.

Government intervention to fund and produce culture could also temper the market and confer autonomy for producers. Moorhouse and Ellis left regular jobs at the ABC when their independent published work had sufficient profile for them to qualify for funds from the Commonwealth Literary Fund, land publishing contracts with advances, or earn a living writing books, plays, or opinionated copy in newspapers and magazines. On getting his first 'special purposes' grant in the late 1960s, Moorhouse recalled seeing his name written up in the newspaper by veteran literary critic Elizabeth Riddell: 'from being an unemployed journalist with his first book a phantom, read only by six reviewers in Australia, I had become a "Sydney writer"'.[55] Grants such as these had the effect of anointing emerging creatives, and even Libertarian writers such as Moorhouse and Thoms, opposed in principle to the concept of state patronage in their younger Push days, found the money irresistible as long as it did not mandate aesthetics, with the former calling grants 'superphosphate for culture'.[56]

Thoms and fellow part-time underground filmmakers Peter Weir and Tim Burstall were able to leave their day jobs in television and advertising when the Gorton government established the experimental film fund. All three men received grants to study avant-garde film overseas and to showcase their work at various international film festivals. The inquiry establishing government intervention to create a film industry was undertaken by Phillip Adams, together with Andersonian Liberal Peter Coleman and Labor Fabian Barry Jones, both intellectual politicians with an interest in the arts. They concluded that if left solely to the market, Australian stories would not be told in cinema, and argued for the funding of both an avant-garde and a commercial stream. For the latter, the government established a film bank, the Australian Film Development Corporation, to loan capital to producers to make more commercial films that would win a popular audience. Funding by federal and state government agencies meant Australian directors were free from the power of studios and distributors that limited autonomy within the Hollywood system.

In the spirit of Australian countercultural artists working across markets, one of the first commercial feature films of the 1970s revival was *Stork* (1971), directed by Tim Burstall and set in the sexually permissive and frankly gross shared houses and pubs of the Carlton bohemian scene. In the early 1970s the federal government and some state governments moved rapidly to liberalise the censorship of transgressive cultural works such as *The Little Red School Book*, and introduced the new 'Restricted' classification, allowing adults over the age of eighteen to view films that were sexually explicit, such as Phillip Adams' satirical documentary on Australian sexual habits, *The Naked Bunyip*, and a succession of sex comedies that came in its wake.

BUYING BOHEMIANISM

Perhaps the biggest change by the late 1960s was that bohemian identities themselves were being manufactured and sold in the mass market to young people who wanted to share in the rebel identity. Whereas bohemianism had since Murger been available to aspiring artists with the necessary cultural capital, these options were increasingly marketed to young people of all occupations and classes. Richard Neville described how the Broadway musical *Hair* hit all the right buttons for him when he first saw it in New York: 'I saw my fantasies take wing – sex, satire, soul, pot, rock and revolution, with a draft dodger hero, and the leading lady consorting with two drop outs … Surely the cultural revolution is unstoppable now.'[57]

However, *Hair* was also one of the most blatant examples of the commodification of countercultural identity. In Australia, show-business promoter Harry M. Miller teamed up with underground Ubu filmmaker and theatre director Jim Sharman to produce a local version in 1969 that crashed through the nudity barrier and was a commercial hit. In the late 1960s bohemian personalities – adorning posters, record covers and magazines – became lifestyle guides to a cross-class audience of young people living in the suburbs who yearned to emulate the rebel style, from sartorial extravagance, experimenting with sex and mind-altering drugs, to exotic travel or playing 'progressive rock' in garages.

For a time in the 1970s some Australian commentators and artists – notably Greer, Neville and Sharp, who were most strongly identified with countercultural controversy, but also Humphries and Hughes – became a neo-bohemian 'A list' for the media in Britain and Australia, as famous for their eccentric lifestyles and over-the-top personalities as for their work. There was a backlash within the movement against those with too much success or profile. Sharp fell out with Neville, a self-confessed 'headline junkie', accusing him of being an 'opportunist' who rushed off to the BBC 'to play leader of the Underground … [whose] motives are questionable – the stirring up of predictable controversy in search of applause.'[58] However Neville and Greer were doing no more with their skills – as writers and talking heads – than Sharp was doing as an illustrator for commercially successful rock bands, playing the popular as well as the avant-garde cultural field.

The accusation that the countercultural leaders and artists 'sold out', or were 'co-opted' misses the point. The movement between markets was a deliberate negotiation in which counterculture commentators and artists debated in articles and books the aesthetic and political reasons for being popular. Craig McGregor was impatient with the elitism of the older left and applauded the young intelligentsia when it found common cause with the creativity of working-class suburban youth. Greer argued that the Rolling Stones' commercial corruption was necessary to reach the unconverted; to help 'thousands of kids to burst out', music 'must reach a mass audience'.[59] More radically, Frank Moorhouse believed that the growing diversity of society made the distinction between fringe and the popular irrelevant and argued for an art of media disruption.[60] Neville argued that anyway, the media was different from drab, routine jobs in the straight world, because 'media is substitute play', an 'element fizzled out [in] established culture in the nineteenth century, when work was sanctified' but 'media has kept play alive'.[61] He is perhaps alluding to the history of the bohemian carnivalesque in the media, which I have argued made newspapers, magazines, cinema and other popular culture industries sites of genuine contestation between creators, managers and audiences, from the time of Marcus Clarke and the early *Bulletin*.

The enthusiastic participation of the bohemians of the 1960s and 70s in the popular culture industries as consumers, producers and promoters of youth styles played an important role in making identity itself into a consumer item by the 1970s, 80s and 90s, extending to everyone who was interested the old bohemian trick of signifying identity by a particular ensemble of fashion, music, décor, behaviour and argot. Countercultures introduced into wider consumption the bohemian skill of 'aestheticising' style to convey a subcultural distinction from other consumers. This was a far cry from mass conformity, but as the trend accelerated over the next two decades some sixties radicals came to lament the cult of the self they had helped to popularise. In 1979 British literary academic Malcolm Bradbury observed that 'there are bohemians on every street corner, self-parodists in every boutique, neo-artists in every discotheque'.[62] By contributing to the identity and image industries of late twentieth-century capitalism, countercultures since the 1960s democratised among a wider population a field of creative expression that in the past had largely been the privilege of bourgeois bohemians on the fringe.

• • •

It is wrong to single out the 1960s countercultures as either purist idealists or as 'sell-outs'. Bohemians had always tried to have a bet each way. Tamed-down versions of bohemia had long been sold as products in Australia, beginning with theatrical shows, magazine articles and items of clothing such as Trilby shirts in the 1880s and 90s. The oppositional narrative of autonomy versus capitalism is as old as romanticism, and it suited artists and their fans to play on it. It influenced how countercultural artists thought about themselves, signified by terms like 'underground', 'guerrilla', 'revolution' and 'counter'.

But while they stressed market independence, shock value and authenticity typical of the older bohemianism of the Heidelberg painters or Angry Penguins, they differed radically in their enthusiasm for producing for the mass market. As with the earlier literary bohemians of the *Bulletin* and *Smith's Weekly*, talented 1960s bohemians found themselves working within mainstream industries, or themselves becoming entrepreneurs within the counterculture. In some cases the young radicals became celebrities, creating themselves as a product to be marketed at consumers.

This synthesis between avant-garde and popular bohemia, of the artist hero with the carnivalesque, harked back to Marcus Clarke's cultural practice before modernist hierarchies of high and low art became entrenched in the late nineteenth century. But it was also the beginning of postmodernity in culture, in the sense of collapsing these boundaries, and more radically because identity itself was now for sale. Equally important was the large youth market's clamour to consume and participate, however vicariously, in transgression and authenticity via fashion, posters, magazines, records, radio, television and mass concerts, resulting in a bohemianisation of popular youth culture where the identity

itself was commodified as a lifestyle option. The trick for creators was to stay ahead of homogenisation and obsolescence. The
late-sixties countercultures' popularity would eventually ebb,
but the bohemianisation of youth culture, now established,
would regularly recur during the 1970s, 80s and 90s. In terms
of Australia's bohemian tradition, by the end of the 1980s the
cultural capital to 'try bohemianism', as Clarke had bid his
readers do, was available to ever more people.

8

THE REVOLUTION WILL BE BOHEMIANISED: COUNTERCULTURES AND RADICAL POLITICS

1965–1980

The blending of the personal and the cultural with the political which had occupied the relatively insulated Push and Drift subcultures in the 1950s and early 60s became the dominant form of a new youth radicalism from 1968, centred on university students, but extending far and wide into artists' communities, the media, left politics and even popular youth culture. Countercultural radicals attempted to hybridise New Left politics with a bohemian valuing of the symbolic, the outrageous and the playful. But as in the 1890s they had to negotiate longstanding tensions between bohemianism and political activism, individualism and the collective, spontaneity and bureaucracy, cosmopolitanism and nationalism. These tensions had frustrated earlier attempts to transform bohemia's opposition to the bourgeoisie into a more explicit bohemian politics in the 1890s and between the wars. Conflict arose again as the countercultural radicals ran the gauntlet of harsh government censorship, the class politics of the traditional left, and the temptations of patronage by the Whitlam government. Yet during the 1970s media, culture and identity itself became important to politics.

The new cultural radicalism was born of conflict between countercultural groups and the state over censorship and, most spectacularly, the war in Vietnam and conscription. But their entry into politics brought them into conflict not only with conservative Coalition governments, but with older activists and intellectuals of the left who were hostile to the countercultural emphasis on the symbolic, the body and the inner world of the mind, on play and popular culture. Writing in 2002 Alan Barcan, who had been a player in the liberal New Left that emerged in the 1950s and early 1960s, despaired that a profound cultural shift occurred in Australia and the west from 1967, most keenly felt in progressive politics and education and driven by student protests and the countercultures. A romantic and irrational new radicalism had been set loose distinguished by lifestyle, personal and 'special interest group' politics and a nihilism destructive of the enlightenment project.[1] For many labourites and radicals, including some Libertarians, long-haired 'hippies' staging sit-ins and street theatre created disorder that obstructed the cause of reform.

'MY GENERATION' AND THE POLITICS OF YOUTH

A belief in state socialism and class lost its centrality for many of the radicals at university in Australia in the first half of the 1960s.[2] While the change was in part due to the influence of anarchism and Libertarianism within, especially at Sydney University, there were also other causes. Old left illusions about the radical potential of the proletariat were replaced by the regret among some left intellectuals in working-class 'embourgeoisement' and conservatism, fuelled by the impact of postwar consumerism and rising home ownership in working-class communities. But most significant was the emergence of a new 'youth' consciousness. While clearly linked to the new teenage youth market of the 1950s and 60s, the concept of 'youth power' also had its origins in the experiences of bourgeois university students attracted to a déclassé bohemian form of radicalism.

Whereas bohemian radicals involved with the late nineteenth-century labour movement or the Communist Party in the 1930s had romanticised the egalitarianism or revolutionary potential of the working class, student radicals from the mid-1960s began to romanticise themselves as a new force for change. Students could imagine themselves as a mass force because for the first time in Australia there were so many of them, thanks to the baby boom, and to federal and state government policies expanding places and access to university through funding increases and scholarships. It is ironic that in expanding tertiary education Menzies created the conditions for a vocal opposition to his other policies. While journalistic retrospectives have focused on the conflict between young radicals and the right-wing conservatives in the Liberal and Country parties and the RSL, the new youth radicalism revived an older bohemian critique of class-based solidarity politics. By deploying the idea of idealistic youth and a 'generation gap', cultural radicals such as Richard Neville could avoid tensions that had arisen over the past century when bohemians joined with working-class movements.

Bohemia was essentially a bourgeois movement that portrayed itself as classless. In the past, separation from the bourgeoisie could be conveyed by identification with the working class, in the manner of the *Bulletin* bohemians or the Push, but in the 1960s the identity of 'youth' was an even more effective way to appear déclassé. University students, while heading for the professions, management within the private or public sector or the expanding technocratic intelligentsia, were temporarily outside their parents' class and denied the positions to which background, education and qualification would eventually entitle them.

Among the young sixties cultural radicals, Richard Neville, Martin Sharp, Robert Hughes, Jim Anderson and Craig McGregor were typical of a large proportion of student bohemians who had attended elite private schools and came from professional and business backgrounds. Neville attended Knox on Sydney's north shore. His father had risen to the rank of colonel in the Second World War and was publisher of the conservative journal *Country Life*, and his mother, the daughter of opera diva Bertha Fanning, was an occasional short-story writer. Sharp, 'the son of a high-society skin specialist', and McGregor attended Cranbrook in the eastern suburbs.[3] A survey of Monash University radicals in 1971 found sixty per cent came from upper middle-class families.[4] By identifying with youth they distinguished themselves from the ruling class from which they sprang.

By making youth itself the radical class of change, bohemians from bourgeois backgrounds, or heading to bourgeois futures, could still identify as the agents of history – at least while young. Sharp wrote to his father: 'It's age against youth, conservatism against inevitable change, whether the actual form of suppression is obscenity, vagrancy or the illegal possession of substances. This change will come as certainly as I, too, will age and become more rigid in my thoughts.'[5] Neville has since argued, quite validly, that '[b]eing white and privileged, as we were, gave no immunity from a feeling of cultural suffocation, a sense of deadness at our nation's core'.[6] However the new youth discourse meant Neville did not have to romanticise the proletariat, arguing that '[t]he Workers know the revolution's done for fun – not them. And anyway, they hate the dirt and hair and polysyllables'.[7] The abandonment of class could reflect upper middle-class prejudice. Alienation could cut across class boundaries. The difference was that these bourgeois rebels had the cultural know-how and contacts to take risks and 'get away with it' when it came to showdowns with the state. Neville complained that his encounters with working-class people were chiefly with hostile police and customs officers and he had little time for manual workers who acquiesced in their own exploitation and alienation. What of socially mobile students from lower middle-class and working-class families? Like the hip mod hero Colin in the novel *Absolute Beginners*, students from non-bourgeois backgrounds, such as Ellis, James and Greer, could leave those identifications behind and begin again in the cause of youth, though it was a harder slog for James and Ellis.[8] James described his parents as a 'prime example of the suffering proletariat in the 1930s'. Ellis's father was a coalminer. Both James and Ellis were candid in their memoirs about the game of getting on, the necessity of working harder and being 'a social climber' when you were not born with networks, confidence and a sense of entitlement.[9]

As with emerging generations of bohemians in the 1890s and interwar years, the counterculture radicals played generational rhetoric hard. While British rock band The Who, decked out in costumes referencing late eighteenth-century dandies, may have sung 'I hope I die before I get old' in the baby-boomer signature song 'My Generation', the concept of youth was in practice elastic. Older bohemian radicals such as Greer, Moorhouse and

Hughes, who were thirty in 1969, cooperated with the younger people still in their twenties such as Neville, Sharp, Bacon and Fell, lending their career networks and qualifications to countercultural projects such as *Oz* and *Thorunka*. These late-1950s undergraduates were intrinsically cool, and still young enough in spirit to move their hairstyles and fashions with the times and surf the youth wave.

The danger in the new generational myth was a tendency by some participants, such as Neville, to impose a unifying mass youth identity that universalised the experience of the white, university-educated and well-off, squeezing the vibrant diversity of countercultural groups into one 'Movement' as he did in *Play Power*.[10] Where communists had claimed to be a vanguard for workers in general, countercultural radicals claimed to speak for the revolutionary potential of all youth, never mind that most were working as apprentices, labourers or junior clerks in offices and shops. Tertiary students were a minority among Australian youth in the late 1960s, and those involved in protest or the counterculture groups smaller still. Most students were neither political nor cultural radicals. Percy Allen, president of Sydney University Student Representative Council in 1969, estimated that radical activists made up about two per cent of the student body, with their followers comprising about one quarter of the students. Yet the dominant image of sixties youth is that of the radical student or countercultural dissident.

The idea of a generation gap and even conflict entered mass media, and the teenage delinquent attained a threatening political edge as the student protester, especially after the student unrest of May 1968 in Paris and at the Democratic Convention in Chicago later that year. By the early 1970s popular consciousness was saddled with the notion of a new generational class that was changing the world. The catchy theme of the American TV show *The Monkees*, claiming that America's confected answer to the Beatles were spokespeople for a 'generation', said it all.

An emphasis on bohemianism, rather than youth, demonstrates the continuities rather than generational rupture. In the area of politics a strong case can be made that countercultural activists who moved through the Push took Libertarian ideas of anarchism and pluralism out of the subculture and into the public sphere. The 'Libertarian Line' stimulated an anti–authoritarian, intellectual culture sceptical of the state in the countercultures, especially in Sydney, and even later in postmodern politics of difference and identity. In his 1997 memoir Neville paid tribute to the earlier generation of Libertarians in nurturing his youthful brand of bohemian politics.[11] He recalls being inspired by Paddy McGuinness, 'a bearded and mumbling Economics lecturer who slouched about the campus in bare feet and corduroys, promoting the creed of anarchy'. Inspired by the Libertarian *Broadsheet*, Neville plucked up the courage to brave the Push watering hole, the Royal George Hotel, where he underwent his bohemian baptism amid '[s]moky alcoves, the juke box blasting Roy Orbison's "Working for the Man", paperbacks of Kafka and Camus protruding from pockets, people in black sweaters espousing free love'. He did not become an inner member of the Push subculture, but Thoms confirmed Neville became a constant at Push pubs, where he broadened the Libertarian ideas he took into *Oz* and the counterculture. Neville agreed that '[t]he Push stance of "permanent protest" had struck a chord'.[12]

Within the late 1960s and 70s countercultures, Thoms, Greer, Moorhouse, Jim Anderson, Wendy Bacon and Liz Fell explored ways to transform Libertarian ideas into political action while insisting on opposition to party politics, governments and unifying institutions. The Push also demonstrated that personal action was political, that freedom could be achieved by carving out an alternative society to the mainstream and sexual freedom was an act of political protest. Most importantly, Sydney Libertarians contributed an anarchist hostility to the state and nationalism that divided the new countercultures from the institutional left in the Communist Party and the ALP. However a crucial difference was that where the older Libertarians had sought freedom in a subculture, the younger Libertarians, who called themselves Futilitarians, were inspired by a post-'68 sense of possibility to bring sexual freedom out of subcultural privacy and into public political debate, taking on government obscenity laws in the media.

• • •

THE POST-MATERIALIST AGENDA

While *Oz* and the Futilitarians drew on the personnel and ideas of the Libertarians, they took issue with their immediate predecessors in campus activism, the academic New Left of the late 1950s and early 60s. Neville characterised the conflict as one of the 'Pranksters versus the Politicos'. While the Eureka Youth League and the Communist Party of the 1950s and early 60s had supported cultural activism through Australian folk music, the New Theatre and the Waterside Workers documentary unit, the old left party hierarchy mandated socialist realism and denounced American-style teen culture. The first New Left revisionists endorsed 'higher' modernist taste such as abstract expressionist painting and jazz, but rejected rock'n'roll and the new consumer youth culture as devoid of creative values and irrational. In 1966, left-wing historian Ian Turner lamented that where once his students exercised their minds with jazz, they now backed into the 'retreat from reason' of pop, an inferno of 'sensation' and 'self immolation in a pre-adult, asexual dream world'.[13] A heated debate ensued.

In *People, Politics and Pop* Craig McGregor criticised the snobby elitism of older left intellectuals, arguing they despised the pop music now embraced by young radicals because, ironically for socialists, they did not much like ordinary people who made up the audience for popular culture. Unlike Neville's youth politics, McGregor believed that an alliance between the countercultures and the young working-class of the suburbs was happening through pop culture. Popular culture could evoke dissent, pointing the way to a new left-wing cultural politics that could be glimpsed in the countercultures.

For Richard Neville, *Play Power* represented the necessary renovation of the left by a young generation raised in the media age. While Neville has been dismissed by some commentators as an incurable romantic, superficial thinker and self-promoter, he must be treated as a central figure in the countercultural political debate owing to his contributions as an editor of the influential *Oz* in Britain, the writer of *Play Power* – which attempted to explain the countercultures politically – and his spirited defence of *Oz* before the courts, which he made explicitly political. At the obscenity trial of London *Oz*, Neville explained how the naïve 'peace' and 'love' mantra of 1967 matured into harder politics directed to inequality in society in the face of brutal institutional opposition in 1968:

> you don't hear so much about love nowadays, because the alternative society has become more practical and political. People got tired of turning the other cheek ... When you see long-hairs or black people or women marching in the streets, they are not there because they want to destroy everything that you believe in; they want to rebuild it and redistribute it, so that everyone receives a fair share.[14]

The brand of countercultural politics promoted by London *Oz* was basically a return to the romantic critique of modern, industrial capitalism — a post-materialist agenda. In the lead-up to the Paris 'uprising' of May 1968, countercultural radicals throughout the west were searching for an elusive authenticity not just within modern industrial society, as bohemians and political romantics had before, but also within a society saturated by mass media — the beginnings of a postmodern rebellion. Unprecedented affluence underwritten by Australia's (and the west's) long boom paved the way for the new post-scarcity, quality-of-life politics pursued by the countercultures, but equally important was the impact of electronic media and what French radical Guy Debord called 'the society of the spectacle'. 'In this revolution', declared Jean-Jacques Lebel in May 1968, 'we are trying to reinvent the concept of life, of language and of self expression'.[15]

An agenda formed in the underground press, such as English *Oz* and Wendy Bacon's *Thorunka*, around post-materialist goals that included social pluralism and social transformation through the personal experience of freedoms such as 'sexual liberation' or drug use, a critique of economic and technological modernity through escape to alternative communities, freedom of expression in media (exemplified through publishing in defiance of obscenity laws), and a reification of 'play' in media and lifestyle as both a political tactic and as a social ideal.

The late-1960s countercultures posited the idea that the 'personal is political'. The revolution in the personal embraced a potpourri of lifestyle alternatives such as sexual freedom and homosexuality (the so-called 'sexual revolution') and communal living, to modes of altering consciousness through psychotropic drugs, music, travel, or exotic religions. By connecting personal experience and lifestyles to a 'revolution' the countercultures brought identity rights into the political debate, and laid the groundwork for social movement politics in the 1970s.

'A growing number of people have dropped out of the competitive panic to experiment with a new way of living,' Neville wrote of emerging communes and the 'pot trail' through Asia in the *New Statesman* in January 1968. So-called 'hippy' communities established in rural hinterlands such as Byron Bay in northern New South Wales tried to combine ecological sensitivity and social experimentation. Efforts were made to imitate pre-modern food production (without recourse to fertilisers and machinery), termed 'organic' farming, and to live communally, which meant sharing some property and breaking down nuclear family structures by sharing sexual partners and the raising of children. Bohemian and radical groups had cut themselves off from society before, to try alternative modes of living in utopian communities such as the ill-fated New Australia in Paraguay, or Jorgensens's Montsalvat. Artists' communities in the late nineteenth century and the Heide group in the 1940s had made a show of rusticity. In most cases the young bohemians were dramatically, and usually only temporarily, free from bourgeois life from which they came and to which they usually returned. However, the connection of anti-industrial romanticism of nature to a politics of protest would by the 1970s lead to a thriving grassroots movement of environmental activists.

Even exploring the unconscious became political. Neville, following Timothy Leary's plea for people to 'turn on, tune in, drop out', argued that freedom could be won by altering personal consciousness through drugs such as marijuana and especially LSD.[16] But what made this 'drug culture' different to Marcus Clarke's advocacy of hashish to unlock creativity was the illegality of the substances, which made their use a political act of disobedience against what was considered a bad law. This transgressive appeal was joined by the naïve romantic belief promoted by Leary and *Oz* that psychotropic drug use could disrupt or

even transform society. Worse, *Oz* underestimated the vulnerability of young drug users to criminals who infested the supply
chain, and the impact on mental health of abusing substances.

Jim Anderson, one time Royal George Libertarian and co-
editor of London *Oz*, used the magazine to advocate the
emerging issue of gay rights and teamed up with expatriate
Australian theatre director Richard Wherrett to produce an
issue of *Oz* celebrating homosexuality. *Oz* embarked on a
variety of identity specials, such as Women's *Oz*, edited by
Germaine Greer, and 'School Kid's' *Oz*, put together by a group
of school students. *Tharunka* and its follow-up off-campus publication *Thorunka* (later *Thor*) ran articles on women's liberation,
the land rights struggle of the Gurindji, gay liberation, the anti-
Vietnam movement and ecology. This impulse to heterogeneity
and identity in counterculture politics nurtured the new social
movements around peace, women's equality, homosexuality,
ethnic identity, environmental conservation and Aboriginal

The trio of London Oz editors en route to their obscenity trial at the Old Bailey
5 August 1971, where they were found guilty, fined and imprisoned – martyrs to
free speech. From left: Jim Anderson, Briton Felix Dennis and Richard Neville.
The judgment was overturned on appeal and the three released.

rights that gained impetus and recruits in the 1970s and 80s.

The limitations of the countercultures were also a lesson for social movements in the 1970s. For example, some feminists who participated in the countercultures have argued that it was their experience of sexism within these male–dominated groups, including the Push and the *Oz* network, that convinced them women required their own movement and theory. Neville's long-term partner during the *Oz* years in Australia and Britain, Louise Ferrier, was a founder of the feminist magazine *Spare Rib*, with a statement of aims that stressed an end to 'chick work' such as making tea, answering phones and first-name-only credits. Second-wave feminism was a broad church, with roots in the late nineteenth century back to Louisa Lawson, the old left, New Left and liberalism, but parts of the countercultures influenced parts of the women's movement. The concept of women's liberation that Germaine Greer polemicised in *The Female Eunuch* was developed through a series of controversial articles for *Oz*, and owed much to the Push's belief in sexual freedom and agency and to the author's experiences in the Underground and music bohemias of the late 1960s. Greer applied the countercultural critique of the institutional left to the methods of the second-wave feminist movement, arguing that 'demonstrating, compiling reading lists and sitting on committees are not themselves liberating behaviour'. Instead, women should transform themselves through sexual and social agency.[17]

Media was to be not just the message, but a political issue in its own right. Thanks to the new technologies of portable typewriters, offset printing, Bolex movie cameras and cheap electric guitars, the tools for making, if not distributing, media content were available to more people. Out of the synthesis of art, pop, politics and new media there arose in 1968 more explicitly oppositional strategies of symbolic sabotage such as the Youth International Party – Yippies – of the US and Europe's Situationist International. The situationists emerged in the May uprising and favoured Dada-inspired stunts that held mainstream institutions up for ridicule in order that freedom could be won amid the cracks, confusion and chaos. Its leader Guy Debord advocated using the media's power and need for spectacle against itself, ju-jitsu style, to disrupt and expose artifice for cultural and political liberation. Dadaesque catharsis had seeped into pop culture via arts schools in Britain, inspiring ex-art student Pete Townshend of The Who to smash his guitars on stage or a Yippie takeover of *The Frost Report*. In Australia, escapee Vietnam War conscript Michael Matteson appeared on *This Day Tonight* in the presence of the Federal Attorney-General as an act of civil disobedience to protest against the 'nasho' (conscription for national service in Vietnam), narrowly eluding police who converged on the ABC. The charismatic Matteson gave 'underground press conferences' and dramatically escaped from police when handcuffed at Sydney University with the help of students, all filmed for the evening news. For a time it seemed like the revolution would be televised.

In 1970 Bob Birrell observed that whereas the old left was concerned with the overthrow of capitalism for materialistic ends, the New Left now sought 'personal autonomy, creativity, human communication, love and enjoyment'.[18] Donald Horne has emphasised that despite the revolutionary rhetoric, such romantic goals as freedom, individualism and even 'nature' harked back to the 'nineteenth century bourgeois liberals and patriots', but these were also longstanding bohemian values.[19] Was the revolution becoming bohemianised?

POLITICS OF THE CARNIVAL

'Good rock stars take drugs, put their penises in plaster of Paris, collectivise their sex, molest policemen, promote self-curiosity, unlock myriad spirits, epitomise fun, freedom and bullshit. Can the busiest anarchist on your block match THAT?'[20]

In *Play Power* Neville contrasted the 'turgid' academic articles of the New Left journals that mouldered unread in drawers with the media impact of burning 'draft' cards or the destabilising play of rock. This new politics was essentially carnivalesque: decentralising power, popular, pluralist and using unruliness, obscenity, vulgarity and humour against the centralised power of traditional bourgeois and socialist politics. He argued that 'an ingredient common to Yippie street demos, altered consciousness, Dylan's lyrics, group sex and the Underground arts/media scene was playfulness'. In a similar spirit, Germaine Greer's *The Female Eunuch* advocated 'delinquency' and sexual pleasure among women as the path to female empowerment.[21] As we have seen, the carnivalesque was long part of the performance of Australian literary bohemia. In the 1890s it was not an easy fit with the radical intelligentsia or labour movement, but the countercultures made the carnivalesque central to a new cultural politics.

Marxism and social democracy were criticised for being the mirror image of the society they opposed – hierarchical, technology-obsessed, dedicated to material progress and the management of people and nature. McGregor believed that the routine and undemocratic nature of most work was the cause of alienation, not the ownership of a factory by a businessman.[22] If the traditional left believed in the dignity of work, the counter-cultures, according to Neville, wanted to play. Beginning with Marcus Clarke, bohemians had sought to make an art form of loafing, in order to show their rejection of the bourgeois work ethic. The countercultures made the rejection of work con-formity a radical political act in itself through the popular call to 'drop out' (a term with Push lineage), welcoming differentiation from the working class as much as from the bourgeoisie.

The idea of the 'carnival' drew on the topsy-turvy spirit of riotous festivity, unleashed in the carnivals of Europe in the fifteenth and sixteenth centuries, in which the lower orders deployed misrule, humour and vulgarity to make their rulers squirm. Soviet literary thinker Mikhail Bakhtin noted the later reinvention in novels and other art forms of elements of carnival such as blasphemy, parody, sexual ribaldry and gender confusion. As well as an escape valve for discontent, carnival could also be politically subversive by overturning customary hierarchies. Parody, comedy and the mockery of authority were central, and appeared in the political satire of Max Gillies at La Mama Theatre, the irony of *Oz* and much of the 'street theatre' that attended rallies against censorship and the Vietnam War. Carnival's collapsing of divisions between performers and spectators, its 'pageant without footlights', was evident in experimental theatre enjoining audiences to participate in the action as a political act, in festivals where communal dancing and sex became the performance, and by underground publica-tions like *Oz* inviting others to take over editing for an issue.[23]

Authoritarian hierarchies could also be destabilised by 'vulgar debasings and bringings down to earth', ideally to the level of the body.[24] Rock songs such as Daddy Cool's 'Baby Let Me Bang Your Box', Thoms' and Beresford's faeces-splattered film ... *it droppeth as the gentle rain*, early David Williamson plays and especially the underground press played with bodily functions and other forms of vulgarity. *Oz* articles and images relishing 'cunts', buggery and oral sex were typical of underground press attempts to demystify the body and sex and were theorised as such. *Thorunka* editors Wendy Bacon and Liz Fell used obscenity and bodily functions as a weapon to 'reduce the mystery of rank' and humanise the powerful. Bacon turned up to the *Thorunka* obscenity trial on 17 August 1970 dressed as a nun and bearing a sign reading 'I'VE BEEN FUCKED BY GOD'S STEEL PRICK', dramatically deploying vulgarity to profane the sacred.

The clash between *Thorunka* and the NSW government, like that between *Oz* and the Crown in Britain, was not just anti-government, but a plea for a heterogenous public discourse against totalising and controlling authority. *Thorunka*'s editorial line was to publish as if there were no restrictions, legal or moral. 'We don't know what they'll do,' announced Bacon, 'so let's do it and see what they'll do.'[25] Moorhouse analysed this later as a shift from abstractly advocating freedom of communication, as had the Push and the anti-censorship lobby, 'to freely communicating'.[26] For these late 1960s libertarians 'free media' had taken on the totemic importance that 'free love' had in the 1950s Push, and among the Heide ménage in 1940s Melbourne, though sexual freedom retained its centrality as fundamental to other freedoms. But where the bohemian Push were content to parade their oppositional selves in the pubs and parties of the demimonde, the Futilitarians performed it at the centre of the public sphere, in the court house and in the media. Greer, Neville and Sharp were taking similar action in Britain with London *Oz* – fusing ideas, deviancy, protest and media to shake up expectations and expose the state's authoritarian streak. The mass media was the new arena for politics. Rather than being thought of as monolithic and powerful, the media was reappraised as diverse, contradictory and vulnerable to subversion from within and without.

THE TENT EMBASSY AND BLACK POWER

At the same time a new and more assertive black politics emerged, rapidly moving beyond calls to end discrimination and disadvantage endured by Indigenous Australians to a post-colonial assertion of Aboriginal sovereignty through demands for land rights and self-determination. The injustice of one nation being invaded and colonised by another was dramatically symbolised by the erection on Australia Day 1972 of the Aboriginal Tent Embassy, outside Parliament House in Canberra. This was both a radical political act and a supreme moment of political theatre that inspired a new, more militant phase in the long campaign for Indigenous rights. Beyond traditional creative practices that stretch back millennia, Indigenous people had played a significant role in the colonisers' arts and entertainment since 1788, as actors, musicians, visual artists, story-tellers, circus performers and vaudevillians and were disproportionately represented in gospel, folk and country music. The Tent Embassy provided a stage for a new generation of Aboriginal activist-artists such as Gary Foley, Sam Watson, Roberta 'Bobbi' Sykes, Tony Coorey, John Newfong, Bob Maza, Michael Anderson, Zac Martin, Carol Johnson, Charles 'Chicka' Dixon, Kevin Gilbert, Paul Coe and his sister Isabel, Bobby McLeod, Tiga Bayles, Bindi Williams, Aileen Corpus and Gloria Fletcher who directed their skills as actors, dramatists, musicians and writers towards a carnivalesque style of protest and more left-wing radicalism quite different from the conventional small 'l' liberal campaign for the Yes vote in the 1967 referendum.

Part of the Black Caucus and the Redfern Black Power Movement with Sykes and Paul Coe, firebrand Foley had cut his radical teeth in the 1971 anti-apartheid protests that accompanied the Springbok rugby tour.[27] In 1972 he appeared in the hit satirical, experimental Nimrod Theatre Company's revue *Basically Black*, which the ABC made into a TV show the next year. Foley combined co-establishing innovative institutions such as the Redfern Legal Service and Aboriginal Medical Service in Melbourne with being a key instigator and performer in the National Black Theatre (NBT), and appearing in and championing Indigenous Australian cinema at home and internationally.[28] Sykes was a much loved radical Koori journalist, poet and feminist who was the Executive Secretary of the Tent Embassy where she was among those arrested in the struggle to keep the tents up. She wrote for *Nation Review* and, with a Jimi Hendrix-style afro, she would later become the first black Australian to go to Harvard, earning a PhD in education and authoring various books.

Country music had long been used by Aboriginal people to tell tragic stories of dispossession, imprisonment and even the taking of children, as well as celebrating kinship and the triumph of the human spirit against the odds.[29] But in the political ferment of the early 1970s, the spirit of resistance in Indigenous country that was always present came to the fore as a new protest music in the work of singer-activists such as Bob Randall, Galarrwuy Yunupingu, Vic Simms and Bobby McLeod. They performed songs (for example 'My Brown Skin Baby', 'Stranger in My Country', 'Wayward Dreams' and 'Gurindji Blues') that were explicitly political, shaming white colonisers with powerful stories and buoying Aboriginal people for the struggle.

Few of the Aboriginal cultural activists came from middle-class backgrounds, most had grown up very poor in the regions and the bush, often running the gauntlet of welfare agencies and police, and some like McLeod had been to jail. They were disinclined to meet the authorities' rough attempts to remove the Embassy with the sophistry of the tertiary educated *Oz* defendants. As police dragged a defiant Bobby McLeod from the tents he declared down the barrel of a television camera, 'People of Australia – get Fucked!'[30] While McLeod, Foley and the other Indigenous artist-activists shared interests and practices with other white countercultural radicals of this generation, their political and cultural practices also drew stylistically and intellectually on other non-European struggles for independence, and the Afro-American Black Power militancy (raised fists, berets, and afros), as well as the diversity of local Indigenous folk cultures, many of which had a strong base in rural and working-class ways of living as well as traditional pre-contact cultures.

A NEW NEW LEFT?

Before Gough Whitlam's elevation to the leadership in 1967, Labor was treated by many countercultural radicals as part of the problem, the bastion of old working-class politics and prejudices out of step with youth. Despite the party's opposition to the war in Vietnam, the new politics was beyond the grasp of Calwell's ALP. McGregor criticised the machine men and anti-intellectuals of Calwell's generation for not moving beyond the certainties of 'White Australia' and utilitarian 'big government knows best'. Yet they also despaired of the next generation of 'meritocratic' elitists around the heir apparent, Gough Whitlam.[31]

For their part, many socialists, feminists and slightly older 1950s Libertarians came to find the ideas of the post-'67 counterculture woolly-headed and irrational, and were uneasy with a politics that embraced play, shock and media culture. Economist and Libertarian Paddy McGuinness complained of the peace movement's 'cock eyed' retreat into utopianism – the standard Push putdown of activism. Clive James argued in *Oz* that the counterculture was a contradiction in terms as there was only one shared culture, and an attack on that was an attack on civilisation, though he thought the anti-authoritarianism and 'this new emphasis on youth, music, soft drugs and less uptight sex might have an ameliorating effect'.[32] Fellow expatriate Barry Humphries, by the late 1960s a confirmed anti-socialist who would join the *Quadrant* board in the 1970s, had fun lampooning New Left academics, countercultural filmmakers, radical artists and women's 'libbers' in his monologues and the Barry McKenzie comic strip in *Private Eye*. By the early 1970s some in the organised women's movement were highly critical of Germaine Greer's brand of women's liberation. Feminist and one-time Push member Lynne Segal recalled that the movement 'predominantly dismissed Greer's individualistic anarchism and dismissal of collective action'.[33]

In Australia some younger New Left intellectuals who also had experience of the countercultures, such as McGregor, counselled countercultural groups that 'it was not enough to simply change heads – structures must be changed as well'.[34] He divided countercultures into those who were political through their experimental cultural practices, such as Sharp, Neville or the Australian Performing Group at the Pram Factory, and those who mobilised culture as political radicals, such as Marxist-leaning academics like himself and Dennis Altman. He believed that 'while the alternative cultures can achieve changes in values, perceptions and attitudes ...: this power must at some point be transformed into conventional political power'.[35] The next step for progressive politics in Australia, they argued, was for the pluralism and cultural activism of the countercultures to create or be harnessed to structures that could engage with governments, because state power could not be ignored.[36] But in the early 1970s engagement with the state was anathema to the Futilitarians, *Oz* and many student radical groups that ran the gauntlet of its police and courts.

The countercultures and the more structured left did come together on a number of fronts, not least the growing opposition to Australia's participation in the Vietnam War. Marxism itself enjoyed a revival in universities in the early 1970s, by taking a post-materialist turn away from the Soviet model towards European theorists, such as Antonio Gramsci and Herbert Marcuse who, in his 1968 work *One Dimensional Man*, linked socialism to cultural and sexual liberation. Indeed much New Left Marxist theory was hostile to the Communist Party as a totalising and authoritarian structure. Free of party orthodoxy, intellectual Marxism became diverse, and its scholars and activists began looking at complementary power relations such as gender, sexuality, decolonialisation and ethnic identity, and the role of culture in maintaining what was called 'bourgeois' hegemony. These more complex ideas of power had been of concern to the Libertarians as far back as the 1950s and not surprisingly some of their number, such as George Molnar and Ross Poole, became interested in Marxism in the early 1970s.

Young activists on campus could now refashion Marxism to suit radical, carnivalesque countercultural groups such as Monash University's Socialist Cynics and Orwellians or Melbourne's Acid Liberation Marxists. In his short-story collection *The Americans, Baby*, Moorhouse's student radicals spout neo-Marxist jargon gleaned from lectures while protesting against university as a 'breeding ground for capitalism'.[37] New fringe Trostkyist, Euro-communist and Maoist parties and movements such as

Resistance and the Spartacists acquired a presence on university campuses, where they bonded with countercultural students. Even the Communist Party of Australia, following its split from Moscow in 1968 over the invasion of Czechoslovakia, embraced new Marxist theory and became more attractive to radical students resisting the Vietnam War. Due to CPA involvement in the anti-Vietnam War movement through front organisations such as the Association for International Cooperation and Disarmament, and the journalism of student activists in *Tribune*, the Coalition government MP Andrew Peacock accused communists of infiltrating 'the student dissent movement'. ASIO responded with a counter-intelligence campaign on campus entitled 'Operation Whip', in which hard young men with crewcuts did a poor job infiltrating rallies.[38] However, the relationship between the bureaucratic obsessions of the old left and countercultural activists was not always a happy one. Moorhouse recounts well-meaning anti-censorship Communist Party members keen to relate with the young being repulsed by the anarchistic bohemianism and permissiveness of *Thorunka*.

More successful was participation of countercultural radicals in the mainstream city-stopping marches against the Vietnam War. The Melbourne May Day march of 1969 incorporated the performance of sixty-second sketches about the war by the Carlton Poor Theatre Group (directed by Blundell). 'Street theatre' would be a feature of the two 'moratoriums' led in Victoria by Labor front bencher Jim Cairns – a mass action attracting approximately 80,000 marchers and influencing many more through the mass media. By creating a popular front in the great cause of the day, the campaign could connect the performative and media skills of participating countercultural radicals to a structure provided by traditional progressive institutions like the unions and the ALP, bringing theatricality, spectacle, iconic imagery and photo-ops of police brutality to the protest.

A new form of practical community-based activism emerged that had its most potent cross-fertilisation of counterculture and traditional collectivist politics in the 'green ban' campaign to save Victoria Street, Darlinghurst and Woolloomooloo from developers in 1973, bringing together members of the Push with the Marxist Builders Labourers Federation. As discussed in chapter six, this anti-development campaign moved the union away from an old left obsession with wages and conditions to the post-materialist values of environment, community, heritage and quality of life of inner-city residents.

BOHEMIANS, RADICALS AND THE SOCIAL DEMOCRATIC STATE

The tension in countercultural politics between bohemian libertarianism and the statist instincts of the left came to a head when the election of the Whitlam Labor government in December 1972 tempted long-marginalised cultural radicals with government patronage. In government, Whitlam moved his party significantly away from old-fashioned labourism and towards social democracy, embracing many socio-cultural issues that were dear to the university-educated, such as the abolition of university fees and conscription, withdrawal of troops from Vietnam, ending the last remnants of White Australia and a new pluralist policy of 'multiculturalism', the expansion of public media and community development. Especially appealing to countercultural bohemians would be massive Commonwealth support for the arts.

Many cultural radicals rallied to Whitlam's standard. Bob Ellis, steeped in Labor history, turned his talents to crafting Labor legends, penning a musical on the life of federation Labor leader King O'Malley and extolling Whitlam's virtues in the *Bulletin* and *Nation Review*.[39] Albie Thoms remembered Ellis at university as enamoured of John F. Kennedy's presidential 'Camelot', and discerned in him a romanticisation of political reformers which distinguished him from the Push's scepticism of authority and 'total cynicism about Whitlam'.[40] Ellis appreciated that the Labor vision was as much about cultural change as bread and butter, and that winning the war against the conservatives required cultural bullets – songs, stories, films and oratory that linked Labor's quest for the 'light on the hill' to the national story. During the turbulent years of the Whitlam 'midsummer' he resolved to be a Lawsonian figure for new Labor times, bridging the gap between bohemia and the politicians, the carnivalesque and the technocratic, becoming an eccentric artist-in-residence to the Labor tribe.[41]

Ellis was one of many erstwhile Labor supporters in the arts community who became a Whitlam romantic. Phillip Adams had abandoned the Communist Party in the 1960s for free-floating cultural socialism. He was originally sceptical of Whitlam's weak socialist credentials, as compared with Calwell and Cairns, but was won over by the new leader's enthusiasm for the arts. Adams helped the new government set up the Australian Film Commission and a revamped Australia Council for the Arts, joining both. During the Whitlam government's tenure many graduates and long-term activists from countercultural groups and even former communists who had left in 1968 were recruited into new state bodies.

But to others more rooted in the countercultures Whitlam was a technocrat, even authoritarian. Thoms and his independent film group were critical of Whitlam's initiatives in Australian cinema, believing his government was using patronage to mandate content and style, promoting Australian nationalism to the detriment of experimentation and diversity.[42] Here Thoms split from Push filmmakers Mike Thornhill and Margaret Fink and Carlton La Mama stalwarts Betty and Tim Burstall who supported a government-subsidised Australian film industry. Graeme Blundell complained that the government's 'bureaucratic' directing of funds into a commercial industry 'stymied aspirations for experimental film as an autonomous artistic endeavour'.[43] This would not stop him stripping down to his jocks and beyond to play *Alvin Purple* – a huge commercial hit. For his part Thoms, ever the Andersonian Libertarian, remained sceptical that autonomy could ever be granted by the state, and kept clear of the film 'renaissance'. Moorhouse, Bacon, Fell and other futilitarians also maintained their pessimistic scepticism about the state in the midst of Whitlam's reform rollercoaster. 'No matter who you vote for, a politician always gets in' was their Libertarian mantra, and Moorhouse warned against countercultural 'backsliding' on the 'illusions' of 'nationalism', parliamentary democracy and accepting 'loot' or 'one day we'll all live on grants!'[44]

But many Whitlam initiatives proved enabling of countercultural dissent, by providing funding to creative artists and community groups with few strings attached. The establishment of community radio licences placed public access radio stations like Brisbane's 4ZZZ and Sydney's 2SER at the disposal of countercultural activists, who used the stations as platforms for the emerging social movements and to energise 'alternative' music and other fringe cultures. Likewise, when Labor Communications Minister Moss Cass established a Contemporary Radio Unit within the mainstream ABC in 1975 he insisted that the new station would be autonomous from the national broadcaster's management hierarchy, that reluctantly agreed to a quasi-collective staff decision-making process – an experiment that was a boon to creative freedom at 2JJ until a more formal structure was introduced in 1978. 2JJ specifically programmed music and, importantly, arts and issues that were not covered by commercial radio, providing public space for the counterculture in its first years of operation. It kicked off transmission by spinning the banned (by commercial radio) Skyhooks song 'You Just Like Me 'Cos I'm Good In Bed', and was attacked by conservative newspaper commentators and politicians for 'filth, smut and foul language', damned as part of 'Labor's grandiose plan to ... wreck commercial radio ... through socialised broadcasting'.[45] In keeping with what manager Marius Webb called 'anti-establishment thinking', announcers and journalists with strong counterculture experience and credibility were employed, leading to programs on Aboriginal and prisoners' rights, women's issues and environmentalism.[46] 2JJ broke new ground by playing songs from local independent labels, incubating the local version of the anarchistic 'punk' bohemia of the late 1970s and the array of subcultural music genres that emerged in its wake. The Fraser government became increasingly annoyed by 2JJ's promotion of social-movement protests against its policies, which culminated in the station telling Sydneysiders where to go to march against uranium mining.

In truth the state was important in Australia, and if key countercultural goals such as cosmopolitan diversity, a freer media and enhanced personal autonomy were to be achieved, it was necessary to cooperate with a reforming government while it lasted. In the 1975 election campaign following the dismissal of the Whitlam government, Frank Moorhouse overcame his indifference to governments to give a speech (representing the 'anarchists of Balmain') at the Sydney Opera House in defence of Whitlam's 'contribution to personal freedom in this country ... the ending of conscription, the legalising of homosexuality ... and its abolition of censorship'.[47] The movement of some young radical leaders, academics and cultural entrepreneurs into positions of institutional importance during and after the period of the Whitlam government influenced the style and content of Labor politics, while countercultural radicals surrendered spontaneity and shock tactics for the meetings, minutes and resolutions required by party politics. Some old left and New Left politicians, most famously anti-war leader and, for a time, treasurer and deputy prime minister Jim Cairns, were converted to the alternative lifestyle cause. But Labor was changing too, as evidenced by South Australian premier Don Dunstan wearing pink hotpants, and the frenzy of Hawaiian shirts and bikini-clad research assistants at the notorious Terrigal National Conference – a Dionysian affair that would have brought a throb to Sir Les Patterson's trousers. Highlights included (married) Treasurer Jim Cairns revealing 'a kind of love' for his intelligent and beautiful (married) staffer Junie Morosi, and a Speedo-clad ALP President Bob Hawke pretending to be whipped by a lithe female delegate.

A younger generation of tertiary-educated radicals recruited to the Labor cause during the Whitlam period – such as Meredith and Verity Burgmann in Sydney, Anne Summers in Adelaide and Joan Coxsedge and Peter Steedman in Melbourne – brought countercultural concerns into the party, and would continue to push issues such as civil liberties, multiculturalism, feminism and environmentalism in the 1970s, 80s and 90s. Even arts-subsidy sceptic Moorhouse accepted a position on the Australia Council's Literature Board. The Whitlam government's funding and policy outreach to projects and movements that emerged in the countercultures, such as women's refuges, public and 'ethnic' radio and legal centres, helped seed identity- and community-based politics that over the next two decades would provoke established parties to adapt to the new post-materialist concerns of an 'affluent society'.

By the mid-1970s internally diverse movements had formed around environmental conservation, nuclear disarmament and the rights of women, homosexuals, different ethnicities,

Aborigines and people on welfare. These movements brought together skills in fundraising and lobbying with ideas, symbolic protest and media stunts. This was the type of structural accommodation that Dennis Altman and Craig McGregor had hoped for. Freed for a time from dogmatic and bureaucratic institutional limitations, the new social movements emphasised the individual within communities and identity, both very bohemian ideas. The personal and the symbolic became political, and 'consciousness' of identities and culture began to complement, and at times transcend, traditional class conflict between bosses and unions. Henceforth '[p]olitics ... wasn't what you did – it was what you were'.[48]

The new social and identity movements were to be the most durable and important outcome of the countercultural firmament, an assessment borne out by the political impact of these groups from the 1980s. Of course the Labor Party and even the Liberals sought to court and incorporate these movements, but struggled to graft their post-materialist values onto their faith in material growth. By the 1980s the movements' cultural strategies were shaping media and political agendas, and leaders were invited to join the federal Hawke Labor government and state Labor governments in policy-making and electoral horse-trading. But despite the tensions and at times cynical co-option of social movement leaders and agendas by Labor governments, the party's official platform at the time it lost office in 1996 after thirteen years reflected the profound influence of these movements on mainstream politics. From gender equality to Aboriginal land rights, multiculturalism to the environment, governments of all persuasions had to contend with a new paradigm.

LARRIKINS FROM THE EDGE:
EXPERIMENTS IN AUSTRALIAN IDENTITY
1960–1980

In 1972 Barry Humphries, collaborating with director Bruce Beresford and producer Phillip Adams, caught an emerging mood in their generation of artists with a film about a gormless young Australian larrikin in London named Barry McKenzie. 'Bazza' was vulgar and irrepressible, perpetually sucking on 'ice cold tubes of Fosters', trying unsuccessfully to get 'a sheila into a game of sink the sausage', and 'chundering' at will on unfortunate 'poms', trendies and countercultural 'ratbags' who crossed his inebriated path. The character allowed Humphries to have a spray at everything he disliked about Australia and England. Based on a cult comic strip Humphries penned for *Private Eye* magazine that had been banned back in Australia, *The Adventures of Barry McKenzie* became one of the first government-funded films of the Australian cinema revival of the early 1970s. Its journey from contraband to flagship for the 'new nationalism' was not without controversy, but luckily the movie was a smash hit. Suddenly ocker comedy was everywhere, from the David Williamson-penned *Stork* and *Don's Party* (plays and then movies) to Tim Burstall's *Alvin Purple* and the ABC's *Aunty Jack*.

Most Australians got the joke, but Max Harris, now a conservative contrarian, was not amused. He condemned *The Adventures of Barry McKenzie*, *Alvin Purple* and Williamson's work in his newspaper column, in *Nation Review* and on ABC television, and even wrote a book, *Ockers*, polemicising against 'the Bad Old New Australia': 'We thought we had won the

battle in the decades since the 1940s. But clearly we lost the war
… Now we're back where we started. Mr Adams, Bob Hawke,
Barry Humphries et al have taken advantage of the so-called
new nationalism … Ocker is celebrated. Ocker is phoenix.
Ocker is King.'[1]

On witnessing the popularity of the ocker films in Britain,
the *Age* fretted that they 'would only serve to confirm the
world's suspicions that we are a *Wake in Fright* nation of Bazzas
and Storks'. The convict streak was exposed to the world like a
grimy stain on the national underpants.

Rallying with fellow sophisticates of art and literary circles
Sidney Nolan, Albert Tucker and Patrick White, Harris criticised
the 'new nationalism' promoted by the Whitlam government
as 'a backward shift to uneducated attitudes', a 'reversion to
proletarian tribalism'.[2] Adams gleefully replied that Harris may
have once been an Angry Penguin but he was now 'a muddle-
headed wombat'. As concerns about Australia's image overseas
escalated, Humphries laughed that no one disparaged *Macbeth*
for misrepresenting Scotsmen.[3] Ocker comedy had provoked
a major stoush between different bohemian generations over
popular culture, class and Australian identity.

Harris had missed the irony of ocker art. Still an avant-
garde elitist at heart, he was too distracted by the vulgarity and
suburban audiences mouthing Bazza's colourful slang to notice
the satire of an Australian society in flux. The people behind
these popular plays and films were far from mere commercial
showmen, and they smuggled into them all sorts of critical
insights and visceral pleasures from the experimental avant-
garde projects at which they laboured in the 1960s. Along with
new magazines and pop music, the ockers of stage and screen
interrogated key tensions in our culture at the time – between
provincial Australia and the British metropolitan centre, the
artist and the working-class larrikin, the wowser and the libertine, authority and unruliness, cosmopolitanism and white
Australia. Far from a philistine regression, the ocker mask was
the other face of the 1970s bohemian, a larrikin performance
long rehearsed in the pubs of Sydney and Melbourne, and toured
abroad as travellers and expats to critical acclaim.

However there is a paradox at the heart of the ocker moment.

In the early 1960s, most of the young bohemian artists were loudly hostile to Australian nationalism, whether the old British race patriotism of the RSL, or the radical nationalism of the left. Yet by the early 1970s most of this generation working at home and in Britain were fast moving away from the international aesthetic to obsess instead about what it meant to be Australian in art funded by the governments of John Gorton and Gough Whitlam under the 'new nationalist' banner.

THE NEW INTERNATIONALISTS

The idea of an international youth bohemia was made tangible from the mid-1960s by cheaper, faster air travel and 'hippy' backpacking across Asia and Europe, international distribution networks for underground publications, a series of mass festivals around music, art, and shared experience with American and other western protest groups opposed to the Vietnam War. Northern hemisphere countercultural celebrities connected with Australian audiences through the globalised mass media of music, television, cinema, magazines and promotional tours, while Australian artists joined their European and American compadres as travellers. The century-long trickle of Australian bohemians to London became a flood in the mid-1960s, swelling an expatriate community of artists, writers, journalists and students. Australians felt they were participants in this global community, and some expatriate activists even became spokespeople for underground activism on the international stage. How had the experience of bohemianism in Australia in the 1960s encouraged a cosmopolitan outlook?

The Libertarians of the 1950s had dismissed Australian nationalism as an authoritarian and homogenising illusion. In the early 1960s *Oz* was highly critical of the institutions that spoke for a conservative idea of nation, such as governments, the courts, police and army, the RSL and service clubs. Labourist and old left nationalism centred on trade unions or the radical nationalist writers of the 1890s seemed equally passé, and often bigoted. The postwar spruiking by ad men, developers and politicians of the 'Australian way of life', with its emphasis on suburban living and consumerism, was also despised by bohemians for its conformity and materialism – especially if they themselves had grown up in the suburbs with a Holden and Victa mower. Richard Neville complained that '[r]acism was entrenched. The Labour [sic] Party pursued a "White Australia" immigration policy, and Aboriginals were outcasts in their own land', which together with the Anzac cult of the older generation reflected 'a sense of deadness at our nation's core'.[4] Sixties activists Neville and Sharp found in the emerging cosmopolitan counterculture an inspiring alternative to an Australia they hated.

Like earlier generations of bohemians, young people in the sixties looked overseas for inspiration, to London, Paris and, increasingly, the United States. Neville checked off in his memoir a list of the latest international bohemian trends that he and his fellow students eagerly consumed: European New Wave cinema; the American Beat poets; the British theatre's Angry Young Men; the 'sick' humour of Lenny Bruce; and 'an exotic range of polemicists like Sartre, Bertrand Russell and Simone de Beauvoir' now available to a new generation in 'saucily jacketed' paperbacks.[5] It is significant that articles in *Oz* and Thoms' writing, for example, make reference to surrealists, anarchists, revolutionaries and romantics in Europe, but ignore Australian variants in the not-too-distant past. This generation encountered bohemians of an earlier generation as icons, such as Lawson shorn of his socialism and honoured on the 1966 banknote, or as the living conservative fossils Norman Lindsay and Packer editor Kenneth Slessor – part of the problem, not the solution.

As happened with the Heidelberg School and interwar modernists, international trends were used by young bohemians to distinguish themselves from their immediate predecessors. The young Barry Humphries condemned the Push as hopelessly parochial and unsophisticated for its failure to appreciate modernist aesthetics such as surrealism, and mocked 'Sinny's' older literary bohemia as coarse and compromised by journalism.[6] He later described Slessor witheringly as 'a tame literary hack for Frank Packer' and 'Australia's greatest poet, whose work would fit quite snugly into any respectable anthology of later Georgian verse, between W.J. Turner and Wilfred Childe', and was rendered speechless when the old poet dismissed him with the remark 'why don't you get your fucking hair cut'.[7]

At the centre of things in New York, journalist and rock connoisseur Lillian Roxon always found seats in the back bar of Max's Kansas City for touring Australian musicians like the Easybeats. However her real enthusiasm was for the iconoclastic art pop of the Velvet Underground and the whirl of cool creativity around Andy Warhol and his Factory scene. *Oz*'s bohemia of satire and rebel rock looked to the international trendsetters Dylan, the Beatles, Lenny Bruce and the *Village Voice*. Like the modernists of the 1930s and 40s, the *Oz* group deployed the latest artistic and cultural developments from overseas, but whereas the modernists were interested in how to apply aesthetic innovations like surrealism to Australian conditions, the countercultures of the mid to late 1960s had little time for national expression. For example, London *Oz* opposed the very concepts of nations and national identity – Australian or British – and stressed the connections between countercultural groups and young people throughout the (western) world, sometimes in a homogenising 'movement' way, but predominantly in a cosmopolitan way. Likewise, Albie Thoms was proud in the late 1960s that there was nothing very Australian about local avant-garde films, that rather reflected a mood to experiment in the international underground filmmaking community and the influence of international figures like surrealist André Breton.

The increasing global interconnectedness of media through multinational company distribution and satellite international television broadcasts from 1967 meant that developments in the new youth protest movements in the northern hemisphere were instantly communicated to young people in Australia. The global corporate media flow between countries and from north to south had a countercultural parallel in the distribution and syndication of underground magazines and films.

While opposing Australia's involvement in the Vietnam War as a folly of 'US imperialism', the form and style of countercultural protest was influenced by American models such as the 'Students for a Democratic Society'. The paradox of the young Australian protesters' love-hate relationship with America, and the influence of American literature and innovative styles of dissent, was explored ironically in a number of Frank Moorhouse short stories, such as 'The American Poet's Visit', and the collection *The Americans, Baby*, which compared the simplistic slogans of student demonstrators to their generation's intrigue with American culture. Moorhouse adopted an ironic distance in these stories, playing with the combinations made possible by diversity and sending up his own subcultures – bohemians, writers, left-wing activists, even conference-goers. This was a return to the ironic, detached observations of Marcus Clarke's fictitious flâneur of the 1870s, the 'Peripatetic Philosopher' for the age of fragmentation.

Aesthetic and political developments in Britain, France and America were sources of inspiration to the countercultures' brand of radicalism as they had been for earlier generations of Australian bohemians, distinguishing them from established players. However by the early 1960s the cultural old guard who came of age in the 1930s and 40s – whether mainstream journalists such as Donald Horne editing the *Bulletin*, the old left producing social realist theatre, or the nuanced cosmopolitanism of Clem Christesen and George Munster, respectively at *Meanjin* and *Nation* – were engaged with national questions about what it meant to be Australian. The turning point for the younger internationalists would be their own experience of Australianness as a way to make a mark while living and working overseas, especially in Britain in the latter 1960s.

LARRIKINS IN LONDON

For Australian expatriates like Richard Neville, Germaine Greer, Albie Thoms and Martin Sharp, the countercultures proved to be an international passport to bohemian pleasure. For over a century Australian bohemians had journeyed to Britain (and in the case of visual artists to France) to seek training, mentoring and, if possible, some artistic success in the larger and more prestigious European markets. Charles Conder, J.F. Archibald, Tom Roberts, Henry Lawson, two generations of Lindsays (most successfully Jack Lindsay, who established himself as a publisher and writer in the Bloomsbury bohemia), P.R. Stephensen, Sidney Nolan, Albert Tucker and Brett Whiteley were just a small part of a creative exodus stretching through each generation of bohemians. A significant number of university graduates from the Libertarian Push and the Drift subcultures had made permanent homes in London, the Continent and even the United States, representing themselves as refugees from Menzies' political and cultural conservatism. Bob Ellis observed in his memoir of the early 1960s that '[n]ot to go in those days was a failure', regretting that he 'stayed, stayed too long'.[8]

The move to London was a final destination in a metropolitan journey that had begun with the move from country towns or suburbs to the inner city of the capital. They arrived in such numbers during the late 1950s that by the early 1960s a connected expatriate community of Australian university graduates and creative artists, many of them working in the media, was replicating the Push style of bohemianism, alongside those 'expats' who passed themselves off as Britons. According to Jack Lindsay's calculations, by 1963, 32,000 Australians travelled to Britain per year, and 'a large proportion are members of the arts or professions', an 'exodus of intellectuals'.[9] But from the mid-1960s cheaper jet travel and the publicising of the 'hippy trail' through Asia, the Middle East and Europe brought an even greater number of young travellers from Australia to Britain, many explicitly to participate in countercultural pleasures indulged in by a young expatriate community that had escaped the censure of parents back home. Self-conscious Australian neighbourhoods arose around bedsits and pubs in Notting Hill and Earls Court. This was the moment the *Barry McKenzie* comic strip captured so vividly.

This generation of Australian bohemian expatriates differed from their predecessors in a number of ways that helped them cut through in the British market. They enjoyed enhanced interaction not just with other Australians abroad, but also with their homeland via improved transport and communication, which was an antidote to naturalisation into the host culture. Neville admitted that the resource that gave his new London *Oz* 'an edge over rivals' was an 'extensive network of transient Australians in London' who did not ask to be paid.[10] *Oz* became a magnet for all those travelling Australians who were intrigued by media publicity about Haight-Ashbury and the 'Summer of Love', and many who had their first experience of sexual liberation and drugs on the hippy trail. Some of the Australian

bohemians who gathered to *Oz*'s standard included Martin
Sharp and Jenny Kee, filmmakers Bruce Beresford, Albie
Thoms and Philippe Mora (son of Mirka), Germaine Greer, Jim
Anderson and to a lesser extent the more sceptical Clive James
and Robert Hughes.

The countercultural expatriates focused on what they had
in common with dissenting young people in Britain. London
Oz, for example, accentuated themes of personal transcendence
and heterogeneity within and across borders. *Oz* converted the
very status of traveller from the antipodes into cultural capital
by promoting exotic journeys through the developing world
and the Mediterranean. A prized pilgrimage (that Neville and
Sharp had undertaken) was trekking east to west from Australia
as backpackers through favoured stops such as Thailand, India,
Nepal, Afghanistan, Turkey and Greece, and joining transient
communities in these outposts on the way to London. Hashish,
free love, communal living and the experience of eastern religion
were just some of the transgressive experiences the underground
press promised the adventurous pilgrim. This became a favoured
way for young middle-class Australians to combine their journey
to the metropolis with an experience of the Dionysian delights
of the counterculture en route. Where to pick up some Indian
trinkets, a cool Afghan sheepskin coat or a block of hash became
the talk of the hippy trail. The cult of the backpacker was in
sight.

Neville and Greer became translators of the counterculture
to the British mainstream via the BBC and the broadsheets,
and headed up a sex festival in Amsterdam. Australian activists
circulated from country to country. In 1969 Thoms toured his
surrealist film *Marinetti* through Europe and North America in
arthouse cinemas. Other underground filmmakers journeying
to Britain and America included Peter Weir, Phillip Noyce,
Philippe Mora, Tim Burstall and Bruce Beresford, some on
grants made available by the Gorton government. Hughes wrote
Heaven and Hell in Western Art in 1968 and landed the prestigious
posting of art critic for *Time* magazine in New York in 1969,
and made art history documentaries for the BBC. Clive James
became a leading Fleet Street television critic, published his
first book, *The Metropolitan Critic*, in 1974 and was admitted

into Soho's journalistic and literary bohemia. Barry Humphries was more overtly Australian in his subject matter, but from a metropolitan perspective. As well as introducing the sophisticated readers of *Private Eye* to the uncouth innocent abroad, Barry McKenzie – a comic-strip leveller of English pretension – Humphries graduated from Peter Cook's fringe Establishment Club to enjoy mainstream success on stage with his satirical monologues about Australians disorientated by cosmopolitan change.

Why did Australians come to play a prominent part in the international underground, and even mainstream British media culture? Ian Britain, in his book *Once an Australian*, argued that the 'famous four' – James, Humphries, Greer and Hughes – owed much to the contrasts of Australian provincialism with their sophisticated university education, producing highly articulate 'malcontents and tearaways' keen to try harder than the locals to demonstrate their mastery of metropolitan culture and grab what it had to offer.[11] However he does not consider the contribution of their bohemianism and its Australian nuance, forged before leaving home, to their metropolitan success.

Richard Neville argued that, paradoxically, Australia's isolation gave its young people an internationalist outlook; 'despite of, or because of, Australia's remote and unexciting image, the You Beaut land is compulsively tuned in to the rest of the world, thirstily absorbing the pop products of its culture and sociology; a half way market between England and America'.[12] Australians had the potential to be more culturally literate than either Americans or the British because they were obsessed with world 'pop culture' – for Neville the lingua franca of the new countercultures. As an Australian living in Britain, Neville had a vested interest in turning provincial marginality into an asset. Rather than the modernist dichotomy of province and centre, scholars of postmodernism have made a virtue of Australia's peripheral status to argue it offers a superior perspective aware of many cultures and their various contributions. Catharine Lumby has argued that Australians' view from the fringe, so distant from the source of images and power, makes the received culture appear second-hand, and ironic.[13] In their use of irony to probe both the metropolis and their homeland, were bohemian expatriates of the 1960s early postmodernists?

There was a noncommittal and ironic observer status in *Oz*, for example, that allowed it to let a thousand flowers bloom and enjoy the interesting combinations, while other underground publications, such as the UK's *IT*, took a particular line partly dictated by its team's entanglement in British class relations and politics. The act of crossing a border, in the case of the Australian expats, from province to metropolis could be distancing, turning the traveller into a detached observer of both place of departure and arrival. One of the ingredients distinguishing the countercultural art of the Australian expatriates from much of the English and American work is a sense of mocking humour crafted back in Australia, linking the underground stunts and 'play' of Greer and Neville at *Oz* to the humorous work of Humphries and James, described by the latter as writing 'wear[ing] a putty nose and revolving bow tie'.[14] Frank Moorhouse applied the same ironic detachment in his writing about Australia's domestic response to the cosmopolitan, and this approach would seep into the vary marrow of the new nationalism of the early 1970s.

Some Australian writers, painters, actors and journalists, notably Leo McKern, Dame Joan Sutherland, Peter Porter and Sidney Nolan, had done well in 1950s London. Typical of the earlier style of expat was Charm School alumnus Jocelyn Rickards who left Australia in 1949. She began a successful career in design, immersed herself in London bohemia and played a leading role as a costume designer and art director in British new wave cinema of the 1960s, helping to craft the distinctive cool black and white Mod look of quintessentially English films such as the *Look Back in Anger, Morgan: A Suitable Case for Treatment, Blow Up* and James Bond films. But what changed from the mid-1960s into the 1970s was that Australians in London built careers in the arts and media as 'Australians' rather than Austral-Brits, and in fact made an outrageous show of it. Albie Thoms and Nick Waterlow argued that it was the quality of Australian larrikinism that distinguished Australian artists in the metropolis and enhanced the quality of their projects.[15] Their exhibition 'Larrikins in London' showcased an Australian style that valued egalitarianism, humour, vulgarity, informality, sexual freedom and disorder.

Australian cultural activists in London during the 1960s and 70s have been criticised for performing a familiar version of the wild colonial for the British establishment. Stephen Alomes found the approach of the expatriates was disempowering as it reinforced the superiority of coloniser over colonised.[16] But this does not explain why Australians among the many different colonial émigrés in the metropolis should be so feted. Nor does it come to terms with why the Australian bohemian style of 1960s expats was effective in this time and place. I would argue that the larrikin carnivalesque of the Australian bohemians, far from the disempowering cringe, could cut through and cross class barriers that corralled Britons and helped shake up the middle-class British culture of the home counties.

Although travelling in search of cosmopolitan experiences, the Australian bohemians in Britain could not help but be self-conscious about their otherness before the gaze of their British hosts, leading either to attempts at masking their identity as faux Britons (in the past) or the performance of an exaggerated Australianness, drawing on folk types and behaviours available at particular times. This performance was both satirised and deployed by Barry Humphries, who recently admitted that Barry McKenzie provided 'a good outlet for my Australianness'. However, the larrikin style performed in Britain in the 1960s and 70s owes a great deal to the bohemianism that Humphries, Beresford, James, Greer, Hughes, Thoms, Neville, Sharp and Anderson had already played at in the Sydney Push and the Drift pubs from the 1950s. As noted, the Push in particular performed an urbane and urban larrikinism that grafted their Libertarian ideas to older traditions of the *Bulletin* and *Smith's Weekly* which bohemians kept alive in Australian journalistic circles.

In Australia, the combination of the stylised working-class ensemble of beer, betting, cursing and carousing allowed the slumming young bourgeois and the socially mobile student alike to cross borders between markets and classes as artists on the make. Could it perform the same trick in the metropolis? The antics of Neville, Greer, James and Humphries, combining larrikinism with sophisticated academic capital, along with countercultural transgression and pluralism, was novel and overturned elite British expectations of provincial Australians. The expatriates were not playing by the coded rules and condescension of the British class system. James explained his resolve to 'exploit the [Australian] image but only by countering its negative expectations, and never by reinforcing them', thus producing surprise.[17] The larrikin carnivalesque declared them to be exotics outside that system who did not care about the rules of British class gradations, and could therefore deliver seemingly original insights. Clive James noted his media appeal increasing 'the more I played the visiting Aussie with the unexpectedly confident perspective on disintegrating Britain'.[18] In the same way, Humphries' characters Edna Everage and Barry McKenzie were loaded dogs rather than pet Australians, their ironic observations of both the metropolitan and Australian cultures cutting through to their creator's advantage.

This larrikinism, which may have been dismissed as boorish provincialism in other times, worked to the advantage of Australian artists in the London of the 1960s and early 70s. They exaggerated behaviours already ascendant in the countercultures such as play, humour, wildness and intoxication. Elevating Australian artists, journalists and academics suited the mood of social mobility encouraged in Harold Wilson's Britain and typified by the homegrown provincial working class like the 'Angry Young Men' playwrights and the Beatles and an assortment of northern and Celtic celebrities who came to work in metropolitan cultural institutions at this time, such as Sean Connery, Dennis Potter and Michael Parkinson. In this context it is revealing that both Greer and James first had their British television break on Manchester's Granada Television. Finally, in the cosmopolitan potpourri that was 'Swinging London' the very familiarity of Australians may have made them preferable in English eyes to their competitors from the West Indies and the Indian subcontinent.

Historian of national identity Richard White has shown with reference to nineteenth-century expatriates how colonial Australians abroad performed an idea of Australianness that the English could read.[19] The West Indians had a profound influence on the style of youth subcultures in Britain, and were demonised in media moral panics around race, deviancy and crime.[20]

Exotic yet familiar, Australians enjoyed an early advantage in London over other immigrants from the Commonwealth, like Jamaicans, Indians and Pakistanis, by being middle class and white. In a country confronting rising racial tension and radical challenges to white Englishness from mass immigration, the Australians' countercultural style was a much less threatening form of difference. This larrikin style of bohemianism was no less authentic than the West Indian Rastafarian or rude boy styles, and could even be destabilising of English moral and gender codes.

But while helping the expatriates participate as exotics in the metropolitan market, the larrikin style of bohemianism also encouraged them to think of themselves as Australians, underpinning a cosmopolitan nationalism that many brought back with them in the early 1970s. *Oz* cover girl and Carnaby Street fashion designer Jenny Kee related how for the first time she felt free to be not just radical, but simultaneously Asian and an Australian.[21] Free from intimidation by cultural conservatives in their homeland, travelling cultural provocateurs such as Humphries, Beresford, Weir and Kee found the opportunity to play with Australian identity on the public stage in Britain a liberating experience. What was emerging was a distinctively levelling, ironic and permissive dialogue with what it meant to be Australian that would be welcome within the cosmopolitan nationalism of the Whitlam era.

'CULTURE UP TO OUR ARSEHOLES'
A 'new nationalism' became an enthusiasm for many creative artists and activists working within local countercultures in the early 1970s. The trend began during the prime ministership of small 'l' Liberal John Gorton, and was accentuated after the election in 1972 of the Whitlam government, which pursued a program of arts funding across genres and media for cultural production with an Australian focus. This largesse was lampooned by Barry Humphries and Bruce Beresford who had Barry McKenzie, played by Barry Crocker, advise a struggling expat in Paris that '[t]he Government's shelling out piles of bloody moolah on any prick who reckons he can paint pitchers, write pomes or make flaming fillums'. Bazza is incredulous that drunken film critic

Paddy (a caricature of then reviewer McGuinness, played by Clive James) 'copped $20,000 to come over here to go to the flicks!' Despairing of the palace of Versailles as an 'old ruin', Bazza boasts to the bemused French that 'in Australia we've got culture up to our arseholes'.[22] Rather than reviving earlier radical nationalist romanticism about their homeland, younger artists, many of whom had spent time abroad, were clearly poking fun at what it meant to be Australian, playing with the older identities by exposing them to the freer society that was emerging. Film and theatre directors, playwrights, journalists and writers depicted Australians navigating a choppy sea change.

The Whitlam government was committed to 'help develop a national identity through artistic expression' and to use the arts to 'project Australia's image in other countries'.[23] The new government's arts adviser, veteran public servant H.C. 'Nugget' Coombs, believed that the arts in Australia had been 'too little influenced by the environment, dreams, prejudices, interests and values which are peculiarly Australian' and for this reason 'the arts have often been regarded as suspect by so many of our people'.[24] Whitlam's 1972 policy speech stated that Labor would use the arts to 'help establish and express an Australian identity'. A new Australia Council for the Arts was established as a statutory authority headed by Coombs with appointed boards in each art form acting autonomously to assess projects and dispense grants to successful applicants. Grants to the Australia Council increased from $5,098,000 in 1972 to $14 million in 1973, $21 million in 1974 and $24 million in 1975.[25] In 1975 Whitlam formed the Australian Film Commission, modelled on the successful South Australian Film Commission.

On the back of its heroic support for the arts, the Whitlam era became known for a 'cultural renaissance'. This was often said with irony by the very artists most identified with it, for an important element in the artistic new nationalism was a sense of self-mockery. For example *Barry McKenzie Holds His Own* is introduced by a fictional (Labor) Minister for Culture, Senator Doug Manton (Humphries as a proto Sir Les Patterson) with a model of the Opera House in front of him, a huge Fosters ad behind him, and the buzz of blowflies just audible in the background. Doug boasts about the wave of Aussie 'artistic endeavour' sweeping the world, comparing it to the 'Italian Renaissance' while leafing through his copy of *Venomous Toads of Australia*. 'The fillum you're about to see,' he puffs, 'makes me proud to be an Australian.' Showing he appreciated the joke, Gough appeared in the film's finale as himself to welcome home the Australian travellers and Dame Edna.

Whitlam's attitude to Australian nationalism was as important as government patronage of arts. The new prime minister had as little time for the racially based radical nationalism still nostalgically revered by some elements of the left (including in the ALP) as he did for the crimson ties of Britishness. Whitlam had come of age during the modernist rebellion of the 1940s and shared with former leader H.V. Evatt and left liberal intellectuals of his generation a commitment to an Australia that was simultaneously more independent of Britain and the United States and also more cosmopolitan. He rejected a monolithic nationalism for one embracing Australia's increasing diversity. An 'authentic Australianism can readily accommodate foreign influences and foreign cultures', he declared in a speech at the anniversary of the Eureka Stockade.[26] Whitlam's nationalism was 'new' precisely because it was cosmopolitan, and this would harmonise with the sensibilities of counterculture artists reconnecting with the local as they matured, or returned home, and put down roots in the 1970s. Indeed one consequence of Labor's support for culture was a hiatus in the exodus of graduates and artists out of Australia and the return of many left-leaning expatriates hoping to secure work.

While the new Labor government recognised through its cultural policy the critical and commercial legitimacy of the modernists of the 1940s and 50s – such as Sidney Nolan, Arthur Boyd and Patrick White, who had been shunned during the long Liberal years – it also enabled young artists from the countercultures who had different ideas to the modernists about mass media and the carnivalesque to focus on Australian themes and styles. Yet the derision of national institutions, colonial deference to great and powerful friends and the suburban homogeneity of 'Alf and Ethel' culture begged the question – what would these young critics put in its place?

Since the bohemian identity had first appeared in Australia

in the nineteenth century, artists had sought to combine its more cosmopolitan elements with nationalist sentiment, partly in opposition to colonial 'groveldom', partly to win audiences for their own work against overseas imports, but also because of a romantic belief that artists should connect with the people and land. While each of these was a factor in the early 1970s new nationalism, there were other causes as well. Paradoxically, many new nationalists were inspired to go local by overseas trends. Internationally, countercultural play with identity was leading to romantic nostalgia for 'authentic' roots – always a strong element in bohemian discourse. This had a popular culture and political dimension. By the late 1960s the Beatles had ditched their eastern exotica and hippie apparel for the garb of Edwardian dandies, and on their *White Album* sought to explore traditional English and American musical forms. In America alternative rock bands such as The Band, Creedence Clearwater Revival and Crosby, Stills, Nash and Young were turning away from acid-inspired surrealism and exploring older styles of 'roots' music like bluegrass, blues and country and western. In Australia Martin Sharp moved from psychedelia to nostalgically referencing Australia's cartoon legacy and Tin Pan Alley tunes with Tiny Tim. Captain Matchbox also looked to 'roots' sounds such as hillbilly 'jug' music, while fellow Carlton band Daddy Cool played a stripped-back 1950s style Australian rock'n'roll in the anthemic 'Eagle Rock'.

Politically, New Left focus on the culture of oppressed people as a form of resistance translated to Australia as a post-colonial identity distinct from British or American 'cultural imperialism'. The protest against the Vietnam War, in particular, was encouraging of a postcolonial perspective that affected the arts. Looking back in the 1980s, filmmaker Peter Weir explained that it appeared to him that the war had 'unleashed energy and conflict, passion. You always have to look at movements in society, to look at any such movement in the arts. You never get a sudden rash of painters, opera singers, dancers or filmmakers just like that from nowhere.'[27]

The questioning of Australia's military subservience to the US spilled over into ambivalence about the impact of American culture on Australian distinctiveness. The Australian Performing

Group campaigned for Australian rather than imported plays to be performed, and filmmakers and their political allies pushed to establish an Australian film industry.

In 1972 Geoffrey Serle expressed the hope that the new generation of artists, with the nationalist/internationalist synthesis of Patrick White and Sidney Nolan for inspiration, 'are no longer tortured by the "complex fate" of being culturally colonial Australian artists'.[28] However the anxieties apparent in the rhetoric of the Whitlam government and of young artists themselves suggests that the dilemmas of the 1940s and 50s were being revisited by a new generation. For young artists interested in pop culture, it was necessary to rerun in film and TV, and also bourgeois theatre, the exploration of Australianness that the 1940s generation had conducted in avant-garde painting and literature.

Whereas the modernist avant-garde looked to their own vision and the power of myth to interpret the Australian landscape and its cultural malaise, Richard Walsh in journalism, Graeme Blundell and David Williamson in theatre, and Bruce Beresford and Tim Burstall in film looked to the way people lived now.

As the 1960s generation of bohemian artists grew up, travelled overseas, then established families and settled in neighbourhoods, the sustained opposition to the Australia of their parents' generation transformed into a critical engagement with local culture and institutions during a time of change. Arguably, a critique of traditional Australian life born in countercultural bohemia became the essence of the new nationalism, as exemplified by the feisty weekly newspaper *Nation Review*, Carlton's avant-garde Australian Performing Group, the cinema revival and even 1970s pop music.

A NATION REVIEWED

Established in 1970 to promote an original and radical Australia, the weekly, first known as *Sunday Review* and later as *Nation Review*, owed its genesis not to the Whitlam government, but to the vision and money of Push entrepreneur and Australia Party founder Gordon Barton. Granted control of style and content, editor Richard Walsh plugged the Melbourne-based magazine into his network of young illustrators and writers who had emerged from 1960s underground publishing. A flick through *Review*'s pages reveals many of the names associated with student publications in the early 1960s and the countercultural creative projects of the late sixties, the Push and the expatriate Australian arts community in London: Bob Ellis, Richard Neville, David Williamson, Mungo MacCallum, Michael Leunig, Barry Oakley, Wendy Bacon, Frank Moorhouse, Phillip Adams and Barry Humphries. In 1971 Walsh was upfront, listing as a principal objective the need 'to explore the possibility of being Australian'.[29] The editor and his team were seized by the idea of creating a contemporary, funny yet influential national paper. Walsh, like Archibald at the *Bulletin*, encouraged a 'heady mix of iconoclasm and wit', combining cartoons, news, culture and humour. The paper's irreverent style came both from a conscious awareness of the larrikin tradition of journalistic bohemia reinforced by the older reporters on the staff – including John Hepworth, Richard Beckett and George Munster – as well as drawing on the countercultures of the 1960s, which had been the formative experiences of its mainly young team.[30] Ellis preferred the subjective celebrity style of the American new journalism as the way forward, though the nineteenth-century *Bulletin* was novel precisely because it also looked to the United States and an earlier form of new journalism.

Review was comfortable with diversity in Australia, and assumed its readers had an informed interest in international affairs, especially the Asian region, and was sophisticated about global trends in art and media. Donald Horne correctly recognised the strong connection to the style of postwar intellectual bohemia, observing that *Review* 'developed something new, an Australian intellectual vernacular – tough, sardonic, racy, hardy, meaty, an idealisation of progressive intellectuals' conversation'.[31]

Review, based in Melbourne, balanced Sydney Libertarianism's pluralism and scepticism of power with the Carlton scene's commitment to creative arts and the older liberal left intellectual tradition in that city, which believed the state and nation mattered and could make a difference. Still, *Review* deployed the countercultural approach of ridiculing traditional

Australian institutions such as political parties, vice-regal office holders and the churches. The young cartoonists Michael Leunig, Patrick Cook and Peter Nicholson, who had worked on *Oz*, brought existential and non-materialist themes to the Australian black-and-white tradition. Unlike the uniformity of Australian newspapers at the time, *Review* was heterogeneous in opinions and contributors. But it rejected the more esoteric obsessions of the counterculture to build a bridge between radicals and the institutions of Australian society that they wanted to change. This national direction was confirmed when *Review* amalgamated with the older *Nation* in July 1972 to produce *Nation Review*. It not only sought to influence opinion leaders but, more ambitiously, to transform sixties iconoclasts into mainstream commentators on national life to rival the established voices by presenting positive, constructive alternatives. *Nation Review*'s writers had matured from rejecting Australia to trying to remake it.

Nevertheless, *Review* remained sufficiently countercultural to cause occasional embarrassment to Barton, who complained of 'the gap in values between people of my generation and the people who are creating *Review*'. Whereas his 1950s generation of intellectuals was dedicated to 'the dispassionate and reasonable approach to all issues', the young approach in *Review* was 'wrapped up in something called commitment, in which it is not a vice to be passionate, but a virtue'.[32] Notwithstanding its proprietor's misgivings, it was the opinionated and trendy approach *Review* took from the underground that distinguished it from other older 'objective' newspapers and won it young readers who found this refreshing. By 1971 *Review*'s readership numbered a respectable 40,000, though it needed regular cross-subsidisation from Barton's other businesses.[33] As with Archibald's *Bulletin*, a genuine radical nationalism had emerged from a playful, satirical engagement with the local scene and a critique of the media status quo.

'GET OUR OWN STORIES ON STAGE'

The new wave of Australian theatre in the early seventies associated with the Pram Factory in Melbourne and Sydney's Jane Street and Nimrod theatres was an outgrowth of local and international countercultural experimentation in performance art. The Australian Performing Group (APG) emerged from the Carlton bohemia that began as the Drift in the 1950s and diversified into theatre, film, music and visual art in the 1960s. It began life in 1968 at La Mama Theatre, in an ex-shirt factory in Carlton, and gained an additional theatre in a disused pram factory in 1970 – the premises by which the company was better known. Key playwrights were David Williamson, Barry Oakley, Alex Buzo and Jack Hibberd, and noted performers were Graeme Blundell, Max Gillies, Jane Clifton, Greig Pickhaver (H.G. Nelson), Evelyn Krape, Jack Charles, Sue Ingleton, Peter Cummins, Kerry Dwyer, Red Symons, John Duigan, Jude Kuring, Yvonne Marini, Bruce Spence and Jenny Kemp. The APG was a testing ground for new ideas and styles that went from having small audiences to enjoying mainstream popularity with playes re-versioned in film and television.

Student theatrical satire and drama was an important local incubator and the university community and graduates provided the sympathetic core audience for the experimental theatre groups in all capital cities necessary for talent to be nurtured and themes massaged before works were taken to larger mainstream audiences. The APG members were intertwined with other art forms, especially rock'n'roll and avant-garde cinema. More importantly, Carlton's student bohemia was immersed in the protest movement against the Vietnam War and conscription that was sweeping Australian university campuses. Jim Davidson has commented on the direct relationship between the protest on the street and the political iconoclasm of the new theatre, suggesting: 'If the small Carlton roughhouse was the pressure cooker for the new drama, then it was fired over the crucible of Viet Nam.'[34]

At first, frustration over the conservative form of the mainstream theatre, rather than the established companies' cringe against Australian plays, motivated the formation of independent companies such as Jane Street, the Nimrod, Mews, Q and APG. The APG founders were enamoured of the innovation promoted in the American avant-garde journal the *Tulane Drama Review*. La Mama stalwart Graeme Blundell described his application of the latest American avant-garde methods in his acting workshops, where '[w]e tossed around dramatic ideas on confrontation and environment from Chaikin, Grotowski, Schenner, Julian Beck and Judith Malina, and Jerry Lewis ... We got into psychotherapy, group gropes and encounter training.'[35] Phillip Adams referred in the *Bulletin* to the popularity of the *Village Voice* among La Mama audiences. Betty Burstall even took the name La Mama from her favourite avant-garde theatre in New York. Their engagement with new American experimentation distinguished the younger generation from an establishment enthralled by older British forms.

The APG abandoned theatrical conventions to create new hybrids of cabaret, satire, slapstick, musicals and serious drama. Initially, interest in Australian content ran second to an emphasis on experimentation in form, such as the collapsing of boundaries between audience and performers. It was argued in journals like *Tulane* that theatre could be invigorated by replacing the authoritarian director with a 'collective' that undertook group workshopping of ideas and performance. *Marvellous Melbourne*, the first play to open in the Pram Factory in 1970, was created collectively by the cast around a local theme.

Despite the international genesis of the new wave, by the early 1970s the APG, Nimrod and Q had 'turned their gaze inward and backward, particularly to popular forms and styles from within Australia'.[36] The impetus was a national assertion of Australianness against the perceived dominance of overseas product in Australian theatre, as in other art forms, like cinema. In 1970 Sydney's Jane Street Theatre performed *The Legend of King O'Malley*, the story of a self-invented Federation-era Labor politician written by Bob Ellis and Michael Boddy, to commercial acclaim. In Carlton, Hibberd's *Dimboola* and Williamson's plays also proved that Australian stories and language were popular with audiences and critics. At a seminar on 'Indigenous Theatre' in 1972, organised by the APG, the director of the Melbourne Theatre Company was attacked for his Eurocentric neglect of local plays.[37] Williamson recalled in 2004 that

> at last we were going to get our own stories on stage spoken in our own accents, reflecting our own life, because up to that stage Australian plays had been few and far between.

> There were no Australian films, no Australian television,
> and our stories were simply not being told. And so there
> was an anger about that, but also an excitement and a
> determination to get the Australian way of life on stage.[38]

Oblivious to the work of the New Theatre movement or
women radio dramatists in the 1950s or the gritty TV drama of
Crawford Productions of the 1960s, Williamson's generation was
engaging with Australianness in the context of anti-imperialist
cultural activism. APG stalwart John Romeril recalled that
'you felt false, unreal, hollow … alienated, unlocated' because
'you didn't speak like you really spoke, weren't relaying what
you heard on the street, you were an outpost of empire'.[39]

Despite the inspiration drawn from the New York avant-
garde, this postcolonial protest was also directed at 'US cultural
imperialism', with La Mama performing a number of plays on
this theme. By 1973 the APG was claiming that its experimentation was directed 'towards the development of a truly indigenous
theatre, strongly rooted in the community and dealing with the
myths and realities of life in Australia; a theatre built from the
fabric – past, present and future – of Australian society itself.'
Such a mission dovetailed with the postcolonial mood emanating from the protest movement, with which APG claimed
close affinity. However, the plays that attracted both critical
praise and commercial success were those such as Williamson's
The Coming of Stork, *Don's Party* and *The Removalists* that used
slang, humour and vulgarity traditionally associated with the
larrikin carnivalesque. Typical of counterculture art, the new
wave theatre was conceived as experimentation that should also
be popular, and reworked traditional popular forms such as the
musical, music hall and comedy to develop a style that appealed
to younger Australian audiences. The decisive move of some
members of this generation into commercial film dominated by
'realism' most clearly signalled a departure from the avant-garde
approach of mid-century modernists.

'EVERYBODY WANTED TO BE NUDE'
The origins of the Australian film revival are to be found in both
the theatrical new wave and the network of filmmakers who had

honed cine skills in a vibrant local 'underground' experimental filmmaking scene and television-based advertising, drama and documentary-making. There was substantial crossover between the theatre and cinema practitioners, and both groups were connected within Sydney, Melbourne and expatriate bohemian communities. Some of the fringe-theatre-to-popular-film translations were Williamson's plays *Stork* (1971), *Don's Party* (1976) and *The Removalists* (1975), directed by Tim Burstall, Bruce Beresford and Tom Jeffrey respectively, and *The Rocky Horror Picture Show* (1975), in which director Jim Sharman reprised his camp stage musical of 1973. All these commercial films delighted in the body and sex, reflecting the common experience of the filmmakers in avant-garde theatre and cinema. As Graeme Blundell fondly recalled (in the 2008 documentary *Not Quite Hollywood*) of the Pram Factory where he acted and directed, 'Everybody wanted to be nude. People were nude in the streets … Nude at parties … Nude at home. People were proud of their bodies. Men of their beer bellies. It was a celebration of fleshliness.'

During the second half of the 1960s Bruce Beresford, Mike Thornhill, Margaret Fink, Bob Ellis and Albie Thoms enjoyed their own filmmaking bohemia within the ecumenical Sydney Filmmakers Co-op and the avant-garde Ubu Films. Melbourne directors Fred Schepisi and Tim Burstall were in the Carlton scene and participated in the Producers and Directors Guild of Victoria. As with theatre, the filmmakers participated in international film networks that interfaced with both experimental avant-garde projects and mainstream film production. Beresford, Thoms, Tim Burstall and Weir all left Australia in the late 1960s to study filmmaking trends in the metropolitan centres, and exhibited in underground film festivals. By their own admission they were at this time more interested in the art of filmmaking and experimentation in form rather than in Australian stories. Weir remembered the cosmopolitan mood of his generation of filmmakers in the 1960s: 'Australia was of no interest to me. None. I couldn't wait to leave, and I left at twenty.'[40]

They cut their teeth making short, experimental films in the late 1960s, taking advantage of the Experimental Film Fund established by Gorton in 1970. Some films, such as *The*

American Poet's Visit, focused on the filmmakers' bohemian milieus and others parodied genres like horror and spy thrillers – for example, Sharman's *Shirley Thompson Versus the Aliens* and Thoms' *Blunderball*. By 1972 over one hundred short films had been funded by the scheme.

Then, in the early 1970s, many of the same filmmakers turned their gaze to Australian stories like *The Adventures of Barry McKenzie*, *Alvin Purple*, *The Cars That Ate Paris* and the Williamson plays. Was the move to national themes a cynical ploy to increase audience share by artists tired of avant-garde obscurity? Albie Thoms thought so, but he was most critical of the surrender to Hollywood narrative style. He criticised the feature films of Weir, Beresford, Schepisi and Burstall for abandoning the deconstructed surrealism and exposure of artifice that had dominated underground cinema in the late 1960s, accusing them of everything from obsequious capitulation to pseudo realism.[41] A strong case can be made, however, that the Australian film revival owed its style of nationalism and its popularity with local audiences to its underground origins.

The 1960s underground cinema's rejection of studios and sets in favour of documenting actual life, attributed by Thoms to 'the desperate attempt by this generation to understand itself and the world in which it lives', compelled these filmmakers to focus on the local Australian life around them.[42] Parody and a permissive attitude to sexuality and the body continued from the experimental into commercial films, encouraged by Coombs, who had argued controversially that sex could help revive the industry. The relaxation of censorship and introduction of the R certificate forged common ground between the permissive counterculture and suburban audiences enamoured of 'risqué, vulgar, vaudevillian titillation as old as Australian popular culture itself'.[43] The early films of the revival, especially the cycle of ocker comedies in the first half of the 1970s, shared with *Review* and the Australian Performing Group a strong sense of carnival, which thanks to distribution into suburban cinemas and drive-ins proved to be a hit with mass-market audiences.

Both the federal government and the filmmakers themselves came to recognise that commercial and 'quality' were not mutually exclusive. Beresford had wearied of the conventions of avant-garde film while commissioning this genre for the British Film Institute and creating visual effects for 'happenings', and had purged himself by making a parody of the genre to be used as a clip in a Barry Humphries character sketch – underground filmmaker Martin Agrippa. In developing the Barry McKenzie films, both men sought to marry the transgressive qualities of their art such as Dada, cathartic vulgarity and the grotesque with commercial appeal.

LIVIN' IN THE 70S: POP-MUSIC DANDIES

The Carlton art precinct also gave Australia the bittersweet music of Skyhooks, an innovative band that brought together tertiary-educated musos Greg Macainsh and Red Symons with cheeky, good-looking tradie Graeme 'Shirley' Strachan, who became the frontman. At Swinburne Tech film student Macainsh had directed an experimental documentary about Melbourne's skinhead-like sharpie subculture, and Symons was a cultured computer science graduate who had acted with the Pram Factory. From the interests of this creative and radical milieu came songs like 'Whatever Happened to the Revolution' and 'Carlton (Lygon Street Limbo)'. But the charismatic carpenter Shirley provided the much-needed larrikinism and street grit to win working-class audiences. While outraging with gender-bending fashion and over-the-top make-up inspired by the British glam movement and Melbourne's cabaret scene, Skyhooks were unmistakably Australian in accent and humour. Hits like 'Livin' in the 70s' and 'Horror Movie' dealt with the contemporary city- and mediascapes, heralding a new era of rock flâneurs in Australian pop culture. There was transgression, too, including Symons' jaunty ditty 'Smut', about a teenager in a crowded cinema sneakily masturbating into a greasy Twisties bag. The song 'You Just Like Me 'Cos I'm Good in Bed' was deemed sufficiently offensive and corrupting of teenagers to be banned by commercial AM radio stations.

Skyhooks united its fanbase of hip inner-city connoisseurs with beer-barn boyos and even the delinquent sharpies, but with the added and all-important demographic of smitten teenage girls. The band's successful parlay from fringe to famous owed quite a bit to the promotional skills of cultural entrepreneur

Michael Gudinski and his Mushroom Records label, but even more to the ABC's new national music television show *Countdown*. The band's theatrical clobber and cosmetics, their cheeky on-camera antics, the twinkle in Shirley's eye and the sense of haughty menace emanating from Red conspired to make Skyhooks perfect stars for the age of colour TV. Their camp style also resonated with *Countdown*'s own, which owed something to the humour and showbiz sensibility of executive producer Michael Shrimpton and 'talent coordinator' Ian 'Molly' Meldrum's den-mother enthusiasm. But the music was also very good, and the diverse audiences responded to energising, intelligent and often sexually explicit songs about where and how young people now lived in Australian cities and suburbs.

Another edgy amalgam of bohemia and blue collar was the Adelaide band Cold Chisel, which brought together the powerful songs of hyper-educated Don Walker with raspy-voiced Glaswegian immigrant Jimmy Barnes. As the name implied, Cold Chisel understood the hard working-class life of the new outer suburbs like Elizabeth, where Jimmy learned to fight and drink. But even more than Skyhooks the band had an acute, and indeed romantic, sense of place. In 'Khe Sanh' Walker's countercultural sensibilities left him acutely aware of the scars gouged in the psyche of Australian men returning without fanfare from Vietnam in the 1970s. Later, in 'Flame Trees', Cold Chisel would come close to a classic rendering of the melancholy nostalgia and hope that greets the weary time-worn prodigal returning to the small town of his youth. A struggling pub band in the late 1970s, Chisel sharpened its act in the sweaty bloodhouses of steel towns like Newcastle and clapped-out Kings Cross nightclubs to emerge into the national spotlight, first via public radio and 2JJ and then *Countdown*, with a repertoire that spoke truths about Australians from the other side of the tracks. Barnes and his band were also wild boys, and became notorious for their hard-partying lifestyle of sex and drugs and rock'n'roll. And booze, plenty of booze.

• • •

What made audiences applaud the theatre, films, writing and rock music of the 1970s was the injection of a sense of play and engagement with modern reality that owed much to the young artists' bohemia. Unlike the older left, they took an irreverent and permissive approach to contemporary Australian society and the past. The portrayal of Australian identity in journalism, theatre and films showed people as sexually active, out of control, frequently funny, contradictory and sometimes frightening. The ocker trend in cinema combined 'low' vaudeville traditions and Carlton countercultural obsessions with the body. The Barry McKenzie films referenced cultural traditions Australians had found diverting, including black-and-white cartoons, music hall, burlesque and musicals, student and TV revue, and satirical magazines of the 1960s, together with Humphries' more avant-garde passions for Dada, surrealism and Wildean irony.

It was the satirical, humorous streak in the popular art of the seventies that produced an Australianness closer to the spirit of the early *Bulletin* writers than the earnest radical nationalism of Vance Palmer in the 1930s and 40s and the postwar left. Carnivalesque elements in *The Adventures of Barry McKenzie*, for example, included drunkenness, gluttony, parody, sexual ribaldry, obsession with genitals and bodily excretions, gender confusion and riot. Creative use of slang was apparent in *Stork*, *Petersen*, *Don's Party* and especially the Barry McKenzie movies, where Humphries recalled '[i]t was marvellously liberating to lift slang from C.J. Dennis, Geelong Grammar, Bluey and Curley, the mural felicities of divers memorable dunnies' as well as from builders' labourers employed by his father. Sampling the older larrikin carnivalesque became a conscious cultural strategy in the early 1970s. Wearing his other hat as publisher of Angus & Robertson (which Barton had also purchased), Richard Walsh systematically rereleased the back catalogue of Australian classics, such as *The Sentimental Bloke*, *On Our Selection* and the humorous fiction of Norman Lindsay. Phillip Adams, a contributor to *Review* and producer of *The Adventures of Barry McKenzie*, explained how in making contemporary satire he, Beresford and Humphries were conscious that 'Australian cinema has a larrikin tradition dating back to *The Sentimental Bloke*, to the early films of George Wallace, to the *Dad and Dave* series', that was worth modernising.[44]

Sydney playwright Bob Ellis signalled that whereas cultural

conservatives and modernists alike shared a prejudice of Australia being a 'barbaric, working-class, provincial, ignorant nation of under-stimulated slobs', his generation of artists would look at the reality of the country for inspiration.[45] The new nationalism was an effective way for the young generation of filmmakers, performers and writers to be simultaneously subversive and popular, and to distinguish themselves from the older modern-ists such as Patrick White and Max Harris who considered it a return to the bad old parochial Australia they had rebelled against in the war years. But was the new nationalism the undoing of cosmopolitanism, or an engagement with it?

'OCKER IS KING!' A NEW COSMOPOLITAN NATIONALISM?

Since the nineteenth century, Australian bohemians had enjoyed a love/hate relationship with the working class. At different times lower-class characters had been a source of human drama, a cause and/or a butt for humour. Lawson enjoyed the fraternity of working men's pubs but feared a brutality lurking in their way of life. Bohemians of the 1950s and 60s in the Push had derided lower-class suburban 'Alfs', while imitating the Australian working-class male's slang and love of the pub and gambling. An exaggerated larrikinism, as we have seen, became an inte-gral part of the expatriate bohemianism in London. Then, in the early 1970s, the working-class male was repackaged as the appalling yet appealing ocker, especially in new nationalist films and plays where he became a foil for conservatives, earnest left intellectuals, prudes, trendies and the English motherland.

The late 1960s and 70s was a period of rapid change like the 1890s. As blue-collar work made way for white-collar work, more and more women entered the workforce and tertiary education expanded. Social mobility increased and mass migra-tion brought new diversity, while ever-expanding suburbia threatened to domesticate the old-style Australia of bush, push and war. Like their *Bulletin* forebears, Humphries and Beresford, but also Williamson and other artists, looked to the disappearing Australian working man with both satire and nostalgia to say things about a culture emerging from isolation. The Barry McKenzie character is badged as a relic from a bygone era by his double-breasted suit and especially his hat, and set loose among the foreigners, artists, hippies and feminists that made up Swinging London. There were few new social movements of the 1970s that McKenzie did not drive to distraction, allowing Humphries and Beresford to remind audiences how intransigent the old suburban Australia could be in the face of these changes. Satirising the attitudes of 'white Australia' *Barry McKenzie Holds His Own* shows a bunch of Anglo-Celtic blokes terribly anxious about other races. Despite having come from a country in the throes of a massive immigration program and a government pledged to land rights and a racial discrimination act, Bazza and his mates don't care much for 'abos', 'heathen chinee', 'yellerens', 'frogs', 'wogs' and 'dagoes'. Humphries' and Beresford's ockers

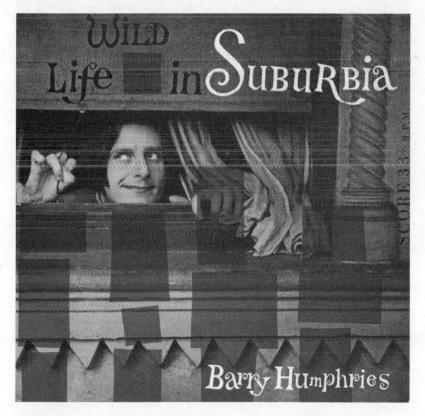

Barry Humphries, Dadaist, aesthete and satirist, in an early record *Wild Life in Suburbia*, vol. 1, 1958, introduced Australians to Moonee Ponds housewife Edna Everage.

mouth the slang of the streets and playground rather than the sanitised language of government tolerance programs.

The emergence of ocker art was a satirical reworking of the larrikin, the bush worker, even C.E.W. Bean's 'digger' as popularised by *Smith's Weekly*. Prototype ocker characters first appeared in John O'Grady's satirical novel *They're a Weird Mob* and the film of the same name, where white Australian 'originals' were thrown into relief and made 'weird' by the novel's (and film's) Italian immigrant narrator. These characters had become exotic because Australia was becoming more ethnically diverse.

While the ocker character gave centre stage to the performance that bohemians had long rehearsed in the subcultural confines of Sydney and Melbourne pubs, and had toured abroad as travellers, he lacked the cultural capital of the bohemian to successfully cross over borders and instead made a loud nuisance of himself as he became stuck between classes, genders, ethnicities and nationalities – this was his value as an artistic device. The ocker was an anti-bohemian mask that allowed artists as different as Humphries, Williamson, Burstall, Beresford, Grahame Bond and Garry McDonald to expose old Australia to a cosmopolitan world at home and abroad. Ockers like Barry McKenzie, Stork, the loutish labourites at *Don's Party*, *Petersen*, *Alvin Purple* and *Aunty Jack* allowed bohemians to identify with Australia while simultaneously mocking how incomplete was its cosmopolitan journey.

On TV the 'sex 'n' sin' television soap opera *Number 96*, which first aired on the Ten Network in 1972, boasted some impressive ocker characters pitted against various eccentrics, migrants, socialites and countercultural types who made up the gentrifying inner-city suburb of Paddington. The avant-garde playwright Steve J. Spears worked on the early scripts. The absurdist performance troupe of Grahame Bond, Garry McDonald and Rory O'Donoghue that emerged from Sydney University's Architecture Revue in the 1960s created a number of Australian grotesques for their popular ABC comedy programs, including the drag-wearing pugilist Aunty Jack, weedy regional television reporter Norman Gunston and bodgie butcher Kev Kavanagh. As with Humphries' work, comedy was extracted by bringing provincial Australia – symbolised by Wollongong – into contact with metropolitan sensibilities.

Appalled by the vulgarity of Barry McKenzie, Alvin Purple and their ilk, Max Harris used his considerable media profile to condemn the younger artists. Ocker satire triggered a stand-off between two different generational perceptions of Australian creative culture. The avant-garde art of the Angry Penguins had explored nationalist themes, but in an elitist way, seeing them-selves as prophets in a philistine wilderness. The new nationalist artists of the early 1970s were exploring identity in the popular media of film and television with themes they were confident would resonate with the mass audiences across classes, as this had been their bohemian practice throughout the 1960s.

Judging by the commercial success of the ocker films, the working-class market in the suburbs enjoyed watching stories about ordinary Australians in extraordinary situations, and perhaps enjoyed the use of characters such as Petersen and McKenzie to puncture pretensions. But these characters were ambiguous, and were also satirising the inability of the working-class Australian male to adapt to the new cosmopolitanism. Through the ocker, Australian cultural producers such as Burstall, Humphries and Williamson had a bet each way, making art that appealed to the public's residual hostility to intellectuals, artists and authority, while inviting the more discriminating to have a knowing laugh.

• • •

Following the ocker cycle in the second half of the 1970s was the history film. Beginning in theatre with *The Legend of King O'Malley* and *Marvellous Melbourne*, this series of films included bawdy colonial bodice-ripper *Eliza Fraser*, the confronting *Chant of Jimmie Blacksmith* and dystopian bushranger shocker *Mad Dog Morgan*, the last directed by Philippe Mora after his return to Australia. While these films appeared to revive the older radical nationalism, on closer inspection they often buffeted the radical nationalist myths with contemporary concerns, such as toadying to great and powerful friends read in the context of the Vietnam War, or vexed, exploitative white/black relations. Certainly they borrow from radical nationalism's championing of the Australian underdog making do in a world deformed by imperial powers, greedy pastoralists and corrupt police. Lawsonian virtues such as mateship, humour and solidarity were pitched against the powerful in *Sunday Too Far Away*, *Breaker Morant* and *Newsfront*. But countercultural sensibilities modified the tradition, which in these seventies films can incorporate women heroines such as Caddie and Eliza Fraser and the Aborigine Jimmie Blacksmith (based on the story of Jimmy Governor). Australia's past was also invested with a bawdiness and vulgarity hitherto absent from historical films and television, once again marrying countercultural carnival with larrikinism, and exploiting the general permissive mood within 1970s media following the relaxation of censorship.

Harking back to Marcus Clarke, some filmmakers such as Weir developed an Australian gothic that explored menace in the bush and the outback. It is interesting that a 1970s generation of cinematic storytellers too urbanised to romanticise the bush as a sylvan arcadia returned to a gothic treatment of the outback as a force beyond human control. Picturesque cinematography of the bush and rural Australia – in part inspired by the Heidelberg landscape aesthetic – harboured hidden menace: supernatural forces, eccentric villagers, rednecks, Aboriginal dreaming. Building on an earlier cycle of late-1960s films by overseas directors – *Wake in Fright* and *Walkabout* – the seventies movies *Long Weekend*, *The Cars That Ate Paris*, *Picnic at Hanging Rock*, *Inn of the Damned*, *Summer City*, *The Chant of Jimmie Blacksmith* and *The Last Wave* portrayed the bush, the outback and nature itself as creepy, mysterious, unpredictable places that could devour and destroy the unwary. For the urban, cosmopolitan bohemians of Sydney and Melbourne who made these films, the bush was an alien place, evoking terror in the stranger, rather than the folksy romanticism of the *Bulletin* and the Heidelberg School. Peter Weir, in particular, like Marcus Clarke a century earlier, was seized by the gothic idea of the unknown, primeval and malevolent lurking in the Australian landscape.

BOHEMIAN KNOW THY SELF

In the 2008 documentary *Not Quite Hollywood*, Bob Ellis described the counterculture within theatre and other media from which the early 1970s film revival sprang as 'a young aristocracy which were making things and preferring fornication and hallucination to what had preceded'. A number of the plays and films that followed were self-reflexive about this milieu, exploring the place of artists, intellectuals and changing mores in Australian society. David Williamson pillaged his bohemian networks for stories and characters that gave his plays about maturing artists and intellectuals an edgy authenticity. *Stork* and *Petersen* dissected the plight of socially mobile young men from the other side of the tracks thrust into bohemian milieus through tertiary education. Williamson sympathised with working-class aspirationals, depicted in characters such as *Petersen*, whose mobility became a plaything for supercilious dilettantes in academia. *Don's Party* looked at ageing radicals dispirited and bitter in the mire of suburban compromise, disorientated by the individual freedom promised by the new counterculture.

Like Moorhouse in Sydney, Williamson looked at his own bohemia anthropologically, and with irony. The Carlton scene went under the scalpel (and starred) in *The Coming of Stork*. The intellectual pretensions of this bohemia were exposed by the loudmouthed, anarchistic character of Stork, a university dropout unfit for either the working class or bourgeoisie. This self-critical ambivalence of bohemian artists towards their relationship with ordinary Australians is a recurring theme in 1970s Australian film.

Sydney filmmaker Mike Thornhill adapted Moorhouse's *The American Poet's Visit* about the encounter between the Libertarian Push and the eponymous condescending cosmopolitan. Thornhill's feature *Between the Wars* pitted a sophisticated internationally oriented psychiatrist who is friendly with Germans into totalising environments hostile to his curious cosmopolitanism such as outback Australia and the home front of the Second World War. The film places the life of the mind, the passions of the body and intellectual complexity on a collision course with nationalism and order. Carlton filmmaker Bert Deling journeyed among the demimonde of Melbourne's seventies heroin culture in the 1976 black comedy, *Pure S.* (censored from *Shit*) The film featured actors from the Carlton scene, including Helen Garner, Greig Pickhaver and Max Gillies, and captured the interesting mix of bohemians with the criminal subculture that supplied their drugs. These films and plays confronted the uneasy relationship of bohemians and intellectuals in Australia to others such as the underclass, the criminal and the bureaucrat.

Feminist, multicultural and postmodern critics have criticised the new nationalist artists of the 1970s for presenting a totalising white male version of the national story, blind to the heterogeneity of Australia, then and now.[46] While it is true that the new journalism, cinema and theatre of the late 1960s and 70s is frequently masculine and Anglo-Celtic, it is saved from the monoculturalism of the earlier radical nationalist or imperial British identities by a cosmopolitan countercultural bohemianism more sensitive to the increasing diversity within society.

• • •

Countercultural nationalism was playful, critical and questioning rather than patriotic and idealising, and proved a creative and popular way to reconcile the cosmopolitan and nationalist tendencies that had long been in tension in Australian bohemia and were now being played out in the wider Australian society. This countercultural Australianness harmonised with wider changes in Australian society, reflected in the election of the Whitlam government, foreshadowing the emerging policy of 'multiculturalism'. But this popular, pluralist and frequently transgressive nationalism was in tension with older versions of radical nationalism and modernism on the left, and the idea of an Anglophile, suburban Australian way of life promoted by conservatives. These tensions would be played out at the level of government funding and so-called mainstream values and became a focus of culture wars over national identity in the 1980s and 90s.

BOHO TO POMO

1980–2012

There is a strong argument that punk began in Australia – in Inala, Queensland, to be specific. For it was in a garage in this south-western suburb of Brisbane that a trio of schoolboy mates formed the Saints in 1974, preceding New York band the Ramones with the buzzsaw high speed sound of punk.[1] Frontmen Chris Bailey and Ed Kuepper, with their keyboard player turned drummer Ivor Hay, may not have used the word punk back then, but their DIY debut song 'Stranded' leaves no doubt as to genre. Belted out in stripped-back vocals and simple power chords, Bailey sang the familiar bohemian refrain of the frustrated creative soul stranded in the somnolent suburbs distant from the action. An Irish immigrant, he felt exiled in the sticky heat, stifled under the right-wing rule of the long-running Joh Bjelke-Petersen government with its violent early-morning raids on share houses and venues. Like Marcus Clarke and Charles Conder before him, Bailey yearned to be where the action was. As their gigs were constantly closed down mid-song by police, the Saints learned to play fast as well as loud. Bailey and Hay turned their share house in inner-city Brisbane into the 76 Club and advertised their wild gigs by word of mouth. Their homemade demos were played on Brisbane's public radio station 4ZZZ and Sydney's 2JJ. But the mainstream media and recording industry rejected their discordant 'amateurish' sound and cynical take on society, abrasive to ears (and advertisers) accustomed to the high production values of seventies supergroups like the Eagles and Supertramp. It was the greatest irony that EMI Sydney only signed the Saints after being ordered to by the punk-savvy London head office when '(I'm) Stranded' was made single of the week by major British pop paper *Sounds*. (The Brisbane office of EMI, having angrily evicted the band from their offices earlier, refused to be involved.) Their debut album, *Stranded*, was recorded in two days and (briefly) swept the world. The 'mouse that roared' narrative appealed to Australian notions of the battler, and with international vindication the Saints' grainy clip shot in an old terrace with graffiti-splattered walls was aired on *Countdown* to the suburban teenagers of Australia.

The punk explosion of the late 1970s across the west sought to expose all art as a commodity, taking the message of Warhol's soup cans to the street. At an aesthetic level punk was the solution to the romantic dilemma that had dogged bohemia since its inception: how to be a rebellious artist when art is just another capitalist product. The Sex Pistols held the filthy lucre of commerce up for all to see and made sport of authenticity and virtuosity. With a wink at the consumer worthy of Marcus Clarke, a Saints follow-up single was called 'Know Your Product'. Always about far more than anarchy or leather-clad cockney gel-heads spitting on the establishment, the punk explosion was a signal that the boundaries between high and pop culture, past and present, male and female were collapsing. The Dadaists, surrealists and situationists had said similar things before, but not on *Countdown*. Postmodernity had landed in the centre of Australian pop culture and would inspire the work and subcultural style of a new generation of aesthetes and intellectuals coming of age in the 1980s.

By the late 1970s, qualities that had for a century been practised by bohemians such as identity play, sexual permissiveness, and media tools were increasingly available to a larger part of the population. Likewise, at this time politics itself came to hinge more and more on symbolic actions and identity rights. This process rapidly accelerated through the 1980s and 90s, as younger people complemented national, local and class belonging with a smorgasbord of subcultural identities based on style obsessions, sexuality or an array of post-materialist causes, many of which entered mainstream culture via 1960s countercultures. US cultural critic Fredric Jameson described a rapid cultural shift from high modernism to postmodernism, beginning around 1967 and characterised by: a fragmenting of society accompanied by an intellectual celebration of heterogeneity for its own sake; the collapsing of hierarchies separating art and entertainment; a rejection of once-influential 'grand narratives' such as Marxism, and the death of the 'subject', including the artist genius; a focus on textual surfaces dismissive of deeper meanings; and an art of pastiche, nostalgia and parody.[2] Postmodern culture coincided with capitalism's transformation in the west from an industrial economy where factories manufactured goods to a new economy characterised by an increased trade in symbolic commodities and media saturation, and the dominance of the global over national markets.

Just as romanticism and modernism were associated with particular forms of bohemianism, so postmodernism as a creative practice – and theory in its defence – was associated with new generations of creative young people in the 1980s and 90s. While the 1960s countercultures began the process leading to postmodernism, in Australia those who acquired market and sanctifying power in the 1970s came to defend much of the modernist agenda their boundary-busting cultural production had undermined, leaving the next generation to use postmodernist ideas to win new space through conflict. But is bohemianism still possible under the conditions of postmodernity? As Elizabeth Wilson has argued in relation to the northern hemisphere, postmodern bohemia could be difficult in an era where symbolic protest is lost amid the fragmenting cultural diversity and even the most deviant transgression is meaningless.[3] However, the desire to find authenticity under capitalism, the central problem around which the bohemian myth revolved, did indeed continue. From the 1980s through to the present, Australian cities were host to a plethora of inner-city music scenes, spectacular youth subcultures, sexual and other identity movements, grunge writers, zine publishers, performance artists, a street art movement, DIY short filmmakers and a comedy and burlesque boom. Since the 1990s they were joined by digital artists, anarchic cyberpunks and libertarian hacker communities who have colonised the social spaces of the internet as virtual bohemias. This creative ferment and the persistence, indeed intensification, in Australia of a conservative wowser element still determined to find offence suggests that the ambiguities raised by postmodernity may have left a space for bohemia.

THE NEW URBAN TRIBES

A general postmodern aesthetic interested in 'sampling' retro cultures led to the revival of past bohemias and youth styles, mainly from Britain, in Australian cities in the 1980s and 90s, manifest in the appearance on the streets of distinctive youth subcultures in the wake of punk. One of the first were 'mods' looking like they stepped off the King's Road, London, circa 1964 wearing sharp mohair suits, riding Lambrettas and Vespas around on hot summer days and dancing to bands like the Sets at Sydney's Sussex Hotel. Quizzed by a reporter for the 1984 documentary *Tribes of Sydney* about whether he was hot in a suit and parka the young mod replied that he was 'hot on the outside but cool on the inside'. Australian rude boys and girls wearing pork pie hats danced to ska bands, but like their mod brethren seemed to be yearning for Old Blighty, and probably Brixton. In quick succession 'New Romantics' and 'goths' (both nineteenth-century looks), and revivals in the styles of 1950s beatniks and rockabillies, and then 1960s psychedelics and hippies and early seventies skinheads colonised inner-city pubs and clubs – to the point where the different subcultures existed simultane-ously and some determined, if schizophrenic, stylists tried them all! Devotees were drawn from universities, many attended art school and a lucky few worked in the creative industries as cub reporters, photographers or museum attendants. Others were unemployed and looking for a place to belong. They were all wanting to experiment with ways of living and in revolt against the uniformity and sartorial indifference of Australian yob youth culture, whether surfies or the suburban working-class look that would come to be known as 'bogan'. New subcultures would continue to emerge, such as the anti-fashion grunge fans and techno music-loving ravers in the early 1990s, and others, notably goths and punks, would be revived again and again to the present, morphing each time, and engaging with new art forms, styles and even technologies.

But the global flows of information and pop culture from the metropolitan centre meant that Australian youth subcultures drew inspiration from international bohemian movements in their general iconography and pop culture memory, rather than demonstrating an awareness of local bohemian traditions.

Ignorant of a local lineage, these groups have continued the traditional bohemian practice of using emerging (if 'retro') European and American identities to distance themselves from older subcultural groups, and a mainstream constructed as sub-urban, 'yobbish' or philistine. However, what was homegrown about the inner-city youth subcultures was the often truly original live music their social life was based around, and the art, media and of course fashions that the fans themselves produced.

THE INNER-CITY SOUNDS

Since the beginning of the 1980s elements of 'traditional' Australian bohemian styles have re-emerged within an inde-pendent post-punk 'music scene' that crisscrossed the capital cities, where bands became the focus of small peer-based bohe-mias drawn mainly from university and art school students. Growing in artistic credibility since the 1960s and energised by punk, new music variously dubbed 'the inner-city sound', 'new wave', 'alternative' and 'indie' attained status among the creative young bourgeoisie just as poetry, painting, satire and film were embraced by earlier bohemian generations. Some achieved mainstream success in Australia in the 1980s but many others were denied airplay on radio and television and remained corralled in the fringe market.[1] Frustrated, the more ambitious, following the exodus of earlier generations, fled their homeland for Britain, France and even Germany.

In their own ways, 'indie' punk and post-punk bands that formed in cities around Australia wanted to take rock'n'roll back to its 1950s and early 60s simplicity, restore its youthful energy, poetics and hint of danger. Music historian David Nicholls notes that Sydney's Radio Birdman and the Saints were influenced by local legends from the 1960s the Missing Links and Masters Apprentices.[5] The new bands wanted melodies that people could dance to very fast, and lyrics they would talk about and quote over beers and bongs at night's end. The Brisbane band scene was typical of that in Melbourne, Sydney and Perth – a hot-house of styles dedicated to the proposition that rock music had taken a wrong turn as the overproduced plaything of stars of the sixties grown old, far removed in their Learjets from the lives of ordinary people, or the energy of youth.

Post-punk acts as diverse as Sydney's Mental As Anything, Melbourne's Bad Seeds and Perth's Triffids created a total aesthetic package that involved the look, the gesture, the surrounding media and especially the relationship with the audience. They thought of themselves as performance artists in an almost avant-garde way. Like the old avant-gardes, many were first recorded by a small independent labels that surfed the 'new wave' that followed punk, such as Regular, Au go go and Phantom, often set up by the bands' mates. Wary of mass rock festivals and stadium pageants, these musicians wanted a more intimate relationship with audiences, who contributed to the bands' evolving art by publishing DIY fanzines, producing public radio shows, writing reviews for the emerging music street press, directing video clips, helping with record covers and posters and loyally turning up to gigs in small, raucous pubs every weekend to dance – or just sway with a look of discerning connoisseurship, lest they be thought uncool. These close-up and personal networks shared subcultural tastes in fashion, style and often art, movies and literature, and coalesced in university common rooms, indie record stores and the bars of venues like Melbourne's Esplanade Hotel, Brisbane's Cloudland Ballroom and Sydney's Trade Union Club as new bohemias.

• • •

One of the brighter post-punk bands was Mental As Anything, who emerged from Sydney's inner-city art school scene in 1976 to become a fixture on 'Top 40' commercial radio and the country's favourite party act by the 1980s. Most of the band's members were painters who exhibited together and their first film clip was shot amid the silk screens and acrylics of Sydney University's Tin Sheds. The Mentals were a colourful outfit, from their garish fifties clothes fusing bodgie and beatnik, to the imaginative artwork that promoted their records and gigs. Their first hit, the controversially titled 'The Nips Are Getting Bigger', was an ode to the solace of the bottle when love goes wrong. Like many Mentals songs to follow, its catchy tune and clever play on Australian slang enabled it to break out of the inner-city garrets and on to *Countdown* to become a beer-barn favourite. A far cry from the angst of British punk, the music had a bright

breezy early sixties sound reminiscent of Roy Orbison, Gene
Pitney and the Monkees, but given a Pacific Island twist via
Hawaiian-style guitar courtesy of the two Kiwis, brothers Chris
(also renowned for his striking irreverent cartoon stylings on
the breakout Mambo surf label clothing and beyond) and Peter
O'Doherty. But the lyrics betrayed the band's art school sensibilities in a postmodern fascination with media and pop culture,
evident in songs like 'Possible Theme for a Future TV Series'.

The Mentals owed their commercial appeal in part to their
cheeky larrikin streak. As the name implied they were very
irreverent. Most members assumed self-mocking stage names
that revelled in artifice or showbiz schtick such as Martin Plaza,
Greedy Smith and Reg Mombassa (aka Chris O'Doherty). Like
Madness in England they were jesters of the new music, but
where the latter drew inspiration from cockney housing estates,
the Mentals drank from the same suburban garden hose as the
comedy of Barry Humphries and the art of Howard Arkley.
Mental As Anything's songs play with the picket fences, school
socials and weatherboards of the suburbs; their record covers,
vivid music videos and posters were adorned with sprinklers
and lawnmowers. In the early 1980s the band was a seminal
influence on the 'pomo' revaluing of suburban iconography by
finding both irony and romance where earlier bohemians had
only found wasteland.

• • •

More than most, Brisbane post-punk band the Go-Betweens
(formed in 1977) made explicit their connection to a bohemian
tradition, littering their songs with references to bohemian heroes
past. Like so many indie bands, the Go-Betweens' nucleus came
together at university. Lanky, intellectual Robert Forster wanted
to be a writer, and the stockier, sunnier Grant McLennan had
ambitions to be a filmmaker. The band's name itself is redolent
with cultural literacy, derived from Harold Pinter and Joseph
Losey's 1970 film adaptation of the L.P. Hartley novel. Both
young men were rebels who, like bohemians before them, felt
Australia's culture was moribund and middle-aged. McLennan
was affected by the early death of his father, boarding school
and family relocations, including to a distant cattle station in far

north Queensland. Forster urged him to learn to play as he had never picked up a guitar before they formed the Go-Betweens – this was to be a partnership formed around aesthetic sensibility rather than being musos. Their eccentric and modern urbane romantic visions expanded as they learned to play, sing and write, striking up long-term romances with their key fellow band members, drummer Lindy Morrison (Forster) and multi-instrumentalist Amanda Brown (McLennan).

Without really managing to score hit records, the Go-Betweens toured Australia and internationally, especially in Europe, scored lovesick reviews from the music press and released a string of classic albums which failed commercially but became the soundtrack to the lives of their young devotees. The Go-Betweens brought a sense of sophisticated lyricism to spiky punk songs about coming of age in the provincial Queensland landscape of 'Cattle and Cane' and the journey into the metropolitan 'world of books, a bigger brighter world', that self-consciously used the language of flâneurs to describe the garrets and pretenders encountered among the demimonde of their 'Darlinghurst Nights' in the 1980s. In a salute to Slessor's bohemian verse, this later song – almost a memoir – made explicit their creative growth in an imaginative, though pretentious, bohemian seedbed of wannabe novelists, film-makers, actors and hangers-on:

> And always the traffic, always the lights
> Joe played the cello through those
> Darlinghurst Nights
> One more coffee and I must go
> Back to my room more chapters to go
> We'll meet up in an alley with more places I know
> I'm going to change my appearance everyday
> I'm going to write a movie and then I'm going to
>   star in a play
> I'm going to go to Caracas because you know I'm
>   just going to have to get away.[6]

• • •

If punk in Britain owed a great deal to dole queues, in Australia it owed more to private music lessons. Here many of the young rebels who took to the stage as punks from the late 1970s through the early 1980s had attended elite schools and sandstone universities. Born in 1957, Nick Cave was a wilful, moody choirboy, raised in the dust of unfashionable Victorian towns Warracknabeal and Wangaratta, where he went to church three times a week. Cave's mother was a librarian and his father taught English, reading him Nabokov's *Lolita* as a bedtime story. Around the age of thirteen, after committing serial offences while at Wangaratta High, he was sent to board at Melbourne's Caulfield Grammar for a year in 1970 before the family moved to Murrumbeena in Melbourne's south-eastern suburbs. At school, Cave, who had been forced by his mother to take piano lessons, befriended guitarist and songwriter Mick Harvey and drummer Phill Calvert. Harvey and Calvert would accompany their theatrical frontman in his tangled musical ascendancy. They next collected bass player Tracy Pew and Rowland S. Howard for glam pop band the Boys Next Door.

The band's mix of Cave originals with covers of Lou Reed and David Bowie alienated half of the exploding Melbourne inner-city punk scene – not hard to do since most of the bands in this hotbed of heroin, speed and hangovers loathed each other only slightly less than they loathed most of the satin pants-clad, overproduced bands on *Countdown*. 'The Boys Next Door weren't welcome over the other side of town,' remarked Rowland S. Howard, who did not go to a private school. 'We were seen as phoneys and rich kids.'[7]

Other key figures connected to the scene were filmmaker Richard Lowenstein, who directed the first clip by band Hunters and Collectors and the feature film *Dogs in Space* – starring Michael Hutchence – and rock journalist and author Clinton Walker, who recently recalled in Lowenstein's 2009 retrospective documentary *We're Living on Dog Food*: 'We were all simpering, snivelling bohemians and dilettantes, really. You know, nobody was tough. I hated flares. I wanted stovepipe pants and winklepickers.'[8]

In 1980 the Boys Next Door went to London, where they began to deconstruct into the raucous post-punk performance act the Birthday Party. Returning to Melbourne and now sporting a swept-back mane of black hair, a long face set off by a high, intelligent forehead and immense dark eyes, the brooding, menacing singer looked like he'd stepped out of a 1920s German cabaret. Diving as though fainting into surging inner-city crowds to lie like a baby tossed by waves, Cave helped create the phenomena of crowd surfing and the mosh pit.

Cave and his bandmates embraced the libertine lifestyle of sex, heroin and deviancy guaranteed to shock polite middle-class Melburnians like their parents. The Birthday Party built a small but dedicated following in their hometown, and then through 2JJ, 4ZZZ and other public radio stations attained cult status – in part through their radical film clips – with the arty, serious end of the inner-city scene, not just in Australia, but in Japan, Britain and Europe.

In Europe Nick Cave forsook the seeming anarchy of the Birthday Party for the gothic aesthetic, and became an esteemed bohemian figure in Berlin, even adorning a postcard promoting the creativity of that most cultured of cities. Cave co-scripted the postmodern prison feature film *Ghosts … of the Civil Dead* in 1988, wrote a gothic novel meditating on Christianity entitled *And the Ass Saw the Angel* (1989), crossed into the pop market in a dark duet with Kylie Minogue drawn from the Edgar Allan Poe poem 'Annabel Lee' about a young woman's murder by her lover for his album *Murder Ballads* (1996), noiring up the image of Australia's favourite 'singing budgie'. He then returned home and transposed the gothic to the Australian frontier by scripting the dark movie western *The Proposition*.

• • •

Singer-songwriter Paul Kelly has been described as 'the closest thing we have to a poet laureate'.[9] Raised in Adelaide, he dropped out of an arts course at Flinders University and drifted around Australia, doing odd jobs and playing folk music. At the age of twenty-one he settled into the Melbourne band bohemia of the late 1970s, but rather than join the arty punk poseurs of the St Kilda Crystal Ballroom set, he headed north of the river to Carlton, where he reckoned 'young lords walked the earth – brainy, serious music architects'.[10] In the early eighties he was fronting new-wave pop outfit the Dots, but the increasingly hit-orientated Mushroom dumped him when his records failed to chart.

His reaction was to hit the road north 'from St Kilda to Kings Cross', where he created the self-funded album *Post* (1985) and with new band the Coloured Girls (later the Messengers) enjoyed huge mainstream success with audiences who responded to intimate, gentle tales evocative of Australian place and heroes like Vincent Lingiari and Don Bradman. But like the short stories of that other dreamer, Henry Lawson, Kelly's best songs deal with the demons and tiny triumphs of ordinary people's lives. His memoir *How to Make Gravy* offers 'Advice to Young Singer-Songwriters' worthy of libertine bohemians past: 'Sleep with whoever the fuck you want to, take what you want from old songwriters, and leave the rest.'[11]

• • •

The Triffids came from Western Australia and blew away the post-punk initiates of Melbourne and Sydney with their Nullarbor-caravan romanticism, innocent minimalism and almost-Wagnerian pomp and splendour. Their frontman and songwriter was David McComb, striking with a combed-back tangle of a pompadour, acne scars rendering his handsome head human, and a haunted look in his eye.

Self-managed as a type of naïve collective, they never recorded with a major label. When they came to Sydney, everyone who was blessed to catch one of their gigs wanted to be on their unsteady bandwagon with them. McComb had the Australian landscape etched into his face, and returned the favour with odes to 'The Treeless Plain' and the 'Wide Open Road'. While university students – invited on stage to play the maracas at refectory gigs – and literate critics loved them, the Triffids remained secret bohemians' business, unknown to the 1980s Oz rock establishment and airwaves. Like so many others before them, they left for London.

• • •

In reaction to the hippies' retreat to arcadia, punks and their 'indie' descendants placed the city back at the centre of their

A simple irreverent poster promoting the highly original and idiosyncratic Triffids, as a covers-band, conveying the ironic sensibility of 1980s inner-city band culture.

songs, images and writing: parading through its public spaces, revelling in its squalor and decadence, exaggerating their urban alienation and artifice. Old cafes and pubs like Sydney's Piccolo Bar and the Piccadilly, still flickering with a bohemian afterglow from mid-century, were reoccupied by a new generation, as young bourgeois cultural rebels, drawn by the popular memory and continued promise of sites such as Darlinghurst.

The new inner-city music bohemians connected with wider

radical political and social activism of the 1980s, such as the anti-nuclear and environmental movements, and Aboriginal land rights. The successes of the left-of-centre Labor government elected in 1983 had the effect of legitimising more left-field causes and politics. The 'benefit concert' became an important fundraising activity for a variety of causes. Brisbane in many ways had never let go of the political passions of the late 1960s. A radical anarchist edge was sharpened by the persistence into the late 1980s of the authoritarian National Party government of Joh Bjelke-Petersen, who had controversially banned street marches and even gatherings, curtailing a fundamental civil liberty. If this was a red rag to Brisbane's punks, the late-night demolition of the Cloudland Ballroom, the hub of Brisbane's band bohemia, was an act of war. The venue had been a cultural gathering place since the 1920s, and its destruction at the behest of the Queensland government and developers in the dead of night in 1982 was an act of vandalism symbolic of the government's corruption and philistinism.[12] The campaign against Joh and his cronies united anarchist punks and artists with unions and the left in a model of community activism and symbolic protest not unlike the Sydney green bans of the early 1970s.

On Sydney's northern beaches, a tall, imposing young law graduate named Peter Garrett – passionate about both politics and rock'n'roll – decided to forsake the barrister's wig for a defiant shaved head as the frontman for Midnight Oil. The Oils married punk's gritty urban sensibilities with a far more suburban outreach and increasingly radical political messages. The Oils' hardcore fans were not inner-city trendies, but the westies and surfies of the suburban beer barns and beachside pubs. Like the Mentals, Midnight Oil were able to parlay inner-city aesthetics to a much wider commercial audience, partly through musicality, professionalism and astute management, partly due to their striking performance style, but also because they engaged with Australian life in a way that resonated with ordinary people as well the educated harbour-huggers. The Oils' songs did not pander to the prejudices of their working-class audiences; Garrett communicated empowering messages about nuclear disarmament, the environment and Aboriginal rights. They tackled the thorny question of national sovereignty in the still-topical 'US Forces' and the rights of ordinary people to be free of exploitation in one of their finest songs, 'The Power and the Passion'.

But Garrett did not abandon more organised politics, and he lent his radical celebrity and integrity to the fledgling Nuclear Disarmament Party, running for the Senate in the 1984 federal election. Older members of the Hawke cabinet, astonished at the bald singer's polling, were said to remark incredulously, 'But who's he?' Though unsuccessful, his campaign politically mobilised many young people who later joined the ALP or the Greens. Garrett had become a glue activist, bringing together not just rock and politics, but young working-class audiences and the values agendas of the eighties' social movements, via outreach such as the new black–white Australian rock'n'roll reconciliation initiative Building Bridges.

• • •

In the early eighties young Aboriginal musicians moved decisively from the Australian country music tradition to which their forebears had contributed so much to an engagement with a variety of rock'n'roll genres, including reggae, rap and ska. While much of the white new music was apolitical, Indigenous bands such as No Fixed Address delivered songs on land rights, discrimination, poverty and demands for a treaty. Aboriginal activists worked across media, with the band featuring in the independent feature film *Wrong Side of the Road*. Radical actor Gary Foley appeared in the post-punk film *Goin' Down*, where he administers some rough justice to a white inner-city wastrel who has stolen the takings at a benefit concert. Yolngu band Yothu Yindi drew nourishment from their overtly political country predecessors, taking the demand for a treaty to the dance floor.

Long before Sydneysiders walked across the Harbour Bridge with Indigenous people in support of reconciliation in 2000, Paul Kelly and Midnight Oil were building bridges with remote communities and some of the legends of Aboriginal country and rock music. Kelly's collaboration with storytellers was deep and genuine. He wrote 'Maralinga' about the H-bomb tests on occupied land, produced the beautiful *Charcoal Road* album for

Archie Roach, and resurrected the career of 'Australia's black Bob Dylan' Kev Carmody (with whom he co-wrote 'From Little Things Big Things Grow') with the double album and live show of his compositions *Cannot Buy My Soul*. With Yothu Yindi he co-wrote the powerful political anthem and international hit 'Treaty'. Like Cave, Kelly branched into other media, starring in the haunting opera hybrid *One Night the Moon*, playing and singing against type as a racist landholder. This collaboration with Carmody and Indigenous filmmaker Rachel Perkins told the tragic tale of a lost child in the outback condemned to die because of the impasse between white and Aboriginal world views.

Midnight Oil worked closely with Aboriginal musicians like Warumpi Band (touring the remote interior communities), and Yothu Yindi (the United States), producing stirring hybrid music on the themes of identity and land. In the 1980s and 90s white musicians like Kelly and Midnight Oil collaborated with their black colleagues to help encourage a growing awareness of Indigenous Australia and its political issues, first in the educated inner cities, then in the regions and suburbs, and ultimately at the closing of the Sydney Olympic Games in 2000 when, with his band in black emblazoned with the word 'sorry', Garrett sang 'How do we sleep when our beds are burning?' before the world, and a presumably uncomfortable prime minister John Howard.

• • •

Like artists and writers of previous generations, many bands left Australia for supposedly more sophisticated cultural markets overseas. Unfortunately, by the time the Saints hit London their raw style was deemed passé and they were rejected by audiences and the music press alike. (They had a better reception in Ireland and France.) The Go-Betweens and the Triffids had more success. Both created enough buzz in Britain to be accorded the honour of cover stories in *NME*. The Triffids, looking like latter-day Beat poets, were lauded as 'The Band of 1985'! But the London music press is fickle, ever on the lookout for the next trend, and when the moment of praise passed, and audiences did not grow, the cold bedsits lost their appeal. As with

Lawson eighty years earlier – and many expats since – some exiled musicians became broke, disorientated and medicated.

Band bohemia had its share of tragedies. One was inner-city rock'n'roll wild man, guitarist Stevie Plunder (Anthony Hayes), one of the frontmen for the Plunderers and also a driving force in the Whitlams. On Australia Day in 1996 his body was found in the bush at the bottom of Wentworth Falls in the Blue Mountains, a presumed suicide. Hundreds of devotees from the Sydney band scene attended the memorial service, and Whitlams' singer Tim Freedman dedicated the band's debut album *Eternal Nightcap* to his friend. Triffids singer-songwriter David McComb was born with a congenitally weak heart, and composed jaunty ditties in the 1980s joking about life's brevity, describing it as 'beautiful waste' and declaring he was 'ready to die now'. McComb underwent a heart transplant in the 90s but it was ultimately unsuccessful and he died in 1999 at the age of thirty-six.

Most of the music bohemians of the 1980s shot across the weekly gig guide like comets, only to fizzle out after their members graduated, took on professions, married or suffered breakdowns. But some of the musicians, by dint of the quality of their music and the lasting impressions it made on their inner-city audiences, became legends of Australian music. Many of the fans took the production skills they honed in the inner-city band scenes into careers in mainstream creative industries as designers, journalists, writers, publishers, television and radio producers, and digital pioneers. Some became successful authors, filmmakers, media gatekeepers and even cultural entrepreneurs in the 1990s, authoring 'secret histories', creating festivals like the Big Day Out and TV retrospectives like *Long Way to the Top*, which ensured that the unfairly marginalised music of their youth was finally recognised, vindicated, even canonised.[13]

GENERATION X BOHEMIAS

While without a generational label until the 1990s, a postmodern 'sensibility' became apparent from the 1980s, informing the work, vision and lifestyles of younger creative and intellectual subcultures in these decades. Its hallmarks were a rejection of modernist ideas of genius and high art and – building on punk and camp – an embrace of pop culture and commerce, a celebration of contradictions and surfaces. Romantic utopianism of the 1960s gave way to cynical irreverence. Nostalgia came to be lived in the present, as young people consciously reappropriated iconography from the history of art and pop culture, including bohemia's past – beatnik meets Weimar cabaret meets paganism with an ironic sampling of the *Brady Bunch* thrown in. While there was no single postmodern 'aesthetic', it is commonly understood to embrace an ironic self-reflexivity about its own creation, scepticism about authenticity, appropriation of pop iconography and history and a sense of play. Suddenly, art and media that did not include the history of pop culture and the media itself in the frame seemed passé. This aesthetic moved rapidly from the fringe 'indie' scene into mainstream popular culture in the early 1990s via hit TV programs *The Simpsons* and *Seinfeld* and in the movies of Quentin Tarantino. In Australia the leading practitioners of this sensibility were cabaret comedians like the Doug Anthony All Stars and Bob Downe, transgressive theatrical bands like Machine Gun Fellatio, the filmmaker Baz Luhrmann and the comedians who came together on the ABC's *Late Show*. The hit film *Muriel's Wedding*, which used a mindscape of Abba songs to unlock an awkward young woman's hopes and fears, was an exemplar of the genre that struck a (perfect pop) chord with a generation.

A feisty in-your-face urban comedy scene arose in the 1980s, drawing on the post-punk band bohemias for both audiences and sensibility. 'New wave' comedy, especially stand-up, was strong in Melbourne, which had the small bars, pubs and Carlton cabaret tradition to sustain a lively circuit. Like the 1960s satire boom there was a synergy with university revue and student papers, and as with *Aunty Jack* the ABC played a crucial role in harvesting the crop in radio and television sketch comedy. In 1986 young graduates from the University of Melbourne came together as the *D Generation*. Not to be outdone, Channel 7 assembled the *Fast Forward* team headed by Steve Vizard, Gina Riley, Jane Turner, Magda Szubanski, Peter Moon, Michael Veitch and Margaret Downey. These programs moved beyond the standard political satire to have fun with the contemporary mediascape of advertising, current affairs and daytime chat shows and television's own history, from *Lost in Space* to *Skippy*. Most ambitiously, a studio was made-over as a Melbourne comedy club called *The Big Gig*, hosted by Wendy Harmer, in which every Tuesday night the cream of Australian stand-up performed in front of a heckling audience. The connection to band bohemia was made explicit by live bands and especially in the all-singing, all-dancing threesome, the Doug Anthony All Stars, comprising Paul McDermott (the nasty one), Tim Ferguson (the good-looking one) and Richard Fidler (the nice one). The transgressive trio from Canberra sang and pranced in harmony to lively original ditties outrageous for references to the flotsam and jetsam of trash culture, such as Kylie's preferred sexual position or the rumoured deviancies of popular TV personalities. They went on to make the absurd space series *DAAS Kapital*. After the success of the *Late Show* in 1992–3 the D-Gen became cultural entrepreneurs as Working Dog, producing *Frontline*, *Funky Squad* and *The Panel*, which in their different ways ironically mined the same pop cultural seam.

Another ingredient of the new sensibility was 'camp'. Sexual libertarianism continued to assert itself through the last decades of the twentieth century, increasingly focused on the gay and lesbian communities, and their network of pubs and dance parties pumping out pulsating disco-style music till the small hours, and publications like the *Sydney Star Observer*. Male homosexual communities had long embraced a camp aesthetic and humour that was an influential precursor to the postmodern ironising of artifice in the arts, especially in older Sydney bohemias around theatre and the Charm School. The gay community was also a driving force for the carnivalesque, which in the 1980s and 90s had its apotheosis in Sydney's Gay and Lesbian Mardi Gras, its bacchanalian after-party, and the Sleaze Ball, held at the Sydney Town Hall. These were hedonistic successors to the old Artists' Balls, where homosexual men in the 1920s and 30s had been known to 'come out'. An examination of the photographs and newsreel of the Artists' Balls and their parade of floats reveals an uncanny similarity in costume, pagan iconography, celebration of the body, even movement, to the Mardi Gras.

While the Mardi Gras continued to outrage some church

leaders and politicians, with the legalising of homosexuality in
the 1980s the event moved from marginal criminalised protest
to a city-wide celebration and eventually a tourist attraction.
As the community aged and became an established fixture in
the Sydney social and cultural set, some younger people began
to critique slogans like 'gay pride' as essentialist and worthy,
and sought a new cutting edge in the ambiguity of bisexuality,
'queer' theory and its practice through performance art. The
various gay and lesbian communities across Australia's cities
fostered their own theatrical and music scenes, from traditional
drag and burlesque to the new vogue for syncopated rhythmic
dance music, which for a time created a new urban aristocracy of club DJs. By the second half of the 1980s dance music

Melbourne performance artist Moira Finucane at 'Club Bent', c. 1995 – an art
of body play where gender and sexual identities were subverted to shake up an
increasingly mainstream Gay and Lesbian Mardi Gras.

distinguished by a pomo sampling and mixing of songs and sounds was de rigueur for many hip heterosexuals of the inner-city demimonde in a vibrant, if decadent, club scene.

Avant-garde-like constellations gathered around particular star performers, such as the legendary burlesque- and carnival-inspired Moira Finucane in Melbourne and the Sydney pop culture ironists Barbara Karpinski and Pauline Pantsdown. In gender-bending salutes to pantomime, women played men dressed as women. As Karpinski's stage character said, 'Gay, lesbian, bi, straight – what's a label anyway?'[14] At venues such as Sydney's Performance Space the red-tracksuited trio Frumpus amused with clownish mime referencing the media landscape, creating a cultural collage combining British slap-and-tickle comedian Benny Hill with the lost girls from *Picnic at Hanging Rock* and the belly birth from *Alien*.

From the early 1990s this postmodern aesthetic became popularly identified with the so-called 'Generation X', people born between the mid-1960s and early 80s, who grew up immersed in TV and pop music. The label derived from the popular 1989 book by Douglas Coupland identifying the retreat into irony of a generation denied meaningful careers by economic change and job-hog baby boomers who refused to make way for the young. However, in a wider sense postmodernity was perhaps lived more artfully and loudly by those younger people self-consciously seeking out the cutting edge in Surry Hills, New Farm or Fitzroy.

WHEN GANGLANDS COLLIDE: CONFLICT AND CONTINUITIES

With a regular newspaper column and frequent media appearances, McKenzie Wark was the accessible public face for a network of mainly young academics who found in postmodernist theories tools to understand Australia's increasingly diverse culture and politics. But he quickly became the fall guy for postmodernism as a backlash occurred, from the right and the left and also from one-time radicals from the countercultures. Many on the left took their lead from Fredric Jameson, arguing that postmodernism was no more than the aesthetic and ideology of late twentieth-century consumer capitalism that 'seemed to threaten culture and the quality of civilisation'.[15] This view had strong support in Australia from one-time countercultural rebels such as Richard Neville, David Williamson and Phillip Adams, who once championed a popular culture revolution and media activism. Both conservatives and many on the left complained that postmodernism was amoral and threatened the western literary canon, even the principles of enlightenment itself. Wark countered that asking questions of orthodoxies, such as what is studied at school or the division between high and popular culture, was the very essence of enlightenment thinking.[16] Williamson wrote the play *Dead White Males* in 1995, sending up the urge of the new generation to deconstruct and devalue the great classics of literature, perhaps a little anxious about the fate of middle-aged playwrights. Wark's response was to remind critics of the popular culture origins of much of the canon: 'I'm sorry but Dickens was trash, Shakespeare was trash ... for the masses which on inspection later turned out to have extraordinary values in it ... the thing about high culture is it comes to you pre-sorted ... it comes pre-filtered ... it's actually a packaged kind of thing.'[17]

As to the accusation of being defenders of consumer capitalism, postmodern critics Wark and Catharine Lumby stressed that commercial popular culture and state activity were the sites of contradictory messages and a diversity of meanings. In a bizarre echo of the interwar Norman Lindsay rounding on modernism, Richard Neville, by the 1990s settled with his family in the Blue Mountains, criticised the amoral art of a new generation who would never quite match up to his. Neville has remained a committed left-wing radical on many of the major geo-political issues of the day, but in a case of poacher turned gamekeeper, he wondered whether community standards should be protected from sado-sexual and violent films and other antisocial messages, and singled out Madonna, Tarantino and splatter movies for particular scorn.[18] Neville's new-found illiberality saw him – with this issue – unusually on the same side as many of his one-time enemies, but also other former Libertarians opposed to postmodernism, notably Paddy McGuinness and Keith Windschuttle.

In memoirs released from the 1990s the veterans of the 1960s and 70s countercultures followed the tradition of bohemian myopia, having little time for predecessors and either failing to recognise any heirs or attacking the younger generation for pursuing aesthetic and intellectual agendas that they believed betrayed the achievements of the 1960s generation. However, from the long-term vista of an Australian bohemian tradition we can appreciate that the criticisms levelled at 'postmodernists' and 'Gen X' were not so different to the hostility of Max Harris to the 'ocker' artists in the early 1970s, or Lionel Lindsay's rejection of modernists such as Harris in the 1940s. Likewise, pomo authors Mark Davis, McKenzie Wark, Catharine Lumby and others in the 1990s turned to the same language of rejuvenation, innovation, internationalism and even Australian distinctiveness made by the Heidelberg painters, *Bulletin* writers, and the teams around *Angry Penguins* and *Oz* in defence of postmodern aesthetics and theory. Certainly, postmodernism's critique of modernist verities such as the cult of the exceptional genius enabled new players to de-legitimise their predecessors' claim to being special, while suggesting the entitlement of youth to take their place in the sun. Catharine Lumby, who wrote *Bad Girls*, arguing for a renovation within cultural politics generally and 1970s feminist attitudes to media and women specifically, declared that 'young women like myself want to have an argument with the older generation about things like censorship, their attitudes to mass culture, to popular culture, which I think many of us see as patronising and authoritarian'.[19] McKenzie Wark was more direct, telling the 1960s and 70s veterans in 1996, '[s]o if you want to be true to your ideals get out of the way … if you want to become an establishment that is going to be resisted and resented you are going about it the right way'.

The stoush reached its climax with the publication of *Gangland* by Mark Davis, a bestseller that identified a 'baby boomer cultural establishment' that had captured the commanding heights of the media, journalism, creative industries like cinema and publishing, public cultural institutions, universities and the all-important power to review and award. The thesis was potent because Davis outed a power bloc of individuals across the left and right, and interconnected since the 1960s, who circulated seemingly effortlessly in powerful media roles.

Radicals and counterculturalists from the previous generation such as Anne Summers, Robert Hughes, Paddy McGuinness, Richard Neville, David Williamson and Phillip Adams were singled out for constipating Australia's creative and intellectual life, and the Sydney Push attributed with the covert power of a Masonic Lodge. From the perspective of this history, Davis discounted the profound divisions between individuals and groups and the reality that the middle-aged of any time will tend to enjoy such incumbency. However *Gangland* mounted sound arguments in defence of new ideas and aesthetics and became a rallying point for young people impatient to attain some creative control and access to public space.

But the 'culture war' between the generations, between baby boomers and Gen X, counterculturalists and postmodernists, was the way the bohemian tradition worked. While useful for maintaining relevance or advancing in the cultural field, the stand-off belied the continuities, and indeed friendly and fertile cooperation, between creative people not all that distant from each other in age. Whether working as essayists, media commentators, novelists or conceptual artists, 'postmodernists' came together in the 1980s and 90s in social formations that resembled either avant-gardes or looser bohemian networks. The lateral-thinking Wark understood this. Working with me on the documentary *Bohemian Rhapsody* in 1996 and in his subsequent book *The Virtual Republic*, he described a university-based postmodern Sydney scene in the 1980s practising a 'technique of the self' not unlike the bar-hopping, paper-giving bohemianism of the Libertarian Push. He excavated an intellectual lineage from the Libertarians through the Futilitarians to Sydney postmodernists in the 1980s and showed this to be based not just on academic institutions and connections between teachers and students, but also on a bohemian style of gathering in bars and cafés practised by his circle in the 1980s and 90s that he traced back to the critical drinking of the Push. This was a cultural tradition hostile to authoritarianism and censorship, that valued pluralism, conflict and the exposure of 'illusions', that was sceptical of utopias and unifying doctrines. But for Wark the actual bohemian lifestyle – groups drinking and arguing together in pubs – was also important to recreating a critical, open disposition.

Many in his circle of postmodernists had been educated by former Libertarians at the Institute of Technology Sydney or the Fine Arts Department of the University of Sydney. Connections could be more personal. Catharine Lumby was formally mentored by Frank Moorhouse, and is writing his biography. Another academic in this group, Fiona Giles, was the inspiration for Moorhouse's *Forty-Seventeen*.[20] Leading postmodernists like Meaghan Morris and John Docker had for a time associated with the later Push.

Likewise it was an exaggeration to paint all of the older bohemian generation as closed to the energy of youth. The irrepressible Bob Ellis went on the road with edgy indie band Custard in an inspired trek through the Queensland landscape that included a jovial visit to the farm of Joh Bjelke-Petersen. Ellis, a generous man, has made a point of befriending young writers, actors and culturally literate politicos, introducing them to arts, media and Labor folklore. Although it is true that, in a fit of anger, he hurled a copy of *Please Just F* Off, It's Our Turn Now*, the Gen Y answer to *Gangland*, in the direction of its author Ryan Heath on reading his criticism of projects Ellis supported, as a writer he brought together younger performers with his older collaborators in the Wharf Revue, and was a catalyst for engaging a young cast on a Newtown revival of Tom Stoppard's play *Travesties*. Other older notables, such as Frank Moorhouse and Richard Walsh, have mentored or published several generations of young writers, and in the visual arts Ray Hughes has encouraged and given space to young painters.

LARRIKINS FOR A NEW CENTURY

In the wake of the debate over postmodernism, and as part of the trend towards sampling the past, an explicit revisiting of Australian bohemian traditions and traces occurred. In the late 1990s attempts were made by media workers to revive the older larrikin bohemianism of the press, staged in both clubs and looser pub gatherings. Sydney's 'Primates', a monthly lunch party of writers, journalists, editors and politicians presided over by cartoonists Bill Leak ('Minister for Nocturnal Affairs') and

Warren Brown ('Pusher of the Brown Rod') tried to revive through regular events the ritualised journalistic bohemia of the *Bulletin* and *Smith's Weekly*, while *Strewth!* magazine sought to reignite the pub bohemia of the Push. Reasons offered by the organisers include providing an antidote to the new office-bound corporatisation of the journalistic profession ('bring back the long lunch') and the hijacking of Australianness by the social exclusion of the Howard era, but these revivals have also served as a way to network and attract attention to projects via notoriety.

In the tradition of the Dawn to Dusk Club, the Primates (motto: 'with thumbs we oppose') bring to their events mock parliamentary debates and titles, cascading wit, the performance of 'turns' such as a song or poem, and an annual dinner at the Parliament House of New South Wales. In keeping with post-1968 transgressive tastes, humour frequently revolves around bodily functions, sex, and political incorrectness. Though the only criterion for entry was hating John Howard, the founding membership in 1997 favoured people who had made a name in their fields or are in some way notorious, and included Meredith Burgmann (then President of the NSW Legislative Council), Bob Ellis, Kevin Jacobsen (events promoter), Judy Nunn (actor and author), Richard Fidler (comedian and broadcaster), Ignatius Jones and Pat Sheil (libertarian journalists and authors and former members of bad-taste punk band Jimmy and the Boys), actor Bruce Venables, the late Dick Hall (journalist and ex-Whitlam staffer) and Reg Lynch (*Bulletin* cartoonist). As a cross-generational network the Primates (a revival of a 1950s journalists' bohemian club begun by Fidler's father) transfers an older Sydney tradition to younger journalists who are invited along. Its projects have included a magazine, *Spleen* (Baudelaire worked on a journal with this name), and group ownership of a greyhound.

Less formal than the Primates is a weekly lunch hosted by painter and art dealer Ray Hughes in his Surry Hills gallery, where artists, writers, filmmakers, broadcasters, academics and journalists mix with the business and managerial end of the culture industries. Hughes' stated aim is to create informal opportunities for young artists such as he enjoyed in bohemia when he first started out as a painter. (It was at such a lunch that Bob Ellis threw the offending Gen Y tome.)

Launched at the Harbour View Hotel in The Rocks in 1998, *Strewth!* sought to revive the look of both underground papers like *Oz*, and the black-and-white larrikinism of the *Bulletin* and *Smith's Weekly*, but without the racism and gender chauvinism. Its targets were good taste, lazy orthodoxy, poseurs and cosy cliques. When *Strewth!* saw a comfortable bunch of backslappers it just had to heckle: SOCOG, Fox Studios, the ALP, post-modernists, Australians for a Constitutional Monarchy, actors, the ABC, the Bradman industry, John Howard's cabinet, New Zealanders, Working Dog, TropFest and, last but not least, Tim Freedman of the Whitlams and his Newtown-via-north-shore acolytes. It took aim at the political correctness of both right and left, though had greater synergies with Labor than the Liberal Party. *Strewth!* liked to crash through the taste barrier, and a personal favourite was 'Australia Shits', an earthy trot through the trots written by a respected *Bulletin* journalist under a nom de plume that culminated in a sift through the sewage works at Malabar to get closer to Sydney's entrails. The paper worked on the maxim that vulgarity can be liberating. Just to keep the wowsers at bay it ran a popular competition entitled 'Australia's Most Earnest'.

The magazine's motto was 'Truth is Beauty, Bewdy Strewth!' and the *Daily Telegraph*-style headlines screamed out insults such as 'Bloody Whingers Rampage Frenzy', 'We Blame You' and 'Big Sooks'. I was a member of the editorial team that was headed up by a mix of twenty- and thirty-somethings who had footholds on various media career ladders, but were frus-trated that they could not get the material they most liked published. The editor was ABC journalist Steve Cannane, sup-ported by cartoonist-of-the-absurd Reg Lynch, who gave the rag its look, investigative reporter Jackie Dent, authors Chris Mikul and Ed Wright, raconteur and eccentric James Scanlon (who had previously hosted 'In Bed with James Scanlon' on the ABC's *Blah, Blah, Blah*), whimsical cartoonist Fiona Katauskas, Newtown pub anthropologist Cath O'Brien and *Australian Financial Review* journalist Grant Butler. In deference to the think tanks then sprouting around town, *Strewth!* declared itself a 'drink tank', and had launch parties in inner-Sydney pubs that deliberately brought together several generations of that city's bohemian spirits, including veterans such as ABC radio's inspirational troublemaker in chief Tony Barrell, Bob Ellis and Paddy McGuinness.

The emergence of this more knowing celebration of a local bohemian tradition among some younger cultural workers in the late 1990s and new century was more than just fun. For younger people it was a way to simultaneously draw on the legitimacy of being a part of a bohemian lineage, and create a splash in the time-honoured bohemian fashion. Thanks to the publicity created by the magazine and especially the launches, many of the contributors were able to get articles republished in the Fairfax and News Ltd press, and soon some were commissioning op-eds themselves, somewhat altering the tone of what was permissible. As Ellis would say, so it goes.

● ● ●

Strewth! was a creature of the margins. A far more ambitious revival of the larrikin tradition was a weekly newspaper started at the same time by a group of young men straight out of university. They called it *The Chaser*, a name by which they came to be known as a comedic group. Some of the team had featured

The Chaser – twenty-first century torch-bearers for the 'larrikin carnivalesque', who mock political spin, corporate humbug and media mendacity. From left Chris Taylor, Chas Licciardello, Julian Morrow, Craig Reucassel and Andrew Hansen.
Courtesy Giant Dwarf Productions, Sydney.

in a 1996 ABC documentary, *Uni*, which aimed to catch a glimpse of Australia's cultural future by taking a fly-on-the-wall look at who was editing *Honi Soit* and directing student revues at the University of Sydney. A couple of years into the new century, the Chaser's style of satire had proven such a powerful antidote to the Howard government's greyness that they secured investment for the paper from maverick ocker ad man John Singleton, a public radio show and were approached by cultural entrepreneur Andrew Denton to try their hand at television.

It is the Chaser ensemble who, over the past decade, have channelled the truly subversive elements of the larrikin carnivalesque – anarchic anti-authoritarianism, Dadaesque stunts, the parody of other media, and flirtation with obscenity and offences against good taste. When I asked Chaser co-founder Charles Firth if they were left wing he said they were 'cynicalists', meaning they apply the bullshit detector to the powerful whatever their political persuasion or ideology. Both Labor and conservatives cop their fair share. But like Humphries and *Oz*, the Chaser is interested in hypocrisy and the abuse of power wherever they lurk: in corporations, the public service, the media, celebrity culture, religion. What makes the Chaser fresh satire for our time is its exposure of the spin, managerial gobbledygook and corporate humbug that annoys everyone. Pollies who come out best are those who laugh along. That's the point of their style of guerrilla humour – to catch the powerful unawares and knock off the public mask. Like the *Oz* team four decades earlier, the Chaser team has been pilloried by the great and worthy but not yet imprisoned. They came close, though, with an inspired stunt during the APEC summit in Sydney in 2007, driving a black limo carrying Chas Licciardello dressed as Osama bin Laden effortlessly through check points, exposing the spin and incompetence of the security as a police officer told them, 'The road is yours.'

Nevertheless, the Chaser can be blind to left-of-centre power. This problem may stem from private school guilt and romanticism about the left. In 2008 a newspaper and online site *Manic Times*, published by Chaser alumnus Charles Firth and devoted to lifting the lid on Sydney, pulled up stumps, which was a pity. Where Firth's newspaper was on a hiding to nothing was its acceptance of assistance from Unions NSW. The problem with this is manifest; Unions NSW is one of the pillars of power in the state of New South Wales, a state mostly run by Labor, which is mostly run by the unions.

• • •

Over the past decade the twin bogeys of patriotism and political correctness never stood a chance against the revival of the larrikin carnivalesque. Dame Edna and Sir Les remain incorrigible, but the ear for accent and social nuance passed to a younger generation. The ocker mask has been worn with style by philosophical sports commentators Rampaging Roy Slaven and H.G. Nelson. Kath and Kim have confirmed Edna's secret that women do indeed rule the childlike men of the suburbs, and they now do so not by shushing male pleasures but by out-ockering them. The Anglo-Celts lost their monopoly on larrikinism in the nineties as 'wog humour' emerged from new-wave comedy with big-haired Greek chick Effie, alter ego of comedian Mary Coustas, and another popular movie where the naïve but vulgar innocent triumphs: Nick Giannopoulos's *Wog Boy*. Today it is Paul Fenech's *Pizza* franchise, like the ockers of the 1970s, that has the power to offend and shock. Today a show about rude, vulgar, sexually explicit, hip-hopping homeboys of Mediterranean or Middle Eastern appearance can only outrage middle-class good taste – especially when it makes Australianness itself ridiculous.

We are also living in the era of the 'She Larrikin'. Two of the more transgressive of the latter day Queens of Bohemians are Sydney singer and performance artist Christa Hughes and Melbourne writer and broadcaster Marieke Hardy. Both have bohemianism in the blood and are adept at making themselves into works of art.

Charismatic jazz chanteuse Christa Hughes is the daughter of legendary pianist Dick Hughes, whom she has accompanied from a young age. As an expat in Paris, she made a name for herself as a Piaf impersonator, gargling the song 'La Vie en Rose' in a television advertisement for mouthwash. Back in Australia she wrote and starred in a series of one-woman cabaret shows and became front and centre of the anarchistic rock'n'roll performance troupe Machine Gun Fellatio. Here Hughes' poise and operatic voice was used to deliver meditations on love such as 'Let Me Be Your Dirty F★★★ing Whore', where the un-PC pleasures of sexual degradation are celebrated. She has a finely honed sense of theatrical, comic and performance history, describing herself as a 'Vaudeville Vamp', 'Rock'n'Roll Hellcat', 'Burlesque Babe' and, ambiguously, 'Raucous Ring Mistress', and revels in mixing high art with the explicitly vulgar and bodily. Her mission to put the carnal back into carnival was on show in her performance as the brothel madam Myrtle in Julian Temple's avant-garde cinematic opera *Eternity Man*. Hughes is also very funny, as was apparent in her larrikin one-woman show *Beer Drinking Woman*, which prompted Barry Humphries to declare: 'She gives vulgarity a good name.'

Child TV star Marieke Hardy – the granddaughter of radical novelist and bohemian Frank Hardy, and grand-niece of irrepressible comedienne and Logie award-winning TV personality Mary Hardy – reinvented herself in the new media age as a blogger, television writer, radio host on the ABC's Triple J, an occasional columnist and most recently a controversialist on *First Tuesday Book Club*. Her output has been prodigious, including several TV comedies and a novel delivered over mobile phone courtesy of the *Age*. Though Hardy is in her thirties, she has become something of a symbol of rebellious bohemian youth. Much of her work takes a self-deprecating approach to youthful inner-city milieus in which she has participated that orbit around indie bands, art and media and is refreshingly upfront about sexuality and other transgressions, such as trysts with prostitutes and running the soggy gauntlet of a swingers' night.

Marieke's celebrity has snowballed through her appearances on the ABC and in the *Age*, and she has written a memoir, *You'll Be Sorry When I'm Dead*, in part anchored in Melbourne's current-day bohemia. Just like Clive James' premature first memoir, the book is a surprise, for in its exposure of Melbourne's artistic underbelly and grungy, deviant beer-guts, Hardy reveals herself to be an acute and witty observer of her generation's urban life, worthy of our most diverting flâneurs. Yet she is criticised by some women, and fewer men, for performing predictable transgression for the titillation of a middle-aged, middle-class

audience. To her credit, Hardy is open to the wisdom (and corruption?) of the older bohemian generation, and has confessed
to an 'unhealthy' obsession with Bob Ellis, whose romantic
leftism she admires. Hardy had the example of her carnivalesque
great-aunt and radical grandfather and gives her work a punky
iconoclasm, but as a work of art herself she also echoes the
model of that other show-off in a short skirt, Dulcie Deamer.

BOHEMIAS IN THE AGE OF NOSTALGIA

The word 'bohemian' is largely deployed in a nostalgic discourse, a 'retro' term to make sense of creative, urbane groups
from the past or to describe gentrifying inner-city precincts
rich in cafés where students rent and older cultural professionals
renovate. However, as we have seen, the term was already nostalgic when Murger described bohemia in Paris, and in Australia
it was always used to describe a creative, transgressive group
retrospectively, after its youth and time had passed. Audiences
have maintained their fascination with bohemian nostalgia
into the new century. Director Baz Luhrmann enjoyed commercial and critical success with theatrical productions of *La
Bohème* and the film *Moulin Rouge*. Bob Ellis wrote and directed
The Nostradamus Kid, a feature based on his experiences in the
late 1950s and early 60s as an innocent discovering sex, drink
and student journalism at Sydney University. It starred the
striking but nerdish Noah Taylor who, as a genuine Melbourne
teen bohemian of the late 1980s, made a career of playing boys
on the cusp of bohemia from the early 1960s, most spectacularly
helping director John Duigan relive his coming of age in *The
Year My Voice Broke* and *Flirting*. Duigan also directed *Sirens*,
set in Norman Lindsay's Springwood and starring Sam Neil as
the artist, with Elle MacPherson and Kate Fisher as Lindsay's
sometimes nude models. At the same time the weekend colour
supplements featured nostalgic articles by or about Australian
bohemians, such as the artists at Heide or the Charm School,
film directors, writers, journalists, broadcasters and controver-
sialists who came through the Push, Drift, *Oz*, the Yellow
House, *Nation Review* or 2JJ, and, more recently, the elders of
Australian punk like Nick Cave.

Both the Primates and *Strewth!* deployed nostalgia to bring together several generations of bohemians working in the press, politics, the ABC and the mainstream cultural industries for recreation but also to promote independent publishing projects and attest to the continued value of the larrikin carnivalesque. *Strewth!* always had a historical mission to revive interest in Australian cultural traditions, publishing articles on legendary larrikins and eccentrics like Marcus Clarke, Frank Thring and Les Murray and spearheading revivals of then-forgotten Australian films from the seventies like *Pure Shit* (at last able to be screened under its full title) and *Barry McKenzie Holds His Own*.

But what of the bohemian milieus of new generations? Semi-autobiographical films about young 1980s and 90s artist rebels attracted to bohemian living in inner-city terraces and pubs have continued to be made and attract audiences, spanning *Monkey Grip* and *Dogs in Space* in the 1980s to *Love and Other Catastrophes* in the 1990s and *He Died with a Felafel in His Hand*, *Garage Days* and the ABC homage to Newtown pub bohemia, *Love is a Four Letter Word* (featuring the Whitlams) in the new century. Most recently the St Kilda punk bohemia was raked over in the gritty documentary *We're Livin' On Dog Food* and *Autoluminescent* by its filmmaker in residence, Richard Lowenstein. Likewise the music series *Long Way to the Top* on ABC TV and *Great Australian Albums* on SBS have essayed the salad days of the Saints, Go-Betweens and the Triffids. These films testify to the desire for Australian filmmakers, like bohemian writers and artists before them, to revisit their own stories about coming of age and getting laid and possibly famous amid the demimonde of the inner city, but also to the continued popularity of the romantic bohemian narrative with audiences.

CYBER- TO STEAMPUNKS

Not everyone looked back to create a culture of pastiche in the last years of the twentieth century. Some embraced the future. New technological innovations such as personal computers in the 1980s and the internet and cheap digital video cameras and editing software in the 1990s brought the tools of professional cultural production and mass and niche distribution, previously limited to a small number of creative industry specialists, to a wider part of the population, democratising much further the Bolex and offset revolution of the 1960s. But the digital revolution would also inspire revolutionaries with a new idea of liberty.

An early night rider of the digital revolution was a highly intelligent, slightly arty, shy pale youth named Julian Assange. Fired up by the ferment of the late 1960s, his mother Christine Hawkins, daughter of a Melbourne academic, left home and hit the road to become an artist. As revealed by journalists David Leigh and Luke Harding in their book *WikiLeaks: Inside Julian Assange's war on secrecy*, Christine met a charismatic radical at a Sydney anti-Vietnam War demo, they became lovers in the passion of the moment, parted, and Julian was born in 1971.[21] A true child of the countercultures, the boy lived an itinerant but stimulating life, for a time with stepfather Brett Assange, a travelling actor and theatre director, then a new-age musician.

Always on the move, Assange attended thirty-seven schools, and though classed as 'gifted' and a voracious reader of science found his real education fiddling with PCs in a Sydney computer store in the mid-1980s. The 1997 book *Underground: Tales of hacking, madness and obsession on the electronic frontier*, researched by Assange, provides an insight into his state of mind: 'The school system didn't hold much interest for him. It didn't feed his mind … The Sydney computer system was a far more interesting place to muck around in.'[22]

At sixteen the curious, rebellious teenager had a modem, and by the early 1990s was an accomplished hacker, who pulled off the big one by penetrating US Defense network, MILNET. This was subversion beyond the anti-American rallies of his parents' generation, and plunged Assange into the shadow world where bohemia meets the revolutionary secret cell, 'a veiled world populated by characters slipping in and out of the half darkness … not a place where people use their real names', according to *Underground*.[23]

Assange became immersed in the 1990s youth subculture where technology met art and nerds with attitude played with a coded style blending science-fiction aesthetics with rebellion and even criminality – cyberpunk. The scene and its ideals could be found in films, novels and especially online, but its

hardcore 'hacker' manifestation passionately believed in the need
to gather surreptitiously in shared houses, garages and abandoned
warehouses, where they tinkered with technology, swapped
knowledge and refined their programming skills. Colombian
ex-hacker turned academic Daniel Angel, who has researched
the persisting Melbourne scene, argues that these hacker communities are a digital-age manifestation of nineteenth-century
bohemia, evident in the use of terms like 'punk' and in avant-
garde style manifestos extolling libertarian principles, especially
a brave new world of freedom of information on the internet.[24]
Like the traditional avant-gardes, Assange published a hard-
copy magazine in the nineties to promote such views called
International Subversives.

That utopia was yet to be and Julian Assange was arrested in
1994 for hacking offences, after a prolonged period on the run,
during which he moved between squats and terraces with his
girlfriend, and for a time slept out in the Dandenongs. Found
guilty he avoided prison, and redeemed himself by lending
his hacker skills to the federal police tracking down an online
paedophile ring.[25] But Assange was not about to become an
agent of the state, and would later claim, quoting Solzhenitsyn,
that '[s]uch prosecution in youth is a defining experience. To
know the state for what it really is! To see through the veneer
the educated swear to disbelieve in but still slavishly follow with
their hearts.'[26] Looking like a cross between Andy Warhol and
the alien super children from *Village of the Damned*, Assange
became a cult personality traversing the international hacker
underground, and began discussing on his blog the philosophy
that would lead to WikiLeaks, arguing: 'the more secretive
or unjust an organisation is, the more leaks induce fear and
paranoia in its leadership ... mass leaking leaves them exquisitely
vulnerable to those who seek to replace them with more open
forms of governance'.[27]

In 2006 the domain name WikiLeaks.org was registered by
Assange in the name of his biological father, in honour of his
'rebel genes'.[28] With the help of his hand-picked hacker cells,
a network of leakers and an ensemble of wary broadsheets,
WikiLeaks presided over the largest leakage of secret information from the US government – any government – in history.

It was all the more potent for the inclusion of documents about America's friends and foes around the globe, including indiscreet information relating to Australian politics. Assange would later boast: 'We had the activist experience and the will to disempower. We had our laptops and our passports. We had servers in different countries. We knew that we would be the most secure platform for whistleblowers the world has ever known. We had gumption. We had philosophy. Game on.'[29]

But Assange's gotcha moment was shortlived as the Swedish government seeks to extradite him for alleged sexual offences, and an American grand jury convenes to draw up charges for stealing state secrets. Like the *Thorunka* and *Oz* editors who endured prison for publishing freely, there is every chance that Assange may end up in a US penitentiary – a postmodern rebel cum martyr for the digital age, defending the recurring bohemian ideal of free expression. Underlining the connection from one counterculture to another, he has engaged Geoffrey Robertson, the Australian barrister who defended Richard Neville and his fellow *Oz* editors at the Old Bailey back in the year Assange was born.

● ● ●

Another species of technobards, who do not much care for hurrying up the cyber future, have instead harked back to the nineteenth century, exploring an alternative timeline where the gadgetry of the digital age is re-versioned for the steam age. Like cyberpunks, the steampunks are enamoured of science fiction, but it is the imaginative worlds of Jules Verne and H.G. Wells that inspire, from elegantly crafted time machines to the ornate fish-like submarine from *Twenty Thousand Leagues Under the Sea*. According to participant Lisa Townsend, steampunk is based on 'an Edwardian-Victorian aesthetic that imagines an alternative future where the atom was never discovered'.[30] The young men and women dressed in corsets and top hats, who have taken to promenading through Melbourne lanes in recent years, embrace the arcane beauty of polished brass contraptions, dials and steam-hissing pumps.

Part of the subcultural performance is to aesthetically remake today's communication devices like mobile phones, laptops and iPads so they look as they might have in a Verne novel. Opposed to sharp modernist lines and design, steampunks, like nineteenth-century gothic revival promoter John Ruskin, are keen that form be highly decorative and definitely not follow function.

However, the deceivingly genteel look, a parody of the dandies and dames, rakes and wenches of an idealised Victorian London, is subverted by an anarchic punkish attitude that, like the speculative fiction they adore, plays imaginatively with 'what if' history, identities and narratives. Fashion accessories such as bustles, parasols, fans, fob watches and top hats are mixed with dreadlocks and body piercings. Of course there was another side to the Victorian city, as its bohemians and flâneurs knew well. As night falls the subculture seeks to recreate a gothic mise-en-scene more akin to the fog, chugging industrial engines and sideshows of David Lynch's *Elephant Man*. At boudoiresque warehouse parties across Melbourne the bodices come off in performances where burlesque, cabaret and a sleazy style of circus tempts this Jekyll-and-Hyde bohemia from restraint into pleasure.

Why Melbourne? Apart from a climate conducive to dress-ups, much of the city's nineteenth-century streetscape remains intact, and in a way that is both nostalgic and also reassuringly Melbourne – with its rather serious fun of the Spiegeltent, horse-drawn carriages for tourists, mighty stone buildings and the Paris end of Collins Street – never really let the nineteenth century go. In their dandy fashions, play with carnival and imaginative journey into the gothic, steampunks are strolling the cobbled lanes in the footsteps of Marcus Clarke.

FRINGE TO FAMOUS

Since the 1980s, there has been an increasingly fertile crossover between 'alternative' arts practice and popular culture industries. The mainstream market itself has become a delta, fragmenting into an array of style-based youth subcultures and identity movements and a proliferation of 'do-it-yourself' independent media initiatives, beginning with public access radio, multicultural television and 'indie' records in the 1980s, proceeding through fanzines, community TV and affordable video and editing technology on to internet-based interactive websites, magazines, blogs, 'mash-ups' and social networking sites. Bohemias have formed around many of these sites of cultural creation, and some of them have taken advantage of the shift in the 1990s and 2000s to contracting and outsourcing by major cultural institutions such as the ABC and large and small publishing and media firms alike to become cottage industries selling services to broadcasters, publishers, cinema studios and festivals hungry for content. Punk iconoclasts of the 1980s, such as Nick Cave and Paul Kelly, have become national institutions, and Working Dog and the Chaser have leaped from university revue to mass appeal. The art of Reg Mombassa and many other punk-inspired artists found itself literally on the sleeves of the masses in funky fashions produced by iconic indie surfwear designers Mambo.

As occurred in the past, cultural entrepreneurs have arisen within bohemias or out of the corporations that leverage ideas from the independent into mainstream markets. Steve Vizard was quick off the starting block with Artist Services, supplying both commercial TV and the growing pay TV channels with risky comedy like the schooner-fuelled precursor to *Q&A*, *Mouthing Off*. Working Dog branched from TV into popular quirky films *The Castle* and *The Dish*. Andrew Denton formed Zapruder's Other Films to parlay space and some genuine creative freedom from the nervous nellies in ABC management for new risk-taking artists like the Chaser and Lawrence Leung, and then, in a further quest for autonomy, the Chaser group formed their own company.

Perhaps the most spectacular move from fringe to famous is that of Peter Garrett from rock rebel to the face of Greenpeace Australia and then into federal parliament in 2004 as the Labor member for the Sydney seat of Kingsford Smith. Garrett's long music and activist career, followed by ascendancy to Cabinet as the Minister for Arts in 2007, demonstrated that values, ideas and symbols had become central to our politics – though building bridges between the suburbs and the inner-cities, the bohemians and the battlers, remained elusive.

As the current Labor government develops Australia's first National Cultural Policy the challenge is how to enable the fertile cross from the cultural fringes to mainstream creative industries. In the age of the National Broadband Network, can governments intervene to encourage public and commercial cultural institutions to harness new digital technology to reach further into risk-taking bohemias and the creativity of the wider community? Politicians had better not wait too long, as the artists, journalists and radicals are simply bypassing the old institutions and narrowcasting peer to peer, peer to many, and virally to the world. Whether in garages or garrets, for emerging young content producers, making and self-curating their songs, satire, films, poetry, short stories or journalism on YouTube, Facebook or Twitter, the internet is the contemporary theatre, community hall, Domain soapbox, mechanics institute, School of the Air, TV network, journal, radio and fanzine all rolled into one. Bohemias, avant-gardes, the countercultures and youth subcultures like punks, hippies, culture jammers and cyberpunks have all sought to empower their members to make their own art and media while trying to change and subvert the mainstream companies where they toiled for their coin. Now William Morris's romantic nineteenth-century socialist ideal of a do-it-yourself arts-and-crafts revolution may be about to become (virtual) reality. Cheap, interactive media technologies have the potential to enfranchise a creative culture in the suburbs and end the bohemian versus bogan divide. One time Push Libertarian and academic Sylvia Lawson has shown that it was an interactive dialogue with the *Bulletin*'s readership in the cities and the bush that created a passionate community around the project in the late nineteenth century, and produced some of the magazine's best writers. Just as many of Australia's past bohemian artists and writers came from the suburbs to find inspiration in the metropolis, it may now be that inspiration is to be found where most Australians live.

• • •

Of all the talented young to emerge in the 1990s it was novelist Christos Tsiolkas who best rendered the polyglot identity confusion that is a crucible of creativity out in the suburbs. Through the character of Ari, the troubled young man living between worlds, in his novel *Loaded*, Tsiolkas revealed – and continues to reveal – how the boys and girls of the 'burbs assemble multi-identities from the material surrounding them as they grow up – the immigration experience, family, religion and politics, sexual options, global TV, the internet, blogs, Facebook, music culture and neighbourhood. Cultural differences – ethnic, life-style, sexual, regional, religious – and their difficult negotiation is the great narrative of contemporary Australian life. This is why so many of us have responded to his novel *The Slap* and its recent television adaption as authentic. The clash and fusion of cultures in the suburbs may be a new wellspring of hybrid art, just as cubism, jazz and rock rolled out of the cities in the last century.

Is bohemianism still a meaningful way of life for artists in a postmodern culture where ironic self-reflexivity about commodification became widespread and the performance of authenticity, transgression, cosmopolitanism, creativity and identity play were available to all? Postmodernists may have danced on the grave of the avant-garde but in the passion with which some young adherents proselytised their credo were echoes of the modernist challenge of an earlier era. Bohemia first emerged as a way young creative people might deal with the problems of cultural atrophy and exclusion, as a strategy to dislodge an incumbent older generation, and win public space for themselves and new aesthetics. This dialectic intensified, rather than disappeared, in the 1980s and 90s in conflicts over art, media, music, sex and technology and became even more acute in the new century as culture wars were waged between liberality and conservatism, libertines and a new wowserism. Bohemianism was reinvented in bands, dissident subcultures, performance troupes and media projects that pushed against the edge of acceptability, created new media spaces and sometimes crossed into a popular culture that they were helping to frag-ment. Yet it was in their struggle with the controlling older generation over new ideas, visions and ways of living that the postpunks and postmodernists of Gen X most clearly relived the romantic urge for artistic autonomy that lies at bohemia's heart.

CONCLUSION:
THE BOHEMIAN LINE

Making the case for an Australian bohemian tradition requires attention to connections, transmissions and patterns of living often invisible to the historical actors themselves but apparent to the historian who takes the long-term perspective. As Greil Marcus asked on perceiving a connection between the Sex Pistols and Dada, is history 'not the result of moments that seem to leave nothing behind, nothing but the mystery of spectral connections between people long separated by place and time, but somehow speaking the same language?' Raymond Williams embarked on a similar project over fifty years ago, linking writers, painters and philosophers to an unconscious English tradition of reaction to industrial capitalism. Williams believed that 'the discovery of patterns ... unexpected identities and correspondences' helped society move on, because 'establishing new lines with the past, breaking or redrawing pre-existing lines – is a radical kind of contemporary change'.[1]

From the 1860s through to the early twenty-first century Australia has had an ongoing bohemian tradition. It has been constituted by successive and overlapping generations of culture creators who formed groups in which to perform a bohemian identity that ranged from explicitly bohemian clubs and circles such as the Cave of Adullam and the Dawn to Dusk Club to project-based teams, such as those focused on *Colonial Monthly*, the Heidelberg painters' camps, or *Oz* to larger networks and subcultures bonded by their own style and argot such as the Libertarians of the Sydney Push or Melbourne steampunks. It was a dynamic, ever-changing tradition, encompassing novel forms like the modernist avant-gardes in the 1930s and the various countercultures that emerged in the 1960s.

Whether garret painters in the 1890s or university students in the 1950s, the 'bohemian moment' for most artists and intellectuals is the free space they enjoyed in precocious and hungry youth. But equally important, as Murger well knew, was the *memory* of youth. Bohemia is in part created in the act of its telling, or more particularly, remembering. In any decade the last true bohemia is usually the counterculture identified with the youth of the middle-aged cohort that currently dominates the arts, media and intellectual life. But this history has sought to liberate bohemianism from safe consignment to the past, and instead consider bohemia as a potent solution to the problem of making a living and a life as an artist in Australia. As this problem persists from generation to generation, bohemianism is something of a 'permanent protest', to borrow from the Libertarian lexicon.

It was common for Australian bohemian artists and writers, once established and grown older, to recycle the bohemianism of their youth as nostalgia in memoirs, journalism, exhibitions, television documentaries and even semi-autobiographical films. Across the generations they close down the possibility of tradition by denying the credentials and credibility of younger artists who came after them. 'We were a true bohemia, not poseurs as they are now,' 1920s 'Queen of Bohemia' Dulcie Deamer declared about beatniks.[2] '[S]omething a little too calculating, a little too prudent, a little commercial has corroded the joie de vivre,' Kenneth Slessor said regretfully in 1965 of the passing of authentic bohemia in Kings Cross.[3] Forty years after the sixties, Sydney Push artist Jan Cork lamented: 'The world is so cutthroat now, there's no room for bohemians.'[4] Martin Sharp declared in 2007, at the height of the Chaser's notoriety, 'I'm a little surprised more young people today aren't carrying on our tradition – but I guess it's a pretty rare moment when an idea comes together like *Oz* did.'[5] This inability by established cultural players to acknowledge, or even see new bohemias emerging around them was common in France as well, leading Pierre Bourdieu to conclude that different generations involved in cultural confrontation don't actually inhabit the same present, and eventually become 'conservative' in the sense that they only recognise 'their contemporaries in the past.'[6]

Despite the rhetoric of generational uniqueness, the continuities are manifest. The tradition was organised and reproduced by cultural work spaces and training institutions that brought people together, such as print media, art schools, studios and artists' camps and universities, and by recreational spaces such as cafés and pubs. These sites played a key role in transmitting the romantic idea of bohemianism from older to younger people, as new recruits came to work in journalism, or to be trained in art schools or universities. The *Bulletin*, *Smith's Weekly* and *Nation Review* encouraged camaraderie and community. The ABC hosted crazy experiments like Double and Triple J in the 1970s and 80s. Today that happens in virtual hubs but also in old converted warehouses where small start-ups fashion the latest animation or digital game. In a few cases families were also important transmitters of bohemianism through generations, for example in the McCrae, Lindsay and Mora dynasties.

For the emerging young, bohemia has been a potent weapon to wield against rivals and the already famous. Bohemia was born of intergenerational conflict at the Paris premiere of Victor Hugo's drama *Hernani* in 1830, when fights broke out between eccentrically attired young romantics *les Jeunes France*, and the conservative classicists. In the Australian colonies, the *Bulletin* pitched the bush nationalism of the native born against the urbane cosmopolitanism of British immigrant Marcus Clarke. Similarly, the young Heidelberg painters launched themselves with the provocative *9 x 5* exhibition in a calculated bid to rerun the Whistler–Ruskin stoush over impressionism. As romanticism developed during the nineteenth century, it came to emphasise the necessity of continuous innovation in art. Emerging artists had little to lose and much to gain from parading their uniqueness and disparaging established artists as obsolete. By attacking new artists or their work, established players elevated them in the field, and the critical 'buzz' became part of the work's value. By introducing difference, bohemians pushed a whole cohort of artists and tastes into the past and thrust another forward. Far from negating a tradition, competition, conflict and refusal of recognition make up the necessary relationship of each new generation of bohemian group to its predecessors and successors in the nation's creative culture.

Bohemia needs to 'outrage the bourgeoisie'. In Australia this was commonly achieved through a carnivalesque spirit of subversion that surfaced in the *Bulletin*'s romance of the bushman; Norman Lindsay's art of pagan pleasure; the Dionysian play of Artists' Balls, the Yellow House and the Mardi Gras; the larrikin sensationalism of *Smith's Weekly*; the satire of *Oz* magazine; and the levelling vulgarity of Barry Humphries' ocker creations. This style of dissent, whether lampooning the powerful, profaning religion or transgressing accepted boundaries of sexuality, has attracted not just social censure, but censorship and even imprisonment.

Bohemia's embrace of sensation, difference and diversity has long been a source of creativity and novelty. It acted as a crucible where class and ethnic differences are hybridised, from modernist painting in depression-era Melbourne to Christos Tsiolkas' *Loaded* in the 1990s. The common bohemian pastimes of intense conversation, showing off, dining, drinking and drugging, and experience of the urban spectacle enhance networks and creativity. Being a bohemian is a licence to take risks and gives the creative youth the touch of glamour and danger that the bourgeois consumer craves, if only for one night's entertainment. The carnivalesque may seem to provide little more than a safety valve for discontent rather than promoting focused political change. But the crossing of arbitrary borders of society and the disruption of expectation could stimulate new ways of thinking, and radically transform culture.

Yet a number of bohemian writers, journalists, visual artists and performers in Australia did make a stand as political agitators, contributing their talents to radical causes as varied as the union movement, the Labor Party, socialist and anarchist groups, the Communist Party, 'Green Bans', and agitation around the environment, decolonisation, gender, race and sexuality. Where British bohemians drifted up the social scale to merge with a decadent aristocracy, Australian bohemia has reached down into labour and revolutionary politics in the 1890s, the 1930s and 40s, and during the radical countercultural upsurge of the 1960s and early 1970s to lend assistance as cultural activists. But this relationship could be vexed, with bohemian individualism, hedonism and spirit of topsy-turvy coming up hard against the solidarity, hierarchies and puritanical streak that can be found in left politics. This tension was partially resolved with the emergence in the 1970s of a more individualised, symbolic social-movement politics that valued cultural identity over class, partying over party.

The clubs and circles of nineteenth-century literary bohemia also excluded women of all classes, mirroring their exclusion from careers in journalism, but also expressing a 'masculinist' form of bohemia that exaggerated women's role in caring for the family into a threat to male pleasure. While women gained entry to club bohemia in parallel with their entry into the media workforce as journalists after the First World War, they continued to be excluded from pub bohemia until the Push and Drift in the 1960s, and even then participated on men's terms. A more female-friendly bohemian space developed from the society salon in the 1930s, exemplified by the rituals of domesticity introduced by Sunday Reed at Heide.

The declaration of independence from commercial compromise was important to bohemians, especially the avant-gardes and countercultures, stressed through stories of fights with uncompromising editors, galleries and reviewers, failed projects, and accounts of material poverty and abuse endured for stubbornly adhering to principles. But the reality was far more ambiguous and interesting, as Australia's bohemia reveals a productive engagement with the market by bohemian and avant-garde artists going back to the nineteenth century. In our small population, bohemian artists commonly breached the artificial borders between so-called high and mass cultures, cross-fertilising each with critical values cultivated in the subcultural margins. Popular writers such as Peter Carey, Frank Moorhouse and Christos Tsiolkas first published in countercultural literary journals and later carried their critical values into the mass market. Performers who began in university or underground scenes such as Barry Humphries, Nick Cave or the Chaser have danced back and forth in their careers from fringe to mass markets just as they move across media forms.

These artists invigorated commercial cultural industries and also appealed to mass and niche audiences eager to consume the 'authenticity' they signified, whether badged as 'avant-garde', 'alternative', 'underground' or 'indie'. A minority acknowledged and played with this reality, like Marcus Clarke at the beginning of Australian bohemia, seeking to stand aloof from the commodification of their work by ironising it in their bohemianism and their texts. This knowing mockery of complicity was evident in the showbiz satire of Barry Humphries, the pessimistic anarchism of Moorhouse's 'futilitarian' literature and became more widespread in a late twentieth-century postmodern aesthetic revelling in artifice, kitsch and suburbia.

Outreach to bring the work of alternative artists from niche to mainstream audiences has hinged on the active role of cultural entrepreneurs who were themselves bohemians moving between sectors and often changing cultural industries. Innovative public intervention has also played its part, such as the establishment of an Australian Film Commission and 2JJ by the Whitlam government. Crucially, audiences – especially as subcultures – and not just 'artists' contribute to the value of art, especially when it is first being developed within the fringe. At certain times, the confluence of social and institutional supports for bohemian subcultures, commercial and public sector outreach to bohemia, and portals encouraging popular participation led to periods connecting artistic achievement, audiences and national self-expression. We see examples in literature, journalism, cartooning and painting in the 1890s, the new nationalist culture in the 1970s and music in the 1980s.

Australian bohemia was formed and changed within the wider cultural problem of a colonial settler society becoming an independent nation while remaining provincial in relation to imperial Britain. A repeated refrain was the colonial dilemma of a 'David versus Goliath' struggle for national expression under threat by the metropolitan culture from Britain or the United States. But, paradoxically, memoirs also emphasised their authors' cosmopolitan sensibility, especially familiarity with the latest aesthetic and intellectual trends and the urge to describe precincts such as Kings Cross as 'our very own Montmartre, Soho or East Village'.[7] The performance of different versions of cosmopolitanism and Australianness by bohemian artists, such as a romancing of the bush, ostentatious Francophilia, playing the larrikin as expatriates in London, trekking the hippy trail through Asia, wearing the ocker mask in comedy and cinema, or building bridges to Indigenous songlines appealed to particular consumers in a competitive market, but also produced a unique Australian art spanning the ballads of Henry Lawson and Paul Kelly, to the suburban Dada of Barry Humphries and Mental As Anything. From the early 1970s the ever vital and diverse creativity of Aboriginal and Torres Strait Islander people was explicitly connected to an agenda of decolonisation by a new generation of artist–activists like Gary Foley and Roberta Sykes, and carried to the world where in many forms and medias it is the aesthetic most recognised as authentically Australian.

Despite the partial accommodation with the nation, there remained in Australian bohemianism an ongoing yearning for the metropolis, explicit in the founding bohemian texts of Clarke, and evident in the journeys of bohemians from the country towns, suburbs and outlying states in which many were raised to the inner cities of Sydney and Melbourne and sometimes on to London, Paris or New York. This odyssey to the centre was balanced by a contrary romanticism of the landscape and folk of the countryside that emerged at particular times alongside a revulsion against the city as a site of capitalist exploitation and artifice. The tendency was apparent in the rural romanticism of the late nineteenth-century *Bulletin*, in the hinterland artists' communities spanning the 1880s into the mid-twentieth century, and in the back-to-nature alternative communities advocated by some late 1960s and 70s countercultures. Yet bohemia was constituted in the spaces of the inner cities and embraces its modernity. Although the art of bohemians is troubled by urban alienation and fragmentation, the lifestyle itself is a celebration of city living, its hustle and anonymous proximity, even intimacy, with strangers.

Bohemia first emerged as the other face of the bour-geoisie, the acting out by its fringe of the French Revolution's radical promises of individualism and self-development – of 'doin' your own thing'. But now we live in an era of global capitalism, where individualism and self-realisation through hyper-consumerism are transcendent. By the late twentieth century the qualities that had for a century been practised by bohemians were increasingly available to a larger part of the population. Likewise, at this time politics itself came to rely more and more on symbolic actions and identity rights. While a postmodern culture and new information technology have helped bring the bohemian tool kit of cultural creativity and identity play to more people, the nature of Australian capitalism, public institutions, class relations and even land use have conspired to limit the impact of bohemianisation outside the metropolitan precincts, university campuses and alternative hinterland villages. An outer-suburban and regional culture anchored in low-density home ownership, old-style media and information inequality may even resent urbanity, diversity and cultural novelty, suggesting bohemia remains distinct and even challenging. Certainly conservatives in politics and the media expend much rhetoric divining a division, if not war, between the suburban 'battlers' and those they disparage as 'caffe latte'-drinking inner-city elites.

Some postmodern scholars were confident that their generation had discredited the idea of the avant-garde and bohemias, but they protest too much. In Australia's current utilitarian political and corporate climate over-regulation and the bureaucratisation of the arts is as much a menace as parsimony for creative workers and dreamers. The long years of cultural conservatism under John Howard, the narrow managerial materialism of Labor's new generation of leaders, and the determination of old commercial media oligopolies to resist change suggest that there is still a place for bohemian dissent and its quest for autonomy in the twenty-first century. As long as capitalism's promises of freedom continue to be frustrated by its other demands for work discipline, social order and sovereignty of market forces, there will be young rebels who find identity and advantage in Murger's romantic myth.

NOTES

INTRODUCTION

1   M.R. Brown, *Gypsies and Other Bohemians: The Myth of the Artist in Nineteenth Century France*, University of Michigan Research Press, Ann Arbor, 1985, p. 1.

2   F. Pyat, 'Les Artistes', *Le Nouveau Tableau de Paris*, no. iv, 1834, quoted in M.R Brown, *Gypsies and Other Bohemians*, p. 9.

3   H. Murger, *Scènes de la Vie de Bohème*, Nouvelle Edition, Michel Lévy, 1851. Murger published under the Anglicised 'Henry', presumably exotic in France.

4   For example: C. Baudelaire, 'Le Dandy', in *Ecrits sur l'Art*, 2, Livre de Poche, Paris, 1971, pp. 171–6; C. de Kay, *The Bohemian: A Tragedy of Modern Life*, Charles Scribner's Sons, New York, 1878; G. du Maurier, *Trilby: A Novel*, Harper and Bros., New York, 1894.

5   J. Richardson, *The Bohemians: La Vie de Bohème in Paris, 1830–1914*, Macmillan, London, 1969, pp. 11–15; E. Wilson, *The Bohemians: The Glamorous Outlaws*, London, I.B. Taurus, 2000, pp. 159–178; A. Parry, *Garrets and Pretenders: A History of Bohemianism in America*, Dover, New York, 1960, pp. *ix–xxviii*, pp. 376–395.

6   M. Clarke, 'Peripatetic Philosopher', *The Australasian, Argus*, 23 Nov. 1867, in L. Hergenhan (ed), *A Colonial City, High and Low Life: Selected Journalism of Marcus Clarke*, University of Queensland Press, St Lucia, 1972, p. 5.

7   Two groundbreaking Australian books that eschew romanticism are P. Kirkpatrick, *Sea Coast of Bohemia: Literary Life in Sydney's Roaring Twenties*, UQP, St Lucia, 1992; and A. Coombs, *Sex and Anarchy: The Life and Death of the Sydney Push*, Viking, Ringwood, 1995.

8   H. Murger, 'Preface', *The Latin Quarter (Scénes de la Vie de Bohème)*, trans. E. Marriage and J. Selwyn, Collins' Clear Type Press, London, 1930, p. *xi*.

9   A. de Calonne, *Voyage au pays de Bohème*, 1852; and Anonymous, *La Silhouette*, 1849, both quoted in J. Richardson, *The Bohemians*, p. 13.

10–11 H. Murger, 'Preface', p. *xxiii*.

12   P. Bourdieu, 'The Production of Belief: Contribution to an Economy of Symbolic Goods', *Media, Culture and Society*, vol. 2, no. 3, July 1980, pp. 261–289.

CHAPTER 1

1   M. Clarke, *The Peripatetic Philosopher*, George Robertson, Melbourne, 1869, p. 31.

2   M. Clarke, 'Austin Friars', *Australian Monthly Magazine*, May 1866, in L. Hergenhan (ed), *A Colonial City*, p. 99.

3   M. Clarke, 'La Béguine', *Australasian*, 8 Feb. 1873, in M. Wilding (ed), *The Portable Marcus Clarke*, UQP, St Lucia, 1976, p. 611.

4   B. Elliott, *Marcus Clarke*, Oxford University Press, 1958, pp. 105–106, p. 253.

5   W. Benjamin, *Charles Baudelaire: A Lyric Poet in the Era of High Capitalism*,

trans. H. Zohn, Verso, London, 1973, pp. 170–71

6   G.M. Hopkins, quoted in L. Hergenhan, K. Stewart and M. Wilding
        (eds), *C. Hopkins' Marcus Clarke*, Australian Scholarly Publishing, 2009,
        p. 33. Cyril Hopkins, who remained in England, maintained a lifelong
        correspondence with Clarke.

7   M. Clarke, 'Human Repetends', in M. Wilding (ed), *The Portable Marcus
        Clarke*, p. 583.

8   H. Mackinnon (ed), *The Austral Edition of the Selected Works of Marcus
        Clarke, Together with a Bibliography and Monograph of the Deceased Author*,
        Fergusson and Mitchell, Melbourne, 1890, p. *iii*.

9   M. Clarke, 1865, in *C. Hopkins' Marcus Clarke*, p. 62.

10   Anonymous, 'Mercantile Morality', *Colonial Monthly*, Oct. 1867, p. 86.

11   M. Clarke, 'Democratic Snobbery', 11 Jan. 1868, 'Democracy in Australia',
        4 Sept. 1877, in *A Colonial City*, p. 12, p. 387.

12   M. Clarke, 1865, in *C. Hopkins' Marcus Clarke*, pp. 145–46.

13   M. Clarke, 'Austin Friars', p. 86.

14   S. Mead, *Bohemia in Melbourne: An Investigation of the Writer Marcus Clarke
        and Four Bohemian Clubs During the Late 1860s–1901*, PhD thesis, School of
        Culture and Communications, University of Melbourne, 2009, p. 24.

15   M. Clarke, 'Preface to Adam Lindsay Gordon', *The Portable Marcus Clarke*,
        p. 645.

16   F. Adams, 'Melbourne and her Civilisation', 1886, *C. Hopkins' Marcus
        Clarke*, p. 58.

17   H. McCrae, *My Father and My Father's Friends*, Angus & Robertson,
        Sydney, 1935, p. 31.

18   M. Clarke, 'The Peripatetic Philosopher', *Australasian*, 23 Nov. 1867, p. 4.

19   M. Clarke, 'Balzac and Modern French Literature', *The Portable Marcus
        Clarke*, pp. 622–23.

20   M. Clarke, *The Peripatetic Philosopher*, pp. 1–2, p. 31.

21   M. Clarke, Jan. 1865, Modified in *C. Hopkins' Marcus Clarke*, p. 75, p. 77.

22   M. Clarke, 'Café Lutetia', *Weekly Times*, 28 Feb. 1874, *The Portable Marcus
        Clarke*, pp. 667–68.

23   A. McCann, *Marcus Clarke's Bohemia: Literature and Modernity in Colonial
        Melbourne*, MUP, Carlton, 2004, p. 6, p. 75.

24   M. Clarke, 'Austin Friars', p. 99; *Café Lutetia*, p. 670.

25   H. Mayer, *The Press in Australia*, Lansdowne Press, Sydney, 1968, p. 11.

26   M. Clarke, *Humbug*, 5 Jan. 1870, p. 80, B. Elliot, *Marcus Clarke*, p. 194.

27   M. Brodzky, 'Preface', *Ben Israel: A Mixed Marriage*, quoted in A. McCann,
        Marcus Clarke's Bohemia, p. 27.

28–29   H. Kendall, 'A Colonial Literary Club', 'Old Manuscripts', and 'On
        a Street', in M. Ackland (ed), *Henry Kendall: Poetry, Prose and Selected
        Correspondence*, UQP, St Lucia, 1993, p. 91, p. 160, p. 185.

30   M. Clarke, 'Review: The Luck of the Roaring Camp', in *The Portable
        Marcus Clarke*, p. 637.

31   A. McCann, *Marcus Clarke's Bohemia*, p. 75.

32   M. Clarke, 'On Advertising', in L. Hergenhan, *A Colonial City*, p. 216.

33   M. Wilding, 'Weird Melancholy', in M. Wilding, *Studies in Classic*

Australian Fiction, Shoestring Press, Leichhardt, 1997, p. 17.

34   M. Clarke, 'The Haunted Author', *Australasian*, 6 May 1871, extracted in *C. Hopkins' Marcus Clarke*, pp. 217–19.

35   C. Bright, 'Marcus Clarke', *Cosmos Magazine*, 30 Apr. 1895, p. 422.

36   H. Kendall, 'A Colonial Literary Club', p. 163.

37   C. Baudelaire, 'Le Dandy', in E. Wilson, *Bohemians*, p. 164.

38   M. Clarke, 'Balzac', in *The Portable Marcus Clarke*, p. 625.

39   M. Clarke, 'On Loafing Round', *Humbug*, vol. 1. no. 12, 1869, p. 6, p. 11.

40   T. Carrington, *The Yorick Club*, Atlas Press, Melbourne, 1911, p. 9.

41   H. McCrae, *My Father and My Father's Friends*, p. 34.

42–43 T. Carrington, *The Yorick Club*, p. 11; J.M. Forde, *The Yorick Club*, 1911, MSS Mitchell Library, p. 9.

44   M. Clarke, 'The Peripatetic Philosopher', in H. Mackinnon, *Selected Works*, p. 467.

45   M. Clarke, 'Obituary, Alfred Telo', *Leader*, 11 Oct. 1879, in *A Colonial City*, p. 372.

46   H. Kendall, 'A Colonial Literary Club', p. 160.

47   Anonymous, 'Clubs', *Colonial Monthly*, vol. 5, Sept. 1867, p. 3.

48   M. Clarke, *Twixt Shadow and Shine*, Swan Sonnenschein, London, 1893, pp. 125–27, p. 134, p. 137.

49   T. Carrington, *The Yorick Club*, p. 13.

50   M. Clarke, 'A Quiet Club', *The Peripatetic Philosopher*, p. 49.

51   T. Carrington, *The Yorick Club*, p. 29.

52   M. Clarke, 'Henry Kendall', *Leader*, 19 Mar. 1881, *A Colonial City*, p. 375.

53   H. Kendall, 'A Colonial Literary Club', p. 163.

54   H. McCrae, *My Father and My Father's Friends*, p. 35.

55   M. Clarke, *The Peripatetic Philosopher*, p. 34.

56–57 M. Clarke, 'A Night at the Immigrants' Home', *Australasian*, 12 Jun. 1869; 'Balzac' in *The Portable Marcus Clarke*, p. 651, p. 623.

58–60 M. Clarke, 'The Chinese Quarter' and 'In Outer Darkness', *Australasian*, 21 Aug. 1869; 'Melbourne Streets at Midnight', *Argus*, 28 Feb. 1868, *A Colonial City*, p. 114, pp. 119–20, p. 124, p. 169, p. 103.

61–62 M. Clarke, 'Port Arthur', in Parts 1, 2 and 3, the *Argus*, on 3, 12, and 26 Jul. 1873, in M. Wilding, *The Portable Marcus Clarke*, pp. 511–530; and quote at p. 530; letter to C.G. Duffy in *C Hopkins' Marcus Clarke*, p. *xxxi*.

63   M. Clarke, quoted by C. Bright in *Cosmos*, p. 422.

64   M. Clarke, 'Cannabis Indica', *The Portable Marcus Clarke*, pp. 542–43, p. 555.

65   M. Clarke, letter to C. Hopkins, 1874, in B. Elliott, *Marcus Clarke*, p. 172; M. Brodzky, quoted in A. McCann, *Marcus Clarke's Bohemia*, p. 225.

66   M. Clarke, May 1877, in B. Elliott, *Marcus Clarke*, p. 179.

67   H. McCrae, *My Father and My Father's Friends*, p. 47.

68   Letters written by R. Lewis and M. Clarke, Dec.–Jan. 1872–3, extracted and discussed in B. Elliott, *Marcus Clarke*, pp. 188–198.

69   J. Dane and A. Miller, 'The Tasmanian "Black War of 1830"', letters to the *Argus*, 5–25 Jul. 1873; *The Portable Marcus Clarke*, pp. 531–37.

70   M. Clarke, 'On Republicanism', *A Colonial City*, p. 464.

71   M. Clarke, 'The Peripatetic Philosopher Answers His Critics',

in *A Colonial City*, p. 54.

72   C.M.H. Clark, *A History of Australia IV, The Earth Abideth For Ever
      1851–1888*, Melbourne University Press, Carlton, 1978, pp. 230–31.

73   H.G. Turner, *Spectator*, 1867, in A. McCann, *Marcus Clarke's Bohemia*, p. 5.

CHAPTER 2

1   B. Lawson, 'Memories', in B. Lawson and J. Le Gay Brereton (eds), *Henry
      Lawson by His Mates*, Angus & Robertson, Sydney, 1931. p. 94.

2   J. Ashton, 'Charles Conder in Australia', in A. Galbally, *Charles Conder:
      The Last Bohemian*, MUP, Carlton, 2002, p. 22.

3   C. Harcourt, quoted in S. Mead, *Clewin Harcourt Information Sheet*, Ian
      Potter Museum of Art, University of Melbourne, Melbourne, 2003, p. 1

4   A. Jose, *The Romantic Nineties*, Angus & Robertson, Sydney, 1933, p. 3;
      G. Taylor, *Those Were the Days: Being Reminiscences of Australian Artists and
      Writers*, Tyrell's, Sydney, 1918, p. 9; N. Lindsay, *Bohemians at the Bulletin*,
      Angus & Robertson, Sydney, 1977.

5   S. Stephen, '"Women, Wine and Song": The Bohemians of Melbourne',
      Royal Historical Society of Victoria Journal, vol. 55, no. 3, 1984, p. 34.

6   L. Lindsay, *Comedy of Life: An Autobiography*, Angus & Robertson, 1967, p. 49.

7   J.F. Archibald, 'Genesis of the *Bulletin*: Being the Memoirs of J.F.
      Archibald', unpublished manuscript, (ML MSS B670), 1907, Mitchell
      Library, State Library of New South Wales, Sydney.

8   V. Daley, *Bulletin*, 1902, in S. Stephen, 'Women, Wine and Song', p. 32.

9   H. McCrae, *My Father and My Father's Friends*, Angus & Robertson,
      Sydney, 1935, p. 13.

10   See H. Mayer, *The Press in Australia*, p. 11. The circulation of the *Sydney
      Morning Herald* rose from 25,000 in 1875 to 100,000 in 1910. In Victoria,
      the *Age*'s circulation grew from 23,000 in 1874 to 120,000 in 1899.

11   N. Lindsay, *Bohemians at the Bulletin*, p. 12.

12   A. Jose, *The Romantic Nineties*, p. 3.

13   R. Quinn, 'Glimpses of Henry Lawson', in *Henry Lawson by his Mates*, p. 177.

14   S. Lawson, *Archibald Paradox: A Strange Case of Authorship*, Penguin,
      Ringwood, 1987, pp. *ix–xii*, p. 3.

15   G. Taylor, *Those Were the Days*, p. 99.

16   E.J. Brady, 'Wage Writer', in B. Scates, *A New Australia: Citizenship,
      Radicalism and the First Republic*, Cambridge University Press, 1997, p. 21.

17   H. Lawson, '"Pursuing Literature" in Australia', *Bulletin*, 21 Jan. 1988, in
      L. Cantrell (ed), *The 1890s: Stories, Verse and Essays*, UQP, 1977, p. 12.

18   J. Mendelssohn, *Lionel Lindsay: An Artist and His Family*, Chatto & Windus,
      London, 1988, pp. 60–61, p. 68, pp. 78–9.

19   H. McQueen, *Tom Roberts*, Pan MacMillan, Sydney, 1996, p. 64.

20   *Lone Hand*, 1914, in S. Stephen, 'Women, Wine and Song', p. 34.

21   H. McCrae, 'Passage to Forty-seven', *Southerly*, vol. 15, no. 4, 1954, p. 205.

22   S. Stephen, 'Women, Wine and Song', p. 34.

23   G. Taylor, *Those Were the Days*, p. 100.

24   A. Jose, *The Romantic Nineties*, p. 24.

25   R. White, *Inventing Australia*, Allen & Unwin, Sydney, 1981, p. 94.

26   F. Broomfield, in M. Sharkey and J. Saunders, 'Another Bohemian Haunt in Sydney: The Century Club', *Notes and Furphies*, no. 23, 1989, p. 5.

27   J. Le Gay Brereton, address to University of Sydney Literary Society, 25 Jun. 1928, *Sydney Morning Herald*, 7 Jul. 1928, p.11.

28   V. Daley, in G. Taylor, *Those Were the Days*, p. 9, p. 13.

29–30 For these observations and quotes for the Dawn to Dusk Club that follow see G. Taylor, *Those Were the Days*, pp. 9–14.

31   J. Le Gay Brereton, 'In The Gusty Old Weather', in *Henry Lawson by His Mates*, p. 3.

32–33 G. Taylor, *Those Were the Days*, p. 10; A. Jose, *The Romantic Nineties*, p. 10.

34   M. Lake, 'The Politics of Respectability: Identifying the Masculinist Context', *Historical Studies*, vol. 22, no. 86, Apr. 1986, pp. 116–31, pp. 119–21.

35   H. McQueen, *Tom Roberts*, p. 50.

36   B. Lawson, 'Memories', p. 107.

37   N. Lindsay, *My Mask*, Angus & Robertson, Sydney, 1973, p. 82.

38   E.J. Brady, 'Mallacoota Days and Other Things', in *Henry Lawson by His Mates*, p. 133.

39–40 G. Taylor, *Those Were the Days*, pp. 63–64.

41–42 S. Mead, *Bohemia in Melbourne*, pp. 58–65; pp. 70–71.

43   T. Fink, quoted in D. Garden, *Theodore Fink: A Talent for Ubiquity*, MUP, Carlton, 1998, p. 60.

44   W. Moore, quoted in S. Stephens, 'Women, Wine and Song', p. 31.

45   L. Lindsay, *Comedy of Life: An Autobiography*, Angus & Robertson, Sydney, 1967, p. 88.

46   R. Bedford, *Nought to Thirty-Three*, Currawong, Sydney, 1944, pp. 274–76.

47   L. Lindsay, *Comedy of Life*, p. 117.

48   G. Taylor, *Those Were the Days*, pp. 19–20.

49   L. Lindsay, *Comedy of Life*, p. 19.

50   E.J. Brady, in P. Kirkpatrick, *Sea Coast of Bohemia*, p. 52.

51   L. Esson, 'Fasoli's', in L. Esson, 'Let Us Go To Fasoli's', *Focus*, vol. 2, no. 6, 1947, p. 4.

52   *Australasian Art Review*, 1 Jun. 1899, p. 13; C.H. Hunt, *In a Sydney Café*, 1899, and discussed in *Australasian Art Review*, 5 Oct. 1899, pp. 8–9.

53   *Argus*, 28 May 1898, p. 4.

54   P. Kirkpatrick, *Sea Coast of Bohemia*, p. 47.

55–57 G. Taylor, *Those Were the Days*: pp. 47–52, p. 77, p. 80, p. 95; p. 47.

58   R. Waterhouse, *Private Pleasures, Public Leisure: A History of Australian Popular Culture Since 1788*, Longman, South Melbourne, 1995, p. 67.

59   G. Taylor, *Those Were the Days*, p. 52.

60   H. Lawson, quoted in P. Kirkpatrick, *Sea Coast of Bohemia*, p. 52.

61   N. Lindsay, *Bohemians at the Bulletin*, p. 54.

62   P. Kirkpatrick, *Sea Coast of Bohemia*, p. 147

63   E.J. Brady, 'Mallacoota Days and Other Things', p. 130.

64–65 N. Lindsay, *Bohemians at the Bulletin*, p. 7; p. 54.

66   N. Lindsay, *My Mask*, pp. 83–4.

67   G. Davison, 'Sydney and the Bush: An Urban Context for the Australian

Legend', *Australian Historical Studies*, vol. 18, no. 71, Oct. 1978, p. 208;
R. White, *Inventing Australia*, pp. 101–06.

68   G. Taylor, *Those Were the Days*, pp. 54–60.

69   L. Astbury, *City Bushmen: The Heidelberg School and the Rural Mythology*,
        Oxford University Press, Melbourne, 1985, pp. 2–3.

70   L. Astbury, 'Cash Buyers Welcome: Australian Artists and Bohemianism
        in the 1890s', *Journal of Australian Studies*, May 1987, p. 33.

71   C. Conder, letter to Margaret Conder, August 1889, in J. Rothenstein,
        The Life and Death of Conder, Dent, London, 1938, p. 30.

72   J. Ashton, 'Popular Errors About Art and Artists', in L. Astbury, 'Cash
        Buyers Welcome', p. 30.

73   A. Cherry in S. Mead, *Bohemia in Melbourne*, p. 106.

74   B. Smith, 'Notes on Elitism and the Arts', in B. Smith, *The Death of the
        Artist as Hero: Essays in History and Culture*, OUP, Melbourne, 1988, p. 5.

75   G. Lambert, 'lecture to art students', n.d., in B. Smith, *Place, Taste and
        Tradition*, OUP, Melbourne, 1979, p. 160.

76   H. McCrae, in S. Stephen, 'Women, Wine and Song', p. 30.

77   Anonymous, *Table Talk*, 22 Jun. 1888, p. 9.

78   F. Blair, 'In Sydney Studios', *Argus*, 28 May 1898, quoted in L. Astbury,
        'Cash Buyers Welcome', p. 26.

79   F. Blair, 'In Sydney Studios', p. 35.

80   J. Ashton, 'Some Recollections of Charles Conder', quoted in A. Galbally,
        Charles Conder, p. 22.

81   A. Galbally, *Charles Conder*, pp. 23–24, p. 40.

82   H. McCrae, *Story Book Only*, quoted in A. Galbally, *Charles Conder*, p. 39.

83   D.H. Souter, 'Tom Roberts, Painter', *Art and Architecture*, vol. 3, no. 4,
        Jul.–Aug. 1906, p. 137.

84   C. Conder, letter to M. Conder, 11 Feb. 1889, in A. Galbally, *Charles
        Conder*, p. 40.

85   D.H. Souter, 'Tom Roberts, Painter', 1906, p. 137.

86   C. Conder, letter to M. Conder, in A. Galbally, *Charles Conder*, p. 40.

87–88   A. Galbally, *Charles Conder*: p. 34, p. 5, p. 41; p. 2.

89   C. Conder, 25 May 1889, in A. Galbally, *Charles Conder*, p. 42.

90   J. Mendelssohn, 'Back to the Bohemians, our "Golden Summers"', *Bulletin*,
        4 Jun. 1991, p. 99.

91   A. Galbally, 'Aestheticism in Australia' in A. Bradley and T. Smith (eds),
        Australian Art and Architecture: Essays Presented to Bernard Smith, OUP,
        Melbourne, 1980, p. 130.

92   A. Streeton, 1890, in A. Galbally, 'Aestheticism in Australia', p. 130.

93   A. Streeton, 'Eaglemont in the Eighties', *Argus*, 6 Oct. 1934, p. 49.

94   J. Smith, 'An Impressionists Exhibition', *Argus*, 17 Aug. 1889, p. 10.

95   Anonymous, 'The Impressionist Exhibition', *Table Talk*, 19 Jul. 1889, p. 5.

96   Anonymous, *Table Talk*, 28 June 1889, p. 3.

97   T. Roberts et al., 'Letter', *Argus*, 3 Sept. 1889, p. 7.

98   J. Smith, *Argus*, 17 Aug. 1889, p. 10.

99   S. Long, in W. Moore, *The Story of Australian Art*, vol. 1, Angus &
        Robertson, Sydney, 1934, pp. 168–69.

100   P. Bourdieu, 'The Production of Belief', pp. 268–69.

101–02 Anonymous, in S. Stephen, 'Women, Wine and Song', p. 35, p. 38.

103   A. Streeton, Jul. 1895, in L. Astbury, 'Cash Buyers Welcome', pp. 32–33.

104   A. Galbally, *Charles Conder*, pp. 3–4, p. 15, p. 40.

105   A.P. Martin, 'The Bohemian', *Australasian*, 22 Apr. 1876, p. 519.

106   N. Lindsay, *My Mask*, p. 169; *Bohemians at the Bulletin*, p. 39, pp. 41–42.

107   H. Lawson, 'A Song of Southern Writers', 1892, in *The 1890s*, p. 18.

108   J. Rothenstein, *The Artists of the 1890's*, Routledge, London, 1928, p. 151.

CHAPTER 3

1–2   J. Le Gay Brereton, *Knocking Round*, Angus & Robertson, Sydney, 1930, pp. 32–3.

3   G. Davison, 'Sydney and the Bush: An Urban Context for the Australian Legend', *Australian Historical Studies*, vol. 18, no. 71, Oct. 1978, p. 198.

4–6   B. Scates, *A New Australia: Citizenship, Radicalism and the First Republic*, Cambridge University Press, Cambridge, 1997: p. 13, p. 17, pp. 20–22, p. 26, pp. 54–56; p. 40.

7   H. Lawson, 'Pursuing Literature', p. 5.

8   F. Bongiorno, 'Constituting Labour: The Radical Press in Victoria, 1885–1914', in A. Curthoys and J. Schultz (eds), *Journalism, Print, Politics and Popular Culture*, University of Queensland Press, St Lucia, 1999, p. 71.

9   T. Mutch, 'Lawson', in *Henry Lawson by His Mates*, p. 151.

10   J.S. Noonan, 'My Friend' in *Henry Lawson by His Mates*, p. 193.

11   E.J. Brady, 'Mallacoota Days', in *Henry Lawson by His Mates*, p. 125.

12   R. Bedford, *Nought to Thirty-Three*, p. 239.

13   H. Lawson, 'Pursuing Literature' in Australia', p. 5, pp. 8–12.

14   V. Daley, in *Henry Lawson by His Mates*, p. 62.

15   H. Lawson, 'Freedom on the Wallaby', in L. Cantrell, *The 1890s*, p. 109.

16   F. Bongiorno, 'Constituting Labour', p. 74; H. Murger, *Bohemian Days*, c. 1895.

17   *Free-Lance*, 4 Jun. 1896, in F. Bongiorno, 'Constituting Labour', pp. 77–8.

18   F. Bongiorno, 'Constituting Labour', pp. 78–82.

19–20   N. Lindsay, *My Mask*, p. 107.

21   W. Lane, *The Workingman's Paradise*, Sydney University Press, Sydney, 1980, pp. 54–61;

22   E.J. Brady, 'The Red Objective', in B. Scates, *A New Australia*, p. 21.

23   H. Lawson, 'The Roaring Days', 1889, in W. Stone (ed), *Poems of Henry Lawson: Illustrated by Pro Hart*, Lansdowne Press, Sydney, 1980, p. 79.

24   G. Davison, 'Sydney and The Bush', p. 200, p. 208.

25   H. Lawson, 'In the Days When the World Was Wide', in *The 1890s*, p. 119.

26   V. Daley, 'The Workers Worst Foe', in *The 1890s*, p. 135.

27   H. Lawson in C.M.H. Clark, *Henry Lawson: The Man and His Legend*, Sun Books, South Melbourne, 1978, p. 53.

28   H. Lawson, 'Song of the Republic', 1887.

29   H. Lawson, in the *Republican*, 1888, in C.M.H. Clark, *Henry Lawson*, p. 4.

30   H. Lawson, 'Faces in the Street', 1888, *Poems of Henry Lawson*, p. 57.

31   V. Daley, 'In Arcady', 1911, in *The 1890s*, p. 147.

32   H. Lawson, 'Up the Country', 1882, in *The 1890s*, p. 152.

33   H. Lawson, 'Song of the Republic'; 'Pursuing Literature', p. 5.

34   A.G. Stephens, '*Bulletin* Story' in *The 1890s*, p. 25.

35   E.J. Brady, 'Mallacoota Days', p. 126.

36   H. Lawson, 'A Song of Southern Writers'.

37–38   Quoted in S. Lawson, 'Print Circus: The *Bulletin* from 1880 to Federation', in A. Curthoys and J. Schultz (eds), *Journalism*, p. 90; p. 83.

39   P. Bourdieu, 'Flaubert's Point of View' in R. Johnson (ed), *The Field of Cultural Production: Essays on Art and Literature*, trans. C. Verlie, Polity Press, Cambridge, 1993, pp. 198–99.

40   J. Le Gay Brereton, 'In the Gusty Old Weather', p. 14.

41–42   H. Lawson, 'Pursuing Literature': p. 6; p. 8.

43   M. Lake, 'The Politics of Respectability', p. 127.

44–45   H. Lawson, in C.M.H. Clark, *Henry Lawson*, p. 104, p. 94–96, p. 99.

46   H. Lawson, 'Rise Ye! Rise Ye!', 1892; 'The Union Buries Its Dead', 1893.

47   H. Lawson, 'A Song of Southern Writers'.

48   J. Le Gay Brereton, 'In the Gusty Old Weather', p. 14.

49   H. Lawson, 'The Cant and Dirt of Labor Literature', in C. Roderick (ed), *Collected Prose*, Angus & Robertson, Sydney, 1972, pp. 26–7.

50   Quotes from J. Mendelsson, *Lionel Lindsay*, pp. 63–64; F. Bongiorno, 'Constituting Labour', p. 80.

51   H. Lawson, 'Pursuing Literature', p. 5.

52   B. O'Dowd, 'Our Land', quoted in H. McQueen, *New Britannia: An Argument Concerning the Social Origins of Australian Radicalism and Nationalism*, Penguin, Ringwood, 1978, p. 102.

53   G. Hage, *White Nation: The Fantasy of White Supremacy in a Multicultural Society*, Pluto Press, Annandale, 1999, pp. 193–97.

54   A. Parker, 'Beginnings', in *Henry Lawson by His Mates*, p. 27.

55   E.J. Brady, 'Mallacoota Days', in *Henry Lawson by His Mates*, p. 128.

56   R. Williams, *Marxism and Literature*, Oxford University Press, Oxford, 1977, p. 114.

CHAPTER 4

1   D. Deamer, *The Queen of Bohemia: The Autobiography of Dulcie Deamer*, P. Kirkpatrick (ed), UQP, St Lucia, 1998, p. 73, p. 75.

2   J. Lindsay, interviewed by T. Moore, *Bohemian Rhapsody: Rebels of Australian Culture*, written, directed and produced by T. Moore, ABC Television Documentaries, Australian Broadcasting Corporation, 1997.

3   D. Deamer, *The Queen of Bohemia*, p. 120.

4   For example G. Serle, *From Deserts The Prophets Come: The Creative Spirit in Australia, 1788–1972*, Heinemann, Melbourne, 1973, pp. 89–118.

5   D. Deamer, *The Queen of Bohemia*, p. 76.

6   D. Deamer, ABC Radio, c. 1965, in *Bohemian Rhapsody*, 1997.

7   J. Lindsay, *Roaring Twenties*, in *Life Rarely Tells: An Autobiography in Three Volumes*, Penguin, Ringwood, 1982, p. 225.

8–9   N. Lindsay in P. Kirkpatrick, *Sea Coast of Bohemia*, p. 59, pp. 75–80, pp. 89–96, pp. 111–58.

10   E. Ridell, interviewed by T. Moore, *Bohemian Rhapsody*, 1997.

11   K. Slessor, 'To a Friend', *Poems*, Angus & Robertson, Sydney, 1972, p. 116.

12   *Smith's* anecdotes from G. Blaikie, *Remember Smith's Weekly?: A Biography of an Uninhibited National Australian Newspaper*, Rigby, Adelaide, 1966, p. 48, pp. 60–61, p. 73, pp. 85–86; L. Lower story from P. Sheil, 'Twang! That's my sides splitting', *Sydney Morning Herald*, 20 Sept. 2003.

13   G. Finey, *The Mangle Wheel*, Kangaroo Press, Kenthurst,1981, p. 24.

14   G. Blaikie, *Remember Smith's Weekly?*, Rigby, 1966, p. 24.

15   D. Deamer, *The Queen of Bohemia*, p. 130.

16   K. Slessor, *Bread and Wine: Selected Prose*, Angus & Robertson, Sydney, 1970, p. 29.

17   R. Lindsay, quoted in P. Kirkpatrick, *Sea Coast of Bohemia*, p. 124.

18   D. Deamer archive, *Bohemian Rhapsody*, 1997.

19   J. Lindsay, interviewed by T. Moore, *Bohemian Rhapsody*, 1997.

20–21 In P. Kirkpatrick, *Sea Coast of Bohemia*: p. 225; p. 225, pp. 219–34.

22   K. Slessor, 'The Prisoner of Darlinghurst', *The Home*, 1 Mar. 1923, p. 32.

23   N. Lindsay, quoted in M. Ryan (ed), *Angry Penguins and Realist Painting in Melbourne in the 1940s*, South Bank Centre, Melbourne, 1988, p. 79.

24   K. Slessor, 'The Prisoner of Darlinghurst', p. 32.

25   P. Kirkpatrick, '"When Skyscrapers Burst into Lilac": Slessor's *Smith's Weely* Poems', P. Mead (ed), *Kenneth Slessor: Critical Readings*, UQP, St Lucia, 1997, pp. 182–84. Discusses 'Gardens in the Sky', 'Cucumber Kitty' and 'It, If and Also'.

26   K. Slessor, interviewed by J. Thompson, ABC TV, 1964, archive in *Bohemian Rhapsody*, 1997.

27   M. Stewart, *Autobiography of My Mother*, Vintage, North Sydney, 2007, pp. 118–19, pp. 138–52, pp. 199–207, pp. 223–24.

28   D. Deamer, *The Queen of Bohemia*, p. 73, p. 75.

29   P. Kirkpatrick, *Sea Coast of Bohemia*, pp. 99–109.

30   J. Lindsay, K. Slessor, F. Johnson, Foreword, *Vision*, no. 1, May 1923.

31   N. Lindsay, in J. Lindsay, *Roaring Twenties*, pp. 302–03.

32–34 J. Lindsay, *Roaring Twenties*: p. 275; p. 210; p. 287.

35   D. Deamer, *The Queen of Bohemia*, p. 102.

36   P. Kirkpatrick, *Sea Coast of Bohemia*, p. 96.

37   J. Lindsay, *Roaring Twenties*, p. 122.

38   L. Poland, 'Out of Type: Bessie Mitchell (Guthrie) and Viking Press', in *Hecate*, vol. 29, no. 1, 2003, pp. 24–27.

39   B. Kennedy, *A Passion to Oppose: John Anderson, Philosopher*, MUP, Carlton, 1995, p. 96.

40   J. Anderson, 'Liberty and Spontaneity', 1932, in M. Weblin (ed), *A Fighting and Passionate Life: Political Writing of John Anderson*, Pluto Press, North Melbourne, 2003, pp. 95–105.

41   J. Lindsay, *Roaring Twenties*, p. 266.

CHAPTER 5

1   M. Harris, 'I am an Anarchist – So What?', *Bohemia*, no. 5, Jul. 1939, p. 12.

2   M. Harris, 'Modernist Criticises His Critics', *Bohemia*, no. 7, Oct. 1939, p. 16.

3   J.A. Allan, 'Open Letter to a Modernist', *Bohemia*, no. 5, Jul. 1939, p. 5, p. 13.

4   Episode title in Robert Hughes, *Landscape with Figures*, ABC TV, 1975.

5   G. Serle, *From Deserts The Prophets Come*, p. 178.

6   J. Burke, *The Heart Garden: Sunday Reed and Heide*, Knopf, Sydney, 2004, p. 213.

7   R. Haese, *Rebels and Precursors: The Revolutionary Years of Australian Art*, Penguin, Sydney, 1981, pp. 1–2, p. 6.

8   A. Tucker, interviewed by T. Moore, *Bohemian Rhapsody*, 1997.

9   M. Harris, 'I am an Anarchist – So What?', p. 12.

10   A. Tucker, 'The Social Origins of Surrealism', in J. Burke, *Australian Gothic: A Life of Albert Tucker*, Knopf, Sydney, 2002, p. 143.

11–12   B. Smith, *Modernism's History*, University of New South Wales Press, Sydney, 1998: pp. 16–22, p. 129, p. 132; p. 129.

13–14   M. Heyward, *The Ern Malley Affair*, p. 27, pp. 30–5; pp. 29–33.

15   J. Burke, *Australian Gothic*, pp. 27–39.

16   A. Kershaw, *Heydays: Memories and Glimpses of Melbourne's Bohemia 1937–1947*, Angus & Robertson, Sydney, 1991, p. 41.

17   S. Reed, 'Three Poems by Arthur Rimbaud', *Angry Penguins*, no. 4, 1943, p. 42–44.

18–20   A. Kershaw, *Heydays*: p. 3; p. 1; pp. 40–42.

21–22   D. Friend and J. Rickards in G. Dutton, *Innovators: The Sydney Alternatives in the Rise of Modern Art, Literature and Ideas*, Macmillan, South Melbourne, 1986, pp. 100–01.

23   A. Tucker, 'Art, Myth and Society', *Angry Penguins*, no. 4, 1943, p. 50.

24   M. Heyward, *The Ern Malley Affair*, p. 4.

25   A. Tucker, 'The Flea and the Elephant', *Angry Penguins*, no. 7, Mar. 1944, p. 55.

26   V. O'Connor, interviewed by T. Moore, *Bohemian Rhapsody*, 1997.

27   J.F. Williams, *Quarantined Culture: Australia's Reactions to Modernism 1913 1939*, Cambridge University Press, Oakley, 1995, pp. 3 14.

28–29   J. Burke, *Australian Gothic*, p. 36, p. 73, p. 79.

30   A. Tucker, *Argus*, 29 Aug. 1940, in J. Burke, *Australian Gothic*, p. 140.

31   M. Harris, 'Modernist Criticises his Critics', p. 16.

32   M. Harris, 'The Saturday Night Mind: A Psycho-sociological Study of Film', *Angry Penguins,* no. 8, 1945, pp. 36–44, pp. 47–52.

33   A. Tucker, 'Art, Myth and Society', p. 54.

34   R. Williams, *Culture and Society*, Chatto & Windus, London, 1958, p. 289.

35   A. Barcan, *Radical Students: The Old Left at Sydney University*, MUP, Carlton, 2002, pp. 36–127, pp. 150–73.

36–37   M. Heyward, *The Ern Malley Affair*: pp. 43–4; pp. 82–89.

38–40   B. Fitzpatrick, J. Passmore and J. McAuley, quoted in 'Alf Conlon' in J. Thompson (ed), *Five to Remember*, ABC TV and Lansdowne Press, Melbourne, 1964: p. 98; p. 105; p. 120.

41   M. Harris, interview with P. Ross in *Max Harris*, ABC TV, 1993.

42   J. Burke, *Joy Hester*, Vintage, Sydney, 2001, pp. 85; J. Burke, *The Heart Garden*, pp. 186–248.

43   A. Tucker, interviewed by T. Moore, *Bohemian Rhapsody*, 1997.

44   S. Reed, interviewed by J. Burke, 5 Jun. 1978, in J. Burke, *Australian Gothic*, p. 121.

45   R. Haese, *Rebels and Precursors*, p. 217.

46   G. Dutton, interviewed by T. Moore, *Bohemian Rhapsody*, 1997.

47   A. Kershaw, *Heydays*, p. 34.

48   Tucker paintings: *Pick-up*, 1941; *Victory Girl*, 1943; *Image of Modern Evil: Spring in Fitzroy*, 1943–44; *Image of Modern Evil 14*, 1945. Arthur Boyd: *Melbourne Burning*, 1946–47; J. Perceval, *Flinders Street at Night*, 1943.

49   A. Tucker, 'Art, Myth and Society', p. 50.

50   P. Bourdieu, 'The Production of Belief', pp. 267–88.

51   R.G. Menzies in M. Ryan, *Angry Penguins*, p. 79.

52   V. Cobb, 'An Artist's Reflection', *Bohemia*, Apr. 1939, p. 15.

53–54   A. Tucker, in J. Burke, *Australian Gothic*, p. 139.

55   M. Harris, 'I Am an Anarchist – So What?', p. 12.

56   15 Sept. 1942, in R. Haese, *Rebels and Precursors*, p. 9.

57   L. Lindsay, *Addled Art*, Angus and Robertson, Sydney, 1942, pp. 59–60.

58   E. Channin and S. Miller with J. Pugh, *Degenerates and Perverts: The 1939 Herald Exhibition of French and British Contemporary Art*, Miegunyah Press, Melbourne, 2005, pp. 209–17.

59   A. Tucker, in J. Burke, *Australian Gothic*, p. 60.

60   M. Mora, *Wicked but Virtuous: My life*, Penguin, Camberwell, 2002, p. 42.

61   G. Serle, *From Deserts the Prophets Come*, p. 178, p. 230.

62   M. Heyward, *The Ern Malley Affair*, pp. 12–13.

63   J. McAuley and H. Stewart, 'Ern Malley, Poet of Debunk', quoted in full in J. Tregenza, *Australian Little Magazines 1923–1954*, Libraries Board of S.A., Adelaide, 1964, p. 66.

64   M. Harris, 'I Am an Anarchist – So What?', p. 12.

65   N. Counihan, 'How Albert Tucker Misrepresents Marxism', *Angry Penguins*, no. 5, Sept. 1943, n.p..

66   A. Tucker, 'Man, Myth and Society', p. 50.

67   A. Tucker, 'The Flea and the Elephant', p. 55.

68–69   J. Anderson, *Art and Reality: John Anderson on Literature and Aesthetics*, Hale & Iremonger, Sydney, 1982: p. 80; p. 71.

70–71   B. Smith, *Place, Taste and Tradition*: p. 238; p. 227.

72   J.A. Allan, 'Open Letter to a Modernist', p. 5.

CHAPTER 6

1   C. James, *Unreliable Memoirs*, Random House, New York, 1981, p. 138.

2   J. Anderson, *Honi Soit*, 14 Oct. 1954, p. 5; D. Horne in B. Kennedy, *Passion*, p. 150.

3   D. Ivison, *Honi Soit*, 11 Jun. 1953, in A. Barcan, *Radical Students*, p. 292.

4   P. McGuinness, interviewed by T. Moore, *Bohemian Rhapsody*, 1997.

5   R. Lupton, 'The Push: The Inside Story of Bohemian Australians', *People*,

14 Aug. 1963, p. 7.

6   I. Davison, 'The Failure of Australian Bohemia', *The Australian Humanist*,
        no. 3, Spring 1967, p. 13.

7   A.J. Baker, 'Libertarianism and the Push', *Broadsheet*, no. 81, Mar. 1975.
        Online at http://www.takver.com/history/aia/aia00026.htm.

8   A. Barcan, *Radical Students*, p. 291.

9–11   A. Coombs, *Sex and Anarchy*: R. Smilde p. 13; p. 52; p. 18.

12   M. Fink, interviewed by T. Moore, *Bohemian Rhapsody*, 1997.

13   J. Gulley, interviewed by T. Moore, *Bohemian Rhapsody*, 1997.

14   A. Thoms, interviewed by Tony Moore, Sept. 2003.

15   C. James, *Unreliable Memoirs*, p. 138.

16   R. Gerster and J. Bassett, *Seizures of Youth: 'The Sixties' and Australia*,
        Hyland House, Melbourne, 1991, p. 48.

17   G. Molnar, *Honi Soit*, 12 Mar. 1959, in A. Barcan, *Radical Students*, p. 320.

18   A.J. Baker, 'Sydney Libertarianism', paper delivered to London Anarchist
        Group, March 1960; A. Barcan, *Radical Students*, p. 292.

19   R. Pinkerston, 'The Ideology of Chastity', *Libertarian*, no. 1, Sept. 1957,
        pp. 22–32.

20   M. Wark, *The Virtual Republic*, p. 62.

21   G. Molnar, 'Anarchism', *Libertarian*, no. 1, Sept. 1957, p. 12.

22   A. Coombs, *Sex and Anarchy*, p. 170.

23   I. Davison, 'Failure of Australian Bohemia', p. 13; F. Moorhouse, 'The
        Inspector and the Prince', *Bulletin*, 14 Feb. 1971, in F. Moorhouse, *Days of
        Wine and Rage*, Penguin, Ringwood, 1980, p. 26.

24   A.J. Baker, 'Libertarianism and the Push'.

25   P. McGuinness, *Bohemian Rhapsody*, 1997; S. Varga, 'Twice the Man',
        Spectrum, Sydney Morning Herald, 9 Aug. 2003, p. 6; F. Moorhouse, 'The
        Inspector', p. 26.

26   J. Docker, *Australia's Cultural Elites: Intellectual Elites in Sydney and Melbourne*,
        Angus & Robertson, Sydney, 1974, pp. ix–x.

27   A.J. Baker, 'Libertarianism and the Push'.

28   R. Smilde, speech launching *Sex and Anarchy*, 1996.

29   J. Gulley, interviewed by T. Moore, *Bohemian Rhapsody*, 1997.

30   A. Coombs, *Sex and Anarchy*, pp. 52–56.

31   M. Fink, interviewed by T. Moore, *Bohemian Rhapsody*, 1997.

32   G. Harrison, *Night Train to Granada*, Pluto Press, Sydney, 2001,
        pp. 103–04.

33   P. McGuinness, 'Investing in Human Capital Costs Money', *Sydney
        Morning Herald*, 10 Apr. 1997.

34–36   I. Davison, 'Failure of Australian Bohemia', p. 13; R. Lupton, 'The Push',
        p. 6.

37   D. Ivison, 'What is this libertarianism?', *Honi Soit*, 30 Sept. 1964, p. 5.

38   M. Fink, quoted in A. Coombs, *Sex and Anarchy*, p. 78.

39   J. Ogilvie, *The Push: An Impressionist Memoir*, Primavera Press, Leichhardt,
        1995, p. 114.

40   E. Morris, 'The Patriarchal Push', *Quadrant*, Jan.–Feb. 1979, p. 76.

41   F. Fink, interviewed by T. Moore, *Bohemian Rhapsody*, 1997.

42   A. Coombs, *Sex and Anarchy*, p. 69.

43   J. Ogilvie, *The Push*, p. 114.

44   S. Varga, 'Twice the Man', p. 6.

45   I. Davison, 'Failure of Australian Bohemia', p. 13.

46   A. Thoms, interview with Tony Moore, Sept. 2003.

47   I. Davison, 'Failure of Australian Bohemia', p. 13.

48   A. Coombs, *Sex and Anarchy*, p. 163.

49   G. Chandler, *So You Think I Did It?*, Sun Books, Melbourne, 1969.

50   A. Coombs, *Sex and Anarchy*, p. 18, p. 64; C. Wallace, *Greer: Untamed Shrew*, Macmillan, Sydney, 1997, p. 72.

51   Editorial, *Libertarian*, no. 1, Sept. 1957, p. 38.

52   A. Coombs, *Sex and Anarchy*, p. 19.

53   A. Thoms, in C. Wallace, *Greer*, p. 101.

54   C. Wallace, *Greer*, p. 100.

55   A. Thoms, interviewed by Tony Moore, Sept. 2003, p. 27.

56   C. James, *Unreliable Memoirs*, p. 138.

57   R. Smilde, quoted in C. Wallace, *Greer*, pp. 84–85.

58   B. Ellis, *Goodbye Jerusalem: Night-thoughts of a Labor Outsider*, Random House, Sydney, 1997, p. 311.

59   R. Milliken, *Mother of Rock: The Lillian Roxon Story*, Black Inc., Melbourne, 2010.

60   B. Humphries, *More Please: An Autobiography*, Viking/Penguin, Ringwood, 1992, pp. 148–49; C. Wallace, *Greer*, p. 56.

61   T. Burstall, *The Memoirs of a Young Bastard: The Diaries of Tim Burstall, November 1953 to December 1954*, MUP, Carlton, 2012.

62   Quote from interview by C. Wallace in C. Wallace, *Greer*, p. 64.

63   A. Thoms, interviewed by T. Moore, *Bohemian Rhapsody*, 1997.

64   G. Greer, in C. Packer, *No Return Ticket: Clyde Packer Interviews Nine Famous Australian Expatriates*, A&R, North Ryde, 1984, p. 94; and G. Greer, *Cities: Germaine Greer's Sydney*, quoted in C. Wallace, *Greer*, p. 86.

65   C. Wallace, *Greer*, p. 64. As one friend reported to Wallace, Melbourne tolerated Greer but Sydney loved her.

66   B. Humphries, *More Please*, p. 169.

67   D. Ivison, *The Sydney Line*, in A. Barcan, *Radical Students*, p. 322.

68   R. Lupton, 'The Push', p. 7.

69   H. de Balzac, *A Prince of Bohemia, 1840*, in M.R. Brown, *Gypsies*, p. 10.

70   J. White, *Sun Herald*, 2 Jun. 1996.

71   J. Docker, 'Sydney Intellectual History and Sydney Libertarianism', May 1972, in A. Barcan, *Radical Students*, p. 323.

CHAPTER 7

1   R. Neville, 'We Were As Good As It Gets', *Australian*, 4 Feb. 1998, p. 13.

2   T. Roszak, *The Making of a Counter Culture: Reflections on the Technocratic Society and its Youthful Opposition*, Double Day, New York, 1969.

3   R. Neville, *Play Power*, Cape, London, 1970, p. 18.

4   F. Moorhouse, 'I Say Whitlam Doesn't Matter', in *Days of Wine and Rage*, p. 78.

5   C. McGregor, 'What Counter-Culture?', 1971, revised for *Soundtrack For the Eighties: Pop Culture, Australian Politics, Suburbia, Art and other Essays*, Hodder & Stoughton, Sydney, 1983.

6   R. Neville, 'We Were As Good as It Gets', p. 13.

7   G. Blundell, 'Sold on the Sixties', *Review, Weekend Australian*, 27–28 Oct. 2007, p. 6.

8   B. Humphries, *More Please*, p. 206, pp. 250–51; C. James, *North Face of Soho*, Picador, London, 2006, pp. 26–30.

9   R. Neville, 'The Dreams, The Trips, The Trials', *Australian Magazine, Weekend Australian*, 22–23 Apr. 1995, pp. 12–18. On screen: *Growing Up Fast*, ABC TV, 1994; *The Nostradamus Kid*, B. Ellis, 1992; *Vietnam*, Kennedy Miller, 1988. Exhibitions: *The Sixties: A Tumultuous Decade in Review*, Performing Arts Museum, Melbourne Concert Hall, 21 Sept. 1987 – Feb. 1988.

10   R. Neville, 'The Business of Being Human', *Good Weekend, Sydney Morning Herald*, 23 Aug. 1997, p. 57.

11   R. Gerster and J. Bassett, *Seizures of Youth*, p. 11; M. Davis, *Gangland: Cultural Elites and the New Generationalism*, Allen & Unwin, Sydney, 1997.

12   For example, G. Greer, 'The Universal Tonguebath: A Groupie's Vision', *Oz*, no. 19, London, 1969, in G. Greer, *The Mad Woman's Underclothes: Essays and Occasional Writings 1968–85*, Picador, London, 1986, pp. 6–11.

13   B. Humphries, 'Adventures of King Arthur', *Spectrum, Sydney Morning Herald*, 17–18 Nov. 2007, p. 37.

14   B. Ellis, 'A Book That Never Came', in R. Walsh, *Ferretabilia: Life and Times of Nation Review*, UQP, St Lucia, 1993, p. 169.

15   G. Greer, 'Million-Dollar Underground', *Oz*, July 1969, London, p. 15.

16   R. Neville, 'We Were As Good As It Gets', p. 13.

17   A. Ashbolt, 'Myth and Reality', *Meanjin Quarterly*, no. 4, vol. 25, 1966, pp. 373–88; I. Turner, 'The Retreat from Reason', *Meanjin Quarterly*, no. 2, vol. 25, 1966, pp. 133–43.

18   S. Alomes, 'Cultural Radicalism in the Sixties', *Arena,* vol. 62, 1983, pp. 28–54.

19   J. Heath and A. Potter, *Nation of Rebels: Why Counterculture Became Consumer Culture*, Harper Collins, New York, 2004, p. 322.

20   C. Hamilton, *Growth Fetish*, Allen & Unwin, Sydney, 2003, pp. 109–111.

21   S. Frith and H. Horne, *Art into Pop*, pp. 1–16.

22–23   R. Neville, *Play Power*, p. 20, p. 98.

24   C. McGregor, *People, Politics and Pop*: *Australians in the Sixties*, Ure Smith, Sydney, 1968, pp. 158–175.

25   G. Greer, 'A Groupie's Vision', p. 7.

26   B. Ellis, 'Sydney University in the Sixties', speech at Adelaide University, Feb. 2006.

27   G. Greer, 'The Million-Dollar Underground', p. 16.

28   B. Ellis, '*Sidere Mens Eadem Mutato*: Sydney University 1959–64' and 'Please Do Not Adjust Your Sets', in *Letters to the Future*, Methuen Haynes, North Ryde, 1987, pp. 23, p. 27, p. 30.

29   C. James, *North Face of Soho*, p. 21.

30–31   R. Neville, *Hippie Hippie Shake*, p. 18, p. 27, p. 34, p. 56.

32   *Oz,* no. 1, Apr. 1963, p. 13, p. 14; *Oz,* no. 16, Jan. 1965, p. 12, pp. 14–15, p. 18.

33   Anonymous, 'Queen versus *Oz*', *Oz*, no. 12, Aug. 1964, p. 13.

34   P. Bourdieu, 'The Production of Belief', pp. 288–90.

35   R. Neville et al., 'The Story of *Oz*', *The Weekend Australian Magazine*, 18–19 March 2006, pp. 18–23.

36   F. Moorhouse, *Days of Wine and Rage*, p. 5.

37–38   A. Thoms, 'Sunshine City: 1972' and 'Surrealist Cinema: 1973', in A. Thoms, *Polemics for a New Cinema*, Wild and Woolley, Glebe, 1978, pp. 156–57; pp. 255–60, pp. 9–13.

39   T. Creswell and M. Fabinyi, *The Real Thing, Adventures in Australian Rock and Roll*, Random House, Sydney, 1999, p. 55.

40   Quoted in R. Neville, *Hippie Hippie Shake*, p. 98.

41   G. Blundell, 'Sold on the Sixties', p. 6.

42–45   C. James, *North Face of Soho*: p. 54; p. 217; p. 55, p. 106; p. 29.

46   R. Neville, *Hippie Hippie Shake*, p. 74, pp. 99–100, p. 120.

47   G. Greer, 'Mozic and the Revolution', *Mad Woman's Underclothes*, p. 18.

48   G. Greer, 'A Groupie's Vision', pp. 6–11.

49   G. Greer, 'The Politics of Female Sexuality', *Oz*, May 1970; and G. Greer, 'Lady Love Your Cunt', *Suck*, 1971, both in. *Mad Woman's Underclothes*, pp. 36–40, pp. 74-77.

50   C. James, *North Face of Soho*, p. 217.

51   T. Creswell and M. Fabinyi, *The Real Thing*, p. 55.

52   D. McKnight, 'Rupert Murdoch and the Culture War', *Australian Book Review*, Feb. 2004.

53   C. James, *North Face of Soho*, p. 168.

54   R. Walsh, *Ferretabilia*, p. 59; R. Walsh, 'Eulogy to Gordon Barton', Memorial service, University of Sydney, 3 Sept. 2005.

55–56   F. Moorhouse, *Days of Wine and Rage*: p. 3; pp. 78–84, p. 102.

57   R. Neville, *Hippie Hippie Shake*, p. 109.

58   M. Sharp, 'Letter', c. 1970, in R. Neville, *Hippie Hippie Shake*, p. 247.

59   G. Greer, 'Mozic and the Revolution', p. 19.

60   F. Moorhouse, *Days of Wine and Rage*, pp. 8–12.

61   R. Neville, *Play Power*, p. 261.

62   M. Bradbury, 'A Dog Engulfed in Sand II', quoted in E. Wilson, *Glamorous Outcasts*, Rutgers University Press, New Jersey, 2000, p. 222.

CHAPTER 8

1–2   A. Barcan, *Radical Students*: p. 307, pp. 323–25, p. 327; p. 309, p. 375.

3   R. Neville, *Hippie Hippie Shake*, p. 19.

4   B. Birrell, 'Student Attitudes to the Left', *Arena*, no. 24, 1971, p. 63.

5–6   R. Neville, *Hippie Hippie Shake*: M. Sharp quote p. 120, p. 123.

7   R. Neville, *Play Power*, p. 257.

8   C. James, *North Face of Soho*, p. 26; B. Ellis, *Goodbye Jerusalem*, p. 136.

9   B. Ellis, 'Sidere Mens Eadem Mutato', p. 11, p. 19.

10   R. Neville, *Play Power*, pp. 18–19.

11–12   R. Neville, *Hippie Hippie Shake*: pp. 16–18; p. 18.

13   I. Turner, 'The Retreat from Reason', pp. 185–86.

14   R. Neville, *Hippie Hippie Shake*, p. 325.

15   J. Lebel, 1968, in R. Neville, *Play Power*, p. 45.

16   R. Neville, *Hippie Hippie Shake*, p. 93.

17   G. Greer, *The Female Eunuch*, Paladin, London, 1970, p. 15.

18   B. Birrell, 'Student Attitudes to the Left', *Arena*, no. 24, 1971, p. 58.

19   D. Horne, *Time of Hope: Australia 1966–72*, Angus & Robertson, Sydney, 1980, p. 43.

20   R. Neville, *Play Power*, p. 108.

21   G. Greer, *The Female Eunuch*, p. 25.

22   C. McGregor, *People, Politics and Pop*, pp. 170–71.

23   M. Bakhtin, in S. Vice, *Introducing Bakhtin*, Manchester University Press, 1997, pp. 151–52; 'School Kids' *Oz*, no. 28, London, May 1970.

24   M. Bakhtin, *Rabelais and his World,* trans. Hélène Iswolsky, Indiana University Press, Bloomington, 1984, p. 74, pp. 78–9, p. 81.

25–26   F. Moorhouse, *Days of Wine and Rage*: pp. 10–11; W. Bacon quoted p. 11.

27   H. Goodall, *Invasion to Embassy: Land in Aboriginal Politics in New South Wales, 1770–1972*, Allen & Unwin, Sydney, 1996, p. 351, cited in G. Foley, 'Black Power in Redfern 1968–1972' introduction, 5 Oct. 2001, Koorie History Website www.kooriweb.org/foley/essays/essay_1.html.

28   K. Lothian in 'Moving Blackwards, Black Power and the Aboriginal Embassy', in I. MacFarlane and M. Hanah (eds), *Transitions: Critical Australian Indigenous Histories*, ANU E-Press, Canberra, pp. 22–23.

29   C. Walker, *Buried Country: The Story of Aboriginal Country Music*, Pluto Press, Annandale, 2000.

30   C. Walker, *Buried Country*, p. 150.

31   C. McGregor, *People, Politics and Pop*, p. 172.

32   C. James, *North Face of Soho*, p. 28.

33   L. Segal, *Is the Future Female?: Troubled Thoughts on Contemporary Feminism*, Virago, London, 1994, p. 88.

34   C. McGregor, *People, Politics and Pop*, p. 83.

35–36   D. Altman, *Rehearsals for Change*, in 'What Counter-Culture?', p. 111.

37   F. Moorhouse, *The Americans, Baby: A Discontinuous Narrative of Stories and Fragments,* Angus & Robertson, Sydney, 1972, p. 108.

38   D. McKnight, *Australia's Spies and their Secrets*, Allen & Unwin, St Leonards, 1994, pp. 214–18.

39   B. Ellis, *Letters to the Future*, pp. 178–83, pp. 184–92, pp. 198–203.

40   A. Thoms, interview with T. Moore, Sept. 2003.

41   B. Ellis, *Goodbye Jerusalem*, p. 311.

42   A. Thoms, 'Australian Cinema at the Zero Point', 1976', *Polemics*, pp. 339–45.

43   G. Blundell, 'Sold on the Sixties', p. 7.

44   F. Moorhouse, 'I Say Whitlam Doesn't Matter', p. 80, pp. 84–85. In Moorhouse's own case this prediction proved prescient.

45–46   P. Ross-Edwards, Victorian Country Party Leader, quoted in the *Sun*,

16 Jan. 1976, and M. Webb, in B. Elder and D. Wales, *Radio with Pictures!: The History of Double Jay*, Hale & Iremonger, Sydney, 1984: p. 25; p. 4.

47 F. Moorhouse, *Days of Wine and Rage*, pp. 101–02.

48 J. Farrell, *The Spirit of the Sixties: Making Post-War Radicalism*, Routledge, New York, 1997, p. 229.

CHAPTER 9

1–3 M. Harris, *Ockers: Essays on the Bad Old New Australia,* Maximus Books, Adelaide, 1974: p. 2; p. 3; B. Humphries quote, p. 33.

4–5 R. Neville, *Hippie Hippie Shake*: p. 20, p. 25, pp. 48–50; p. 10.

6–7 B. Humphries, *More Please*: pp. 155–72; p. 171.

8 B. Ellis, 'Sidere Mens Eadem Mutato', p. 22.

9 J. Lindsay, 'The Alienated Australian Intellectual', in J. Lee, P. Mead, G. Murnane (eds), *Temperament of Generations*, p. 173.

10 R. Neville, *Hippie Hippie Shake*, p. 113.

11 I. Britain, *Once an Australian*, OUP, Melbourne, 1997, pp. 9–14.

12 R. Neville, *Play Power*, p. 23.

13 C. Lumby, interviewed by T. Moore, *Bohemian Rhapsody*, 1997.

14 C. James, *North Face of Soho*, p. 52.

15 N. Waterlow (ed), *Larrikins in London: An Australian Presence in 1960s London,* exh. catalogue, Ivan Dougherty Gallery, UNSW/COFA, 2003.

16 S. Alomes, *When London Calls: The Expatriation of Australian Creative Artists to Britain,* Cambridge University Press, Cambridge, 1999.

17–18 C. James, *North Face of Soho*: p. 165; p. 236.

19 R. White, 'Cooee Across the Strand: Australian Travellers in London and the Performance of National Identity', *Australian Historical Studies*, no. 116, 2001, p. 117.

20 D. Hebdidge, *Subculture: The Meaning of Style*, Methuen, 1979, pp. 36–43.

21 J. Kee, 'Larrikins in London' seminar, UNSW/COFA, 2003.

22 B. Humphries with B. Beresford, *Barry McKenzie Holds His Own: An Original Photoplay*, Sun Books, South Melbourne, 1974, p. 3, p. 14, p. 72.

23 Australia Council for the Arts, *Annual Report*, 1973, p. 9.

24 H.C. Coombs, quoted in T. Rowse, *Arguing the Arts: The Funding of the Arts in Australia*, Penguin, Ringwood, 1985, p. 74.

25 E.G. Whitlam, *The Whitlam Government: 1972–1975,* Viking, 1985, Ringwood, pp. 560–63.

26 E.G. Whitlam, 'Eureka: The Birth of Australian Democracy', speech at Art Gallery of Ballarat, 3 Dec. 1973.

27 P. Weir in S. Mathews (ed), *35mm Dreams: Conversations with Five Directors about the Australian Film Revival*, Penguin, Ringwood, 1984, p. 84.

28 G. Serle, *From Deserts the Prophets Come*, p. 230.

29 R. Walsh, 'Founding Principles', *Nation Review*, 1971, in *Ferretabilia*, p. 49.

30 R. Walsh, Apr. 1971, in *Ferretabilia*, p. 20.

31 D. Horne, 'The New Nationalism?, *Bulletin*, 5 Oct. 1968, p. 37.

32 G. Barton, interviewed in *Review*, quoted in R. Walsh, *Ferretabilia*, p. 59.

33 S. Forde, 'The Development of an Alternative Press in Australia', *Media International Australia*, no. 87, May 1998, pp. 122–23.

34   J. Davidson, 'Mr Whitlam's Cultural Revolution', *Journal of Australian Studies*, no. 20, May 1987, p. 83.

35   G. Blundell, 'Introduction', in J. Romeril, *I Don't Know Who to Feel Sorry For: A Play*, Currency Press, Sydney, 1973, pp. 7–11.

36–37   D. Pulford, 'America and the Australian Performing Group', *Antipodes, Journal of the American Association of Australian Literary Studies*, Dec. 2000: p. 111; p. 112.

38   D. Williamson, interviewed by G. Negus, *George Negus Tonight*, 9 Sept. 2004, ABC TV.

39   J. Romeril, *Meanjin*, 1978, in G. Blundell, *Australian Theatre*, p. 174.

40   P. Weir, interview by K. Ward, 'Weir'd Tales', *Tabula Rasa*, 1994, p. 4. Accessed at www.tabula-rasa.info/AusHorror/PeterWeir.html.

41–42   A. Thoms, 'Australian Cinema at the Zero Point' in, *Polemics*, p. 339.

43   T. O'Regan, 'Australian Film in the 1970s', *Australian Film in the Reading Room*, p. 6.

44–45   P. Adams, *Age*, 1974, B. Ellis, 1971, quoted in M. Harris, *Ockers*, p. 34.

46   M. Arrow, *Upstaged: Australian Women Dramatists in the Limelight At Last*, Currency Press, Sydney, 2002, pp. 195–97; K. Wark, *Virtual Republic*, pp. 75–77; M. Davis, *Gangland*, p. 29, p. 108.

CHAPTER 10

1   C. Walker, *Stranded: The Secret History of Australian Independent Music 1977–1991*, Macmillan, Sydney, 1996, pp. 9–17.

2   F. Jameson, 'Periodizing the 60s', in his *The Ideologies of Theory: Essays 1971–1986, Vol. 2 Syntax and History*, Routledge, London, 1988, p. 191–95.

3   E. Wilson, *Bohemians: The Glamorous Outcasts*, p. 246.

4   C. Walker, *The Inner City Sound*, Wild & Woolley, Sydney, 1982.

5   D. Nichols, 'Bending Corners', chapter in 'Dig', unpublished, p. 7.

6   'Darlinghurst Nights', words and music by Grant McLennan and Robert Forster. Reprinted with permission. See imprint on p. *iv* for details.

7–8   *We're Livin' on Dog Food*, directed by R. Lowenstein, Ghost Pictures, 2009.

9   P. Kelly interviewed by A. Denton, *Enough Rope*, ABC TV, 5 Jul. 2004.

10–11   P. Kelly, *How to Make Gravy*, Penguin, Camberwell, 2011: p. 279; p. 273.

12   A. Stafford, *Pig City: From the Saints to Savage Garden*, UQP, St Lucia, 2006, p. 139–40, p. 149.

13   *Great Australian Albums*, SBS TV, 2007; D. Nichols, *The Go-Betweens*, Allen & Unwin, St Leonards, 1997.

14   B. Karpinski, performance at Club Bent, Performance Space, Feb. 1996, *Bohemian Rhapsody*, ABC TV, 1997.

15   A. Barcan, *Radical Students*, p. 17, p. 326.

16   M. Wark, *The Virtual Republic*, p. 83.

17   M. Wark, interviewed by T. Moore, *Bohemian Rhapsody*, ABC TV, 1997.

18   R. Neville, 'The Business of Being Human', pp. 56–58; R. Neville, 'Baby Boomers' on *The Hub*, Foxtel, 1997; R. Neville, 'The Cook, the Thief, His Wife and the old Hippy', *Sydney Morning Herald*, 2 Jun. 1990, p. 75.

19   C. Lumby, interviewed by T. Moore, *Bohemian Rhapsody*, ABC TV, 1997.

20   R. Guilliatt, 'His Dark Material', *Weekend Australian*, 1 Dec. 2007.

21   D. Leigh and L. Harding, *Wikileaks: Inside Julian Assange's War on Secrecy*, Guardian Books, p. 34.

22   S. Dreyfuss with research by J. Assange, *Underground: Tales of Hacking, Madness, and Obsession on the Electronic Frontier*, Random House, 1997, quoted in *Wikileaks*, p. 42.

23   S. Dreyfuss, research by J. Assange, *Underground*, quoted in *Wikileaks*, p. 41.

24   D.A. Bradford, 'From Campus to Hackerspace: The Origins of the Hacker Subculture', unpublished 2011, Monash University, Melbourne.

25   R. Manne, 'The Cyberpunk Revolutionary', *Monthly*, Mar. 2011, www.themonthly.com.au/ julian-assange-cypherpunk-revolutionary-robert-manne-3081.

26   J. Assange, 17 Jul. 2006, quoting A. Solzhenitsyn, *First Circle*, extracted in R. Manne, 'The Cyberpunk Revolutionary'.

27   J. Assange, 31 Dec. 2006, extracted in 'The Cyberpunk Revolutionary'

28   J. Assange, quoted in D.Leigh and L. Harding, *Wikileaks*, p. 46.

29   J. Assange, *Julian Assange: The Unauthorised Autobiography*, Text Publishing, Melbourne, 2011, p. 130.

30   L. Townsend, 'Steampunk Lets Me Slip into a Corset', *Australian*, 13 Sept. 2010, p. 20.

CONCLUSION

1   *Lipstick Traces: A Secret History of the Twentieth Century*, Harvard University Press, Cambridge, 1989, p. 23; R. Williams, *The Long Revolution*, Chatto & Windus, London, 1961, p. 47.

2   D. Deamer, quoted in T. Moore, *Bohemian Rhapsody*, ABC TV, 1997.

3   K. Slessor, 'My King's Cross', in D. Haskell (ed), *Kenneth Slessor: Poetry, Essays, War Despatches, War Diaries, Journalism, Autobiographical Material and Letters*, UQP, St Lucia, 1991, p. 86.

4   J. Cork in N. Barraclough, 'This Bohemian Life', *Sydney Morning Herald*, 6 Mar. 2004, p. 29.

5   M. Sharp in R. Neville et al., 'The Story of Oz', p. 23.

6   P. Bourdieu, 'The Production of Belief', p. 290.

7   A. Kershaw, *Heydays*, p. 1; L. Jaivin, 'From Boho to Poho', *Monthly*, Jul. 2005, p. 39.

INDEX